# THE POWER OF
# GOD'S
# CONSCIOUSNESS

JAMES GRANT

ISBN 979-8-88616-858-7 (paperback)
ISBN 979-8-88616-860-0 (hardcover)
ISBN 979-8-88616-859-4 (digital)

Copyright © 2022 by James Grant

All rights reserved. No part of this publication may be reproduced, distributed, or transmitted in any form or by any means, including photocopying, recording, or other electronic or mechanical methods without the prior written permission of the publisher. For permission requests, solicit the publisher via the address below.

Christian Faith Publishing
832 Park Avenue
Meadville, PA 16335
www.christianfaithpublishing.com

Printed in the United States of America

# Contents

Acknowledgments ......................................................... v
Preface.................................................................... xxvii
Introduction............................................................ xxix
The Definition of Consciousness.................................1
Defining Our Meaning and Being in Life.....................38
The Christian's Lifestyle and God's Consciousness ........50
The Comfort Zone......................................................56
The Biblical Word of Consciousness? .........................95
++Understanding Our Trials and Temptation .............125
Understanding the Nature of Trials and Sins ..............146
Understanding the Conditions of Our Sins .................238
Minister's Perspective on Sin ......................................270
Looking at Our Trials and Temptations .....................291
The State of Leadership and Authority .......................307
God's Consciousness in Our Lives...............................338
The Consciousness of Our Faith .................................343
The Emotion of Our Consciousness.............................352
Understanding the Power of God's Consciousness .......359
There's Power in God's Consciousness and Creation....375
The Difference Between Our Trials and Our Sins........382
People's Word Is Their Bond ......................................396

Transformation of Saul's Consciousness into Paul........414
The Consciousness of God's Discernment...................424
Mankind's Purpose and Reason to Exist .....................428
The Light and Energy of God ......................................433
Defining the State of God's Consciousness .................438
The Consciousness of Good and Evil ........................445
Existentialist Philosophers Believe? ............................453
The Meaning and Being of Our Lives ........................465
Why Did God Create Mankind? .................................469
Why There Was a Need for the Holy Spirit?...............489
The Spiritual Essence of Purpose and Reason .............517
Reasoning with the Scriptures .....................................523
The Dangers of Our Comfort Zones...........................526
Defining Our Purpose through Jesus Christ ...............542
Faith in the Midst of Our Sins ....................................556
The Definition of Consciousness..................................574
Developing Confidence in Our Spiritual Consciousness .......................................................591
The Sculptor's Consciousness of Meaning and Being ..599
God Being the Sculpture of Mankind..........................618

# ACKNOWLEDGMENTS

**M**y spiritual experience in America came when I was at Twelve Baptist Church. My only pastor who is now pastor emeritus Arthur T. Gerald, I thank him so much for being there for me when everyone tried to destroy God's divine faith and talent that He placed in me. My pastor emeritus was also there for me. Thank you for supporting and giving me the courage confidence to continue this race in Jesus Christ. Thank you again, Pastor.

I would also like to thank Deacon Warren who was constantly there and selfishly gave his time and dedication to make sure that the church and the facilities of the church and the security of our house of worship and prayer was safe and secure to the believers of God.

Pastor Bruce Wall, thank you for giving me my first instructions and lessons. Those lessons became the only messages I needed over the many trials and storms. I have faith in my youth and adult life.

Bishop William Dickerson, I appreciate the man that God has shaped your integrity into becoming. You are one of the best examples of a pastor and activist in the community. Your work as a bishop has impacted a lot of people in the community. Bishop William Dickerson, you have even impacted the younger generation. You have made the young men aware of their daily environment and how to better enhance themselves both spiritually and physically and also allowed us to be men who are dedicated to our friends and especially to our families. May God continue to bless you and your family as well.

I would like to thank Deacon Sherman Bartholomew for your support. I would also like to thank you for your words of spiritual encouragement.

Deacon Edwin Wright, I thank you for your wisdom your inspiration and your love and your support once again. Thank you as one deacon to another, giving me the encouragement to be steadfast and strong.

Markel Crockton, thank you also for being that ear, for listening to me, whatever the topic or information that I might be wrestling with. You are always there to listen. May God continue to bless your position as a deacon here at Twelve Baptist Church.

I would like to thank the Twelve Baptist Deacon Board and Twelve Baptist Deaconess for their support and spiritual perspective and guidance. I would also like to give thanks to the deaconess for the hard work and dedication and support to the deacon and deaconess board. The organization, they dedicate the hard work and the effortless time to make this Twelve Baptist Church God's Church possible.

I would also like to extend thanks to the trustees, ushers, ministers, and all the staff and organization at Twelve Baptist Church that makes this church a church that preaches and teaches God's Word.

Thank God for Deacon Hozel Murray, for his strength in God, and his leadership as a man of God. I thank God for your inspiration that has been a strong influence in my Christian life.

I also appreciate Willow Dean Jones Murray. Thank you for your prayers and your inspiration.

I also thank Alma Wright for giving me the encouragement and support I need to complete my book project.

I would also like to thank Deacon Hozel Murray for recognizing my spirituality and maturity and fighting and struggling with others to choose me to become a part of the Deacon Board of Twelve Baptist Church. That's where I reside as a member still today.

Skip Janie, thank you for your wisdom and understanding. I can talk to you, my brother, about anything, and you were able to give me the right answers all because of your life experience, which is the best academic institution for higher learning. I thank you very much for love and support.

I would also like to thank Deacon Learie Blackwell and Andrew Henry, my line brothers that crossover with me as deacons here at Twelve Baptist Church. I thank you for your strength and confidence in me. You brothers have been very supportive to me as deacons and men of God.

I also thank God for Tommy and Mary Campbell. Tommy, thank you for always keeping me focused in my relationship with God. Prayers don't cost anything, but you still get the right answers and results to answer my questions.

Thank God for Marshall Mills who has always influenced me to win the Golden Key Award in photography.

I also thank Susie Gerald, the First Lady emeritus, for taking the time out to read my manuscript and give me your opinion, which resulted in the confidence and courage to complete my book.

Miss Spencer, for her vision of why they made me a deacon: thank you for your honesty opinion. May God continue to bless you and your family.

Pastor Willie Broderick, I am so glad to have you, my brother, as my second pastor. God has blessed you to become one of the most Charismatic speakers of this time. Thank you for spiritual drive, ambition, and motivation in God. I know God is going to use you in this world to achieve and do greater things than He has already done.

Michael Lewis, I thank you for the years we spent as children. I also thank God for using you as a teacher of the Gospel. Thank you for also teaching me.

I also want to thank the Gibbs family—Marlene Gibbs, Althea Gibson, Gillian Gibbs—and most of all, Mother

Gibbs and Beulah Gibbs for their love and spiritual support throughout the years.

Reverend Bernard Spencer and Christine Spencer, thank you for your support. Thank you, Christine, for your spiritual support in Sunday school.

Naomi Smith, thank you for your anointing, prayers, and encouragement.

David Smith, thank you for your spiritual support and influence throughout the years.

Michael Tabb, thank you for your support and the love of your family.

Raymond Nobles, I would keep you also in prayers. Keep singing and shining for God, my brother.

Jay O'Neal, thank you for constantly checking up on me to make sure I keep focus on my spiritual life. Thank very much, my brother.

George Richardson, thanks you for your wisdom and knowledge. Thank you for just being you and helping to give the support I needed to complete this project.

Betty Cambronne, I thank you for your prayers and for mentoring me. Thank you for your academic support as well. May God continue to bless you and your family. You have always been an inspiration to me. Thank you for your spiritual inspiration and knowledge of God.

Johnny Carter, thank you for your support. Please don't change. You have enough knowledge to inspire the world.

Megan Charles, thank you for your love and support in reading and giving me your responses also toward my manuscript.

James Paul, thank you for your support and encouragement.

Andrea Bynum, thank you for your support and love and conversation about the book project.

Louis Bellamy, thank you for patience with me over the years. You were one of my best teachers. Thank you for your stern discipline.

Ronald Spratling, thank you for your patience, discipline, and most of all, I thank you for being my friend and teacher. I learned a lot from you where God has brought me to this time in my life.

Alda Marshall Witherspoon, I thank God for you and for your presence. You have always been an inspiration to me and everything that I am doing, and I really appreciate you for who you are as a person. May God continue to bless you and your family.

Carol Bynum, thank you for your patience with me as a student. Thank you for your guidance your inspiration and always being there for me, especially when I have to reflect on my life itself and my future. I would also like to thank Darrell Smith for his political role in our community.

Linda Solomon, I can always reach out to you for information and spiritual advice. You have always been there for me.

Michelle Madera, thank you for giving me the opportunity to start my career in teaching middle and high school.

Billy Morgan, thank you also that you continuously work with the kids in order that they will develop and we would have a better future.

Jeffrey Brewster, thank you for your friendship and support and your spiritual guidance. May God continue to bless you and your family. From Barbados, West Indies, to America—thank you and your family.

Barbara McInerney, thank you so much for your inspiration and your love and your spiritual perspective on life.

Alma Wright, thank you for your prayers and support and direction. Please don't park over there. It is not safe. Okay?

Brenda Richardson, thank you for your support and your hard work and dedication with the children both in public school and in the church.

Willow Dean Jones / Murray Dean, I appreciate your support and love and your prayers that put me in the right direction.

George Richardson, thank you for your knowledge and your wisdom and always being there when I call you when I have a question about whatever. Thank you, my brother in Jesus Christ.

Sissy Gerald, First Lady Emeritus, I thank you for honesty and directness toward my manuscript. I really appreciate your honesty.

Megan Charles, thank you for taking the time out to look over my manuscript and giving me your spiritual perspective and what has now manifested itself to become a book.

Michael Lewis, thank you for being a true friend over the years. I appreciate you from my childhood right into my adult life. I thank you for your strength.

Johnny Carter, thank you for your friendship as a brother. You're always there to support every effort or whatever challenges I have to face in life. I thank you so much, Johnny.

Kevin Thomas, thank you so much for the years we spent together in our youth and adult life. May God continue to bless you and your family.

Lorraine Mundy, thank you for being so supportive of me in my youth and in my adult life. You have always been an inspiration.

Lynn Mundy, you have been my spiritual sister for years. You have help me mature spiritually in my faith with God.

Tracy Mundy, may God bless you and your family. You are my little sister in God.

Curtis Howe, thank of your friend over the years and even when we were children.

Oscar Reed, thank you, my brother, for the conversation. Keep up the good work.

Zack Ray, I thank you for such a wonderful bundle of joy (Hazel). May God continue to bless you and your family.

Phillip Walker, thank you for always being the inspiration. Thanks for giving me the strength I needed to accomplish the things that you wanted me to do.

Toney Brewer, thank you for working love and hard work in the community.

I thank God for you, Ron Bell, for your hard work and dedication to our communities. You are the community's silent strength.

I thank you, Bruce Wall, for your support and love. Bruce Wall, I thank God for your life as my pastor. I want you to know that you had a great impact on my life. I thank God for you being in my life.

Roscoe Baker, thank you for introducing me to Twelve Baptist Church while I was a teen running around with the Roxbury Boys Club. It was Roscoe Baker who introduce me to my home of worship which is still my home of worship today: Twelve Baptist Church.

I also would like to thank Elder Pastor Herschel Langham and his family for embracing me as child in their family. I never experienced what it was like to speak in tongues, but I did because of this family. I was introduced to my first experience in speaking in tongues at Faithful Church of Christ.

Thank God for Deacon Hozel Murray for his strength in God and his leadership as a man of God on the Deacon Board. I thank God for your inspiration that has been a strong influence in my Christian life.

I also thank God for Tommy who always keeps me focused in my relationship with God and his advice and support toward my family.

Thank God for Marshall Mill who influenced me to win the Golden Key Award in photography.

Thank you, Adrian Clark, for blessing me. You have such an inspirational voice that has touched many hearts even to this day. You were the voice and inspiration of our youth choir.

I also thank Sissie Gerald, the First Lady Emeritus for taking the time to read and give me the courage to complete my book.

Miss Spencer, for her vision of why they made me a deacon, thank you for honest opinion. May God continue to bless you and your family.

Pastor Willie Broderick, I am so glad to have you as my second pastor. God has blessed you to become one of the most Charismatic speakers of this time.

Edward Lewis, I thank you for the years we spend as children. I also thank God for using you as a teacher of the Gospel. Thank you for also teaching me.

Phillip Walker, thank you for always being the inspiration that gives me the strength I need to accomplish the things that you wanted me to do.

Toney Brewer, thank you for your hard work, love in the community, and your political astuteness.

Candace Sealy, thank you for your inspiration and information on politics.

Robert Kenny, I really appreciate you, my brother, for your hard work and determination and trying to maintain Roxbury Community College as a community college that prepares people to further the academic education in colleges and universities. I really appreciate meeting you on the student government for Roxbury Community College.

Dean Bright, thank you for your hard work and determination and acknowledging that Roxbury Community College started in your house. Dean Bright's legacy needs to be brought to the surface and placed on a plaque or a statue in that academic institution.

Sherry Smith, thank you for your guidance when I was a student at Roxbury Community College and one of the members of the student government at the time, and Brother Kenny as well.

Ron Bell, thank you for your hard political work in the community and your determination to make sure that the right candidate is elected for the job of representing our communities abroad.

Shirley Schillingford, thank you for being that light in the community of culture. Thank you for being able to feed the communities of Boston.

Rita Dixon, thank you for your love and your support. Thank you for your courage, and thank you for your drive and ambition to speak up for those that are in need. You have done a wonderful job of supporting people than the politicians that they have voted for in this community, and I must say thank you to you and your family. Really, you have the drive and ambition to help others who are in need and are struggling with everyday issues.

Mattie Maria, thank you so much for your research and your information and your ability to know where to get the right topics from surrounding topics. I thank you and appreciate you and your knowledge and wisdom.

Dave Eastman, thank you, my brother, for everything. Your conversations are enlightening in Boston's political arena. I also thank you for being a man of God.

Brad Howard English High of the 1970s, thank you all for your support and the many varieties and diversity of people. We are still able to come together and love each other all as one without regard to our faults or imperfections.

Kenny Woods, I would also like to thank you. You have always been supportive of me for many years. Thank you for your prayers and support.

Luisa Byron, thank you so much for the years that you have given me and the time that you have spent with me as my teacher. Thank you so much.

Louis Elisa, thank you for your support and your love for your community. Thank you for your encouragement and your words of inspiration. Thank you for giving me the motivation to continuously look into this political arena for leadership.

Ralph Beach, thank you for your art. You reach into the hearts of the children and develop their inability and the talent through your art and leadership. Thank you very much. You are an inspiration as you acknowledge God in your heart. We have walked a long path and we have come a long way. May God continue to bless you and your family.

Mattie De Loah, thank you for your love and your support. Your knowledge and wisdom are immaculate. I am privileged to get to know you. May God continue to bless you and your family.

Christopher Jackson, thank you so much, my brother, for your inspiration, for letting me to run things by you. You were always there. And thank you for you giving me the questions I needed to expand the knowledge that God has given me spiritually and physically. Thank you, my brother.

Annette Simmons Jackson, my spiritual sister, I thank you so much for your prayers your motivation, your spiritual anointing, and your preaching perspective about God.

Carol Peters, thank you for your inspiration and thank you for your support. Thank you for your prayers and your soul. May God continue to bless you and your family.

Jeffrey Jackman of Twelve Baptist Church, thank you so much, my brother. You have always been an inspiration to me through the discussion in the messages that we have talked about. May God continue to bless you and your family as well.

Deacon Warren Montgomery of Twelve Baptist Church, thank you so much for your motivation. Thank you for your patience, for your direction, and for your time that you have spent in God's house and your dedication to God's house and his people. Once again, thank you.

Eleanor Chavez, thank you so much for your support and your love with my son and family.

James Paul, thank you over the years of high school martial arts (MBTA). Thank you so much. You're an inspiration to continuously serve God.

Kenny Osborne, thank you so much for being my mentor, my inspiration while we were in middle school. May God also continue to bless you and your family.

Lamont Penn, thank you so much for your support over the years and the reflection of our childhood. You were always there to support me and help me in any situation that I was in. You're like my extended brother, even as we were in Northeastern University together and majored in criminal justice.

Jean Epps, thank you, my sister, for your endurance and your support throughout the years. May God continue to bless you and your son, Cory.

Lorraine Langham of Faithful Church of Christ, thank you for your inspiration and your motivation as my first Sunday school teacher. I guess you taught me well enough for me to hold onto my faith until my adulthood. I appreciate your teachings and your direction once again. God bless you and your family as well.

Jackie Langham of Faithful Church of Christ, I really appreciate you and your husband for taking me in and teaching me about God and being my first teachers of the spirituality of God. We had experienced speaking in tongues; thank you so much for that.

Buster Langham of Faithful Church of Christ, I guess we like the brothers. Thank you for your father and your mother for opening up the doors for me to experience my first relationship with God.

Yvette Prescott, I thank you so much. You are like a sister to me. Thank you for being my ear.

Diane Prescott, thank you for being like a mother to me. Godey, thank you also.

Euston Brathwaite, Crystal Haynes, Tony Price, Deborah Briggs, Edward Downey Maddie Laroche, Deborah Lyunch, Natalie Hill, Stephen Hendrix, The Roxbury Boys Club, Saiid Jamal, English High, Claudia Stalwart, Rolando Dinking, Wayne Miller, Rodney Dailey, Janine Dailey, Deborah Grant, Aldo Marshall Weatherspoon, Eddie Jenkins, Bishop William Dickerson, Martin Russell, Ruben Dottin, Darlene white Dottin.

For my love, compassion, and change for our community, these are some of the political Candidates I supported: Senator Bill Owens, representative Shirley Owens Hicks, Senator Royal Bowling, Bruce Bolling, Congress Elizabeth Warren, District Attorney Rachel Rollins, City Council at Large Ayanna Presley, Congressman Michael Capouano, Government Duval Patrick, Senator Ed Markey, Congressman Joe Kennedy, Governor Charlie Baker, City

Council at large Michelle Wow, Mayor Charlotte Golar Richie, Mayor Marty Walsh, City Councilor Charles Yancey, Senator Diane Wilkerson (was one of the first candidates that I ever sold silk-screen T-shirts for)—thank you.

Olivia Depeiza, thank you for your friendship over the years. I appreciate you even when we lived as neighbors in Barbados.

Rickie Depeiza, thank for your friendship over the years, especially as children growing up.

Laura Barros, thank you for support and love and being able to reach out to my family. May God continue to bless you and your family.

Toney Barros, keep with the children in Cape Verde. May God continue to bless your movement and your love for the children of Cape Verde, the computer program you have started, and your academic inspiration for the children of Cape Verde.

Wesley Camron, thank you, my brother, for your support love through the years, Sugar Bear.

David Coleman, thank you for being my teacher, and you're an inspiration as my professor and teacher, giving me the right direction in life.

Kayode Bright, thank you for your inspiration over the years and your knowledge.

Dorothea Jones, I have to thank you for your love and support and for always being there for me. May God continue to bless you and your family.

Yvette Prescott and Diane Prescott, I thank you all so much for being so supportive of me and my family. I will always love you, my dear mother and sister.

Natalie Sheets, may God continue to bless you and your family.

Craig Smalls, continue to do the great work in the community. Thank God for you and your family.

Michael Gerald, thank you, my brother, for your love and your support throughout the years and always trying to give me encouragement.

Paul Lockhart, once again, thank you for your family and your love and your support. I really appreciate you and your family.

Lamont Penn, thank you for your love and your support once again throughout the years and now.

Rudell Peeler, I thank you also for your support, your love, and your compassion and always being there when we needed you at the church. Thank you for your family as well. May God bless you and your family.

Thomas Perry, thank you so much for your effort in the church and being one of the consistent people of the kingdom keepers at Twelve Baptist Church. Thank you for every effort that you have made and put into the church to make sure that it is safe. May God continue to bless you and your family.

Nancy Thomas, thank you so much again for your knowledge and your wisdom and your spirituality and your guidance and your support continuously. May God continue to bless you and your family as well.

Rufus Hall, thank you so much, my brother, for your inspiration your hard work, your drive, and your motivation for the community. You are enlightening to the younger generation. May God continue to bless you and your family.

Tyrone Foster, thank you so much over the years, my man. You've been an inspiration to me, even if we don't speak for a long time when we meet up. We've been seeing each other every day. Thank you so much for your love, and may God continue also to bless you and your family and your retirement career.

Steve Barnes, thank you so much, my brother, for your support over the years, even when we were students at the University of Boston. May God continue to bless you and your family.

Wayne Miller, may God continue to bless you as well, my brother. You've always been supportive, instrumental in my life. You were always there when I needed to ask you a question. May God continue to bless your singing career and your acting career.

George Richardson, thank you, my brother, for your inspiration. I thank you for the long travel that we had and how you dropped everything to transport me from Boston to Washington DC. I thank you for that and your time. I also thank you for allowing me to recognize that the family is more important and better than chasing a career.

Please, if I forget anyone, don't blame it on my heart. Please blame it on my mind. It might've been someone that I have forgotten that has been a powerful inspiration and has impacted my life. May God continuously bless you and your endeavors in this life. Thank you once again.

Commissioner Dennis White, thank you for your peace walk in the community. I also thank you for the concerns that people had financial concerns where they might not have been able to pay a bill, pay the rent, or pay for some of the people I could not afford. The thing is that people did not know that you reached out to those who couldn't pay their bills, and when the police and media wasn't around, you were there, walking with the community to bring peace among the community and the police. I thank you.

Also, with Robert Kenny, we organized Roxbury Community College from Dudley Station to Massachusetts College of Art to each location by Roxbury Crossing in order that Roxbury Community College would have their own academic facility in the community that it serves.

Brad Howard and English High School of the 1970s, we are a family from different mothers and fathers. We give each other more support than our original families. Thank God for my high school friends.

University of Massachusetts at Boston:

Logan Richie, I thank you so much for being my brother from another mother and father, even throughout our college years.

Reggie Nicholas, thank you, my brother, for your insight and your knowledge throughout the years.

Marianne Alexander, thank you so much for your support and understanding with the children from our community and what they are up against in the academic institution. I hope that God blesses you and continuously blesses you throughout your career as a student adviser. Your guidance and your confidence in me has allowed me the courage and the strength to write every book that I have written, and the other thing is not knowing what Cliff Notes are.

Elicia Marin Roe, thank your mother for her prayers and conversations about God. It is true that prayers work not at the time we talk but in God's time. I love our conversation about God.

Professor Landy, I thank you so much for your teaching ability, your enthusiasm, and teaching students and making sure that the students that you have taught are able to comprehend the subject that you have been teaching. You are an encouragement and a wonderful teacher. I am glad that I have experienced your teaching and your strength as a teacher. I am your student. Thank you so much, Professor Landy, for your encouragement and strength.

Michelle Marin, thank you for being my friend for so many years.

Elijah Cotte, thank you for our discussions. There were very inspirational and fulfilling.

Glad Amere, you're like a sister I never had, always wanting to help people in the community through teaching.

MBTA Workers.

Annzinethia Jones and family, thank for your support. You have been very helpful.

Anita Scott, thank you for help and support.

Wesner Alexis, thank you for your knowledge and wisdom.

Stephnie Brade, thanks for teaching me about where to place the train in the yard.

Stacie Atkins, thank you for help and support with the trains at Mattapan.

Nicole Manson James, close the window. Stop opening up the window to the office. I thank you for your support and patience.

Kathy Lopes Grant, what is now? Close the window. Thank you also for your support and patience.

Martel Hodges James, do this work, not that work.

Anthony Pipe, James, please, please, James, let me help you pick your work you've been in the pick room too long, and you haven't picked your work yet.

Cheryl Anderson, James, I am going to. James, if only you knew. James boy, you don't know.

April

These are the men and women that helped me during my difficult times of learning how to drive a train. These are also the men and women that I love see and look forward to seeing them at work. When I see them, I already know that I am going to a blessed and wonderful day at work:

Martin Cadet, Kassandre Casame, Shawnta McKay, Gaenslie Procope, Joe Napoli, Wally Holly, Kenny Barnes, Devon Barrett, Abiyou Temesgen, Larango Furgoson, Joseph Dieudoran, Montlhard Blanchet, Steve Biggby, Rudell Luis, Reggie Bragg, Michael Lane, Nicolas Verland, Antonio Grimes, Kim Malone, Noemi Pena, Jeff Green, Geo Huezo, AJ Ajmal, Candido Lopes, Joseph Dieudonne, Elvin Salley, Takisha King, Wendy Chrisotume, Rev. Demetrius Cooper, Perry Spencer, Jimmy Malone, John Cinelli, Brian Court, Reda Direny, and Tove Burnett-Edghill, Dimone Marshall, thank you for your support and your conversations of wisdom.

Victoria Dowe, the president, the secretary, the treasurer, and the boss of our MBTA class and our MBTA big sister.

Boston Legal Services serves as a member.

Philip Walker, father and son, my brother, thank you so much for encouraging words.

Ronald Walker, thank you for your friendship and support. When I think about getting another, I think about your talents and management skills.

Yvette Walker and Denise Walker, I pray every day for your family and their love toward me.

Floyd Cameron, thank you for spiritual enlightenment on many subject on God.

Rita Dixon, I have always appreciated your strength and compassion for others. Rita, you have accomplished more others than the politicians and ministers in our community.

Reuben and Daniela Dotting, thank you for sharing your love every year with the people that you love. Reuben and Daniela, it is good that you bless others with the blessings you get from God. I thank God for you every day.

I also want to thank Lora Mariah Barrose for her friendship and support over the years.

I would also like to thank Rachel Miselman for your political advice. You have a lot of information. I thank you so much. May God continue to bless you and your family.

Shawn Nickson, thank you for being the brother I never had. Thank you for looking out for me. Thank God also for you and your family.

I thank you, Greg Allimoeo, for your friendship over the years.

Roccio Nunes, thanks for being my friend and the three amigos—may God continue to bless you and your family.

Cliff Anderson who worked with me as a teacher in the Boston Public School system—thank you for teaching our children.

Samir Stanley, how are you doing, my brother? I still drive where you lived, looking for you. I miss your presence around the neighborhood.

Lorraine Langham, thank you for being my first Sunday school teacher. I learned a lot from you at Faithful Church of Christ.

Pam Grant, Jennifer Grant, Michelle Grant, Deborah Grant, Janine Grant, Shawn Grant, Brian Grant, Sharon Grant, Shalaine Grant, Amanda Grant, Charlene Grant, Michelle Grant, Marcia Grant, Judy Grant, Paula Fleming, Sean Fleming, Malcolm Niles—thank you.

George Folks, thank you for being my brother.

Brandon Bento, thank for helping me with electronics.

Laura Esther Rivas, thank you so much for your friendship. You are a wonderful person. May God continue to bless you and your family.

# Preface

This is a book that focuses on the power of God's consciousness. Now here is why: it is a book that is able to bring mankind into their own spiritual awareness through God's divine Word. It is through God's Divine Word that mankind is able to embrace the power of God's consciousness. Here is what I mean: it is through God's consciousness that transforms mankind from a physical being into a spiritual creation of existence.

Here is how because it is through the power of God's divine Word that we are able to transform mankind's free will. It is through the power of God's divine Word that we are able to transform mankind's sinful nature and imperfections and bring mankind into a spiritual being.

The power of God's consciousness has to do with God's divine Word. It is through God's divine Word that it is able to reach mankind on whatever level or life condition that mankind is faced with. God's divine Word is able to reach and develop mankind's spiritual potential in order that mankind would become a spiritual being, knowing what his true purpose and reason is for living. That can only be achieved through the Power of God's consciousness that transcends the mind of mankind, and that is where transformation of mankind's spiritualism takes place.

As mankind progresses and matures in God's divine Word, that is what brings mankind into harmony with God. It is the power of God's divine Word that mankind experiences as a spiritual being living in a physical experience that creates all of mankind's human experiences.

When mankind is able to define his true purpose and reason for living in the midst of their physical existence through God's divine Word, that is when mankind is able to enhance their spiritual life to become one with God the Father, the Son, and the Holy Spirit.

# Introduction

The question someone might ask is, how does mankind become in tune to God's consciousness? And why would mankind want to become in tune with God's consciousness? Because through God's consciousness, there is a certain peace, which resonates and surpasses mankind's understanding and comprehension.

Now, is there certain peace that surpasses mankind's understanding? Yes, and here is another question that complements that same question, and that is, why would mankind need to know what this peace is? Because it is a peace that transcends mankind's consciousness in harmony with God the Father.

Another question is, why would mankind want to be in harmony with God and not himself? Because mankind does not have the wisdom to understand and define his true purpose and reason in life.

The only way mankind can define their purpose and reason in life is through embracing God's divine Word. Here is why: God already created us with a reason and purpose to exist, or as some people would say, God created mankind with a spiritual DNA that dictates our reasons and purposes for living for God.

The only way mankind can define their true purpose and reason is in life. I also believe that our purpose and reason in life are determined through our spiritual consciousness and our discipline.

Mankind must first develop a spiritual consciousness. The question one might ask is how mankind develops their spiritual consciousness. The first step is mankind must recognize is that when God created mankind already with a purpose and a reason to exist both spiritually and physically in this life.

Each person created by God's authentic hands was created to serve a purpose or has a reason to be created. Everything in this world was created with a purpose and a reason to exist. When mankind tries to find their reason and purpose in life, that is when mankind is trying to give their life meaning and being to exist, which is within their purpose and reason. But it is designed by mankind's consciousness toward God.

The only way mankind can find a purpose and reason for their lives is when mankind can develop their state of consciousness.

The only way that mankind can develop its consciousness is through God's authentic Word, when mankind embraces God's divine Word in their heart, mind, body, and soul.

In order for mankind to define his or her true purpose and reason in life, mankind needs spiritual guidance in his life. The only way that mankind is able to understand and define himself is through God's consciousness. It gives mankind the purpose and reason for mankind to define and acknowledge their true purpose and reason for living in this world.

How does mankind stay in tune with God's consciousness? By embracing God's divine Word which brings mankind into harmony with God, and it is that state of peace and harmony that mankind finds his true reason and purpose for living.

When mankind is able to find his reason and purpose for living in the midst of his adversities and through the struggles with adversaries in life, this is what brings mankind into his own peace, faithfulness, and righteousness with God the Father, and this is where the power of God's consciousness takes root in people's lives by transforming their minds into a divine consciousness state with God.

# The Definition of Consciousness

The one thing in life that I have come to realize is when I look into the heart of America, what I have come to experience is a society that is in dying need of God's consciousness. Now before I go any further in the text, please let me define consciousness.

Allow me to define consciousness, in the book *The Power of God's Consciousness*. First of all, *consciousness* is defined as "a mental and physical state of awareness."

Now that awareness, that mankind embraces from God's divine Word, is nothing more than mankind's state of spiritual consciousness. It means that God's Word is bringing mankind into a state of awareness, and that awareness is what develops mankind's spiritual consciousness.

Now the knowledge or wisdom one gathers from God's Word chooses one to decide to resonate with good and evil. Now that decision of good and evil is decided upon that person's consciousness or state of awareness. Now when I mention state of awareness, I am referring to the knowledge and wisdom that mankind learns and embraces in their heart and soul as God's divine Word.

That knowledge and wisdom that mankind learned and understands from God's divine Word is what transforms and transcends mankind into developing their true spiritual consciousness in God.

Now that mankind embraces God's divine Word, that is what gives mankind the power, knowledge, and wisdom to understand, comprehend, and interpret, God's divine Word to become mankind's spiritual consciousness and awareness of who God truly is to mankind personally.

Now the information that mankind learns and understands from God's divine Word is what transforms mankind into becoming a spiritual human being, even if mankind has to study God's divine Word as a particular subject or thing.

It is God's divine Word, that is still able to develop mankind's sinful nature, and imperfection, it is also God's Word, which can transform mankind into a spiritual human being.

Now when mankind is studying God's Word to gain knowledge, mankind can comprehend and understand

God's Word. That is nothing more than mankind's state of consciousness that brings mankind into acknowledging mankind's state of awareness and consciousness.

Now the information that I'm referring to is nothing more than God's divine Word that enlightens mankind's consciousness. We must also understand that religion has nothing to do with transforming mankind into becoming a spiritual human being.

It is God's divine Word that can transform mankind into becoming a spiritual being with a divine consciousness of who God is. The only way one gets to know who God is, is through His Word, and we've become privileged to the power and knowledge that is in the Word of God.

When mankind embraces God's divine Word in their hearts and mind, that is when God's Word becomes manifested in the physical existence of mankind's life. When I say the *physical existence of life*, I am referring to how God's Word can transform mankind into a spiritual human being.

Here is how that happens: The Word of God becomes mankind's consciousness through mankind learning and studying God's Word. As mankind study God's Word, it is God's Word that brings mankind into their awareness and enlightenment of who God is.

Now that awareness or enlightenment is the consciousness of mankind. When mankind decides that they are going to live by God's Word or make what they have studied and learned from God's Word a part of their lifestyle or actually live out what God's Word demands of them, that is when we start to believe in God's Word.

Now when mankind tries to apply God's Word to their lifestyle, that means mankind had enough confidence in God's Word to believe that God's Word is the way of life. That belief is what exercise and execute as their faith in God. That is when mankind's belief brings about the power that is in the faith of God's divine Word.

When God's divine Word becomes manifested in mankind's heart and soul, that is when God's Word begins to take control as well as challenge mankind's sinful nature and imperfection.

When God's divine Word takes control of mankind's sinful nature and imperfection, whatever mankind experienced in their sinful nature and imperfection is what challenges mankind's spiritual consciousness toward what mankind needs to do, especially in the eyes of God.

That is what brings mankind's consciousness into the spiritual manifestation of God's divine Word. Mankind's spiritual consciousness and awareness are not developed through any religion.

What some of us have experienced from the religious dogma are sometimes not God's authentic Word but how many religious scholars perceive how God should be worshiped and what type of information should be taught to the masses of people in the congregation. Some people think that when God comes again, He comes for the church that they are a member of.

What we must understand is that the edifice of the churches does not have a spirit or a soul, as you and I do. So why would God want to come back for a building that houses people coming back for wood and brick?

What God is coming back for is the spirit and souls of all men, women, and children. *Spirit* is what I use, who have made up the churches and allowed His spirit to dwell there with them. What makes up the church is the spirit and soul of mankind praising God and giving God His prayers.

We misunderstand that a building is nothing more than wood and mortar. The building does not have any lungs, the building does not have any feelings, the building does not have any emotions, and the building itself cannot exercise love or compassion, like mankind should do for each other.

Here is why: The foundation and structure of the building are built with either break or mortar, but the foundation of mankind's faith is built on God's authentic Word. So that is why God is not coming back for any one particular church or religion that is a house or a building. God's salvation toward mankind is a gift from God, which mankind embraces through their spiritual consciousness.

Once again, mankind's salvation is developed through mankind's constantly studying God's divine Word and the discipline we are taught to live by. When mankind develops their spiritual consciousness, it is through mankind's faith, which gives mankind the discipline mankind needs to better develop their salvation through God's authentic Word.

All of this comes with understanding and interpreting God's scriptures when mankind tries to develop a state of spiritual consciousness. The question is how mankind develops their spiritual consciousness.

Here is how mankind develops their consciousness in God. It is done through studying the Word of God and embracing God's Word in our hearts and souls.

> Yes this is what the Lord Almighty, the God of Israel, says: "Do not let the prophets and diviners among you deceive you. Do not listen to the dreams you encourage them to have. They are prophesying lies to you in my name. I have not sent them," declares the Lord. This is what the Lord says: "When seventy years are completed for Babylon, I will come to you and fulfill my good promise to bring you back to this place. For I know the plans I have for you," declares the Lord, "plans to prosper you and not to harm you, plans to give you hope and a future. Then you will call on me and come and pray to me, and I will listen to you. You will seek me and find me when you seek me with all your heart." (Jeremiah 29:8–13 NIV [https://www.bible.com/111/jer.29.8-13.niv])

The only way that your spiritual consciousness can be developed has nothing to do with you studying the Word of God. Studying God's divine Word is introductory to mankind being introduced to their spiritual consciousness.

The studying gives you the information mankind needs to develop their own spiritual consciousness and character of how mankind should be through the teaching and knowledge, which is in embracing God's divine Word.

Mankind spiritual consciousness begins when mankind actually decides to make God's Word a part of mankind's lifestyle. When mankind makes God's Word a part of their everyday lifestyle, that is when mankind begins to experience their own spiritual consciousness.

When mankind starts to experience their own spiritual consciousness. The maturity of mankind, spiritual consciousness comes when mankind is challenged by their adversities and adversaries of life or when mankind has to choose between what is goodness and evilness.

Now our faith is the belief we have in God's Word. That belief that we have in God's Word is what gave mankind the confidence and courage they need to develop and mature in their faith, in God. We must remember that our faith in God's Word is nothing more than mankind's faith in God.

As we study the Word of God, we learn about our true calling and message: God wants us to do with our lives what is pleasing and acceptable to God Himself. Mankind cannot find their true calling or even understand what they should do if they keep listening to their pastors, preachers, and bishops and not God's Word.

The key to a successful relationship with God is to get to know God for yourself spiritually. That is why we should constantly develop and improve on our spiritual consciousness through God's divine Word.

Here is how that process work. First, become submissive to the will of God by studying and obeying God's Word. Next, interpret God's divine Word as a state of awareness, which brings mankind into their own consciousness of who God is to them.

Also, acknowledge that whatever we study is manifested and inspired by God's divine Word. When we embrace God's divine Word, it should allow our lifestyle to reflect the sermon that we are preaching and teaching to other people instead of allowing our lifestyle to become a hypocritical sermon that we are not living or even preaching.

Whatever our state of consciousness embraces from God's divine Word, it should always be the discipline that God's Word has though us to execute as Christian believers of God's divine Word, especially, in our lifestyle.

When I mention God's divine Word, I am referring to the scriptures that created the Holy Bible. In other words, I am also referring to God's Word or any experience that has been inspired or revealed by God through His prophets and mankind. The Bible is the book that develops the spiritual consciousness of mankind.

Even the lifestyle of such prophets like Noah, Abraham, Moses and, most of all, Jesus Christ. That lifestyle and experience are prime examples of how we should be able to pattern our lifestyle after to live in harmony and fellowship with God.

Especially the inspiration and the revelation of God's Word that brings mankind into a spiritual state of enlightenment, that spiritual state of enlightenment is what allows mankind to develop and mature spiritually in God's wisdom and knowledge.

The other question someone might ask is how someone or some people become conscious of God's Word. Now when I mention mankind's consciousness, here is what I am referring to: mankind studying God's Word with discipline to gather a better understanding, interpretation, knowledge, and comprehension of God's divine Word.

We must understand that our strength in God comes through our discipline and studying God's Word and embracing God's divine Word in our consciousness and transferring that knowledge and wisdom we learn from God's Word into our hearts. As we transfer God's Word in our hearts, that is when we receive the confidence and experience of our faith in God's Word.

Now when we study God's Word, the interpretation and message that we interpreted and understand or do not agree with still bring enough awareness and confidence for us to acknowledge our state of consciousness and spirituality in God. It is that awareness that also acknowledges mankind's state of consciousness.

Mankind needs to study God's Word to gather enough knowledge and information that mankind would be prepared spiritually to overcome the evil that causes bad things to happen to good people like you and me.

Everyone experiences a light-bulb moment in God's divine Word. That light-bulb moment is how mankind can transition and transform their lifestyle from the physical existence of life into the spiritual reality of God's Word. God's Word is the enlightenment of mankind's consciousness and the development of mankind's spirituality.

When we study God's divine Word, we are also trying to get enough knowledge to better educate and enhance our lives on how mankind should develop their relationship with God.

This would help enhance mankind's lifestyle, mankind's spiritually, and mankind's enlightenment. What studying God's Word does to mankind is bring mankind into consciousness where mankind would develop their own selves for mankind to become a better human being.

It is through God's Word that mankind can reach its spiritual perfection even in mankind's state of imperfection and sinful nature. I am referring to how God's divine Word can bring mankind into their spiritual consciousness.

Our sinful nature and imperfection are exposed and revealed in our own state of consciousness as we study and embrace God's Word. It is God's Word that gives mankind the opportunity to develop mankind's faith in God as mankind develop their faith in God through His word.

It is at that moment in mankind's life that mankind has the potential to reach spiritual perfection in God. This is what brings mankind into fellowship and in tune with God.

Now when mankind becomes in tune and has fellowship with God, especially through God's divine Word, submissiveness, and prayer, this is what brings mankind into its state of consciousness. It is through God's divine Word that inspires as well as brings man into their spiritual consciousness.

The only way that mankind can become a spiritual being is when mankind embraces God's Word in their minds and hearts; and that, my friend, is when mankind can become in tune with God the creator.

God allowed His Word to become a way of life for mankind. It is through the knowledge and wisdom of God's Word that mankind embraces the knowledge from

God's divine Word. The ultimate spiritual experience for mankind is when God's Word brings mankind into mankind's own spiritual consciousness and salvation.

The essence and substance of God's Word are what acknowledge and transform mankind into becoming a spiritual human being. Someone might ask this question: What is it in God's Word that can impact and transform mankind's state of mind into a conscious state of mind, which brings about a spiritual experience to mankind being able to transform from the mere physical experience into the spiritual reality of life?

God's divine Word is the spark that has been created within the inner chambers of mankind's soul and brings mankind's spirit into a spiritual consciousness state as one with God our Father.

It is the depths of mankind's souls that produce the spark that starts the fire burning in the spirit and soul of mankind. It is God's knowledge and wisdom that gives mankind the spiritual enlightenment, consciousness, and faith mankind needs to become a spiritual being.

The knowledge and wisdom that one gathered from God's divine Word are what develops and enhances mankind's consciousness and bring mankind into the spiritualism of God's faith As mankind embraces God's divine Word, that is when mankind gets to experience the beginning stages of their spirituality.

The best way for someone, to develop and understand God's divine Word, is to read, and study, God's Word enough, where you create the discipline, needed to develop your faith and spiritual consciousness in God. This is what helps mankind to feel confident while maturing, and understanding, their state of consciousness and spirituality.

Someone might ask this question: What is spirituality? Now from my perspective, spirituality is something that cannot be bought, spirituality cannot be touched, spirituality cannot be felt, and spirituality cannot be experienced through making physical existence.

Spirituality is a learning process that is experienced through mankind's state of consciousness. Whatever mankind learns from God's Word is what resonates and is also stored within mankind's mind; and that is what becomes the foundation of mankind's faith, spirituality, and consciousness. Now the evidence of mankind's spirituality is in the behavior of mankind's integrity and character.

Spirituality can only be defined as something you earned through acknowledging the presence of God's divine Word in your heart and mind. In other words, spirituality is best described through mankind's behavior and actions.

Our actions manifest and dictate our spiritual behavior and maturity in God. All of this is experienced through our state of consciousness. When I mention mankind's state of consciousness, I am referring to how mankind develops and matures in spiritual maturity and development in God.

Mankind's spirituality is a reflection of how mankind can define God's wisdom and knowledge. Now God's wisdom and knowledge can only be manifested in mankind's life and is displayed through mankind's actions. Those actions are displayed based on mankind's faith, integrity, and personality.

The strength and foundation of mankind's consciousness are based on how well mankind develops its knowledge and wisdom of God. The potential of mankind's relationship with God should be a prosperous and harmonious relationship with God, now that relationship develops with nothing more but love, grace, mercy, compassion, and understanding.

When mankind has a prosperous and harmonious relationship with God, that is what develops consciousness and brings mankind's consciousness into an in-tune relationship with God our Father.

Mankind's prosperous and harmonious relationship with God is determined by how much of a sacrifice is mankind willing to sacrifice for mankind to have a better relationship with God. For mankind to mature and make progress in this life and their lifestyle to better enhance mankind's lifestyle.

This reflects the character of God or having a godlike character embedded in us—so strong that people would want to experience God for themselves because they have experienced the reflection of God's character in us.

Once again, your character as a Christian should also manifest God's Word being lived out in our character. Our character as Christians should always be a reflection of God's character. God's character should always be noticed by our friends and family. Our friends and family should be able to experience God's divine character through our lifestyle as Christians.

Also, our character as Christians is the message and witness of how we define God in our state of consciousness, and it should be expressed in our faith and should be expressed in our private lives and in our personal lives. Our integrity and character should also produce mankind's worship and fellowship with God, and that is what develops mankind's faith and worship in God.

Mankind's faith is an exercise through mankind's consciousness. Mankind's consciousness is what produces mankind's belief in God, and it is through mankind's belief that gives mankind the potential to develop their faith in God.

That faith that mankind has believed in is nothing more than mankind's faith in God. When mankind embraces God's faith, that is when mankind begins to give birth to the development of their spiritual potential.

When mankind can develop their potential of faith by simply embracing God's divine Word in both their hearts and soul, now that is when mankind starts to allow the Word of God to resonate and become a part of mankind's consciousness, and it is at that state of mankind's consciousness.

I mean the consciousness that gives birth to mankind's faith. The birth of mankind's faith begins with a belief in God. Now that belief as it matures becomes the strength that mankind needs to develop and enhance one's belief in God. That belief is what shapes one's consciousness to become the faith of God.

Now mankind's consciousness is what develops mankind's belief. That belief transcends and is transformed into mankind's faith in God. It is through mankind's consciousness that gives mankind the potential to develop mankind's consciousness and faith in God.

Someone might ask this question: How do we know that mankind has developed its consciousness or is in a conscious state of fellowship and worships with God?

Mankind's faith is the consciousness that develops and gives birth to mankind's spirituality with God. Mankind's spirituality is very important to mankind and their relationship with God.

Here is why: Mankind's spirituality is the faith that preserves mankind's salvation and relationship with God. Mankind's spirituality is what places mankind in the position to be favored by God. God's favor is an exhortation and spiritual recognition of mankind's development, the spirituality of their faith in God through mankind's state of consciousness.

It is mankind's state of consciousness that gives mankind the knowledge and understanding of who God is to them.

We must also understand that being a Christian is not a state of comfort. It is a lifestyle that is a challenge to good and evil. So our fight is trying to maintain and preserve our spiritual consciousness through our faith while being challenged by what is good and evil.

Our spirituality is determined based on our state of consciousness and how God's Word is stored in our state of consciousness. Our state of consciousness is the energy that houses the knowledge needed for us to maturity in our faith.

Our faith is the belief of our consciousness. The belief of our consciousness is experienced as we mature spiritually in God's grace and mercy. So if we are not in tune with our spirituality, we would not be able to make the right decisions in life or understand what God is calling us to do.

That is why it is imperative for us to stay focused on God's Word for us to have a positive spiritual life. If we don't stay in constant prayer and submissiveness to God, we become vulnerable and easily manipulated by the evil that Satan does to good people.

That is why before every decision, we must pray first. Prayers keep our minds focused on our spiritual consciousness and our faith in God. Now when mankind focused on their prayers, it develops and matures mankind's spiritual consciousness. The power of our belief in God develops and strength our faith in God.

When mankind stays in tune and has constant fellowship with God, that is what gives mankind the confidence and courage that mankind needs to make the right decisions in life where their decisions do not jeopardize their relationship with God.

One of the most interesting things to me is to experience how evil can manipulate and cause so many bad things to happen to mankind, such as the trials that mankind faces, the tribulations that mankind faces, the temptation that mankind faces, and the adversities that mankind. All are caused by Satan's evil desires to destroy mankind.

The question is why Satan would create these bad situations in mankind's life. It is simple: to destroy mankind's goodness, faithfulness, maturity consciousness, and love that mankind has developed for God.

The evil that exists within bad is what causes bad, to create all of the worst situations to destroy mankind's spirituality. The power that exists within God's consciousness is what gives mankind the ability to rise above all evil desires that create the bad situation and circumstances that exist in evil.

The bad that exists in evil is more of a psychological weapon that challenges the spirituality and consciousness of mankind. It is through mankind's consciousness and information that mankind embraces God's divine Word, which allows mankind to rise above all of their evil desires and wants. That is why mankind's spiritual consciousness is the weapon that can take mankind from mere physical into the spiritual realm of God.

The most interesting thing about evil is that the more God wants to do good in your life, the eviler tends to prevail. And if I can summarize how evilness uses bad circumstances, and things to destroy mankind's faith and fellowship in God, I would have to say that evil exists and is created only to destroy the godliness that exists in the faithfulness and righteousness of God's people and throughout the world.

The consciousness of mankind is the knowledge and wisdom that mankind embraces through God's Word. When mankind embraces God's divine Word, it is the knowledge and wisdom that mankind gathers and learns about that protects mankind from the evilness that causes bad things to happen to good people like you.

We must also understand that whenever evil is present, good is also there to challenge evil. We must understand that we need as human beings to develop a conscious state of mind. That consciousness brings about a certain strength of awareness through God's divine Word where mankind's consciousness can destroy the evilness. That causes bad things and circumstances to happen in the lives of mankind.

It has always been interesting to me, how evil seems to be winning in the spiritual battles; and then all of the sudden goodness steps in and destroys the evilness that causes so many bad circumstances, problems, trials, and situations to happen to good people like you.

Evil will always challenge the good to destroy the goodness that exists in people's life. But the goodness of God brings peace and harmony to mankind, although mankind's sinful nature and imperfection exist. It is through mankind's consciousness that mankind can develop the potential to become perfect in God.

One of the things that have puzzled me over the years is how a powerful and loving God has developed in His heart, knowing the sinful nature of mankind; and God is still able to express compassion, grace, and mercy toward mankind's sinful nature and imperfections.

The question someone might ask is how mankind develops a perfect relationship with God. Mankind can never develop a perfect relationship with God. Here is why: mankind can never reach perfection, even in their relationship with God.

When mankind studies God's divine Word, what gives mankind the potential to achieve perfection is the discipline and studying of God's Word that produces mankind's consciousness in God.

It is through the information that we learn and gather from God's Word that places mankind in the realms or environment of God's perfection. Although mankind is in a perfect state of existence, that God has created mankind to be in, mankind still doesn't have the spiritual consciousness to embrace and understand the disciple it takes to reach spiritual perfection that mankind has learned through God's divine Word.

Here is what I mean. God created a perfect world because God Himself is perfect, and God wanted mankind to be perfect, but it seems that mankind's free will is what destroyed mankind's perfection in God.

Now mankind's free will let us know that God did not want to control mankind's decisions or dominate mankind's existence but give mankind or even make mankind a slave or even dominate mankind's existence.

What mankind's free will does is give mankind the opportunity to freely or, even without fear, embrace God's consciousness through God's divine Word without any restriction or obligation to God. Mankind's free will gives mankind the choice and opportunity to serve and pray to God based on their own free will.

It is through mankind's free will that also gives mankind the opportunities that come with mankind seeking his own free will. But it is our choice to become submissive to God through His divine and authentic Word—only to mankind's free will.

This also allows mankind with more than enough knowledge for mankind to make a positive decision about their spiritual consciousness or even a decision about their evil desires. That is also what mankind's free will does for mankind.

God did place mankind in a perfect world and gave mankind a perfect message from His Bible. It is that perfect message that brings mankind into its state of consciousness.

Now that state of perfection that mankind cannot perfect spiritually does not mean that mankind does not have the potential to reach its state of perfection. The only way that mankind can achieve perfection is through studying God's Word and embracing God's message as a way of life.

That is why God, through His compassion of grace and mercy, allows mankind the opportunity to seek perfection, knowing that mankind cannot achieve such perfection just because of mankind's free will. Yet mankind through their spiritual consciousness has the potential through their faith in God to achieve greatness in God, but mankind cannot achieve perfection in God.

The only person that has achieved perfection in God is Jesus Christ. Mankind strives for perfection, but it's judged based on his goodness and faithfulness to God. That is why mankind can never achieve perfection in God.

Now here's something very interesting the reason why mankind cannot achieve perfection in God: Mankind has a sinful nature, and mankind is already perfect from creation. Because of mankind's sinful nature and imperfection, mankind can only achieve goodness in righteousness and faithfulness; and mankind's goodness, righteousness, and faithfulness are what allow mankind to develop the potential to strive and seek perfection in God.

We must also understand that it is God's compassion, grace, and mercy that forgives mankind of their imperfection and sinful nature. Mankind has the opportunity to through their faith, goodness, and righteousness to develop the potential to strive for spiritual perfection; but mankind cannot achieve it.

Now here is how the consciousness state of mankind, impacts mankind's spiritual consciousness and growth. Now here is how the consciousness state works. The consciousness state of mind is what gathers information and stores the information in mankind's mind to give mankind the knowledge and wisdom they need for mankind to overcome their evil desires.

We can use the information that is stored in our minds to protect our faith from the evilness that creates the bad things that happen to Good people like you and me.

The information that mankind studies and knows, that information that mankind studies and understands from God's divine Word, is what mankind needs to do to study God's divine Word. As mankind studies God's divine Word, it brings mankind into a spiritual experience, which is what shapes our divine consciousness.

It is mankind's state of consciousness, that stores the information needed for mankind to seek God's wisdom and knowledge to develop and protect mankind spiritually.

I will discuss further in the book how mankind's faith is not enough to gain salvation in God. Mankind's actions are what manifest the character and integrity of God in their lives. Just like everything that exists in our minds, it is what we remember about God's divine Word. What we remember is nothing more than awareness.

It is that awareness, that brings mankind to understand and comprehend God's consciousness. When mankind begins to comprehend and understand God's Word, that is when mankind can become spiritually enlightened. That is what develop mankind's spiritual consciousness and faith in God.

When mankind studies and embraces God's divine Word, the information that we learn from God's Word is nothing more than the essence and substance of God's wisdom and knowledge. You see, God's wisdom and knowledge do not embrace any schools of thought such as philosophy, theory, ideology, and even theology.

Read the book written by James Grant called *The Theory of Theology* that talks about how theology, theory, and philosophy are not inspired by the Word of God but by mankind's perceptions of who God is; and if God does exist, who is God and why do mankind want to worship God? Also, we must recognize that somewhere in the nature and pride of mankind, mankind always want to replace God, even in the mist of God's creation and His revelation. Mankind's pride, lust, power, and authority always want to take over God's existence and creation. What mankind need to that they can never achieve that greatness, which God has achieved.

Now spirituality can also be expressed in this manner, and that is to bring our physical existence into a divine experience with our Creator God. Now that information that gives mankind the knowledge for mankind to become a spiritual being is stored and embraced mankind's state of consciousness.

When a person mentioned matures or progresses spiritually through their state of consciousness in God, that means they are embracing God's divine Word and making God's divine Word their lifestyle.

We as Christians must also remember that our salvation is based on our faith, submissiveness, spirituality, and how we perceived and apply the knowledge and wisdom of God to our lives. That is what drives and motivates us to become better men and women of God, not religion.

When mankind recognizes that their salvation does not depend on religion. That is when mankind starts to recognize their state of spirituality. We must understand that religion does not bring mankind into spiritual maturity or even spiritual progress with God.

God does not favor religion. Here is what God favors. He favors obedience, submissiveness, compassion, faith, and most of all mankind's favor, spirituality, and obedience to Him.

We must also understand that religion is how a group of people worship God. Religion does not guarantee a persons' faith or salvation in God. The question is if a person or people's religions teach religion more than the doctrine of God. Then one needs to remove themselves from that religion or if religion is more appealing to masses of people then one needs to remove that person from their religion.

Then that means that religion itself cannot develop mankind's spirituality or place mankind in heaven with God. What that means is religion is not teaching the true reality of God's divine Word. What religion does for the soul of mankind is allow mankind to mankind up his or her deathbed.

We must also understand that religion is not mankind's way to salvation. Mankind's salvation depends on the roads that mankind has to travel in their life. For mankind to achieve spiritual perfection, mankind must develop their inner self through their consciousness and spiritual existence of life.

Although mankind is imperfect and has a sinful nature, somewhere in mankind's life, God is still able to inspire mankind enough where mankind can travel the crossroads of life, facing many detours, and still seek salvation in God. Mankind is imperfect and still has a sinful nature.

Mankind is imperfect and has a sinful nature. What is it about God that allows mankind to still be privileged to salvation? However, God already knows that mankind is imperfect and has a sinful nature.

Mankind can only seek salvation through God's grace and mercy. It is through God's grace and mercy that becomes the compassion of God's forgiveness for mankind's sinful nature and the actions of mankind's imperfections.

Now mankind's spiritual perfection is based on mankind's consciousness. Even how mankind thinks and perceives life is based on mankind's consciousness. Now mankind's faith is the actions and discipline of mankind's consciousness.

Mankind's faith is displayed once again in mankind's integrity and character. In other words, the way we act is impacted by our faith in God. It is through mankind's faith that brings mankind in fellowship and tunes with God the Creator.

If we agree that faith is our belief in God, then we must admit that it is through the awareness of our knowledge that our consciousness gives us the information we need to exercise the reality of how we define our spirituality in God.

How is it that our belief becomes the reality of the and actions of our life? Faith is our actions on how we perceive our state of consciousness. Everything that we have learned and gained knowledge of, especially from God's divine Word, is stored and remembered in our minds. Now that is what becomes the essence and substance of mankind's spirituality.

How does mankind define the reality of their faith? The reality of mankind's faith is simple: it has to do with mankind being too submissive to God and how mankind can express and comprehend God's Word in mankind's lifestyle.

Now the knowledge that we get from God's divine Word is our consciousness. It is in our state of consciousness that we become aware of who God is through the essence and substance of God's divine Word. It is through God's Word that the essence and substance of God's Word give birth to mankind's consciousness.

Now it is in our state of consciousness that our belief becomes our faith in God. We must also acknowledge that our belief is the root and strength of God's faithfulness. God's faith brings mankind into harmony with mankind's reality of who God is.

That reality of mankind's faith is nothing more than a belief that comes from the mere physical existence of life. That belief that shapes mankind's faith is spirituality, which brings mankind into the spiritual realm with God our Father.

As mankind matures in their belief in God, it is through mankind's belief that they manifest mankind's faith in God. As mankind develop their belief in God. It is through mankind's belief that mankind begins to experience and understand the true essence and substance of their spirituality with God our Father.

One of the questions that were asked to me is how mankind develops its faith in God. Mankind's faith in God is developing through prayer, study, submission, and discipline that God's Word teaches us and also what God's Word expects of us to do.

Mankind's faith is only challenged through the trials, tribulations, and adversities that mankind faces. Although mankind's trials, tribulations, and adversities cause mankind so much pain and suffering, God's Word somehow becomes an antidote to mankind's pain and suffering.

It is through mankind's pain and suffering that allows mankind to experience the true substance and essence of mankind's faith, spirituality, and strength in God. It is true our pain and suffering that we truly display the action of our true consciousness, faith, and spirituality through God's divine Word. That is what mankind embraces as our way of life.

No one has ever displayed the strength and character of our father during death like Jesus Christ. He died for mankind's sin through Jesus Christ's pain and suffering. He never compromises God's divine Word. Yet Jesus still ministers to thief on the cross in His pain and suffering.

Mankind's pain and suffering to me seem to be mankind's only way to inherit, God's kingdom and salvation. As mankind develops their consciousness through God's divine Word, it is mankind's faith that brings the reality of God's divine Word into the creation and lifestyle of mankind's faith in God.

The elasticity of our faith is stretched and challenged through mankind's pain and suffering. It is through mankind's pain and suffering that mankind can experience and comprehend God's true reality that exists in God's divine Word and is expressed through God's grace and mercy.

## THE POWER OF GOD'S CONSCIOUSNESS

*Consciousness* is a word that has been misused. But when I do mention consciousness, I am making reference to awareness. What I mean by that is being able to grasp knowledge from a particular place, person, or thing. In this case, I am referring to God's authentic Word as the reference that mankind is able to grasp in order for mankind to develop their consciousness through God's divine Word.

The word *consciousness* is defined in so many schools of thought. Such as an academic perspective, theological perspective, metaphysical perspective, philosophical perspective, and most of all, a theoretical perspective. When we read literature that talks about the consciousness of mankind on all of these schools of thought, it is difficult for us to understand the definition that is able to define mankind's consciousness.

Always remember that consciousness means awareness. In this case, it means someone who wants to become knowledgeable of their environment and the many things that we experience in life, such as good or bad experiences that shape and carve our conscious state of mind. Now what we learn from people's experiences and the many obstacles that we face in life is what develops our conscious state of mind.

Consciousness could also mean trying to develop our own ability to understand and comprehend information that is able to develop a person's consciousness spiritually.

When we are able to develop our understanding spiritually, it also means that we are becoming enlightened or what I would refer to as a light bulb moment. A light bulb moment means bringing someone out of darkness and using the Word of God to bring them into the light of

God's wisdom, giving them the knowledge they need in order to develop their consciousness.

Our consciousness does not stop at just bringing someone into the light of God's wisdom but allowing that person to define their true reason and purpose for living through God's consciousness. In God's consciousness, mankind is able to define their true meaning and being in life. The wisdom of God is what develops our consciousness, our state of mind.

When we embrace God's consciousness, what is it that we are embracing? We are embracing our own direction in life which is given to us through our reason and purpose for living. Now to shed more light on consciousness, I would have to say that consciousness from my perspective is a mental state of an awareness that brings mankind into a better understanding of trying to define their true purpose and reason in life. Now mankind's purpose and reason in life can only be defined through mankind's spiritual consciousness, which gives mankind the potential to develop their faith through God's divine Word.

One of the things that I want us to understand about consciousness is that it is a state of awareness. Consciousness is what brings our hearts and minds together with the knowledge we gather from reading and studying the Scriptures.

When we read and study the Scriptures, the Scriptures formulate and interpret in our minds the knowledge we received from them. That knowledge we receive from the Scriptures is what develops our mind. Now the development of our minds or the parts of our minds that the Scriptures have developed are now embraced in our state of consciousness.

Now our state of consciousness that has embraced the Gospel becomes our belief in God. Now it is through our consciousness that gives us confidence we need in God's divine Word that produces the power of our faith in God. That is when our mind becomes transformed into our state of consciousness that gives mankind the confidence and courage they need to act upon their faith in God.

When we act upon God's Word or even God's will for our lives through the reading and studying of God's Word, we are embracing the messages that are in God's Word. Those messages that we receive while reading and studying God's Word are when our consciousness begins to exercise what it has formulated and interpreted in our mind and that develops our consciousness through God's divine Word in order to develop and produce our faith in God. One episode again: When we read and study God's authentic Word, the messages that we gather from God's authentic Word are implemented in our minds through reading and studying God's Word. The messages we gather from God's Word are what develops in our spirit and soul, the power of God's consciousness. It is also at this point in our lives that we believe and begins to develop our faith in God's consciousness.

This is how I define consciousness as it pertains to mankind and God's divine Word or as I would say, mankind's spiritual consciousness. Here is how mankind's spiritual consciousness is what shapes the character and integrity of mankind's consciousness into becoming like the image and likeness of God.

Now as we understand what consciousness is, let us look at it also from a social perspective. With the intentions of what we gather in our thoughts, it becomes who we are as people. Our thoughts pioneer our thinking. Here is what I mean. America could be the pioneer that has the potential to express love to the point where America can become its own example to the world as the society that has reached a perfect utopia in the eyes of God.

Yes, America has that potential of greatness because God has blessed America and the people in America beyond their means. I think the more progress America makes, the more America is trying to leave God behind. America, like most countries, is forgetting where their blessing comes from, and the poor people whom God has used to bless America and work hard are being denied true freedom. It is through the people of America's prayers and consciousness of the faithful people in America that America has survived so long. It has nothing to do with our political structure, economics structure, or academic structure—these are not America's survival mechanisms. It is the people's spiritual consciousness that America is still standing strong and tall, especially those people who attend pray meetings and churches, where the people congregate to praise God to bless America. How can America still deny people their true freedom and justice, which is apart of the masses of people alienable rights—the right that is given to mankind by God?

In America, we have a body of people who are captivated with afflicting so much hate, pain, and suffering on others, especially those people who somehow might not look like the standard and image that America perceives their citizens to be.

In other words, it seems that America looks at the outside of their people in order to paint an image of what they assume is a perfect image of what a person should be or who America protects under the words "Let us make America great again."

America's perceptions of greatness have nothing to do with looking into the hearts and minds of their citizens in order for America to find its greatness in the hearts and minds of its citizens' greatness. It seems that is because of America's philosophical ideologies on, "Let us make America great again."

This statement alone—"Let us make America great again"—has become a statement of deception instead of a statement of love, unity, and progress for a growing nation who want its citizens to make progress in unity, God, love, and progress.

I would assume that statement would be a God-driven statement by a country who teaches "In God we trust." Now that statement has been the backbone to American people's consciousness along with the hate that America has caused its citizens.

To me, when that statement was mentioned, "Let us make America great again," I can appreciate that statement if that statement was referring to idea of "Let us make America great again" if it meant that America was last in education, if it meant that America was last in the Olympics competitions, or if it meant that America was last in poverty. I can accept the statement of, "Let's make America great again" but only for America to use the ideology of "Let us makes America great again."

That is the statement that has brought so much pain and suffering upon people because of the way they look or speak. It is easy to judge people based upon how they look when America thinks like that. It places America in a dangerous position for any nation of people to be in. This statement with its word could bring an internal revolution to masses of people living in America.

The hate that is in these words is developing a consciousness of hate, pain, and suffering that is slowly destroying America to the point of where America's hate cannot acknowledge its own self-destruction. Because in those words, "Let us make America great again," it has developed a consciousness in the minds and hearts of some American people that has caused so much pain and suffering on the terrains of America. It's not a reality of American democracy at all what we are experiencing with. "Let's make America great" are the words that bring harmony and peace to the American people's hearts and souls. But to express and experience it living in America is different from what it truly means.

The words "Let's make America great" are not transparent enough to reach everyone the same way that they should. Some benefit from the words "Let's make America great." Do you understand any statement that we made, especially in America? It means that everybody's nationality and all Americans should benefit from the statement "Let's make America great." This is a prime example of how we allowed deceptions in words to change our consciousness toward God.

It seems sometimes that mankind is afraid to share the material possessions that God has given or blessed them with, but still, they want God to continuously give them the material possessions that they are not willing to give to each other or share with each other.

And others don't, but the one thing I want us to recognize is through it all, in God we trust; and that has always been the changing time to create out of a negative situation or bad situation the positive spiritual consciousness and enlightenment of God, which mankind need to progress spiritually.

From everyone's heart and soul in America that elaborate on "Let's us make America great" and not allow American citizens not to experience that greatness to its fullest ability is the deception of words that sometimes produce and create lots of hate.

That statement, "Let us make America great again," has placed the American people into this type of consciousness that bring about this awareness, and that is what seems to be the truth as being compromised as a lie.

What we know as a lie seems to become more respected than the truth itself. America is supposed to be a country of greatness still, and yet it does not have an appreciation for its own greatness.

America's greatness is twisted in so much pain, suffering, and hate. That same pain, suffering, and hate that is in America is destroying the true love, unity, and progress that America represents to the world.

That pain, suffering, and hate is becoming like a disease or sickness that is destroying America's own social, economic, and political system. That same greatness of America is extending itself into the minds and hearts of the American people.

Now that same statement of "Let us make America great" has extended itself into the edifice of the churches. I know that America is blessed. If we look at oher countries, we would realize how blessed America is or how great America is. America's blessings comes from God. We still have food, water, and food pantries. To be honest with you, God has blessed America because of the people that pray for the conditions of America. These are the people whom God listens to when they say "Let us make America great again."

To me when someone says "Let us make America great again," I assume that they will be working toward a utopia where they would be trying to prevent the crimes that are seriously affecting America. Mankind tries to develop a better way for their citizens, through developing their state of consciousness.

The hate that breeds hate is what is going to intentionally destroy America itself. Many people all over the world thought that the Rome empire would never fall. The Roman Empire fell because of a nation strained. Just like the Roman Empire, though, they were too great to fall.

America will fall also if it does not adhere to the consciousness of God's divine Word, and mark my words, America will fall. The reason why America is standing strong now is because of the people and churches that pray for America to implement God's consciousness, compassion, patients, grace, and mercy in order that God Himself would forgive America.

One of the things that we need to do is have prayer in the schools of America. We also need to implement pray in the schools. God's consciousness, should also be implemented in the workplace just to keep employees focused on God with God's consciousness.

Just to keep God's spirit resonating in the lives of mankind and to keep us in a perfect attitude of love joy and happiness toward each other where we can reflect the same love that God has reflected in us and through us because we acknowledge and study God's Word to enhance our spiritual consciousness.

I would always say that in America, the more that America deviates from God's Word and teachings, the worse of a condition America is going to place itself in, which is going to lead to the destruction of America.

There is still enough time left in America's heartbeat to resuscitate America back into its own state of mind which reflects God's consciousness, God's compassion, God's love, God's grace, and God's mercy for its people based on the person's or people's integrity or character.

The question someone should ask is, what is missing in any society that exercises that type of greatness that is able to produce so much pain, suffering, so much hate toward its citizens?

To be honest, America is a society that, even in its state of greatness, still needs healing. The question one needs to ask is, what does America need in order to heal itself from its own pain and suffering?

America has the answer to heal its own broken heart, and the answer to the question is so simple. Here is what the answer to the question is. I mean the answer to the question about, "Let us make America great again."

America, with all of its hate, pain, and suffering needs to embrace God's divine Word. As America begins to embrace God's divine Word, it is God's Words that becomes the water and that is able to put out the burning flames of America's hate, pain, suffering, and oppression which America has caused their citizens.

America needs that water to flow into the hearts of the American people in order to destroy the hate, pain, suffering, and oppression that America has caused its citizens.

America needs a spiritual cleansing by using God's divine Word which is to develop the consciousness of America if America was to embrace the consciousness of God through God's divine Word.

The consciousness of God can become the spiritual waters that is able to wash away the floods that exist in the hearts and souls of mankind, which can destroy the hate that exist in the world. America needs to resuscitate itself back to life in order to put out the burning flame of America's hate, pain, suffering, and oppression that the people of America have experienced.

While America is embracing God's divine Word, Americans should be in the state of developing the love and compassion that America has built itself upon many years ago.

The question one needs to ask is, what are we referring to when we talk about God's consciousness? We are trying to acknowledge first God's transcending presence in our lives. We are also trying to educate ourselves about God's divine Word in order for us to get a better understanding of God's Word.

When we try to get a better understanding of God's Word, we are acknowledging the truth within God's Word and trying to apply that truth that is in God's Word to become a way of life for us to embrace as we continue to make God's Word a priority in our lives.

We can only do that through our consciousness, and as we embrace God's Word, we are making God's Word a part of our consciousness and letting it become a way of life for us to develop and mature in the presence of God.

When we open up our hearts to let God's presence in, we are acknowledging that through God's presence in our hearts and minds comes a deeper consciousness that gives us a deeper understanding of our spirituality and reality as well.

As we embrace God's consciousness, we are embracing God's authentic wisdom. I am referring to the wisdom that transcends itself through God's Word. God's Word gives us the knowledge we need to strengthen our faith through our consciousness in God.

# DEFINING OUR MEANING AND BEING IN LIFE

For instance, God's consciousness gives us the knowledge we need to acknowledge what is our true meaning and being in life. As we try to define our meaning and being through God's Word, that is when we are beginning to develop a consciousness that is able to enlighten us about God's consciousness.

That thought that teaches us to comprehend God's consciousness is the same thought that starts to develop in our lives, in its spiritual essence; our spiritual essence is what develops God's consciousness within each and every one of us, which comes with the confidence that we need in order to receive God's consciousness within us.

As we try to comprehend our meaning and being in life, even when we are wrestling with our adversities and the chaos that exist in the world, it is through God's wisdom that we have the discipline we need in order for us to make the right choices in our lives, and those choices that we make should always be influenced by God's consciousness. Our consciousness develops our actions which produces our faith in God.

That is why God's consciousness gives mankind a deeper understand of who they are, spiritually and physically, because we become more confident in the decisions we make and because we acknowledge God's consciousness in our lives.

After embracing God's consciousness, we have a tendency to mature and develop in the understanding of God's faith and God's grace and God's mercy. Then to better enhance man's spiritual essence, God is still able to implement His grace and mercy, His salvation, His faithfulness to mankind, and most of all, His compassion.

The only way that God's consciousness plays a vital role in our lives depends on how well we are in tune with God's consciousness and how much of our free will we are we willing to give up in order to follow God as well as embrace God's presence in our lives.

In other words, in order for us to totally understand God's consciousness, it depends on whether we are willing to surrender our lives totally to God, or like most people do, give just a portion of our life to God when it is convenient for us to do so.

We must be willing to give our lives totally to God. The idea behind mankind's spiritual consciousness is not giving God what we think He deserves but giving God total responsibility toward our life. We can grow and mature in God's righteousness, even when we are going through our trials and tribulations in life.

When we start to experience the true essence and substance of God's spiritual consciousness within our lives, that is when we can experience how profound and powerful God's Word is that develops and shapes our own spiritual consciousness is to mankind.

If we don't give God our all and all every day and every second, God does not want a portion of our lives. God needs the total amount of our lives. If we only give Him a portion of our lives, that means we are stagnating the importance and significance of our faith in God. The only time that our faith becomes mature is when we study and embraces God's Word and His love for mankind and stay in constant fellowship with God our Father.

If we give a portion of our lives to God instead of giving all of life to God, what do you think we would get back from God? We would just get back a portion of what we have given to God. Even in the portions, which we have given to God, God is still blessing us abundantly. Think about it. Do you know if we gave our all to God at how much more of God we would have through God's blessings?

Now here is a question: do you know why so many Christians are having a difficult time in their faith? It is simple. They have not given God 100 percent of their lives, and the battle becomes more of a personal issue than a spiritual issue. I will discuss this further in the book.

## THE POWER OF GOD'S CONSCIOUSNESS

The only way that we can become in tune to God's consciousness is by acknowledging God's presence through His authentic Word, which is the Bible. No one can comprehend or understand God's consciousness if they have not experienced reading and studying God's divine Word. Now as we understand God's consciousness, we must keep in mind that we do not have the mental capacity to understand nor comprehend the mind of God. But through God's Word, we have the mental capacity to understand and comprehend God's consciousness through God's divine Word.

The other question is, how do we acknowledge God's presence in our lives? In other words, what do we have to do in order to acknowledge God's presence in our lives? Let us look at it also from this perspective, and that is what we have to do.

When we are able to embrace God's Word in our mind, we are actually saying that we are able to comprehend God's Word with enough understanding to remember it enough to let it become part of our character where we can use the spiritual essences of God's divine Word in order to develop our spiritual consciousness and discipline that we have learned from God's Word.

We have to constantly stay in tune to God's Word and embrace God's Word in our hearts and minds. When we embrace God's Word in our hearts, it means that we acknowledge through God's Word that we have learned enough of His Word to mature in the love of God's consciousness.

When we mature in God's consciousness, we are actually developing our faith in God. As we develop our faith in

God, it is our faith in God that gives us the love we need to let God's will manifest itself in our lives; where the faith that we have in God's Word has given us enough confidence to accept God's Word through our faith in God. God gives us the confidence or enough confidence for mankind to experience their spiritual consciousness progress and mature through Him, and it is in Him we become conscious of God's anointing. Here is what I mean. You see the knowledge and wisdom that mankind gathers from God's Word becomes the power and consciousness of mankind's true reality and existence of their faith in God our Father.

When mankind studies God's Word and is able to comprehend, understand, and allow God's Word to become a way of life. In other words, when mankind is able to comprehend, understand, and make God's Word a way of life, that is when God's Word becomes the spark that ignites, the spark that gives mankind a light-bulb moment as well as an enlightenment for mankind spirit and soul to become mankind's spiritual consciousness with God.

When mankind starts to understand and comprehend God's Word and live by God's Word, that is when mankind also starts to develop their spiritual consciousness.

When mankind develops their spiritual consciousness, mankind can only develop their spiritual consciousness through excepting and living God's divine Word in their heart, mind, body, and soul. This is how mankind starts to develop their spiritual consciousness in God.

Now as mankind comprehend and understand God's Word, this is where mankind starts to develop and allow mankind to mature God's faith. We must also understand that when mankind embraces God's consciousness through

God's Word, that is when mankind is able to understand God's wisdom, and this is what gives mankind the opportunity and privilege to develop their spiritual consciousness in God. Mankind spiritual consciousness can only be developed and matured based on how mankind lives their lives.

Mankind's lifestyle is a true example of mankind's faith in God. Faith is the belief that uses mankind's spiritual consciousness and lifestyle to become the true reality that reflects and exhibits God's consciousness.

The true essence and substance of mankind's faith and consciousness in God. Also, mankind's faith is displayed through mankind's action and how mankind also lives our God consciousness through their integrity and character. Now that is the true reality of life and mankind's relationship with God.

Mankind's belief in God is what gives mankind the spiritual consciousness that mankind needs in order to exercise their faith, which is mankind's belief in God. The power that we have through God's divine Word is the belief that shapes our faith and integrity of who God is to us.

The belief that mankind has in God's faith comes from mankind experiencing God's Word. God's Word is what shapes mankind's faith, and spiritual consciousness in God.

As God's Word shapes our spiritual consciousness and faith in Him, that is what allows mankind to recognize the true essence and substance of God's power through His Word, and that is acted out through mankind's faith in God.

Now as mankind studies, understands, and interprets God's Word, it is in the belief of God's Word that we develop our faith in God our Father; and that is what gives mankind the opportunity to study God's Words.

And when mankind studies God's Word, it gives mankind a sense of physical and spiritual security that builds up their confidence and courage, which mankind needs to live by the Word of God. Now that confidence is what mankind needs to live by the Word of God, and that is what develops mankind's spiritual consciousness.

When mankind develops their spiritual consciousness in God, that is what gives mankind the confidence and courage they need to manifest God's power, which mankind has come to acknowledge through God's divine Word. The power that mankind has come to acknowledge the power of their consciousness can only be achieved through mankind's own faith and consciousness, which mankind receives from studying and reading God's authentic Word.

The power that mankind gathers from God's Word transcends itself in us and through us as we study and read God's Word. The reality of reading and studying God's Word develops our confidence.

Here is why people have confidence in God's Word. We actually make God's Word a part of our lives and also when we make God's Word a part of our discipline and our lifestyle.

When we experienced the honesty that exists within God's Word, just as human beings, we know that we can stand strong in representing God's name and what God stands for. Our confidence comes in knowing that everything that God says, His words come true, and everything that God said to us comes true would do.

The idea that we know that God's Word does not play tricks with us; it does not use intellectual words to deceive us or make us think that something is different than what it is.

Because God's Word is not written to fit into mankind's status or agenda, God's Word does not fit into mankind's status quo. God's Word does not fit into mankind's status. God's Word is not written for one particular group of person or people. God's Word is not written for a particular church, religion, or even a particular congregation. God's Word is written to bring mankind into the mere physical existence of life and into the spiritual reality of mankind's consciousness.

When we embrace God's divine Word and apply God's Word to start to become a part of our discipline and way of life, our confidence that we receive from God's Word comes to us because we experienced the truth and spirituality of God's Word in our lives, which exist within God's Word. We even experienced the authenticity of God's Word, being truthful to the masses of people.

Making God's Word worth dying for is the truth and honesty that God displayed through his Word, and everything that God says He was going to do, He did.

When we are not preparing for the truth, God tells us what the truth is. God is always right. He tells what the truth is, even if we don't want to hear the truth or experience what the truth is. God is always right and just. The truth of God's honesty in His Word is what develops mankind's consciousness and faith in God.

This is especially when mankind already acknowledges to themselves the belief. Now mankind's belief in God has to do with mankind knowing through their spiritual consciousness and belief in God. That is what gives mankind the confidence and the courage of what they can achieve through their belief and faith in God, and it is at this point that mankind's consciousness is what shapes mankind's spirituality.

It is mankind's belief in God that develops mankind's faith and spiritual awareness of who God really is to mankind.

Now it is because of mankind's faith and awareness of who God is to mankind and the experiences that mankind has encountered from the intense studying of God's divine Word.

It is the studying, it is the faith, it is the spiritual awareness, and it is the life's experiences that mankind has learned and encountered. It is all of these factors that impact and develop mankind's consciousness in God, and that is what makes mankind transform from a physical being into becoming God's spiritual creation of life.

It is through mankind's awareness that is manifested through mankind's consciousness that gives mankind the power they need through God's divine Word to exercise the manifestation of their faith, which mankind receives through God's divine Word.

The significance of faith is to let mankind acknowledge the power that God has given mankind through His Word. The power that mankind has received from God's Word gives mankind the power, to overcome all of mankind's principalities and things that are not seen or experienced to mankind's physical eyes.

When mankind starts to mature in God's Word, the knowledge and wisdom that comes from God's Word start to develop mankind's consciousness. As mankind's consciousness starts to develop, at that point, mankind inherited the true essence and substance of mankind, which defines mankind's spiritual gifts and anointing. Mankind's spiritual gifts are what help mankind bring some transparency to mankind's reason and purpose for living.

This is when mankind's consciousness goes way beyond the mere physical existence of what mankind can comprehend or understand in the physical existence of life. When I mentioned principalities and things unseen, I am making reference to what the human eyes and instinct can only experience as his or her physical reality and human experiences.

Once again, mankind's consciousness is created and developed through mankind's intense and dedicated studying of God's Word.

As mankind study God's Word, it is God's Word that opens up mankind's consciousness and intuition, which develops mankind's consciousness, in God. When mankind studies God's Word, it seems that God's Word has a tendency to bring light into man's inner self. This is what gives mankind the ability and confidence to naturally develop their spiritual insight and enlightenment in God.

When mankind develops their spiritual consciousness, it gives mankind the opportunity to experience their own principalities and things that are unseen to mankind physically or things that they cannot understand or comprehend with mankind's natural eyesight.

The consciousness that mankind has developed from God's Word is what gives mankind a certain amount of power to heal the sick and make the blind see without any medical degree or medical influence from this world or academic institution or education.

Here is why our spiritual consciousness is important to us: it allows us to recognize and experience our spiritual adversities and adversaries before they can attack us or destroy us or kill us physically and spiritually.

Mankind's spiritual consciousness gives mankind an advantage over Satan's evil desires to destroy mankind and this world and the spiritual world. Our consciousness gives us another advantage: to see and experience Satan's principalities and the things that are unseen to us in our physical lives and existence.

Our consciousness in God's faith is what prevents us from experiencing so much pain and suffering before these things are able to happen or create serious pain and suffering in our lives. Let me remind you that our spiritual consciousness is developed through God's Word.

Now it is our consciousness that shapes the integrity and character of our faith in God. We must also remember that our belief in God is what develops and matures our faith in God. Our faith is the action that challenges our belief and our actions in God.

Faith is nothing more than the belief that allows mankind to know and to recognize how important our consciousness in God is to mankind. When mankind is able to recognize and develop its spiritual consciousness, mankind's spiritual consciousness is what gives mankind the power over all the principalities and things that are not seen, especially those that do not exist in the physical manifestation of mankind's existence. Faith is the action and expression of how our actions are the belief of the action, which displays the actions of our integrity and personality.

We must also understand that faith is not a belief. Faith is the action that creates and produces mankind's consciousness. Faith is the belief that produces the consciousness of mankind's faith in God.

Now faith is the evidence that expresses and produces the belief that mankind has in God. That belief of our faith is what enlightened mankind's consciousness and awareness about who God actually is to mankind.

Mankind's faith is the actions of mankind's consciousness. Mankind's faith depends on how well mankind interprets as well as acknowledges also how well mankind comprehends the information that mankind receives from God's Word.

The consciousness of mankind's actions is what shapes mankind's integrity and personality and how mankind lives their lives pleasing and acceptable to God. Mankind's actions are displayed and expressed through mankind's consciousness. Our consciousness in God is what shapes our spiritual identity and gives us the confidence, courage, and compassion we need in order for us to do whatever God's will is for our life.

# The Christian's Lifestyle and God's Consciousness

I strongly believe that we must come to an understanding that the Christian life is not a life of convenience but a life that exercises true faith and discipline through God's divine Word, and that is what develops our consciousness in God.

When I say convenience. I mean that convenience is also a state of consciousness that has its moments of convenience but not to the point of where we become comfortable in the state of our convenience. Because we wrestle with many obstacles, that produces many adversities and many adversaries. It is through our consciousness that helps us understand the state of our adversities and how to handle or adversaries.

We must understand that as Christians, we make a commitment to God. Now that commitment is influenced by our consciousness, and it is our consciousness that acknowledges our confession that we made toward God.

Now that commitment that we made toward God makes all Christians a precious commodity here on earth to Satan. I think sometimes Christians don't know our value as it pertains to our spirituality, but what I do know is that Satan does know mankind's worth better than mankind does.

Christians must understand that the existence of life and spirituality does not stop here on earth. It transcends into the many decisions which God has to make in order for us to gain access to our salvation.

The first time that we become conscious of our commitment or confession to God, that places Satan in a position to destroy our worth. We must always try to remember our worth here on earth.

Our worth here on earth is more valuable to God than our faith and consciousness can comprehend. Our worth goes way beyond our salvation in God because our salvation is spiritual, and it is in our state of faith and consciousness that we are still able to comprehend the true reality of God's divine Word which also acknowledges our true worth to God.

As Christians, we must understand how we become a precious people who are also anointed by God, although we are an anointed people. We must also realize that we are created here on earth, but we are spiritually driven by our consciousness to spiritually define what our purpose and reason is to exist. While we are finding our purpose and reason to exist, we must also try to find God through all of our adversities and adversaries in order for us to become successful in our relationship with God.

Satan is working day and night every second to the hour, just to steal our salvation in God by challenging us through our adversities and adversaries. Satan somehow does not have the same compassion or forgiveness that God has for us.

In other words, Satan has no love for you as well, so it does not matter how we think. That is why we should constantly, pray to God, and stay constantly in tune to the message that is given to us by God and deliver it to our hearts and minds through the Holy Spirit.

Our adversities and adversaries are constantly knocking at our doors, trying everything they can to break our spirits and control our state of consciousness.

That is why we are constantly being challenged by our adversaries and adversaries, which means that if we procrastinate, even in our faith, we would give Satan an opportunity to come into our hearts and minds and destroy our relationship and faith in God. As we continue to study God's divine Word, we are embracing God's consciousness as a means to exercise our faith in order to transform our hearts and minds not to become submissive to our adversities and adversaries.

We must always recognize that it is through God's consciousness that prevent us from becoming submissive to our own sins. Our consciousness gives us the awareness to acknowledge the actions of our sin. It is also through our consciousness which caused us to exercise the faith we need that would transform our lives, not to be become the subject of our sins or what we have done that is wrong in the eyes of God.

The Christian life is not a life of convenience because we are constantly wrestling with our adversities and our adversaries and the chaos that already exists in this world.

Convenience is something worth looking forward to as a Christian based on our faith in God. Convenience is not an honor or something granted to us by God. Here is why I say that the Christian life is not a life of convenience but a way of life. Now that way of life comes with many challenges that are able to spiritually draw us closer to the Father.

Here is why we should not depend on the state of mind which causes us to be in a state of convenience. You see, our convenience creates something called a comfort zone. That comfort zone sometimes is what causes us to be constantly challenged by so many obstacles in our lives.

The one thing that we should know about is whatever temptation we are faced with, God is always preparing us through our faith in Him for us to always face our adversities in life. When we face our adversities in life, and we know that God is in the midst of our adversities, we have confidence in God to know that God will bring us through the crossroads and detours of life all because we have embraced God's spiritual consciousness in our lives. That is what gives us the confidence and courage we need to continuously serve God through our mind, body, and soul.

When we reach the crossroads of life, we are approaching some harsh and difficult times in life. We might not know which roads to travel, but the one thing that we do know is that there is a sense of peace as we travel the crossroads and detours of life where we have to make some serious decisions at the crossroads of our life and where we need to make some serious decisions that lead to an intersection of our lives.

But through our intersections in our lives along with our adversities, we will always feel the pressure, tension, and stress of our crossroads and detours in life. But it is our faith in God that gives us a sense of inner peace we need. That peace becomes the confidence to know that we will always be successful, even in the midst of our adversities.

I mean when we truly give our lives to God, we do develop a sense of peace, that peace we experience even when we are going through our trials and temptations. There is still a sense of inner peace that dwelled among God's people even in times of their storms.

Our inner peace comes with knowing that whatever difficulties we are facing, whatever difficulties we have during our trials, whatever difficulties we have during our temptations, the one thing that we do know is God is going to bring us through our trials and temptations.

Although we might not like the outcome of God's answers to our situations and circumstances that we are facing, we already know that God has the answer to our problems, even if the answer is not what we don't want to hear or do.

The one thing we do know is that through our adversities, there are lessons which we need to learn, even in the midst of our adversities, that God is or has been willing to teach us, but for some strange reason, we're not listening or trying to understand or interpret the message, which God has been given us to understand; so the best way that God is going to capture our attention is to bring us face-to-face with our trials and adversities.

But through our consciousness, God is able to teach us a lesson about our spirituality to help us strengthen our faith and love in God.

# THE COMFORT ZONE

**M**any Christians get caught up in something that I call a comfort zone, and that comfort zone prevents many Christians from becoming mature in their faith with God.

The comfort zone also prevents Christians from maturing in their faith with God. It is through our faith that acknowledges the presence of God's consciousness in our lives.

In order for us to understand God consciousness to its fullest potential, we must recognize that being a Christian, we must constantly develop the understanding that the Christian life is a way of life more than a way of convenience.

Let me reiterate we must realize that the Christian life is a way of life. It is not a life that is lived only in a state of convenience. The Christian lifestyle is a state of maturity where we grow, but as we grow, we are developing our consciousness in God's faith. But the more we grow and mature, the more obstacles we are faced with.

While facing our obstacles in life, we must also realize that Satan is responsible for all of mankind's temptations here on earth. Now some people would say that God is responsible for our trials. To me, it does not matter if we are being tempted by Satan or going through some difficult trials that God has placed before us.

The main reason and purpose of our trials and temptations is to use our God's divine consciousness which God has bestowed upon us to defeat the obstacles which we are facing in the midst of our temptations and our trials. Let me reiterate we need God's divine Word to overcome our temptations or our trials. The key is to knowing what to do in the midst of our trials and temptation and how to used God's divine Word to overcome all of our adversities in life.

That is why it is very important for us to study God's Word because our salvation depends on our relationship with God and how well we are able to understand God faith through our consciousness in God.

When we are able to use our consciousness to develop and mature in God's grace, that develops our confidence in God's faith. The confidence that we develop through our consciousness in God's faith is what matures to our faith in God and what we in order for mankind to mature in God's consciousness. It is in that state of maturity that mankind is able to develop their spirituality in God. It seems that our state of maturity comes with how well we use God's consciousness to overcome our adversities in life.

Our trials test our faith in God. It seems that our strength and maturity comes in the midst of our adversities. We must also understand that in the midst of our adversities is where the potential of our faith is easily challenged.

When I make reference to the idea that the Christian life is a way of life than a way of convenience, what I am referring to is letting people know that the life of a Christian is the essence of their spirituality.

If I had to define spirituality, I would define it also in this manner. Spirituality is allowing your belief to develop your consciousness to become in tune to God's righteousness. When we stay in tune with God's righteousness, we are also developing our faith in God.

Let me get back to my point about difficulties and obstacles. What makes our obstacles and difficulties in life easy to bear has to do with the direction in which mankind is directing their faith. In other words, during our difficult moments in life, we need a sense of security and comfort just to help us through our most difficult times in our lives.

What eases the burden of our difficulties and obstacles has to do with how mankind positions their faith in God. For example, if you are a person who places your faith in the world while struggling with your difficulties, then you are placing your salvation in a dangerous place in life.

Here is what I mean. If we place our faith in the world, we already know that our faith is very important to the nurturing and development of our consciousness.

Now if we place our faith in the world, then we are destroying our consciousness. If we place our faith in God, then we become liberated thinkers of our own consciousness. Here is why our consciousness is developed through God's divine Word.

We all can agree to disagree that the world is full of disappointments which is also affecting the churches. In other words, the Churches are also becoming a disappointment to the masses of people in society. Here is why the churches are supposed to be teaching and preaching the Word of God.

Instead, the people who are in authority in the churches—like the pastors, ministers, bishops, and deacons—use their titles as a status to gain enough power from the people and abuse that same power that they get from the masses of people and then turn around and use that same power that they received from the masses of people. That power that the masses of people give to the pastors, ministers, bishops, and deacons is the same power they abuse, especially those people who have a lack of knowledge, understanding, and interpretation of God's doctrine. The pastors, ministers, bishops, and deacons abuse their power to gain monetary rewards from the political system and economic system that speaks against God's divine Word. That is why it is very important that we develop our divine consciousness in God.

We would become still in tune to God's grace that we would begin to mature in God's divine consciousness. As we mature in God's grace, we would be able to recognize those people who are the false teachers of God's divine Word, such as pastors, ministers, bishops, and deacons, even if they were wrapped in beautiful attire to convince the masses of people that they are God's anointed people.

God would reveal to His people through the Holy Spirit who those false teachers are. That is, imitators of the Gospel. The Holy Spirit already knows who the false prophets are in their hearts and minds. The Holy Spirit already recognizes who is faithful and who is not; in other words, who is unworthy to God's divine grace.

Some people, in the congregations already know that there are many pastors, ministers, bishops, elders, and deacons that are teaching more theology, and theory than God's authentic Word to the masses of the people.

They are people who already know, through the conviction of the Holy Spirit, that the Church they are attending is not in compliance with God's divine Word. Now here is where the problem starts. The problems do not start with the false prophets. Let me look at it from this perspective: the problem does not start with the teaching of the false prophets. The problems start when the people of God have no courage. The problem starts when the people of God are afraid. The problem starts when the people of God have more fear in their hearts than they do faith.

In other words, the problem starts when the people of God have more fear in their hearts than they do God's faith and righteousness. We must always remember that our faith is the true manifestation and elevation of mankind's spiritual consciousness in God.

While fear causes mankind not to live up to their full potential of what faith is to them, fear is the destruction of mankind's salvation. Here is why: because God does not create fear in the hearts of His people. God is a God of faith, compassion, righteousness, grace, and mercy. These are the attributes and characteristics of God.

How can we say that we are anointed when we as Christians cannot defend God's doctrine? I mean the righteousness that gives us the consciousness to find the courage within ourselves, to find the faith we need in order to stand up and represent the faith that God has given us.

What I am experiencing in the world, it seems that the churches no longer have God's grace dwelling in the churches. The question one needs to ask is why is God's grace being removed from the churches? Because the consciousness of the people in the churches are not being nurtured with God's wisdom. It seems that God has removed Himself from the edifice of the churches.

What the churches are afraid to admit is that they are facing some prevalent times; the churches are in chaos within themselves. But the question is why? Here is why: the churches are distorting God's Word and are compromising God's Word to fit into their political or economic agenda. Instead, the people who are in leadership positions in the churches are using God's Word to fit into the world's agenda instead of using God's Word to revive and rehabilitate the people in the world that is in dying need of God's Word.

That is why some of us cannot get our lives together because we want what is in the world and we want what God has to offer us. We want it all at the same time. This mindset has stolen many Christians' salvation.

The tension and stress of trying to serve two masters at the same time is what creates the difficulties and stress that is going on in our lives right now. We even tried to master serving two masters at the same time, and what is happening is that our evil conditions that we are constantly faced with. Sometimes, I think that our sins and adversities begin to take complete control over mankind.

Once again, that is why we need to stay in fellowship and in constant harmony with God's divine Word to better enhance and develop our spiritual consciousness through God's divine Word.

Those who give up their lifestyles in the world and are able to follow God still feel the pressure, tension, and stress of their difficulties that they are faced with, but those people who are faithful and righteous in God's eyes are the people who will still able to find peace, security, and tranquility in the midst of their difficulties. Here is why: because of their consciousness in God.

Let me elaborate a little bit more. Even when we are sleeping, we should still be committed to staying in tune to God's consciousness, doing what we can do to stay constantly in tune to God's righteousness.

God's consciousness should always be embraced in our minds and in our hearts. For example, how we live our lives and how we carry ourselves as individuals for God should always be reflected in our integrity and faith.

We must realize that our survival as Christians depends on our consciousness. Here is what I mean: as Christians, we must always stay constantly in tune to God's Word. Our consciousness should always be in tune to anything that has to do with our spirituality which reflects and dictates God's righteousness and true salvation in our lives.

Our consciousness should always develop our spiritual gifts to make us the sculptors of our own faith. Being the sculptors of our own faith, we should always spend time shaping and carving our character in order that we may develop the same lifestyle as Jesus Christ.

The question someone may ask is, how do we shape and carve our own faith to be in the image of God? As Christians, we must always stay in tune to God's consciousness. God's consciousness is the survival and strength of our faith. Our consciousness develops our faith in God. We must always develop who we are through God's consciousness and express who we are through the consciousness of our faith in God.

This is our survival magnesium, something that all people who believe in God should do, and that is we should always develop our consciousness in a way that will allow us to stay constantly in tune to God's righteousness through God's divine Word.

At this point, I would like to ask this question. At what point in our lives should the Christian experience reflect God's consciousness in our lives?

Think about it. When you are around church members on Sundays, when you are in church where people can see how wonderful you look, that is how we judge each other. We judge each other based on how we look and not how spiritually endowed that person's relationship is with God.

Sometimes we use people's status as a means to determine their righteousness with God. When we use people, careers, and academic degrees in order to determine their righteousness with God, that is when we lose focus of the person's or people's divine consciousness.

As human beings, these are the things we use to determine how faithful we are toward God, but our Christian life should always reflect God's consciousness, especially when we are by ourselves where people cannot see the things that we are doing in private.

The Christian life is challenged more in our private lives than in public, especially when no one is around to observe what you are doing. Do you still have that same spiritual consciousness that reflects God both in your private life as well as your public life? Or are both your public and private lives truly different?

Here is the other question: is your private life the same in public? Can people look at your Christian life and recognize that your spiritual life in public is the same in private? Our lives as Christians should be the same in public as it is privately. As a matter of fact, our lifestyle as Christians should be the same all the time. Both your private and public lives should be the same in the eyes of the Lord as well as other people. God should be proud of you or me in private as He is of us in public.

Our lives should always be influenced by God's consciousness. The only way that we can see God's potential in our own life is when we study and accept God's Word as His authentic Word and acknowledge that God's consciousness is a way of life.

This is very important when we are able to experience God's consciousness, so please let me elaborate. If we were to look at God's Word by trying to challenge it authenticity, the question that should come to mind is, what is the right way to define God's doctrine? The first thing we must realize is that God's doctoring means the Gospel, Scriptures, which is the Holy Bible. The Word should be proven based on its authenticity and nothing else.

For example, the thing about God's Word is that God's Word cannot only be defined based on reading God's Word or placing it in academic institutions. God's Word can only be defined in the heart and consciousness of mankind. Now that sounds good, but let me bring some clarity to that statement about how God's Word should be defined.

The reality of God's Word can only be understood through faith. When you are studying and teaching God's Word, in order to validate its authenticity, we must teach the truth. If we don't teach the truth, then we are introducing what I refer to as the "Theory in Theology."

For example, many theologians have not understood the true reality of God's faith, God's mercy, and most of all, God's grace. God's Word was never written to be interpreted by academic scholars or to be define by scholars. God's Word was written to transcend and transform and change mankind's life in order to bring mankind into a spiritual human being in God's consciousness.

God's Word can only be defined through mankind's consciousness. The consciousness of mankind is best expressed in the actions of mankind's faith. The actions of mankind's consciousness should truly be expressed through mankind's faith. Mankind's faith is where we displayed our true characteristic of who God actually is to us. Faith should always be displayed as the human actions of God's divine righteousness.

Here is why faith is the only belief that mankind has where he or she is able to prove their love for God. There are no other actions of mankind which are able to define or prove God's faith without producing the actions that are able to create with it God's divine faith.

The actions of mankind's faith determine the maturity and strength in God. For example, the more love we have for God, the more determined we are to act upon our own faith. The more we act upon our faith, the more we are willing to give up mankind's free will and sinful nature.

Faith is that only belief that stands by itself in the spirit of mankind's heart and soul. Here is why faith is a word of action. What I mean by that is it is the only way we can define the level and maturity of our consciousness in God, which means faith is best defined based on our actions toward God. Faith is practiced as a state of maturity, although there are levels of maturity that bring our faith into perfection with God. Every time we are able to overcome our temptations or trials, that means that we have perfected another level of our spiritual growth and maturity in God's consciousness.

We must also recognize that our stages of growth become our level of maturity in God's grace and mercy. As we mature, and our consciousness of God begins to increase and grow, our consciousness then becomes our true awareness. That divine awareness is able to strengthen our beliefs in God.

As we are able to strengthen our beliefs in God, we must recognize that our beliefs are what strengthen our faith. It is our faith which develops our awareness of who God is to us.

That awareness is what develops our consciousness in God's divine righteousness. It is through our consciousness that we are given the confidence we need to act upon the actions which are needed to strengthen our faith in God.

Our faith is based on how committed we are to God. That is why Christians cannot become comfortable or look for convenience in this life. As a Christian, it is imperative that we recognize this statement that acknowledges to us that we are going to be constantly at war with our adversities and our adversaries. Although we are a people of peace, our circumstances in this life will not allow us to have peace within ourselves.

For example, our faith in God is like a child maturing into adulthood. Just like a young Christian is like a baby who needs nurturing, young Christians need nurturing as well until we run into some difficulties that challenge our faith to make us strong through the stages of its life.

Here is what I am referring to: when a child progresses through these stages of life, and it knows when and how to take its first steps in life, the child's confidence builds, just like the child is able to take their first steps in life and their confidence builds upon their first steps.

As we progress in our faith with God, we are taking baby steps as well. As our belief in God starts to take its steps into God's righteousness, our consciousness matures. As our consciousness matures, it is like us taking baby steps where our confidence starts to take root. As our confidence takes root in God's consciousness, it gives us a sense of confidence.

That confidence is the same confidence that we have in our faith as we grow in God's divine righteousness. Our confidence is our security and strength that we have in God's righteousness.

As we begin to mature and develop, we start to experience the responsibilities that come with us maturing. Do you know that the same way we mature spiritually in the eyes of God is the same as maturing physically in the eyes of God?

Here is what I mean: for example, as a child progresses through the stages of life, in order for that child to mature and develop into adulthood, that child has to experience life for itself. Now those experiences might be good or bad, but whatever these experiences are that the child has experienced, it has to do with strengthening the faith in the child and how that child interprets the concepts of what is good and bad that surrounds their lives.

The child's confidence matures because that child already knows that whatever obstacles that child is going to face, their parents are or their parent is always going to be supportive to them, and that is what gives the child the faith they need to overcome the many obstacles that they would face in life.

When that child knows that their parents or parent is going to support them, that is when that child's faith and confidence grows, developing a stronger relationship with their parent(s).

That is when the child's confidence grants them the confidence they need in order to have faith, knowing that their parent or parents are always going to be there for them always. I know that somewhere in our lives, we have had the same experience with God being the Father and Author of our faith.

We also know that through our faith in God, we can overcome any obstacles in life that we are faced with, all because of our faith in God. We must also understand that it is through our consciousness in God that strengthens our awareness that allows us to develop and mature in our faith with God.

In other words, faith lets us recognize how much confidence we have in God's Word and how developed and mature we are in God's Word. We must be conscious enough to understand that our faith is justified by our love and actions toward God.

Here is why: God's Word is written for us to have a spiritual direction and focus in life and to support each other spiritually and allow God to implement His will in our lives through our prayers, our fasting, and through our learnings and teachings of God's authentic Word so that we can better understand what our reason and purpose is in life.

If we are looking to criticize the Word of God or to find infallible truth in God's Word or try to test or whether or not God's Word is authentic or even try to disclaim the existence of God, we will never experience God's true essence of His authentic Word.

Many people read and study the Bible like it was a textbook or a novel, but in reality, it is not. For example, the Bible is not like a book where you read it and then take a test to find out how much of the Bible is either true or false or multiple choice. In order for you to find out weather, you have passed the test, or what percentage of your Bible is true or false, you need to pass in order to determine how much of God's Word is true or false.

The Bible is a book that is true. It develops mankind's consciousness. The Bible is a book that takes the physical mentality of mankind and transforms it into the spiritual consciousness and existence of life. The Bible is a book that brings mankind into recognizing what is God's truth versus what mankind's truth is.

The Bible develops mankind's gift of discernment. Our discernment is a spiritual gift that God has given to mankind to help mankind's consciousness to become more in tune to God's righteousness. The Bible is a book which leads us into all righteousness. The Bible is a book that helps to give us a direction in life.

The Bible is a book that teaches mankind about their salvation and what roads we should follow, even when we are facing our adversities. God did not develop the Bible to be a book that is full of quizzes and testing but to instruct and develop mankind's spiritual essence and mankind's love for each other.

The Bible is a book that is spiritually motivated and driven by the same God who created the world and everything that is in the world. It is also a book that teaches mankind how to improve their spiritual discipline. The Bible is a book that teaches us about our consciousness and awareness and how mankind should embrace God's Word as a way of life.

The Bible teaches us about Jesus's character, and through the teachings of the Bible, we also learn that we have the potential to become like Jesus Christ. The Bible also introduces mankind to their true God, and it is done not by angels but by normal men and women, like ourselves, who because of their consciousness became submissive to the will of God. The Bible also teaches us how to develop our consciousness from the physical existence of life into the spiritual existence of life.

The Bible also teaches mankind to pattern their lifestyle to reflect the image and likeness of Jesus Christ. The Bible is the blueprint of what we need to do in order to develop our faith and consciousness in God.

The Bible allows us to develop our consciousness enough to recognize that it is through our faith which develops our character and belief in God's divine Word. Now that divine belief is strongly influenced by the Bible. The spiritual character and integrity of a person can only be defined and developed in the reading and studying of God's divine Word.

As we develop spiritually in God's Word, our consciousness matures. As our consciousness matures, the knowledge and wisdom we receive from God's divine Word is what develops our faith in God. The faith that we receive from God's divine Word is divinely inspired by God's Word and can only be acknowledged in the words and messages of God's divine Word.

The words and messages that we receive from God's divine Word become our state of consciousness. As we embrace God's consciousness, we are embracing the messages that is in God's divine Word and through those divine messages which shape mankind's consciousness into becoming a way of life.

Those messages that are in God's divine Word are what shapes the knowledge of our consciousness. As God's divine Word shapes our belief in Him, that is when our consciousness begins to influence our faith in God's divine Word. That is why our consciousness should always be in tune to God's righteousness. As God's Word shapes our consciousness through the messages of the Scriptures, that is when we elevate ourselves to become spiritually driven and motivated through God's wisdom and knowledge.

For example, God's Word gives mankind the power to liberate their minds which develops a certain essence of love in the hearts of mankind. That love that we develop for each other is inspired by God's divine Word.

Mankind should have enough love for each other where we intercede for each other, especially here on earth as we fight against principalities and things that we cannot see or even experience ourselves. That is why we should keep uplifting each other in prayer and support each other spiritually. This is what exists through our spiritual consciousness and love for each other.

It is through God's consciousness that mankind is able to recognize and intercede as well as understand the evil desires that mankind cannot experience or see physically.

Mankind's consciousness is that light-bulb moment that awakes his or her spiritual insight that brings mankind awareness into a state that challenges mankind. Mankind's spiritual consciousness is constantly more than ever all because mankind believes in God. That is why we should pray for each other because we need to understand how can we say we love God whom we haven't seen but still hate our brother whom we have seen.

As mankind on this earth, we all should be in his heart, for each other, where the Word of God is able to cut through the heart of man so much where God's Word is able to pierce through the consciousness of man's mind and develop mankind to become a spiritual being.

Where God's Word is able to liberate mankind's consciousness, by placing mankind in a state of spirituality, where mankind is able to become one in fellowship with God, this is how mankind's character and integrity start to shape itself spiritually in the consciousness of mankind's heart and soul.

Now that same character and integrity can only become spiritually motivated by mankind's faith in God. That faith that I am referring to can only be determined and evaluated based on the actions of mankind. Faith is only based on mankind's actions. It is through mankind's actions that we experience mankind's faith.

But our faith in God allows us to mature and develop spiritually. Our spirituality is based on our submissiveness to whatever God's will is for our life.

Mankind's submissiveness to God is the character in which mankind are able to develop their consciousness. As mankind develop their consciousness, it is in the state of mankind's consciousness that mankind are able to recognize God's righteousness.

When mankind is able to understand God's righteousness, that is when mankind starts to experience God's faith. As mankind experiences God's faith, that is when mankind is able to develop the courage and confidence mankind needs to exercise their faith in God and throughout the world.

In other words, faith is not based on what you tell God but what God tells you to do. Faith does not have to do with how many times and how loud you pray. Faith is a lifestyle that is developed through a person or people's consciousness. Our consciousness develops our love for God.

What should people do for Him? God does not need you tell Him how much you love him if our lifestyle does not reflect God's love. Faith is based on our actions and, again, our submissive toward God.

The way mankind's actions express God's faith determines the level of maturity that mankind has experienced through God's faith—the faith that mankind has in God.

The question is, why is our faith in God constantly being challenged? So God can prove to us, based on our actions, how loyal and faithful we are to Him. God already knows how righteous we are to Him. The question that needs to be asked is, do we know how righteous we are to God?

Now our faith is challenged by our own adversities and by our adversaries. Both our adversities and adversaries are the circumstances and obstacles which occur in our lives which try to prevent the people of God from reaching their full spiritual potential.

It seems that when we are in our quiet moments of life, nothing in life at that particular moment is causing us no problems or stress in our lives. Maybe what I should say is when we are at peace with ourselves and we have no problems or trials or tribulations in our life at the time.

I mean when we have reached total peace or that state of total serenity, that could be a very dangerous position to be in. Here is why: if we are not exercising our faith, that means that our faith is in a vulnerable state.

That state of vulnerability that our faith is in can become a very dangerous place for our consciousness to be in. Here is why: because it is at that point where we become weak in our faith. Some people have become weak where they have allowed Satan to steal their salvation, even in the midst of their vulnerability. That state of vulnerability places us in a very dangerous position.

Here is what I mean: let me be clear. When our faith is not being challenged. We are at a standstill. That standstill, makes us vulnerable. It's just liked a person who is not exercising their body. If you are not exercising your body, what happens is it becomes weak. In other words, if there is no movement in the body, that means that our body is dead. In other words, if we are not exercising our faith in God, then our faith is dead. Dead faith means dead souls.

What we must understand is that when we are in a state of serenity, peace, or calmness, we have a sense of comfort. Now in that state of comfort, we should develop the many areas of consciousness which would give us the motivation we need to study God's divine Word. We should always acknowledge in our state of comfort that it is a time to pray, fast, and meditate on God's divine Word. Here is why: because God is preparing us to get ready for our adversities.

When we have those peaceful moments in our lives, we must recognize that those moments are for us to prep and prepare ourselves for those quiet moments in our lives. That is the perfect time for us to focus and embrace our spirituality.

The one thing we must realize as Christians is we cannot become comfortable in our commitment with God. We must try to motivate each other through the spirit of God. But in order for us as believers to motivate each other in God, we have to always be supportive to each other as Christians because our faith and salvation depends on it.

We must always try to constantly motivate each other faithfully and spiritually. We must recognize that our consciousness needs to be recharged and nurtured. Here's how we can begin to recharge our faith in God. We must constantly place ourselves in a state of motivation. What I mean by that is we must always want to nurture our faith so we can grow and mature in God's consciousness.

The Bible also teaches us about the importance of faith, and when we lose focus of our faith, what we need to do in order to improve our faith in God. That is why it is important for us to stay in tune with God's divine Word.

That is why when we are talking about God's divine Word, we are referring to the authenticity which embraces God's doctoring. What makes God's Word authentic is the truth which is embraced in God's authentic word.

Here is what I mean: when we read and study God's authentic Word, we have to be in the right state of consciousness, or as some people would say, mindset.

Now if a person or people approach God's divine Word with the right consciousness, that person or people would be in tune to God's authentic Word, and their consciousness would develop spiritually and keep them in tune with God's divine truth.

Now if we approach God's Word with the intention of trying to destroy the true reality of the Gospel, that is when the person or people's consciousness is going to become distorted and fallible.

The infallibility of the Gospel has always developed mankind's consciousness to become a positive spiritual force in mankind's life. If we are looking for spiritual reinforcement in the Gospels, we will find it. In other words, if we are trying to find loopholes and imperfections within the Gospel, we will find them.

Let me reiterate if we are looking for imperfections within the Gospel, we will find them. The Bible is a book that is driven by our faith in God, not through the physical interpretation of mankind's philosophies, theories, and ideologies.

The Bible is a book that is spiritually driven and motivated to bring an awareness to mankind's consciousness about who his creator is and what is mankind's purpose, reason, and responsibility to God.

The Bible is also a book that teaches mankind how to develop his consciousness in order for mankind to reached his spiritual potential through God's divine Word. Here is how mankind is able to reach his spiritual potential: by reading and studying God's divine Word.

If mankind is looking for imperfection and loopholes in the Bible, mankind is going to find those loopholes and imperfections.

For example, when I say that they would find those loophole and imperfections in the Bible, I am not saying that the Bible is not authentic or the Bible already has loopholes and imperfections in it. Let ask this question: how can someone say that there are loopholes and imperfections in the Bible when they already say that the Bible is God's divine and authentic word? The Bible is not a book of fallibility. The Bible is a book of infallibility.

If the Bible is authentic, and it is God's divine Word, how can you say, Mr. Grant, that people would find imperfections in the Bible? Here is what I mean: first of all, the Bible is not a research paper or an academic thesis. The Bible is a book that does not try to compare similarities and differences in order to come up with the truth. The Bible is a book that is truthful, an authentic book in its divine right. The Bible is not a book like a research paper or an academic thesis. First of all, the Bible is a book of truth and spirituality. The Bible is also a book which is inspired by God, and the message of God is transcended by Him through mankind.

In the Bible, there is only one opinion, and that opinion is God's opinion, not mankind's theological influence, not mankind's thesis, not mankind's philosophical thought. The Bible is a book that is completed with nothing but God's thoughts and spiritual influences.

We must understand that the Bible is not an academic thesis. We must also understand that the Bible is not a philosophical book. We must also understand that the Bible is not a theological book. The Bible is not an academic term paper or an academic thesis where we are getting graded for comparing similarities and differences for an academic grade. The Bible is a book that is able to develop mankind's consciousness from the mere physical to the spiritual.

Here is why: because the Bible is a book which should be approached with a certain type of consciousness. If I approached the Bible, looking for imperfection, I will find them. Here is why: anyone who is trying to find discrepancies, inconsistencies, or imperfections with the Gospel will definitely find them.

Here is why: because anyone who approaches the Word of God to read and study God's Word must approach the Word of God with a certain state of mind and consciousness.

First, that state of consciousness should be approached by mankind humbling themselves toward God's divine Word.

Second, we must also understand that the person who is reading the Bible must also have a faith based on their consciousness in the Scriptures.

Third, we must pray and ask God for guidance or reveal to us what is the message God is trying to reveal to us while we are reading and studying God's divine Word.

Fourth has to do with how we are going to apply the message that God is trying to reveal to us through reading and studying the Scriptures and how the Scriptures have impacted our lives that people can have a divine experience based on the reflection of our divine character and consciousness.

What people as well as Christians must understand is that the Bible is not just an ordinary book. It is God's divine Word which is God's message which transcends from God to mankind. Many people would assume that because mankind received God's message, mankind might have tampered with God's divine Word.

I think that many theologians and philosophers think that God was desperate and needed mankind to teach and preach His divine Word. So God randomly needed people to preach and teach God's divine Word.

So God was roaming through the world, looking and begging people to teach and preach His Word. So God gave His Word to each and every one to preach and teach His Word. It does not matter who it was; it seems that God gave His Word to everyone and anyone to preach and teach.

Let me acknowledge this. We already have each and every one preaching and teaching God's Word, and those were never people anointed by God. Look at each and every one who is preaching and teaching God's Word. They are doing more damage and abusing God's divine Word. We experience that through the condition that most of these churches are in and are going through.

We already experience how the Gospel of God is being place in the wrong hands, and the world is using the false prophets to disclaim and abuse the Word of God. False prophets are people chosen by man to do a man's job. The prophets of God are men and women chosen by God to do God's work for humanity in order to bring love and peace to heal a broken world.

One of the problems with people in the pulpit is that each and every one is teaching and preaching God's Word, but somehow, the majority of them do not have the God-driven character to become submissive do God's will; the majority of them are doing their own will instead of God's will, and they are doing this at the expense of mankind's salvation.

God does not choose people because they sound good on a pulpit. It does not mean that they are anointed by God to preach. Nor does mankind have the divine right to anoint a person or people to preach God's divine Word. That right is only given to mankind by God. Mankind has to be available to teach and preach God's Word when he or she is called by God to do so.

With teaching and preaching God's Word, it means that a person or people have to have a God-fearing consciousness which matches their integrity and character and which reflects God's divine Word that the person or people are teaching.

Here is why: God was never in a state where He had to depend on mankind in order do His will. Instead, God uses mankind to do His will. If God depended upon mankind to do His will, God's will would have never been accomplished here on earth. Mankind would have never had the opportunity to exercise their free will if God wanted to control mankind or dominate mankind's existence just to do His will. God would never create mankind with an understanding to exercise or give them a kind of privilege to exercise their free will.

What God did was to let mankind know that He is not a God of control or domination. What God was looking for in people was those people who wanted to have enough of awareness to develop their spiritual consciousness to serve God.

What we need to understand is that God did not anoint people who were walking down the street. These men and women were spiritually anointed by God through His Word. We must first try to understand what it is to be anointed by God. It wasn't that God saw people walking down the street, and God reach out to them and gave them His Word to teach and preach to the masses of people.

These men were tested and tried, even in the midst of their trials and temptations, God was looking at their faith in Him. This is how these men and women were constantly being tested in order that God can develop mankind's spiritual consciousness.

Some of the trials and temptations that mankind went through, no normal man would have become successful in achieving their greatness in God's eyes. When I say greatness, I am referring to some of the most difficult trials that the majority of men in this world would have given up.

These men were truly tested for their roles with God, our Father. They test God's prophets. The word *prophets* sounds good, especially reading about them in the Bible, but they were tested beyond what mankind themselves can comprehend through trials and temptations.

I know that a lot of men would have never been able to face the problems that the men of God had faced in order for some of them to become successful in the midst of their trials, tribulations, and temptations.

Not all men have the spiritual consciousness and the discipline to overcome their own trials and temptations successfully if they don't keep their eyes focused on God's righteousness.

We must understand that the nature of mankind is not to worship God but to destroy the mere words that are written in the Bible. Mankind don't want to give up his free will because somewhere in mankind's free will, mankind has congregated in his mind that he has the potential to become like God or mightier than God. So mankind don't want to become submissive enough, in order to give up their free will, to worship God. What mankind must understand is the nature of his free will.

If mankind does not understand the nature of the free will, in order to develop mankind's faith to the point where mankind feel a sense of comfort where mankind knows that in order for him to reach his spiritual potential in God, mankind has to give up his free will in order for mankind to develop his consciousness that would allow mankind to come to the reality which would cause mankind to reconcile his differences with God in order that mankind would become that spiritual beacon in the dark that reflects the light of God's consciousness in his heart and mind.

Now if mankind does not want to reconcile his differences with God, then mankind would always be in denial and confused about their relationship with God by trying to disclaim the true existence and presence of God.

When mankind comes to grips with themselves in a sense of giving up their free will, that means they are recognizing that they must develop their own consciousness. In order for mankind to understand that while they are giving up their own free will, there is an omnipotent being who truly understands the nature of mankind.

If that omnipotent being is able to understand the nature of mankind, then that same omnipotent being must also be in a state of forgiveness. That same omnipotent being must be always in a state of righteousness and compassion. That same omnipotent being that mankind needs to be submissive to has to be God.

Because that same omnipotent being has to be God of mankind, here is why: only God can understand what is the true essence of good and bad.

When God teaches mankind about what is mankind's true essence of good and bad, that is what mankind needs to know in order for mankind to embrace God's divine Word and apply it to their own consciousness and their hearts. That is why it is important that God uses mankind's own experiences and mankind's sinful nature to teach and preach His Word.

It lets mankind know that is why God grants us the gift of grace, mercy, salvation, and compassion because God is not naive to the conditions of mankind's sinful nature, and because God understands mankind's sinful nature better than mankind understands their own sinful nature, it does not mean that God is naïve to mankind's sinful nature.

It was God who experienced mankind choosing their sinful nature over God's divine Word. God, through His salvation for mankind, is letting mankind know that He is not ignorant to mankind's nature of sin. That is why God developed the consciousness of mankind to experience God's grace, mercy, and compassion for mankind.

So that is why it is important for mankind to study God's Word so mankind can achieve God's wisdom. God never wanted mankind to feel like he is alienated because of mankind's sinful nature. God has always opened up His heart to mankind, giving mankind the free will or options to embrace God's love.

And now, because of God's love and salvation, God is able to elevate mankind's consciousness from the physical existence to the spiritual existence of life where mankind is able, through his consciousness, to constantly stay in tune with God's knowledge and love so that mankind would become a spiritual being through God's divine Word.

When mankind is able to embrace God righteousness and develop his or her consciousness in the state of God's righteousness, that is when mankind is able to transform himself or herself from the physical existence of life into the spiritual existence of life. Now the answer also to the question is if God is able to take mankind from the physical existence of life and transform mankind's consciousness into becoming a spiritual being embracing God's wisdom.

So if God is able to transform mankind from their physical existence into the spiritual existence of life, then God is able to accept mankind's sinful nature and transform mankind's sinful nature and mankind's free will in order for mankind to change their consciousness into becoming a spiritual being.

When mankind is able to transform his consciousness into the spiritual realm where mankind is able to stay in tune with God's righteousness, as mankind stays in tune to God's righteousness, that is mankind's inspirational moment where God can influence and use mankind to inspire and reveal His Word to mankind and give mankind the authority to write His doctrine in order for the masses of people to become also inspired by God's doctrine as well.

What happens if the angels wrote the scripture? The masses of people in the world would have this answer. That is, are the scriptures more authentic, or would the scriptures have less authenticity, such as more arguments or more debatable discussions in them, just because the angels wrote the scriptures?

For example, we would have another argument, which would be what we are going to obey, scripture or not scripture. One of the arguments would be how God allows the angels to write the Bible when the angels are not human beings.

The angels do not know or experience the imperfections or sinful nature of mankind. The angels are not human enough to understand what actually challenges mankind's physical nature and imperfections that would cause mankind to sin.

Some people would assume that because the angels are above men, they would assume that if God inspired the angels to write the scriptures instead of mankind, the next argument would be that, that is why the Bible requires mankind to be more perfect than their actual imperfections and sinful nature. The other argument would be that, that is why mankind does not even have the potential to achieve spiritually.

The other perspective is that mankind, about the angels, write the scriptures for mankind to live by. It is that the angels do not know the nature of mankind and imperfections of mankind well enough to be inspired by God to write a book for mankind to live by. It seems that mankind still will find excuses why the Bible should never be the authentic Word of God.

Mankind will also have a question; and that question would be why God would or, if God's Word is authentic, why he would allow the angels to write the Word or why God would inspire the writing of the Bible or the scriptures to be written by the angels if the angels have not experienced the lifestyle that exists in the physical manifestation of our existence.

Oh, why would God get angels to write the scripture knowing that angels do not have any human experience like human beings do? What's the nature of a human being it's different from the nature of angels? So it is very difficult for angels to write the Bible and not experience what maintains and challenges the nature of mankind as human beings.

The angels do not know what it is like to have a human experience, so they can't write anything spiritual documents that are able to relate to the human experience, and that is why God uses mankind who already acknowledge the human experience and uses their experience and relationship with God to bring His Word to enlighten and development mankind's spiritual consciousness.

Just like we know of the angels, the angels also know of us. The angels understand mankind's sinful nature and imperfections, so it would not have given them the opportunity with clarity to write God's Word as it relates to the nature and imperfection of mankind's true existence as human beings.

Because the angels have never experienced mankind's imperfections and sinful nature, I don't think that the angels are competent enough spiritually to write or edit the Bible as it relates to mankind's sinful nature and mankind's imperfection. I still don't think the angels are equipped to write about mankind's imperfection and sinful nature. I can experience and accept the fact that angels are protecting mankind's interest.

I can even experience the angels protecting mankind from the principalities and things that are unseen that challenges mankind's faith and integrity and consciousness with God the Father.

What would happen if God decided to write the Bible without using mankind as a means to inspire His Word through. The other argument that the philosophers would have is that God is too perfect and mankind's nature is imperfect and mankind also has a sinful nature.

No, by many of the philosophers' theories and theologians. They would ask the question of how God wrote the scriptures when God actually doesn't have the human experience that mankind has. The other statement one might basically question, or that is the reason why God decided to use mankind to inspire His words through mankind—that mankind came and wrote God's Word down based on their own experience and the choice of mankind's free will.

Now if God wrote the Bible without any human, help, experience, or influence—I mean, if God took it upon Himself to write the Bible without any help or support from mankind—it would create this type of an argument from the atheist perspective, and that is, how can God write the Bible when God does not have any experience of mankind's nature? Now the question here is asking, what would happen if God wrote the Bible without mankind's influence or experience?

Please let me reiterate: in other words, what would happen if God wrote the Bible without using mankind's involvement? I assume that is a good enough argument by the philosophers and atheists in order for the mankind to distort this claim and stagnate God's divine Word. First of all, how can God write a book for mankind which teaches about salvation when God Himself has never experienced what it is like to be created and being created with a sinful nature, or even being in the state of mankind's nature?

How can God who never experience being created or having such a sinful nature write a book for mankind without experiencing what it is like to be created and have a sinful nature? Think about that statement for moment.

I would have to agree with that question, especially when it mentions that God was never created and was never created with the free will to exercise a sinful nature; yes, that is true.

God answered the question in this manner: by letting mankind know that He has used mankind's nature as a means to write the Bible. In other words, God has used the nature or the sinful nature of mankind and the imperfections that mankind has in order to write God's divine Word which we refer to as the Bible. Here is how God did it:, by developing the awareness of mankind's consciousness through His divine Word which would bring mankind into a spiritual awareness and which would develop mankind's consciousness into becoming a spiritual being where mankind would have the opportunity to become godlike; where mankind is able to come into God's righteousness, and it is in that state of God's righteousness that mankind experiences being a spiritual being in the eyes of God's divine Word.

It is the nature of mankind that causes mankind to sin and fall short of God's Word. It is also the nature of mankind that God's Word is able to develop mankind's nature and bring mankind's nature into a consciousness state of spirituality where mankind can live in harmony with the presence and righteousness of God's existence.

Now here is something that God has done because of the nature of mankind. God has taken mankind's sinful nature and used that same sinful nature to elevate mankind's nature to acknowledge to mankind how it could be that through God's Word, mankind is able to become an imperfect being. With the perfect Word of God, that brings mankind into his own spiritual consciousness with his God where God and mankind can become one in their consciousness and love each other.

The one thing mankind needs—or may I say the atheist needs to know—is that God already knows that mankind's nature is sinful, and mankind is also an imperfect being, but God was still able to use mankind's imperfections and mankind's sinful nature to produce His authentic Word to the masses of people.

In other words, He knows if mankind's imperfection is God's perfection, mankind's sinful nature is God's divine nature. It is through God's Divine word which becomes the power of God's consciousness because God's Word is able to transform mankind from his imperfections and sinful nature to become a spiritual being which is able to relate to the power of an omnipotent God who is able to develop mankind's consciousness spiritually.

Here is what I mean about the transformation of God's divine Word: Somewhere within mankind's sinful nature, God is able to penetrate mankind's heart to the point where God is still able to develop mankind's consciousness into becoming a spiritual being.

God is able to reach mankind through mankind's faith in Him. Here is how mankind is able to reach God's faith. Mankind can only reach God's faith through His Word. Faith is the shaping and carving of our integrity toward God, but the character of mankind's faith is deeply rooted in the subconscious of mankind's heart.

It is in the subconscious where mankind is confident about exercising their faith in God, even if mankind does not understand or know the outcome of their adversities or the circumstances that are causing their adversities while mankind is still depending and exercising their faith in God.

The question is, how does mankind reach that level of spiritual consciousness where they feel comfortable exercising their blind faith for God when some of those same people who have enough confidence exercising their blind, faith for God would not exercise that same blind faith while being asked out on a blind date?

The question arises, how can mankind who is sinful by nature become so much in tune with God's righteousness be able to come to a point in their sinful life where they are able to exercise their blind faith for God?

The question is, what is it about mankind that would transform mankind's consciousness into becoming a spiritual being in mankind's physical existence here on earth? First of all, it is the transcending presence of God's message which is able to develop and mature in the hearts of mankind. That is what develops the consciousness of mankind; now the transformation of mankind can only be achieved by mankind being able to study God's divine Word.

The second perspective is that after studying God's divine Word, this is where mankind acknowledges the purity of his faith and the importance of repentance, knowing that God is able to forgive mankind of their sinful nature, especially when mankind is still in his sinful nature.

Then, through mankind's sinful nature and imperfections, God, through His grace, is still able to forgive mankind of their sins without holding any animosity or grudges toward mankind.

How is this omnipotent God who is all-powerful able to understand mankind's sinful nature enough to accept mankind's sinful nature without destroying mankind? Now if mankind was in the same position as God, being omnipotent as God, mankind would have destroyed each other a long time ago. If we look at the conditions of the world, mankind is preparing themselves for their own self-destruction.

When mankind asked forgiveness from God, God was able to grant mankind His forgiveness. Now God's mercy is how mankind is able to experience God's goodness and righteousness through our sins.

For example, when I say the goodness of God through our sins, I am also referring to God's compassion. Where mankind has experience and understanding God's love through whatever adversities mankind has to face, God teaches mankind all this through His divine Word.

We must also understand that mankind will never be in a position to become smarter than God. Mankind does not have enough knowledge or wisdom to compete with God, especially when it comes to knowledge and wisdom. So why would God write a book, like the Bible, to become a book of judgment toward mankind's salvation without allowing mankind to experience his own sinful nature and mankind's free will? In other words, mankind's free will and sinful nature is the true reality of mankind's existence.

God also allowed mankind to experience his own sinful nature and free will in order to get a better understanding of God's authentic word. For example, mankind's sinful nature and free will can best be understood by mankind's challenges in life, and when mankind is able to use God's divine Word as a means to conquer their adversities, that is when mankind is able to acknowledge their own divine righteousness based on God's divine Word.

Let me reiterate. The only way that mankind is able to become a spiritual being is when mankind is able to embrace God's divine Word. As mankind embraces God's divine Word, mankind must also acknowledge God's divine presence throughout His Word.

Now it is at this very instance that mankind develops their own awareness, and it is in that awareness that allows mankind to develop, improve, and mature in their own spiritual consciousness. Mankind's consciousness is developed through the many pages of God's divine Word.

We must also understand that the reason why mankind has a free will is for mankind to make decisions based on his own free will without God's divine intervention. This has been the message that causes mankind to exercise his own free will and sinful nature without relying on God's intervention.

The question that has puzzled mankind for centuries is, how can an omnipotent God give mankind so much freedom, knowing that mankind already has a sinful nature? This has been the statement, or may I say the question that has puzzled the theologians, philosophers, and theorists for centuries, and that is how God, who is all-knowing, can give mankind so much freedom to make decisions, knowing that mankind by nature has an evil nature.

This question or statement arises because it is in that statement or question that mankind is able to develop their consciousness spiritually where they can become motivated in their faith to do God's will in their lives.

We must also try to understand that God is not trying to manipulate or force mankind into a state of worshipping Him or trying to blame mankind for worshipping Him.

What God is trying to do is give mankind the opportunity to worship Him based on mankind's own free will and sinful nature.

Here is what God has done for mankind: God has given mankind the privileges to use his own sinful nature and free will to understand God's Word and become knowledgeable in God's Word where mankind can use their sinful nature and free will to enhance their spiritual awareness through God.

God does this in order for mankind to understand the importance of giving up his free will and sinful nature. At this point in mankind's life, they are able to use God's Word as a comparison to gain enough knowledge to recognize the importance of why mankind would want to give up their sinful nature and free will in order to develop their consciousness in God.

Mankind is able to develop their consciousness by reading and studying God's divine Word enough where mankind is able to develop their faith and confidence in God's divine Word where they feel secure and comfortable enough in God's faith to better enhance and develop their consciousness in God.

# THE BIBLICAL WORD OF CONSCIOUSNESS?

In other words, how could God write a book with so much spiritual insight and give it to mankind as a means for mankind to become a spiritual human being?

When the consciousness of mankind is not able to comprehend God's wisdom, how is God able to give mankind spiritual insight when mankind is sinful by nature and mankind also relies on his own free will? I guess what I am trying to say is how can God bring mankind from a sinful nature into a spiritual consciousness where mankind can become a spiritual being which is righteous in God's eyes?

So God has used mankind's sinful nature and mankind's free will to become the experience God needs in order to bring mankind into his own divine state of existence and consciousness. But through mankind's faith in God, mankind has become a spiritual being recognizing God's presence in his life.

Here is the other question: how do we know if God's Word is authentic? This question arises because mankind doesn't want to accept the responsibilities that come from God's divine Word.

Within this question also comes a certain fear to believe in God's divine Word. As believers of God, we should be able to give an account for the questions that people ask that pertain to our faith in God. The answers come through the constant studying of God's Word.

We also know that mankind cannot be trusted like God, but sometimes, we ask the questions that pertain to trust and the Bible, and that is how God can trust mankind. With such important and powerful information, how can God, who is omnipotent, in His power, trust mankind with His Word, not knowing if mankind is going to tamper with God's divine Word?

If God already knows the sinful nature of mankind's free will, why would God give mankind the opportunity to be responsible for God's divine Word, which is the Bible?

Mankind's free will and sinful nature do not allow mankind to be honest and loyal or even have enough trust in God not to tamper with God's divine Word. This has always been the question of the atheists, theologians, and philosophers who have used their schools of thought in order to determine that because of mankind's sinful nature and free will, mankind cannot trust themselves; and if mankind cannot trust himself, how can an omnipotent God trust mankind with His Word?

This statement even brought the theologians, philosophers, and theorists to believe that God does not exist or if God exists, He has to be naive because it means that God is naive in His state of omnipotence, and no God that exists with omnipotence such as His is able to do such a thing, so that means that God does not exist.

Now because mankind is not loyal to each other, it does not mean that God is not loyal to mankind. God has always been loyal, and God's actions and words do not change.

Although mankind has free will and a sinful nature, then God should not trust mankind, with His Word. We cannot trust the people that God has chosen to teach and preach His Word. The scriptures which we just read, everything we do, is spiritually driven and motivated by God's divine Word.

Although mankind's free will by nature is sinful, and God has used mankind sinful nature to inspire God's divine Word. It does not mean that the Bible is imperfect that the Bible is still not God's authentic Word.

So that means that the philosophers, theologians, and theorists are looking and digging deep, trying to find many imperfections in the Bible in order to let the world know that the Bible is a book of imperfections and not a book of God's authentic truth.

The truth of the matter is that there is no imperfection and loopholes in the Gospel; if someone approached the Scriptures with a negative disposition, then everything that they interpret from the Scriptures is nothing more than a negative interpretation of the Gospel. That is why we should always pray before reading and studying God's authentic Word.

Whatever the person is that is approaching God's divine Word to find imperfections in the Gospel, their interpretation of the reading of God's divine Word is going to be interpreted as imperfect.

Here is why some people, it seems, spend a lifetime trying to prove to their friends and family and the world that there are imperfections in the Gospel. Sometimes those people who are looking for imperfections find enough perfection in the Gospel to convert themselves not to believe in God's authentic Word. I believe and know in my heart that God's Word is the perfect truth that tries to bring mankind's nature into God's divine consciousness.

Just to let you know, there are some people who would spend a lifetime trying to develop arguments which are convincing enough to distort and destroy the Word of God.

Again, look at the world and how the world is using every philosophical, ideological, and theological arguments in order to distort and destroy God's divine Word. The world is using every argument to distort God's divine Word.

It seems to me that the more the world tries to disclaim or disapprove the existence of God, the world is setting itself up to become more destructive. The more the world disclaims the Bible, the more chaos the world is setting itself up for.

If we are honest and truthful, look at the wars that are causing many nations to fight against each other. The younger generation is becoming more disrespectful toward the older generation. Think about why is that when in our mother's and father's generations, it was imperative for the younger generation to respect, listen, and learn from the older generation.

The question we need to ask ourselves is why is the majority of the younger generation in our society today are so disrespectful and lost. It is like the younger generation has no ethics, morals, respect, and cultural values.

It seems that we have a culture that doesn't care about life or the air that they breathe. Now please stay with me because I want to make a point.

Please let me make this statement, and that is not all of our youth is bad. It is a small amount of our youth that is honest. Yes, we do have a deviant and rebellious young generation. We have a larger percentage of our youth being deviant, which impacts the other wonderful children that are in the world.

It is not difficult to solve the problem. Here is what I mean: The previous generations had respect for God's Word, which shapes, tones, and develops the older generation's integrity, and personality from the cradle to the grave. We believe in God's Word and respect our elders.

Parents demanded that the children, who were carrying their last names, respect others, especially those who were older generations in the neighborhood.

Reading the Word of God, praying, and respecting were implemented in our schools, home, morals, ethics, and the culture of the family. This concept developed the perspective of our neighborhood and community to pray.

All of this was a part of our discipline and, once again, a way of life, I would say, for my generation.

Now when we look into the heart of our society. We experienced the love that once strengthens us as a people and culture. Now as the world turns, it seems that everyone is in chaos spiritually and physically, not knowing what the truth is and what is a lie.

We have evidence from previous generations and how other previous generations were raised, and now we are in a state of chaos and uncertainty. Now the reason why I am struggling with this perspective is that we are not trying hard enough to use God's consciousness as a light-bulb moment to enlighten the younger generations.

It is obvious that the churches played a very important role in the world, neighborhood, and communities at some point in time. Many people would say that I'm looking for the earth to be in utopia.

And what I would say to them is that I'm not looking for utopia because when God created man mankind, the earth was still not a utopia. It was mankind's sinful nature and imperfection that caused sin. I can tell you it was not God's consciousness, which is putting the world in chaos.

Even when Jesus was on earth, mankind was still in a sinful nature and exercises their imperfections and thinking that God's consciousness is a theory, philosophy, and theology. The world was in chaos; and violence and deviant behavior were still roaming the streets, communities, and neighborhoods, which Jesus Himself has studied.

Still the church played a vital role in the socialization and had an active voice in masses of people's lives. But in today's society, we have lost that love, compassion, and change. In other words, the younger generation of today has exercised more deviant behavior than yesterday's generation.

Let us look at how the world is evolving. The world is evolving and going crazy with the increase of crime, murder, family abuse, child abuse, and rape instead of correcting the problem.

Here is why: we are trying to develop a world without God and His consciousness being implemented in the culture, education, morals, ethic, culture, of the younger generation's spiritual enlightenment.

Pride, self-centeredness, and power are destroying our world; and it is trickling down to our countries, communities, neighborhoods, and most of all families. We are still turning our hearts and minds against God's knowledge of the problems of the world, which would save the lives of our children.

Somehow some of the older generations are afraid to express the love we need to inspire and teach the young generation about God's consciousness and His love. So the younger generation is suffering tremendously, and the only thing that can save the younger generation is God's divine Word.

The truth that exists within God's Word is the survival mechanism that can develop the consciousness of the younger generation and bring them into a transformation, which can enlighten and transform them to become better human beings with spiritual enlightenment and experience, which can change the younger generation's life in order that they might become better human beings in our society.

The real weapons that our youth need are for them to develop themselves and mature in God's consciousness. I was always told as a youth that the only weapon I have is my mind, but it is knowledge and education that can develop our consciousness spiritually for the younger generation to achieve greatness in their lives.

The idea of teaching the younger generation is to put them in a spiritual consciousness where, as the younger generation progresses and matures in life, there is development through implementing God's Word in their life.

It is imperative that we teach the younger generation to start developing their own spiritual consciousness of who God really is to them. If the older generation can reach the minds and hearts of the youth through God's divine Word.

Once again, let me reiterate that if we can develop God's consciousness in the minds and hearts of our youth, our youth would become a positive force to be reckoned with in our society. Our younger generation can become that light-bulb moment that lights up the world.

Sometimes in the midst of all of this controversy and hate, they are some of our children that are trying to develop God's consciousness within their lives and help bring themselves into an awareness of enlightenment.

As I grow older and make progress in life, I appreciate my teachers from English High School who gave me the structure and discipline I needed to become successful in this life after graduating from English High School:

Carol Bynum; Ron Spradlin; Ms. Bellamy; John Weeks; and Tippy Johnson, who would take me to play basketball with him in the summer—these are the men and women who have inspired and given some good memories about life. Children can be disciplined with love in order to survive in the world we almost have discipline and this is what English High School teachers have taught me.

These teachers help me because there were full of discipline, structure, and still were able to show how much they love me as a student.

Every Thanksgiving that love between teachers and students is expressed. Even today I had to thank God for my academic experience at English High School.

I know we believe so much in academic institutions, such as colleges and universities. My best academic experience was at Saint Patrick's Grammar School. I can still remember Sister Catherine, who basically mold me and shape me and taught me how to read the scriptures with conviction.

She even showed me how to take control over the narrative of the scriptures based on my tone and mannerism in order to give the scriptures the true feeling and the emotions needed to manifest God's Word in the hearts and minds of those people's consciousness that is listening to me reading God's Word.

And I remembered Father Malloy, who spoke to Pastor at Twelve Baptist Church at the time, where I was at the time member and still is a member of the great historic church. Pastor Michael E. Haynes was the pastor at the time. Father Malloy, from Saint Patrick's Church, wanted to know if I can become an altar boy at Saint Patrick's Church in Roxbury on Dudley Street.

Now everything shifted when I went to college because as a young man, I had some experiences about God's consciousness, especially growing up in the church, as I told you. Here are some most discouraging moments in my life that occurred, especially when I was attending college and at the universities.

Here is what I mean. It is easier for the majority of our youth to get involved in criminal activity such as drugs, gangs, prostitution, youth, violence, and even killings than for them to become successful in college and universities.

Here are some incidents which actually happened to me when I was studying for my bachelor's degree and master's degree.

For example, our students are sometimes placed in a situation of discouragement by their professors. I was one of those students who was discouraged by their professors, who should be given me more encouragement to become successful in life. I have to say that I appreciated my guidance counselor, whom I had called Marianne Alexander. She was surprised at some of the conversations that I was having at a young age with my professors.

Now let's not lose focus on youth respecting, the older generation, and how the youth of today are more deviant than the older generation. Please keep that in mind.

When I attended college, I had the desire and the compassion to learn, I thought college was the place for me to learn, get an education, and support my family. I was the only black male person in classes, and some of the professors wanted to know, why I was interested in taking their course. I told them to get an education. I went to school to get an education to do great things in my community and be able to support my family, that opportunity was almost destroyed by the same professors, who should be giving me the encouragement to become successful academically.

It seems that my professor's encouragement was a discouragement. For example, I took a course about five British writers. I wanted to better learn about the Shakespearean style of writing because it was similar to the biblical text of the Bible.

I had a book report which was supposed to be a three-page paper on *Hamlet*. A Shakespearean play that describes *Hamlet*. I end up loving the play, enough where I got cough in the play itself.

I end up loving the Shakespearean language, and the paper that was supposed to be three pages, came out to be twenty-five pages. I just love the play, and I enjoy reading the play.

As I passed my paper, I thought it was the number of pages I wrote that got a D– on. He appreciated me writing the paper. It had to do with me being a black student. That wrote a paper with so many pages and the paper's content.

The professor told me that if I had that much education and capability to write that type of paper I should have studied for my master's or my doctoral studies. He mentioned that your black people don't, know anything about Shakespearean for you to write such a powerful paper about the play *Hamlet*.

I told my professor that black people and people read the Bible also, and that is why I took the English course—to learn more about Shakespearean writing because it reminds me of the Bible.

My professor argue with me that I was incompetent to write such a paper, and he said to me I need to bring in the CliffNotes which I copied Shakespeare's writing from. I told my professor I didn't know anything about CliffNotes.

Where were the notes that I used to write the paper? I never knew what CliffNotes were. I was a young man who grew up in Boston, Massachusetts, in Roxbury from Barbados, West Indies.

My mother dropped out of school in the third grade in order that her younger and older brothers could go to school and become educated. My mother was not allowed to be educated, and here is why: When she gets married, her name changes, and her brothers' names stay the same. That is why she was kept home from going to school.

The more I tried to tell my professor I didn't know anything about Cliff Notes the worst and angry he became. He was yelling and screaming, at me in his office. I couldn't believe it so then I went home to my mother, trying to figure everything out, of why my professor was yelling and screaming at me. He thought I bought the CliffNotes.

Why would I buy the book? The book was not on your syllabus, Professor. So I told my professor that I did not read the CliffNotes. My professor underestimated my ability as a student. They are some people who do enjoy writing.

They are some people who are trying, to make a contribution to developing God's consciousness, within themselves so they can progress and become better people in life.

That is when I had to dial 1-800-Mom. That is when my mother told me, with her third-grade education, that it would be better for most students to look at their syllabus, purchase the books for themselves, and read and study the books that were listed on the professor's syllabus.

My second experience at the university and college level is when I took a course in liberation theology and one of my professors told me that he had not done so much studying since I was studying and writing since his doctoral thesis.

He also said to me, "I would not call you James. I will refer to you as Mr. Grant because you're very knowledgeable and very well educated about the subject. But your people and the people in your communities will never respect your knowledge." He was degrading the people in my communities and those who lived in the environment of the communities in which I lived.

Remember I was a student at a particular university in Massachusetts where this professor was talking about in class or was talking about the population of people that lived in Boston who are not educated and have no sense of life and reasoning.

So I told him, "You have a lot of people in Boston that are not given as many opportunities as others in different parts of Massachusetts, especially in this country we call America."

He gave me a bad grade I got a D– for the course, and he said to me, "I gave you a bad grade because I wanted to meet with you." He sat down. "Mr. Grant I would never call you James, but I would call you Mr. Grant. You're very well knowledgeable about the subject we discussed. Young man, you know your subjects and your topics very well. But if you were white, I would've written you a recommendation giving you a scholarship to Harvard University and making sure that you get into Harvard University.

"But your people are not conditioned or conscious enough to listen to the things that you have to say because you do not have an academic institution degree in order to solidify who you are as a person and the level of education that you have achieved. So your people in your community will never listen to you because we did not condition those same people in your communities, which you are representing and fighting for to come out and represent you.

"Mr. Grant, your people would never represent you or even respect your knowledge or even listen to people like you, especially if you don't have an academic institution representing your name. Even those people, in your own community, all because you do not have an academic institution behind you in order to validate where your knowledge came from."

The only person I want to validate me is God.

He also said, "I can't give you a passing grade. I can only give you a D– for the course."

It seems that I have been underestimated because of the consciousness and spirituality which God has developed and inspired within my state of consciousness.

I think my professor thought that the statement was supposed to destroy me as a youth and stop me from progressing in life. God has thought me through my faith in Him, which has developed my spiritual consciousness. Through all of my adversities and my adversaries that constantly challenge me and try to destroy me, my strength, and power are in my faith and spirituality, which is able to develop my consciousness in God.

That is when I decided to self educate myself if I wanted to make a difference in my own life and in the lives of other people. I have to stay constantly in and supplication, with God. That is how I develop my God's fearing faith, which exists in me through God's consciousness, which God has manifested in my life and through my life.

I also remember having a job where I was going through training where everybody was getting $11 an hour. I would buy the group of trainees food or pizza because I understood that they had a family, and they were struggling.

I was asked, to sit in a black SUV. Where the two women ask me if I was a drug dealer, or do I sell drugs. All because God has placed me in a position constantly to help others. My behavior was also misinterpreted. I was confronted with that statement several times, all because I was helping others who were unfortunate at the time.

I think people underestimate my potential a lot except God, who already knows who I am. I am viewed as incompetent, and I should not have the knowledge and wisdom that God has placed in me to help others. My mind and how I think have become my spiritual weapon in order for me to develop my state of consciousness. Just to make me a better person in life, to help develop the character and integrity, which is embraced in the communities of Boston and most of all my church, which is Twelve Baptist Church, a historic church. The younger generation is becoming more disrespectful toward the older generation and that is because the older generation is not indoctrinated in God's Word to know the importance of having in administering respect to the older generation to pave the way both historically or even.

It seems that some of the pastors, ministers, bishops, and deacons are believing in the lies which surround the Gospel than the actual Gospel itself.

The pastors, ministers, deacons, and bishops are confused about the true reality of the Gospel.

Here is what I am referring to: The pastors, preachers, and ministers believe in the gospel still. Yet they don't have the courage or strength to stand up to the world and represent the faith that they clamp and believe in that exists as God's divine Word.

It seems that the pastors, preachers, ministers, and deacons prefer to teach a lie than to teach the truth, which surrounds God's authentic Word. The pastors, preachers, and ministers should already have enough, courage, strength, and love in their hearts, which would give them the courage and strength they need to stand up to the world and preach boldly and courageously the love the pastors, preachers, and ministers should have for God's Word.

It seems to me that the world is the one that is manipulating God's Word instead of the passes in the preachers being in tune to the consciousness and allowing the spiritual consciousness to give them the courage they need to manifest God's Word courageously and proudly and lovingly in the hearts and souls for God. Here is what I mean: It seems that the pastors, ministers, preachers, believe in the Gospel. But they don't have the courage or the strength anymore to stand up for the faith that the preacher, ministers, bishops, and deacons believe in. It seems that some of the clergy believe in lies instead of the biblical truths that God Himself has given to mankind.

We must also understand that the Bible is not a thesis paper where we are comparing men's philosophical, theological, and theoretical beliefs in order to get a good grade. The Bible should not be read like a term paper where we are comparing and contrasting ideologies and perspectives to get a better grade. The Bible is not a novel about people's experiences in life. The Bible is not an autobiography.

The Bible is a book that is inspired by God, and it is our guide for living. The Bible is a book that brings mankind in tune with his divine Creator. The Bible is a book that is able to transform mankind's life and develop the consciousness of mankind's faith in God.

Here is what makes the Bible a different book: when we approach the Bible, we must treat the Bible as God's divine Word. We must pray and ask for guidance. But as we pray and ask for God's guidance, what are we actually asking for? We are asking for God to prepare our hearts and mind in order for God to bring us into a spiritual awareness that we can better understand and interpret the messages that God Himself is revealing to us in our hearts and minds.

Let me reiterate. There are some people who spend their lives trying to destroy the authentic words of the gospel. That is why if we listen and believe in those people who are trying to find imperfection in the Gospel, this is when we end up losing all of our confidence and faith in God's authentic Word.

Here is why we lose confidence in God's Word. We must first study God's Word in order to develop and strengthen our consciousness and faith in God's divine Word. We must also study to show ourselves approved of the Gospel.

Here is another reason why we lose confidence in God's divine Word. When we don't apply or even understand that what we have learned from God's divine Word is how we are able to develop a consciousness of discipline, that consciousness state of discipline is nothing more than a way of life.

Our consciousness should bring us into an awareness and understanding of what it means when we try to define what life is to us as Christians. Here is what I mean: For example, how we eat and how we carry ourselves as Christians should also reflect our consciousness and character of God's divine faith.

Also, it is in how we dress and talk, and most of all, how firm and stern we are in representing and standing up for the Gospel of God, even if God's Word is not popular with the masses of the people. We do not speak and teach God's Word based on popularity and convenience for the masses of people. We teach and preach God's Word because of the convenience of God and because our spiritual consciousness has developed to a level where we realize that we should never be intimidated to teach and preach the Word of God, even if it means destroying us or killing us for teaching us teaching and preaching the Word of God.

God's divine Word to the masses of people. We must remember that we don't fear God because of intimidation, distraction, intimidation, destruction, or even us being killed. But we fear God because of His power, compassion, and love.

The person that the pastors, preachers, and ministers should follow is God, not the world. We recognize the power that we have through God's Word, which has shaped and carved our state of consciousness to become men, women, and children of God. The Word of God is not to be thought as a message for the masses of people but to be spiritually influenced for all people even if the masses do not appreciate God's authentic Word at that time. It is very important for the men and women of God to still preach and teach God's divine Word.

As believers of God's Word, we should always preach and teach God's Word in and out of season. In other words, we should preach and teach God's Word even when it is not the popular thing to do, even if it is not appreciated by the masses of people.

We must always remember that whatever we preach and teach of God's Word, we must also liv, and become the actions of the words, which we preach and teach even if God's is not popular to masses of people.

Although the Word of God might not be popular to the masses of people at that particular time, God's Word can still resonate and manifest itself in the masses of people's lives even if God's Word is not popular with the masses of people.

We lose confidence in God when we don't study God's Word as a discipline and as a way life. If we are not studying God's Word and not applying God's Word to our lives, then our confidence in God's Word begins to deteriorate, and when we lose confidence in God's Word, that becomes the downfall of mankind's relationship with God.

When I say God's authentic Word, I am referring to the sixty-six books of the Bible. I am not talking about someone who is taking God's Word and cutting and pasting God's Word to fit their own agendas or to compromise God's Word so they can have a certain position, career, or status in life.

So those people who want to used God's Word for their selfish desire only, those are the people who try to justify and reason with God's divine Word by developing arguments with others about the authenticity of God's divine Word, how God's Word is not authentic enough, and would strongly express how God's Word is filled with some fallibilities.

The majority of the time, people who think with that mentality are trying to justify the wrongs that they like to do or may I say they are trying to justify the sins that they are committing, but they don't want to be reminded of the responsibilities that come with them, committing the sins that they know they shouldn't be committing. Those people or persons want to ease their consciousness and don't want to be reminded of the sins they have committed toward God.

Also, when people are looking for things that are not authentic in the Bible, they are looking for divisions in the Bible. Here is why: some people want to create their own religious preface and premise that would satisfy their religious beliefs but not to be totally committed to the true belief of God's Word.

Let us look at it also from this perspective by asking one of the most profound questions, and that is why we have so many different religions and churches with such long biblical names, as long as Bible verses, and all of these religions and churches have one Bible but many different denominations that share the same Bible verses, and through reading God's divine Word, we have also only one faith. That faith shares the same Bible, but that Bible serves so many denominations.

How could that be? Seriously, think about it. And some of you already have thought about it. Here is the key. It is because everyone wants to copy and paste God's divine Word to fit their sins that they are committing.

So they study God's Word, looking and trying to use one statement or a sentence that would make them feel comfortable to commit their sins and not allowing their sins to convict them of their consciousness they have with God. They don't want their consciousness to convict them for standing and representing God's faith and God's Word.

What God needs in these difficult and challenging times are strong men and women who are able to accept God's Word the way He intended it to be accepted by mankind's mind, body, and soul; in other words, God wants men and women to be able to develop enough confidence in their faith in Him also where ministers and pastors would have enough courage to die for God's Word instead of having enough courage to die for the material possessions that exist within this world.

You see, God never wanted His Word to be theologically, philosophically, and intellectually interpreted to fit other people's agendas. God's Word should never be used to fit into people's situations or circumstances, nor should it be copied and pasted to fit people's situations and circumstances.

People with that type of mentality are people who compromise God's Word to fit whatever situations, circumstances, or problems they have or need just to create their own comfort zone for themselves. Knowing that the wrong that they are doing is not right in God's eyes, what they do is try to compromise or justify their sins in God's eyes.

So those people are trying to create within their lifestyle a comfort zone, whatever that comfort zone might be, to stay constantly in their sins.

One of the biggest problems that Christians has is not taking the time out to allow God's Word to become a part of their consciousness. When we study God's Word, we must let God's Word resonate in our heart and soul. Here is why: just to experience and see how God's Word has manifested and matured itself into the consciousness of our hearts and minds, which is developed through our consciousness.

When God's Word becomes a part of man's consciousness, it is easy for man to acknowledge that God's Word can only become real to that individual or individuals based on how that individual is able to live out God's Word in their lives and see God's Word has manifested itself in their own character.

Now we all can agree that the integrity of a person can sometimes be judged by his or her actions. So when a person allows God's consciousness to shape their integrity, his character becomes that of God's divine essence. When a person's character is shaped by God's divine essence, that means that person is in tune with God's consciousness. When we become part of God's consciousness, we must look at life from a different perspective. Here is what I mean: we are not supposed to become a part of this world, although we exist in this world. For example: part of the world as in John 17:13–19, which simply means that we may live in this world, but we can't make the same choices as those who are living in this world. We cannot let the same things that influence the world's ideologies, theories, moral, ethics, and philosophies have the same privileges and impact in helping to influence the Christian community on the spiritualism and consciousness of God's divine doctrine.

What is happening is the world wants the Christian community to accept how the world defines God for themselves. And not only that but how the world defines the Christian Community as well. To my brothers and sisters, it seems that the world is winning this battle.

As Christians, we cannot allow the world to use the political strategies and philosophies to dictate the spiritual agenda for God's divine Word. It is up to the believers of God to stop being calm, convenient, or comfortable in God's Word and start to rattle the cages of the political strategists and philosophies that keep stagnating God's divine Word. We cannot let the world used their philosophical and intellectual beliefs to define who we are nor can we let the world define who we are as Christians because the world does not have knowledge and the understanding of God's consciousness to make the righteousness and faithful decisions that need to be made in order for us to understand the essence and substance of God's grace and mercy as it applies to mankind's salvation.

The world can only be defined through God's divine Words. The world is not in a position to define God's Word or how Christians should live their lives. Our duties and responsibilities are already defined through God's divine Word and not through the world's philosophical, ideological, and theological beliefs.

It is up to the Christians to understand that God's Word is enough where the Christian community can use God's divine Word through reconciliation to be the Christian's discerning factor to judge their actions toward what is right and wrong in God's eyes and the world.

In other words, we can judge all things based on God's Word which manifested itself in our consciousness, and it is within our divine consciousness that we use our discernment and reconciliation to judge everything, including our lifestyle and the world's lifestyle as well.

We cannot let people in the world influence the men and women of God. We are to influence the world through God's Word and let God's Word manifest itself in our hearts. We must stand strong in God's consciousness.

When we come in to God's consciousness, we are acknowledging the fact that we are all human beings existing in a physical body with the potential of developing our spiritual consciousness. We can only develop our spiritual consciousness through God's divine Word. It seems that this statement has developed one of the most powerful and yet intriguing questions that pertains to man and God, and that question is, how can we reach God's consciousness?

We are able to reach God's consciousness through God's divine Word. There is no other path one can travel that would lead them to God's consciousness except traveling the path that leads to God's righteousness, which is God's divine Word. In God's Word, mankind is able to develop and achieve God's consciousness. It does not mean that you are not going to be challenged by adversities and adversaries of this world. What it truly means is you are going to become a subject of the world challenges that lead to tests, temptation, and sin.

## THE POWER OF GOD'S CONSCIOUSNESS

The first approach that should spark mankind's curiosity about God's consciousness is first being able to look at the true essence and substance of God's creation. We can also understand God's consciousness through God's creation. First of all, when we look at God's creation, we are looking at the heavens and the earth and its beauty thereof.

We also experience from God's creation how something as simple as falling rain brings so much joy and happiness and serves so many purposes to God's creation because of how the rain provides nourishment for our bodies.

Mankind knows there is no better liquid that is able to quench their thirst like the natural waters that God has already created for mankind to drink. So when we begin to look at God's creation, we can agree that in God's creation, they had to be someone who understood the nature of mankind but one who is more omnipotent and one who is more compassionate, one who is more graceful than mankind himself.

What makes God's divine Words so authentic? God's Word develops itself in the hearts and minds of the masses of people as a force or power that transcends through the development of a power or force that is the transcending power that comes from God's Word.

> In the presence of God and of Christ Jesus, who will judge the living and the dead, and in view of his appearing and his kingdom, I give you this charge:
> Preach the word; be prepared in season and out of season; correct, rebuke and

> encourage—with great patience and careful instruction.
>
> For the time will come when people will not put up with sound doctrine. Instead, to suit their own desires, they will gather around them a great number of teachers to say what their itching ears want to hear.
>
> They will turn their ears away from the truth and turn aside to myths. But you, keep your head in all situations, endure hardship, do the work of an evangelist, discharge all the duties of your ministry. For I am already being poured out like a drink offering, and the time for my departure is near.
>
> I have fought the good fight, I have finished the race, I have kept the faith. Now there is in store for me the crown of righteousness, which the Lord, the righteous Judge, will award to me on that day—and not only to me, but also to all who have longed for his appearing. (2 Timothy 4:1–8 NIV [https://bible.com/bible/111/2ti.4.1-8.NIV])

In the beginning was the Word, and Word was made flesh. The Word of God became flesh, those same Word of God is able to transform and transcend Jesus Christ into becoming flesh. Those same words are the words that develop our spiritual consciousness in God.

When mankind embraces God's Word and believes in God with their hearts and souls, it is that belief that inspires mankind's faith in God. It is that belief that also gives mankind the power to heal the sick and raise the dead. All of that is done through mankind's faith in God.

What makes God's divine Word so important? Is it because it is a transcending force that is so powerful it created the world and it is able to bring some of the strongest men to their knees? When I say strong men, I am also making reference to those people who have hardened their hearts toward God so much that they themselves think that they are God the creator.

Those are people who make the Christian community think that God is a figment of their own imagination. Those are the same people that place God on the same level as themselves. They are the same people who think that God does not exist. They are the same people who think that God does not have anything to do with this world.

It is because those people choose not to have a relationship with God. The mentality of those who think that God does not exist have caused so much destruction, pain, and suffering to many people in the world and sometimes death. People do that base on their on their own agenda and material possession and wealth.

Families are being broken up at the expense of people not having a compassion in their hearts for God and for each other. They are violating the rights and freedom of others. The people with this type of attitude is not spiritually or consciously driven by God, it is an attitude that is driven by mankind's sinful nature and imperfection. It is an attitude that is also influenced by mankind's pride and material possessions and not by the spirituality of God's consciousness. The Word of God has softened the hearts of those people with a hardened heart.

The Apostle Paul is a prime example of how God is able to reach those people with hardened hearts toward God. The Apostle Paul persecuted the same people that allow him to find his peace and salvation in God, and that is what gave the Apostle Paul a true sense of spiritual consciousness, faith, and in peace with God and himself.

Although God is able to transform us, we must also recognize some important factors that pertain to the God's transformation. The first one is that God is not looking for perfection from us; what God is looking for from us is our faithfulness and righteousness toward Him. Our faith should always be exercised through our consciousness in God.

The knowledge that we gather from God's divine Word helps us shape who we are as human beings both physically and spiritually as faithful believers in God. We must also understand that God's Word developed a sense of discipline and obedience that is also developed through God's consciousness.

Now with faith comes discipline. With discipline comes divine consciousness; with divine discipline comes faith; with faith comes repentance; with repentance comes God's salvation.

When we talk about being faithful and having discipline through the consciousness of God's Word, what are we making reference to? We are making reference to how the knowledge of God is able to transform our lives into a spiritual state of awareness. Now from my perspective, I would say that faith is taking what you have comprehended and understood from God's Word and reinforcing whatever you have learned or gained as knowledge from God's Word and making God's Word a true reality of your lifestyle.

Whatever you display as your character from reading and studying God's Word, that alone should always reflect the compassion and love in your heart that expresses God's love. That love that comes from learning and understanding God's love. That love should be manifested in our state of consciousness and lifestyle.

As God's Word is able to manifest itself in our lives, it should also become a part of our consciousness. When we allow God's Word to become a part of our consciousness, we are actually elevating ourselves from the mere physical existence of life into the spiritual existence of life.

This is where God and man becomes one in thought and consciousness. When mankind is able to acknowledge God's presence in their state of consciousness, that is when mankind is able to become spiritually mature. Our maturity depends on how well we embrace God's consciousness through God's divine Word. When mankind reaches his state of consciousness, God begins to use mankind's natural gifts by developing mankind's faith through mankind's own consciousness.

As mankind is able to mature in his consciousness with God's knowledge and wisdom, that is when God is able to develop mankind's spiritual gifts. The spiritual gifts or natural gifts that we receive from God are to help improve our natural gifts as well as enhance our spiritual gifts in order for us to stay in constant fellowship with God, and God is able sometimes to manifest His consciousness through us to reach others.

Also, God is able to use our natural gift that He has given us before we became Christians and turn them into spiritual gifts. God's Word develops a sense of spiritual and divine consciousness in our hearts, and that is why God is able to instill in us His spiritual gifts in us. God's gift is manifested through our character and integrity of who God is to us as believers of God's faith.

# ++Understanding Our Trials and Temptation

I want to pause here for minute to elaborate on something that many people, as well as Christians, have been misinformed about. Many people who try to develop a relationship with God assume that because they are faithful to God, they should not have to go through so many trials and tribulations in life.

They assume that because they believe in God and are faithful to God that they should be privileged not to encounter so many trials and tribulations in their lives, and if they do it, they should not be harsh and long, but in reality, God never said that we will not experience or have trials or adversities in our lives. To be honest, because we believe in God, we are going to have lots of trials and adversities in our lives just because we are spiritually conscious of God's divine Word. We will always have trials and temptations—it is part of our spiritual maturity.

Actually, what many people do not know is trials and temptation are the burning desires in our souls that sharpen and purify our faith in God. I believe that if a person wants to mature in God's consciousness, that person should have the potential to face trials and temptations.

Here is why one can never develop in God's consciousness if that person or people are not tempted by the trials and tribulations that God has placed before them. If at any time you want to experience how strong a Christian is in his or her faith toward God, wait until that Christian is faced with a difficult trial.

Jesus Christ said the best time that a Christian can express God's consciousness in their lives depends on how well that Christian handles or faces their trials. For example, if you want to see how strong a Christian is in their faith with God, or if you want to see how strong your faith is in God, wait until you are faced with some difficult trials.

Trials will test the honesty of your faith in God as well as develop your spiritual consciousness in God. Faith is the substance and essence of mankind's belief. That is why our belief in God is so powerful belief. It is that belief that shapes the integrity of our spirituality and love for God. Most Christians lose faith in God when the elasticity of their faith stretches them to a point where they have to make decisions about the face because the trials they are facing are difficult. It is the difficulties in our trials that challenge our faith in God, and this is what tests the elasticity of our strengths in God. I am talking about a trial that we have been faced with in our lives that when we drive through intersections of life, trying to make decisions about where to turn, knowing that whatever choices we make, it impacts our faith in God, especially while traveling through the crossroads of life that we are faced with.

Those crossroads of life that challenge our faith in God through our adversities and adversaries prepare us for nothing but all kinds of accidents while traveling the crossroads of life where these accidents of life become our trials and temptations in life. But as we continue traveling the crossroads of life where we are experiencing many difficulties traveling the crossroads of life, that is where God is able to see how in tune we are to His consciousness. We use God's consciousness to prevent us from getting into accidents that life is trying to cause us. It is God's consciousness that gives us the wisdom to face the accidents that occur in our life as we travel the crossroads of life.

Our faith is having confidence in God's Word, knowing that whatever accidents that we are faced with, while traveling on the crossroads of life, we can only overcome those accidents based on how well we are mature in God's consciousness. I don't want us to forget, but we must always remember that God's Word is what develops mankind's consciousness to have confidence in God while handling the challenges that we are faced with in life.

When we are able to stand up to our trials, we make God proud of us because it shows how faithful we are to Him, especially during our adversities that we are facing while putting God first in our life. It lets God know that in the midst of our trials, we have used every drop of His Word to develop our consciousness enough in order to overcome the adversities and the adversaries that we are facing during our trials.

Here is why: We make God proud because God can experience from our action in the midst of adversities how we use His Word to develop our consciousness to overcome our adversities and adversaries.

Because when you are in tune with God's consciousness, you make Him proud because the only way God knows that you were able to overcome your adversities and adversaries is because we were in tune with God's Word. Being in tune with God's Word means developing one's consciousness in a divine and spiritual manner.

God already knows that in order for us to become successful over our adversities and adversaries, we have to stay constantly in tune with His consciousness. We must understand that the more we stay in tune with God's consciousness, the easier it is for us to overcome our adversities and face our adversaries face-to-face.

I know in my life when I was faced with many adversities and when I had to look at my adversaries in their faces, when I came face-to-face with them, it was through God's consciousness that gave me the courage to overcome all of them.

I can only say that I have grown spiritually in my walk with God. Here is why: because through my trials and adversities, I stood firm in my faith, and I embrace God's consciousness. It gave me the courage to stand firm in my faith with God so that nothing can come in the way and shake and destroy my faith in God.

Here is what our trials do for us and our faith in the midst of our relationship with God. I can never understand why God would want to test my faith in Him through my trials. I remember acknowledging this through my experience as a Christian, the why in my trials, why I have to experience trials in my life as Christian. Here is the answer: trials test our faith in God.

Now that sounds good, but what does that actually mean? It means that God is testing our faith for us to recognize how faithful we are to Him, and the only way that we can recognize how faithful we are to God is through our trials and temptations. We can read Scriptures, we can quote Scriptures, we can prophesy, we can talk about discernment, but our true test is in God's faith, which comes in our trials and temptations.

Trials are for us to recognize to ourselves, not to God, how faithful we are to God. Here is why God who is all knowing already knows what your strengths and weaknesses are.

I have a question. What happens if God places us in a situation that requires more faith than what we have? This is a very important question to those theologians, and that is what would happen if God places me in a situation where I do not have enough faith to overcome the situation. God would teach you about that situation in a dream or in a message. God would walk you through the situation step by step in your dream where it is only you and God, and God would reveal the situation to you through enlightening you about the situation. God would transcend the message through your spiritual consciousness, letting you know that as long as you have faith in God and listen to what God is asking you, you will always become successful in what God has called you to do for Him. God would place the situation before you from beginning to end. God can do all that in a dream.

The other way God is able to reach mankind is through His message. God can use dreams and messages to reveal to mankind their purpose and reason that is in the message that God is trying to reveal to them as a means to give us an understanding of the situation that we face or do. Now if we think that we do not have enough faith to face the situation, then God can use messages or dreams to compensate for your faith, which means that the situations or circumstances that we are faced with require more faith than we have for us to know what our reason or purpose is for us to do. God would reveal what He want us to do through a dream or message to compensate for us not having enough faith to understand what it is that God want us to. He would give a reason and purpose to reveal what He wants us to do in a message or a dream.

What do you mean, Deacon James Grant? Here is what I am mean. When God appears to mankind, He has enough confidence in us, knowing that we are going to be successful in this task that God is asking us to do, but that is not enough. What God is trying to do is to let us build up our own confidence in our own faith. I don't mean to become prideful and selfish. What God wants is for us to have confidence and courage in our own faith. There are two thing that occur at that moment. The first is that God is expressing in us His knowledge and wisdom he has in us for us. This is why God says that he is all-knowing. Second, God is allowing us to recognize our true worth in Him through trying to build up our maturity in our faith for Him. Our consciousness is like a mustard seed, it is constantly growing, maturing, and improving through the soil and fertilizer of our adversities and adversaries. The size of a mustard seed is very important. If one has enough faith as a mustard seed, God can use that faith in dreams, visions, or message to mature our faith in Him.

The size of our faith being like the size of a mustard seed means that a person or people have enough room in their faith where God can use that person or people to mature and grow in God's grace and consciousness.

It also means the size of a mustard seed is all God needs to work with in order to use us, to do His will in our lives. When our faith is small, it becomes the essence of our innocence where God is able to take the innocence of our faith and make us submissive enough to Him where we can mature and challenge the outcome of any situation that God has placed us in.

I would say that God appears to us to increase our faith in Him so we would have enough confidence to complete the task that God has called us to do for Him.

## Temptations

Let's read 1 Corinthians 10:10–13:

> And do not grumble, as some of them did—and were killed by the destroying angel. These things happened to them as

> examples and were written down as warnings for us, on whom the culmination of the ages has come. So, if you think you are standing firm, be careful that you don't fall! No temptation has overtaken you except what is common to mankind. And God is faithful; he will not let you be tempted beyond what you can bear. But when you are tempted, he will also provide a way out so that you can endure it. (1 Corinthians 10:10–13 NIV; https://bible.com/bible/111/1co.10.11-13.NIV)

So during our trials, we have the power within our consciousness to overcome any temptation or trials that we are facing in this life. Here is why: because our faith prevents us from becoming a subject of our trials. God knows whether we are becoming submissive to our trials or becoming submissive to Him in the midst of our trials as well as through our consciousness and faith in God's grace.

I believe that our storms place us in position of trials just for us to experience how faithful we are to God. James 2:14–24:

> What good is it, my brothers and sisters, if someone claims to have faith but has no deeds? Can such faith save them? Suppose a brother or a sister is without clothes and daily food. If one of you says to them, "Go in peace; keep warm and well fed," but does nothing about their physical needs, what

good is it? In the same way, faith by itself, if it is not accompanied by action, is dead. But someone will say, "You have faith; I have deeds." Show me your faith without deeds, and I will show you my faith by my deeds. You believe that there is one God. Good! Even the demons believe that—and shudder. You foolish person, do you want evidence that faith without deeds is useless? Was not our father Abraham considered righteous for what he did when he offered his son Isaac on the altar? You see that his faith and his actions were working together, and his faith was made complete by what he did. And the scripture was fulfilled that says, "Abraham believed God, and it was credited to him as righteousness," and he was called God's friend. You see that a person is considered righteous by what they do and not by faith alone. In the same way, was not even Rahab the prostitute considered righteous for what she did when she gave lodging to the spies and sent them off in a different direction? As the body without the spirit is dead, so faith without deeds is dead.

"Faith without works is dead." So through our pain and suffering, that creates so much chaos in the midst of our trials and temptations. That is where we produce the works that are needed for us to sustain as well as maintain the foundation of our faith in God.

The question is, how do we become successful in our trials? We become successful in our trials based on how faithful we are to God and how thankful we are to ourselves and, most of all, how well we have matured in our state of consciousness toward God our Father and also how faithful we are to ourselves and others. The only times that our trials become a sin is when we break down and give in to our trials. This is when we realize that we need to work a little harder to overcome our trials. For example, what happens if we had that same trial accrue or reoccur three times over in our lives if we stay spiritually grounded in God's consciousness or in a spiritual consciousness of mind?

We would learn how to battle those trials and adversities that we have been faced with, and now that we mastered the trials that occur in our lives, it means that we are understanding the essence and substance of God's Word.

Let us assume we have a particular sin that we want to get rid of, and that sin is constantly defeating us. We prayed, and the sin makes it seems that our prayers and talking to God are not having an impact on our sins, and then all of sudden God send you a revelation, and that revelation that God has sent you has given you power over your sins or that particular sin.

That means that we have matured spiritually and physically because we would be able to use God's Word to defeat our sins or sin.

Now that same sin or sins had so much control and impact over our faith, but through God's revelation, He was able to give us the strength and courage we need for us to overcome our sin or sins.

Now at this point that we overcome our sins or sin, we recognize that the only way that we can come over our sins is through God's love, compassion, grace, and mercy, and also having the ability to stay in tune with God's consciousness and His righteousness.

One of the main reasons that mankind is challenged by our sins is to make us strong, fearless, while preparing us to do battle against Satan and his satanic tricks. The truth also is learning from our sins in order that we will mature physically, spiritually, consciously in God's grace and mercy.

We must also understand that because we overcome a great battle of sin or sins get a battle, it's not over yet.

We have to understand how sin is affecting us spiritually and physically. We also have to understand constantly that we have to fight and stay in tune with God's grace and mercy. Because when our sins overpower our emotions and begin to take control over our faith in God.

I already have enough confidence to know that God would send me a revelation through prayers or revealed to me through my consciousness. I order to help me defeat Satan, even at Satan's best, and win over Satan. Even at Satan's best, I can defeat Satan through God's consciousness. When we defeat Satan, it is like God has placed a spiritual comforter over us to embrace us with His love, mercy, and grace.

And it is through God's authentic Word that gives us the confidence in His faithfulness to continuously fight this fight of spiritual warfare that is constantly brewing, between mankind and Satan. That is why we have to constantly keep in God's consciousness because our spiritual survival depends on our faith in God's divine Word.

Our biggest fight and survival for our spiritual survival and consciousness is fighting a fight that mankind cannot see or experience what they are fighting or what we are fighting and whom we are fighting against. This is what we refer to as the principalities and things unseen to physical eyes and even to mankind's physical existence and creation.

The only thing that is able to recognize the principalities and things that are unseen, which is challenging. To mankind, the spirituality and consistency it takes for me to stay in tune with God's divine Word.

It is through our state of consciousness, which also develop our belief, which is exercised by our faith in God. Our consciousness is the weapon that we need to stay continuously in tune with God for us to defeat Satan even in the state of Satan's principalities and the things that are unseen to mankind's physical eye.

So when we talk about principalities and things unseen what are we referring to? We are referring to a world that exists but mankind has no knowledge of. Although mankind has no knowledge of this world, this world exists and even affects mankind's spiritual life and physical life here on earth.

Now let me bring some transparency or clarity to principalities and things unseen to the naked eye. That we will get a clear understanding when we hear the words *principalities* and *things unseen*. That effect, which affects our lifestyle, both spiritually and physically. What I am referring to when I mentioned principalities and things unseen is making.

First of all, we must understand that because something is spiritual, it doesn't mean it is peaceful, safe, or sinless. What it means, once again, when we refer to the spiritual world, it is a world that exists or when we start to talk about the spiritual world. That we are referring to or talking about a world that exists where mankind cannot touch, feel, or even exist in. Mankind's body cannot even exist in the same world. The only way that mankind can exist in in the spiritual world is mankind's physical body has to be transformed. Here is what I mean:

> But our citizenship is in heaven. And we eagerly await a Savior from there, the Lord Jesus Christ, who, by the power that enables him to bring everything under his control, will transform our lowly bodies so that they will be like his glorious body. (Philippians 3:20–21 NIV; https://bible.com/bible/111/php.3.20-21.NIV)

The term *spirituality* means being able to embrace God's knowledge and wisdom when we embrace God's knowledge and wisdom. It is at that point through the interpretation and comprehending of God's Word.

Whatever we learn from God's divine Word is what develops our character and integrity of mankind's spirituality in God.

Here is why—because it is when mankind is able to live in the essence of God's Word that is when mankind is able to manifest their true spirituality of God in their lives.

The only people that can exist in the spiritual world are God our Father, Satan the destroyer, the Holy Spirit, angels, and Jesus Christ. Those are the people we know that live in the spiritual world, and there are more. Everything that goes on in the spiritual world affects the physical world that mankind lives and dwells in.

When we pray to God, where is God located? In the spiritual world. When we pray, where are our prayers going? When we pray and praise God, we are praying and praising God in the spiritual world. When Satan uses the principalities of this world, he is bringing evilness from the spiritual world to destroy the spirit and soul of mankind.

When God uses His goodness to bless us or protect us from the principalities and things unseen, our blessings and protection. Our belief in God is what produces enough of our confidence and courage where we need through our faith in God—to always become successful over Satan even during the times in which Satan is challenging the men and women of God during their temptations with Satan's principalities and things unseen. When God answers our prayers, it also comes from the spiritual world.

Just as we speak about the Holy Spirit, we misunderstand that the Holy Spirit is a spiritual energy that protects us from the principalities and things unseen to the masses of people living on the earth, but that spiritual world exists because that is where our salvation is. That is what caused the bleeding and suffering come from, which is the spiritual world.

Principalities do come from the spiritual world; principalities exist also in the physical world as well, but it is always willing and helpful to destroy the faith and consciousness of mankind, especially those who are very conscious of God's grace and mercy.

The principalities that exist in the spiritual world are always trying to destroy the consciousness of mankind and distract the men and women of the earth from continuously serving and praying to God.

The term *spirituality* means "a world that exists that is unknown to mankind's physical experience, understanding, and physical existence." Here is why: mankind's only existence and experience are in the physical existence of life.

This is what separated mankind from the spiritual world and the physical world. When I mentioned mankind, I am referring to mankind's state of consciousness, which exists living in the physical existence of life, trying to define our true meaning and being in life based on our spiritualism, and consciousness. I also mean what we can touch, feel, experience, understand, and comprehend through our physical creation, existence, and experiences in life.

Here is another question: Can mankind's body exist in the spiritual world? I would say no. Here is what I mean. The only thing that would exist in the spiritual world is mankind's consciousness. Mankind's awareness of God is what exists beyond mankind's physical body and existence in life. When mankind dies, the only thing that keeps mankind in tune with God is mankind's consciousness.

Now if you are a person who believes that mankind's faith is based on mankind's action toward God, and also if you think that mankind actions of God are the evidence of mankind's faith, then if you believe that mankind's faith is physical, then mankind's faith would get him or her into heaven. When we die, the only thing that exists in our lives is the spiritual existence and experiences of mankind's consciousness.

Now I don't think that our faith exist in our spiritual world. Here is why: When God spoke to Jeremiah, Jeremiah never entered his mother's womb. Now because Jeremiah was from in his mother's womb, God was able to give Jeremiah his meaning and being in life.

That is why when we developed our consciousness in God. It is our consciousness in God that allows mankind to define their true meaning and being in life. We also recognize from the conversation that God created all of us knowing and giving us meaning and being to exist in our lives.

That is why when we go through our lives trying to determine what we are called to do we must become submissive to God, and God would reveal to us what our true purpose and reason are in our life.

Now in the book of Jeremiah 1:4–14 (NIV):

> The word of the Lord came to me, saying, "Before I formed you in the womb I knew you, before you were born I set you apart; I appointed you as a prophet to the nations." "Alas, Sovereign Lord," I said, "I do not know how to speak; I am too young." But the Lord said to me, "Do not say, 'I am too young.' You must go to everyone I send you to and say whatever I

command you. Do not be afraid of them, for I am with you and will rescue you," declares the Lord. Then the Lord reached out his hand and touched my mouth and said to me, "I have put my words in your mouth. See, today I appoint you over nations and kingdoms to uproot and tear down, to destroy and overthrow, to build and to plant." The word of the Lord came to me: "What do you see, Jeremiah?" "I see the branch of an almond tree," I replied. The Lord said to me, "You have seen correctly, for I am watching to see that my word is fulfilled." The word of the Lord came to me again: "What do you see?" "I see a pot that is boiling," I answered. "It is tilting toward us from the north." The Lord said to me, "From the north disaster will be poured out on all who live in the land." (https://bible.com/bible/111/jer.1.4-14.NIV)

That is why mankind's life has to exist with meaning and being. God did not create mankind to just exist without consciousness. God created mankind God created mankind with a reason and purpose to exist. That reason and purpose exist to become the consciousness of mankind's nature.

The nature of mankind is to complete God's reason and purpose in their life. In order for mankind to reach the full potential of their reason and purpose in life, God has to challenge mankind through the obstacles that they have to face and bring in life.

It is interesting but we can only find our meaning and being through our own state of adversities and adversaries, which exist in our life. We face and bring God's reason and purpose for our life in order that we can achieve our potential, which exists before we entered our mothers' wombs.

The only thing that is able to recognize the principalities and things that unseen to mankind is the spirituality and consistency it takes for me to stay in tune with God's divine Word. It is through our conscience, which also develops our state of consciousness. Our consciousness is the weapon that we need to stay continuously in tune with God for us to defeat Satan even in the state of Satan's principalities.

Trials also create more discipline and spiritual awareness in order for us to stay constantly in tune with what God's will is for our lives when our trials are able to break us down or overpower our faith in God. In other words, when our trials break us down so much until we cannot focus, when our trials break us down so much that we become so disoriented, in our focus and walk with God, we do not know what to do.

We must somehow find enough confidence within ourselves to remember that God did not put us through our trials because God is looking for perfection in our lives. God places us through our trials based on our imperfections. It is through our faith in God that determines the elasticity of our faith and consciousness in God's grace and mercy. This is done through God's divine Word, which God gives us the insight to recognize what is right and wrong or what is evil and good, and that is what gives us a better assessment to make spiritual decisions as we mature and grow in God's divine Word.

What God is looking for us to do is to observe within the inner chambers of our soul to find enough faith where we know that God is going to give us the victory over our problems and anything that we face in life. God is not looking for us to be perfect. We are already perfect through Jesus Christ's death on the cross. It is our imperfections God wants us to mature spiritually through His Word and He wants us to use every drop of our imperfections and sinful nature to develop the potential we need to seek our perfections through God's Word and manifest them to become an example of Jesus Christ's lifestyle when Jesus was here on earth.

We must understand that our imperfections is what this omnipotent God is still able to love us for. Our own family cannot love us through our imperfections like God is able to do for us. I would say the closest love that I can see that comes close to God's love is that of a mother's womb because the mother's womb is the creation of life, and within that creation of life is where the mother's love becomes the consciousness of God's extended creation because there is no love like God's and a mother's love. They love their children unconditionally, even threw their own faults.

Through our imperfections, He is the only one person that can love us unconditionally. What God wants us to recognize is that His grace, which is sufficient, is enough for us to recognize that we do have the potential spiritually to mature in God's consciousness by reading, studying, and absorbing God's Word in our hearts and minds where we have the potential to seek perfection within God's grace.

When I mention perfection in God's grace and mercy, I am referring to mankind becoming vulnerable in their sins but learning enough from their mistakes that is causing them to sin, knowing that they don't want to constantly stay in their sin. Here is what I mean:

Do you think that the only way that we can acknowledge God's divine Word is through the study of God's Word to gain His wisdom and knowledge? It is the information of studying and learning God's divine Word that develops our consciousness in God's Word.

Through studying and learning God's Word is what gives mankind insight into God's Word. That insight that comes from God's Word transcended and transform into mankind's consciousness. As God's Word develops in mankind's consciousness, it shapes mankind's faith, confidence, and courage in God's Word; and this is where mankind's action of faith is developed.

We must recognize the only way we can acknowledge God's consciousness is the true essence of His divine Word. Here is why? When we read and study God's Word, we get a better sense or understanding of how God's consciousness is being developed in our hearts and minds.

Our minds and hearts start to evolve and become the reality of man's spiritual existence as well-developed man's consciousness by interpreting to mankind who God is to all men. We experience in God's Word how it develops in each of us the spiritual consciousness; we need to stay focused on what God's will is for our lives.

We also experience how God's character and integrity interacts with man's nature and through our experience if we are honest about God's Word. We would want God's Word to become successful in our lives, and the only way God's Word is going to become successful in our lives is if we embrace God's Word as a way of life and consciousness. Our spiritual consciousness is first is a gift from God. It is what develops who we are in God's consciousness.

Now the reason why mankind does not become successful in their trials is because they depend more on their free will than what God's will is for their lives. That is why mankind is able to challenge God's will. When you become in tune with God's consciousness, you are allowing God to develop what your reason and purpose is for your life. When you deviate from God's will, you become vulnerable to the adversities and adversaries that you face every day in your life. It is through God's consciousness that we get our true salvation in God because we are becoming more aware of who God actually is to mankind themselves. We are interpreting and acknowledging not from a religious or denomination perspective but from God's perspective.

# Understanding the Nature of Trials and Sins

**M**ankind has free will because God has given mankind the opportunity to make their own choices in life based on mankind's free will. We must also understand that because mankind has free will, mankind's free will gives mankind the will, freedom, and power to sin.

We must always remember that mankind's sinful nature and imperfection are what give mankind the action and right to sin. Mankind's sinful nature and imperfections do not give mankind the power, or the right not to sin.

Mankind is given the power to sin because of their own free will.

Mankind's free will gives mankind the power to sin and make the choice and decisions mankind choose to sin or causes mankind to sin. Now mankind's ability to sin can never be removed from mankind's nature because it is mankind's nature to sin. Mankind's free will is influenced by mankind's nature, which causes mankind to sin.

If I can make this statement, it is through God's creation of mankind's free will that gives mankind spiritual freedom of will to sin. Yet it is through mankind's will that gives mankind the spiritual opportunity to sin, and it is through mankind's sins that gives mankind the opportunity to be forgiven for their sins, which mankind has committed.

Now the only control mankind has over sin is developing their consciousness to mature spiritually in God's divine Word. That is why it is important that we stay in tune and in fellowship with God's divine Word.

Because God has given mankind the opportunity to make choices based on their "free will," man's "free will," if it is not exercised spiritually, mankind would never have the opportunity to have the discipline they need to become successful both faithfully and spiritually in their walk with God in God's divine Word.

The question comes to mind, why would God give mankind a "free will" if God wanted mankind to obey Him? When God created mankind, God created mankind with an independent nature, enough to make decisions based on their own free will or whether man's free will conflicted with God's will. This is why it is important for mankind to stay in tune with God's consciousness. Here is why mankind's consciousness can only become successful based on how well mankind has developed their faith in God.

It is through God's consciousness that mankind is able to develop enough discipline to stay in tune with God's consciousness. When mankind stays in tune with God's consciousness, that is what makes mankind become successful in his or her physical life and spiritual life.

When man is able to master his nature, that is when mankind are able to master themselves. The only time man is able to control his or her "free will" is when mankind is able to master his nature, but even if mankind are to master their free will, man still needs God's Word as the primary factor to discipline mankind's nature. Here is why the nature of mankind is destructive and evil: it is stimulated by mankind's pride, jealousy, and lust for material possessions. The stimulation of pride, jealousy, and lust would cause a brother to kill his own brother. For example, when we look into the book of Genesis 4:1–17, we experience from reading the text pride and jealousy can destroy mankind's relationship and salvation with God our father. That is why it is imperative for mankind to stay in constant pray and fasting in order for us to stay focused on our God and father:

> Adam made love to his wife Eve, and she became pregnant and gave birth to Cain. She said, "With the help of the Lord I have brought forth a man." Later she gave birth to his brother Abel. Now Abel kept flocks, and Cain worked the soil. In the

course of time Cain brought some of the fruits of the soil as an offering to the Lord. And Abel also brought an offering—fat portions from some of the firstborn of his flock. The Lord looked with favor on Abel and his offering, but on Cain and his offering he did not look with favor. So Cain was very angry, and his face was downcast. Then the Lord said to Cain, "Why are you angry? Why is your face downcast? If you do what is right, will you not be accepted? But if you do not do what is right, sin is crouching at your door; it desires to have you, but you must rule over it." Now Cain said to his brother Abel, "Let's go out to the field." While they were in the field, Cain attacked his brother Abel and killed him. Then the Lord said to Cain, "Where is your brother Abel?" "I don't know," he replied. "Am I my brother's keeper?" The Lord said, "What have you done? Listen! Your brother's blood cries out to me from the ground. Now you are under a curse and driven from the ground, which opened its mouth to receive your brother's blood from your hand. When you work the ground, it will no longer yield its crops for you. You will be a restless wanderer on the earth."

Today you are driving me from the land, and I will be hidden from your presence; I will be a restless wanderer on the earth, and whoever finds me will kill me." But the Lord said to him, "Not so; anyone who kills Cain will suffer vengeance seven times over." Then the Lord put a mark on Cain so that no one who found him would kill him. So Cain went out from the Lord's presence and lived in the land of Nod, east of Eden. Cain made love to his wife, and she became pregnant and gave birth to Enoch. Cain was then building a city, and he named it after his son Enoch.

Now to explain the nature of mankind and their actions that would motivate the nature of mankind's action toward their brother or even family, mankind would even kill his brother to satisfy the nature of their passion, which is pride, lust, and jealousy. The consciousness of mankind is challenged by mankind's "free will" and mankind's sinful nature.

It is at this point where mankind's nature and free will collaborate together to question what is right and wrong. In other words, to question the true reality of the existence of what is right and wrong or what mankind chooses or acknowledges that is good or evil is first displayed in mankind's actions, which is also reflected in mankind's consciousness and faith. Now the actions that mankind freely exercises are known to mankind as their free will.

That free will is nothing more than mankind's choice. Mankind's actions are nothing more than a choice. Now that choice is driven by mankind's free will gives mankind the choice of good and evil.

Whatever choice mankind chooses between good and evil is nothing more than mankind's free will. Now mankind's free will is challenged by good and evil.

Now whatever choice that mankind decides to choose between good and evil is based on mankind's free will.

Now good and evil is decided on based on the knowledge that mankind has embraced in their own state of consciousness and what experiences mankind went through in life.

Mankind's free will challenges mankind's state of consciousness. Mankind's consciousness or awareness allows mankind to choose good over evil or evil over good. This is also based on mankind's state of consciousness of what is good and evil. Whatever choice that mankind decides on is nothing more than mankind's nature. We must also remember that our choices in life are impacted by our sinful nature and our imperfections

Even when mankind is faced with many adversities in life, which pertains to good and evil, those issues and the decisions that mankind chooses are done based on mankind's free will that God has given to mankind in order that mankind would get a better understanding and opportunity on what is good and evil based on mankind's state of consciousness and the actions, which causes mankind to choose good or evil.

I guess what I'm trying to say is mankind's free will, gives mankind the opportunity to choose whatever lifestyle that mankind wants to live either good or evil. All of that is left up to mankind's state of consciousness.

Now that is when mankind chooses as their choice in life whatever road that mankind chooses and experiences for itself as good and evil.

That is why mankind's free will can only be judged by God. Here is why: God created good, but because of mankind's free will, it was mankind's free will that caused mankind to create the existence of evil. That evil still exists in the world today.

Now this is very important, although God is the author and finisher of mankind's free will. Under mankind's free will is the choice that mankind makes, in order for mankind to exercise their free will. Mankind is still responsible for the choices they make that pertain to mankind's free will.

Now mankind's free will exists in the choices and decisions that mankind chooses, which also pertains to what is good and evil. Now because of mankind's state of consciousness. Mankind has the opportunity to choose what is good and evil.

We must also understand that because mankind, has free will. That freedom of mankind's free will places mankind in a compromising and submissive position with God our Father.

Mankind's free will that mankind exercises gives mankind the opportunity for mankind to acknowledge that their free will has its own responsibilities to God our Father. Because of mankind's free will, that is what gives God the right to judge mankind of their free will.

Now we must also understand that because of mankind's free will. Mankind's free will does not mean that mankind has the right to judge mankind, nor does mankind has the right to judge his own actions of his or her free will of what is good and evil.

Here is why: Mankind did not create each other. That authority is not given to mankind but God Himself to judge mankind of their own good and evil. God is the only person who can judge mankind because God Himself created mankind with their own free will, and that is what gives God authority to judge mankind, not mankind themselves.

We must understand this statement in order to understand why God is the only person to judge mankind of their own free will. First of all, the choice that mankind makes concerning good and evil is made by mankind.

Now mankind's actions of good and evil can only be judged by God himself and once again not mankind. That authority of judgment is only given to God Himself. Although mankind commits the act, the authority that comes with God's judgment is embraced in God's compassion, grace, and mercy.

Mankind cannot judge himself or others because mankind does not have or cannot embrace the qualities of forgiveness and judgment like God can because of God's infallible compassion, grace, and mercy. The capacity in which God is able to embrace is without fault, prejudice, bias, or favoritism. Like God can.

That is why mankind's consciousness is very important to mankind's faith in God. Here is why: Mankind's awareness of the scriptures gives mankind the enlightenment and knowledge to seriously overcome their evil desires. Mankind's consciousness is what develops mankind's faith in God.

What God is responsible for is when mankind makes their choice to accept either good or evil. That choice is left up to God because mankind's salvation depends on God's compassion, grace, and mercy. Mankind's salvation depends on mankind's choice of consciousness, which is good or evil.

Mankind must also remember that whatever choice they make, especially toward good and evil, affects their salvation with God.

I think one of the most important things that Christians need to understand is, for example, just like you have faith in God. There are many people who have just as much faith or more faith in Satan than most Christians do in their own God and evil desires of this world, such as pride, selfishness, hatred, and misjudgment of others.

Some philosophers, theologians, and theorists have developed the argument of if God created mankind with free will. Then God should not judge mankind or condemn mankind. Although mankind has free will, it does not excuse mankind's decisions.

The decisions, which mankind makes under their free will. God makes mankind responsible for the decisions which mankind makes, based on their own Consciousness, state of mind. Now the conscious state of mind gives mankind the knowledge and awareness that mankind needs to make the choice, which mankind chooses evil over good. Now with mankind having the opportunity to exercise their free will, that is what makes mankind responsible for their own choices under mankind's free will.

Now if God gives mankind their own free will, why would God want to judge mankind for choosing what is good and evil or evil over good? God never gave mankind the freedom to choose what is good and evil. God gave mankind the opportunity to choose what is good, not evil. It was mankind who choose evil over good.

Once again for clarity mankind chooses good and evil themselves. It was mankind who choose evil over good. It was God who created mankind and place mankind in a state of peace, which was the garden of Eden. It was here that mankind went against God's laws and principles.

That is why God uses mankind's evil desires to judge and determine mankind's salvation based on what is good and evil. That is why God uses salvation as a means to judge mankind's action of good and evil because of mankind's sinful nature.

Here is another statement: Why would God choose heaven or hell as a means to place mankind in? Here is why: it is because of the choices that mankind made. Those choices that mankind makes of evil and good are choices that have spiritual responsibilities attached to them from God that mankind is responsible for even when mankind thinks that they getting away with the wrong that they are doing.

We must also understand that good and evil need to exist together or that good and evil will survive because it seems that the nature of good and evil is to challenge each other, and that is why they exist to the capacity in which they do.

One of the intriguing and interesting things about good and evil is that good always wins over evil. Even if it seems that evil is winning, you know why: mankind created the desire and opportunity for evil to exist as part of mankind's nature.

Now because God created good and not evil, good would always rule and dominate evil because everything that God has created out of the essence and substance of God's righteousness has always included good. So good will always dominate and rule over evil. Even when mankind does experience good, rising up to destroy the evilness that looks like it is winning to destroy good.

Always remember when you are faced with your adversities, especially in this life, that good will always win. Here is why: God created good, although mankind chooses evil over good. At the time, mankind chooses evil over good.

When mankind goes through adversities and trials in life, I think God allows these trials and adversities to become a part of mankind's sinful nature and imperfection. I think it is because God uses our adversities and trials to remind us that He did not choose evil for mankind.

Instead, mankind chooses evil for themselves first, and now evilness is a choice that mankind choose. The evilness that mankind chooses causes mankind so much pain and suffering. When God put us through trials and adversities, God put us through these trials and adversities to remind us of the day that mankind choose evil over good, and that is the choice that challenges mankind's spiritual consciousness.

Now we might be able to argue this fact, and that is if God did not give mankind free will to exist. Many people would start saying that the God we serve always wants to be in control. Then we serve a God of manipulation.

The God we serve is a God who dominates mankind's life. The God we serve cannot exercise compassion. The God we serve cannot exercise grace, and the God we serve cannot be merciful. Here is why: never allow mankind to make their own choices in life.

That is why it is very important that mankind is able to choose and make their own choices in life, and it is those choices that were given to mankind for mankind to make their choice under the freedom of mankind's own choice. That is why we call those choices, mankind's free will, that God Himself has created mankind with, which is mankind's free will.

We must also understand that God gave mankind one option to choose from, which was good, but mankind created our one option two, which was evil. Now because mankind created or caused another option to exist with good, which is evil, God had to make mankind responsible for the evil that mankind created that causes so many bad things in the world.

We must remember that evil came into existence based on mankind's free will. That is why, we as faithful believers in God, need to respect God's awesomeness. Here is what I mean when I mention the awesomeness of God: mankind created the evilness that causes so many bad things to happen to good people, like yourself.

Because mankind created the evilness of this world, God could have destroyed mankind to the point where mankind did not exist anymore. But through God's faith, compassion, grace, and mercy for you, He understands mankind's sinful nature well enough to give mankind enough compassion, grace, and mercy. God still has enough love to forgive mankind if they ask forgiveness from God.

Now the choices that mankind chooses are embraced in their consciousness. These two choices that mankind embraces are good and evil. In order for us to understand why God had to judge good and evil is simple. We must understand that God did not create evil. God created mankind with free will to become in harmony and fellowship with God our Father. It is mankind's free will that introduces the evilness that exists in the world today.

So we must admit that God never created evil but he allows man's free will to choose and introduce their evil desires to the world, and that is what gives God the authority and power to judge mankind's actions on what is good and evil to mankind.

It also allows God to have a strong opinion on what is good because if we created something, we have a tendency to love it and appreciate it more than anything that challenges what we have created.

I think that is why God judges evilness with such much sovereignty and authenticity the way He does because mankind introduces evilness to compete with God's goodness. So that is why we can experience and understand why God is so harsh toward mankind's sinful nature and imperfection.

Now mankind's state of consciousness is what brings mankind into consciousness and awareness of what is good and evil. Now whatever road mankind chooses to travel, especially when it comes to good and evil, is determined by the choices that mankind makes between good and evil.

# THE POWER OF GOD'S CONSCIOUSNESS

Now that is the choice that mankind makes, especially when it comes to good and evil. Now mankind's choice of good and evil is decided by mankind's free will. Now mankind's free will that mankind is able to exercise is nothing more than mankind's choice of what is good and evil. Now whatever mankind exercises that is either good or evil is all judged by God Himself.

There is a spiritual consciousness that resonates with mankind when mankind's consciousness embraces God's divine Word, which makes God have compassion for the evilness of mankind's actions, especially when those actions are driven by mankind's actions of good and evil. Here is what I mean: We must understand that our consciousness is challenged by good and evil. Now the challenges of good and evil are now judged by God Himself.

Sometimes good looks very vulnerable and weak. The true essence and substance of good are misinterpreted and can sometimes be misinformed by those people who also believe in God. Sometimes good is interpreted as a sign of weakness. While we spend more time rewarding and acknowledging the evilness that causes bad things to happen to good people like you, it seems to me that we appreciate good over evil. Strength itself is only rewarded in the evilness of mankind's actions.

Especially when we are in a situation that challenges our faith in God, now those situations are the ones that challenge our faith and consciousness in God. Those situations that challenge our lifestyle try to create the weakness of our faith and consciousness in God. It is those weaknesses that even challenge the power of mankind's faith in God.

And the only time that we experienced and exercise the power of good being displayed is in the midst of our trials and adversities, and that is what brings mankind's consciousness into harmony with God our creator.

Even in the midst of our trials and adversities, we can still experience the goodness of God, being experienced in the manifestation of God's spirit, being transformed and transcending through the state of mankind's own consciousness. And that is how mankind is able to experience the goodness of God, transforming and transcended just to destroy the will of mankind.

Now we must remember still that God's grace, mercy, and love for mankind will always outperform evil because God did not create the evilness and evil things of this world, especially those things that happen in the world, to the good people like you and me. Mankind made that choice of good and evil, and now the repercussions of all evil this is our sinful nature that is now being judged by mankind's salvation through God Himself.

Because your spirituality resonates and collaborates with your spiritual state of consciousness, now you have developed and matured in your spiritual state of consciousness. It is very easy now for mankind to experience the transparency and clarity of good and evil and what path they have chosen to walk in.

Good and evil exist around us. That is why it is important for mankind to stay in tune and in fellowship with God our Father. Here is why: it is because of God's Word that develops and enhances mankind's spiritual consciousness.

God's Word is what allows mankind to make the right choices, especially when it comes to choosing good over

## THE POWER OF GOD'S CONSCIOUSNESS

evil. God's Word makes this life of good and evil so transparent to the spiritual consciousness of mankind.

The goodness that challenges the evilness of this world. We must also recognize that the evilness that we choose, mankind chooses evilness because mankind does not want to listen to their spiritual consciousness of what God's Word has though us about, what is good and evil. Mankind would not be naive to the reality of what is good and evil. When we choose what is good and evil, mankind is responsible for their own actions as it relates to good and evil. Mankind chooses evilness based on what they are getting out of the choice. If good is not profitable, then when mankind chooses the evilness of this world over the goodness of God, once again mankind's imperfection and sinful nature are played out through mankind's free will. It is mankind's free will that gives mankind the opportunity to exercise their free will to choose evil over good. Here is why mankind chooses the evilness of this world over good.

Sometimes it is wealth, pride, and most of all when mankind wants more than what God has blessed mankind with; and that is what becomes the danger zone for mankind. That is when mankind starts to compromise God's goodness and compassion for the evilness of this world. And it is at that state of mankind's consciousness that determines how it is acted out through mankind's discipline and faith in God.

The question that should come to mind now is how does one acknowledge God's divine wisdom? In other words, how do we rekindle that spark that allows us to embrace God's righteousness in our lives? How does a person embrace God's righteousness while wrestling with their own imperfections in life? For example, here is what I am referring to, and that is, how can a perfect God love an imperfect human being like me and you?

Let me say that again. How can a perfect God love the imperfections of mankind enough to send His Son to die for us? Let me be honest. I know I am an imperfect human being. I have many faults. I have fallen short of God's Word so many times. I can teach you enough to protect you from falling short of God's Word. I can show you as well as tell you what you need to do or what you need to do that will not place you in a vulnerable position to fall short I continuously fall short of God's divine Word.

It has nothing to do with me being smart or spiritually strong. I have a strong faith or belief in God; it is just because I have you and tell you what it is you need to do not to fall short of God's Word.

It is because I have done it so many times, and it comes from learning and experiencing the adversities, adversaries, and allowing me to subconsciously or spiritually recognize how strong and how powerful my spiritual consciousness is in God.

The one thing I don't do is use my imperfections as an excuse to justify my sins. Here is what I mean. My imperfections are those experiences that nurture and mature my spiritual consciousness enough where I have learned to enjoy my trials, temptations, chaos, and adversities. So what I learn proves to me how mature and comfortable I am in God's grace and mercy.

Now when I become successful in my trials, temptations, chaos, and mercy, even if I don't become successful in my trials or temptations, whatever the outcome of my trials and temptations, it still depends on our maturity and spiritual consciousness. One thing I can say is it's all maturity in God's Word that teaches us how our experiences and struggles with our adversities allow our faith to become that belief that strengthens us through God's divine work in the midst of our adversities.

My imperfections relate to how well I overcome my sins during my trials and temptations. It also allows me to recognize the areas I need support in so that I can improve and mature in my faith with God and become strong and submissive to his will.

Here is my main point: I do not use my sins as an excuse to take advantage of God's grace and mercy. Let me elaborate. One of the things I have admired about God is that God is the only person whom I know who is able to forgive mankind of their sins, although He still remembers the actions of mankind's sin that they have committed.

This is the example that makes God separate from mankind: through God's grace and mercy, God is able to forgive although God is able to remember the sins that mankind has committed. God's grace and mercy are extended through generations and generations to come.

There are two things that need to be understood at this point, and that is how God is able to forgive us because of His grace and His mercy, but the one thing that we must realize is never underestimate God's grace and mercy. It could mean that you are abusing God's grace and mercy.

Let me shed some light on the statement about how mankind is able to abuse God's forgiveness by constantly committing sin or sins and using God's forgiveness as an excuse to continuously commit sin.

Mankind must also remember and understand that we strive to become spiritual beings. Although we have the potential to become spiritual beings, even with mankind's sinful nature and imperfection, mankind still has the potential to become a spiritual being based on mankind's maturity of their consciousness and faith in God. Now that is how mankind is rewarded—their salvation in God. We must also consciously try to understand that God's forgiveness is not something that we earn from God. We must also understand that God's forgiveness is nothing more than a privilege. We cannot earn God's forgiveness. Forgiveness can only once again be given to mankind based on their lifestyle as a Christian.

Even when mankind exercises their sinful nature and their imperfections, God, through His grace and mercy, is always willing to forgive mankind of their sinful nature and imperfection.

What we truly need to understand is that God's forgiveness is a blessed privilege and a blessing. In other words, a blessing is what God does for everyone that asks for a blessing. Privilege is a blessing, which comes through the favor of God's grace and mercy.

Our state of consciousness is what we experienced from God's Word and making God's Word's a lifestyle or a way of life. As we embrace God's Word as a way of life, we are actually developing and maturing in our faith with God.

As we mature in God's grace, we are exercising a different lifestyle that makes a difference in our life. Now that difference is what brings mankind into the understanding and comprehension of their faith in God, and it is at this point that we develop our spiritual consciousness in God's grace and mercy.

Now let us get back to the point of why we are blessed to be privileged to be blessed versus being blessed. Here is what I mean: Being privileged in your blessing and being blessed. The best way to define these two words of *being blessed* and *being privileged* in our blessing is this: We are blessed to be living under God's grace and mercy. Our blessing comes when we, through our consciousness, decide to make God's Word a way of life. When we embrace God's Word, we make God's Word a way of life. That is what starts to develop our spiritual journey, which begins to develop our own state of consciousness in God.

When I mentioned spiritual consciousness, I am referring to studying and living the Word of God. I mean inhaling, exhaling, and digesting God's Word to become every drop of our lifestyle. This is when God's Word becomes mankind's spiritual consciousness.

The consciousness of mankind is making mankind aware of God's Word. When mankind becomes conscious of God's Word, that consciousness is what develops and sparks mankind's curiosity to become aware of God's divine Word.

As mankind develops their consciousness through God's divine Word and is living God's divine Word as a way of life, that is when mankind begins to develop its spiritual consciousness through God's divine Word even when mankind is living in its own sinful nature and imperfection.

This is where God we begin to acknowledge the differences between being privileged by God's blessing and not being privileged by God's blessing. For example, let us look at King Hezekiah living fifteen years more years (2 Kings 20:1–7, Isaiah 38:5).

It is something that mankind doesn't want to abuse, especially God's forgiveness. It is something that we don't want to ever abuse or take for granted. Here is why: This is the only thing that gives God the compassion to forgive mankind even in the state of mankind's free will, sinful nature, and imperfection. God's forgiveness is the only passes way to mankind's salvation.

Although mankind's free will is given to him to exercise without any limits of decision or knowledge that they have, it is through God's compassion, such as grace and mercy, that exercises God's forgiveness for mankind's sinful nature and imperfection.

What would happen if you knew that every time you sin, God is forgiving you? Forgiveness is a privilege that we get from God, and we sometimes abuse it because we know that we have been forgiven by God. So we don't want to be placed in a position where we abuse God's forgiveness because when we abuse God's forgiveness, we might be at that point where we might die or death is knocking at your door of life.

We must understand that sometimes we get so caught up in the comfortability of our sins and sinful ways and imperfections that we get comfortable. That comfort zone is a dangerous place, especially when we feel comfortable in the state of our sinful nature and imperfection.

The comfort zone is the place where what we are doing feels so good committing the sin or sins that it feels so good that we forget the act itself is a sin, and that is what destroys mankind's salvation in God.

## THE POWER OF GOD'S CONSCIOUSNESS

That is what I referred to as the comfort zone of comfortability, which can make you feel so comfortable that you don't recognize or understand you are sinning. Sometimes we use Bible verses to help accommodate our own sinful nature and imperfections.

That is what makes sinning feel so good until it is not a sin. We must always remember when we sin to ask God for His forgiveness because of our sinful nature and imperfections.

What we need to consciously acknowledge is that we don't know if we were forgiven for our last sins. Think about it. So why would we continue to do the same things constantly over and over again and explain to God to exercise His forgiveness for us committing our sins? What we need to understand is that God's forgiveness allows mankind to mature in their sin. Here is how: as we mature in our sins, it means that we are striving more into developing our state of consciousness.

When I mentioned maturing in our sins, I am making reference to the idea that as we sin, and from the impact and consequences of our sins, it is at this point that we begin to mature in our sin. It is mankind's spiritual consciousness that keeps us focused and in tune with God's Word so we will not be tempted or become vulnerable and obligated to commit the same sin or sins over and over again in life.

What we do know is that we are blessed and highly favored because we are still able to listen to the words of God. What we truly don't know is if God actually forgave us for the last sins which we have committed.

The one thing that we do know is because we are still breathing, we are still alive all because of God's grace and mercy. It is through God's grace and mercy that we are privileged to receive God's forgiveness that God places upon us because of our sins and imperfections as human beings.

It is through God's grace and mercy that we are still alive to acknowledge that we are still favored and truly blessed, but we cannot acknowledge consciously if God has forgiven us for our last sins that we have committed, even the sins that we don't know about.

What we do know is that God is still allowing us to live, but we would never know the degree or level of God's forgiveness. The one thing that I would tell you is that God, in His state of forgiveness, acknowledges to mankind there is much compassion, love, and understanding that God has taught mankind about our sins and imperfections still, yet God is able to judge mankind as a righteous man or woman are, even if God has to place mankind in hell for the sins that he or she has committed. God's forgiveness is a privilege and we do not know when and at what time God's patients are going to run out on our sins and imperfection.

We already know that through God's grace and mercy, we are able to read this book and we are still alive, even in the midst of our sins. The one thing that mankind is not privileged to know is if God has forgiven mankind of their last sins that they have committed. Everything else is revealed through mankind's consciousness for mankind to know and understand.

What is sin? We can go through the Bible and get a concrete answer that defines sin. But from my perspective, sin is a state of mankind's understanding of where mankind is at during that particular time in their lives, where mankind knows that they can do better and mature in the actions of their sins. What sin does to mankind is give mankind the consciousness to know that through mankind's faith in God, mankind has the spiritual potential to do better in their spiritual walk with God where mankind has the ability to be forgiven. Now knowing this brings about this argument and that is first of all, mankind already knows of God's grace and mercy and how mankind has abused God's forgiveness and mercy through our sins. Mankind knows about God's salvation. We abuse God's salvation when we sin against God and continue to keep sinning without respecting our faith in God. See, we lose respect for God's forgiveness when we can become comfortable with continuously sinning, and having a good explanation for the sins that we are committing does not make it right for us to sin.

Now the one thing that we misunderstand is that because we have a good excuse for why we are committing the sins does not mean that it is right for us to do. For example, we know that taking drugs does destroy the human body, but most people will find many excuses why they take drugs.

Although we ask God for forgiveness and God is able to forgive us, God even manifests himself through us; and because of God's manifestation through us, the drugs that you have taken already have some serious consequences, which causes so much pain and harm to the masses of people's living conditions.

When you feel the pain and suffering that you are experiencing coming from just taking drugs and abusing your body, the drugs that you have done become detrimental to your body as the drugs start to begin to decay in destroying your immune system.

This is all because you're taking drugs. Now think for a moment: you don't think about the drugs that you're taking and how these drugs are destroying your body and how these drugs are affecting your immune system.

Now have you ever asked people why they sin or why they take drugs. The question is this: Why do people sin? Why do people take drugs?

It is because it's acceptable and enjoyable to mankind although we know the danger that is involved in drugs and in the actions of sinning.

Through our sins and drug abuse, at some point in time, we must also acknowledge to ourselves that every action or every reaction has a consequence on everything that we do. That is why it's very important that mankind tries to develop its spiritual consciousness.

Here is why our spiritual consciousness always keeps us focused in the spiritual world. We are constantly thinking about things that we have to do. For example, how do we elevate ourselves from the mere physical existence into developing our own spiritual consciousness? Now our spiritual consciousness is what protects and gives us the power over all satanic powers such as the principalities and things not seen.

Our consciousness needs to be always in a positive light. To do that, we must constantly spiritually think and be positive about our environment. When we deviate from our own spiritual consciousness, that is when we leave room for us to sin.

The most dangerous place that a Christian could be in is not developing the consciousness but using the scriptures as a tool to justify the sense that they are committing.

This is what I call spiritual entrapment or spiritual suicide. This is what is going on in our society today. I think that the majority of mankind is not spending enough time on developing their spiritual consciousness.

It seems to me we are spending more developing a curriculum to satisfy and sit into the world standards instead of God's standards. I think the majority of mankind is spending more time trying to please the masses of people than trying to please God. Here's what I mean.

One of the things that I have come to recognize is that mankind is trying to use God's divine Word to fit into the world or society's agenda and not God's agenda.

Here is what mankind is trying to do with God's Word: they try to create, words, philosophies, and ideologies that remove the discipline, teachings, and authenticity from God's Word.

When mankind removes the philosophy or ideology from God's divine Word and replaces it with philosophy and ideology, that is when the Word of God becomes sugar-coated and watered down with mankind's own version of mankind's ideologies, philosophies, and theories.

This creates spiritual diabetes that sits in the consciousness of mankind's mind, of mankind's hope, for you to commit sin and destroy the world, creating enough conflict to keep people confused about the lifestyle and still yet cause enough dissension and distortion in the Word of God.

We as mankind now have spiritual diabetes that is killing us, and we cannot even get enough supplication or justification from God's grace and mercy to help support our salvation in God. Read the book *The Theory of Theology* by

James Grant. It talks about how mankind is using God's divine Word and destroying the true reality and spiritualism of God.

We also know about the uncertainty of our sins. The uncertainty of our sins means we commit the sins, but we don't understand or have knowledge if God has forgiven us of our previous sins or even our one sin.

The uncertainty comes with us not knowing, if God forgave us of our sins. Forgiveness is a divine state of consciousness which can only be exercised and control by God Himself because forgiveness needs actions in order to be perfected and the only person that is able to exercise perfection in it true state of forgiveness is God Himself.

The true perfection of forgiveness that has been exercised toward mankind is Jesus's death upon the cross where the father has shown a perfect love of forgiveness for mankind.

In the true state of forgiveness, it takes integrity, compassion, mercy, and grace to achieve perfect forgiveness. Someone might ask the question, what does it mean when you mention perfect forgiveness? And most of all, what is the true state of perfect forgiveness? What are you referring to as the true state of perfect forgiveness?

Here is what I am referring as the true state of perfect forgiveness. The true state of perfect forgiveness can only be expressed and exercised by God because with truthful and perfect forgiveness comes also total truthful forgetfulness that only God Himself can exercise toward mankind. Not because God is the creator of mankind or because God created the world. Not because God is omnipotent and omnipresent. But the forgiveness of mankind's sins comes from God because of God's compassion, God's grace, and God's mercy for mankind and race that we want to win is to allow God to forgive us so we can learn and have a consciousness of our sins as human beings. This is what helps us run this race to win our salvation back through God's salvation. Here is why: because God wants mankind to experience and give mankind through his consciousness the understanding to comprehend and exercise the true or perfect state of forgiveness that God Himself has just given to us.

God wants mankind to exercise that same truthful state of forgiveness toward us. We should exercise that same state of forgiveness toward each other also so that mankind can experience and understand how truthful forgiveness works.

The question some might ask is, why do we need to know about the truth in forgiveness from God if God is the only person that is able to exercise the truth that is in forgiveness? Because God is trying to let mankind know that mankind has the same level of forgiveness that God has for us, we should have that same status, greatness, and level of forgiveness that God has for us as we should have for each other, especially when we have experienced God's compassion, grace, and mercy that God has teaches us through His divine Word. How can we say we love God whom we have never seen and hate our brother whom we have seen? It is also good to know that forgiveness also has its own state and level of maturity in the nature of mankind's hearts.

Just like every emotion that mankind has experienced, we must also realize that the things that we have experienced are what bring us into a state of learning and knowledge of our consciousness, where we understand and embrace our learning and experience through mankind's consciousness that is developed through God's divine Word.

Every challenge that mankind has come to face to face with is experienced through mankind's consciousness. Everything that we experienced is nothing more than mankind's true awareness, and it is that awareness that allows mankind to exercise their knowledge and experience to become their true spiritual consciousness.

The knowledge that mankind experiences exist through mankind's consciousness. That is what gives mankind the courage mankind need to face their adversities and the challenges that try to destroy mankind's consciousness, belief, and faith in God. That only is achieved through our state of adversities.

What God is trying to let mankind know is that in His perfect state of forgiveness, He is able to let mankind experience His actions and experience of forgiveness and how mankind should be able to exercise that forgiveness at the same level as God does. Our first example of God's forgiveness is best expressed and experienced through God's salvation, and when we become submissive, asking God to forgive us, I think is the first experience we have with God's divine forgiveness. It is when mankind asks forgiveness and even in their state of repentance.

What is it like to experience and understand what someone like God or Jesus Christ has to do in order to exercise the true nature and actions of forgiveness? I mean forgiveness that produces perfection in the midst of forgiveness as it relates to perfection, and most of all, what is it like to identify with the actions that create perfection in God's forgiveness? What is perfection of forgiveness?

It means being able to exercise forgiveness with the same actions and attitude as God (Jesus Christ). I mean being able to forgive a person without holding any grudges or animosity toward them.

If I had to define forgiveness, I would have to say forgiveness is like faith—it gets better as we mature in our actions—and understanding what true forgiveness is as it is express by God Himself toward mankind. We use our actions as a means to mature in our own state of forgiveness. Our action of maturity means that our faith grows; our consciousness teaches us how to forgive like God, which means that we have the potential to reach the same state of consciousness that God has reached.

I strongly believe that God's forgiveness has been misinformed as well as misinterpreted to mankind. Here is what I mean: every sin that I have committed is forgiven by God. So that means that I can commit thousands of sins and still be forgiven by God. The problem is we do not know if we were forgiven already for the last sins that we have committed. The only person who knows if God has forgiven us for our sins is God Himself, not even the person who has sinned.

Now let me reiterate because my understanding of God's forgiveness toward mankind's sin is it means that God is constantly going to forgive mankind of all of their sin.

So from that interpretation and understanding, that means that we should continue to constantly sin because it seems that before we sin, we are already in a state of forgiveness. Here is how the sin or sins that we have committed become a problem to the person or people who have committed their sins.

When mankind gets accustomed and comfortable with their sins, they might get ready to miss God's heavenly glory. Here is what I mean: it might not be God's will tomorrow for you to wake up because mankind does not control their sleeping conditions. It means that mankind does not have the power to die in his sleep or not, so when we sleep, we don't control the outcome of tomorrow; we don't control the conditions of the weather.

Let me at this point develop this premise. Let us assume that a person who is committing a sin or sins feels comfortable in committing their sins.

Now let me elaborate, especially when I say a person or people feels comfortable in their sins. What I am referring to is that the person who is committing their sins has used every excuse to justify the actions that are causing them to sin.

When I mentioned *justify*, I mean people who would use every excuse to justify their reason and purpose of why they are sinning or even feeling good about the sins that they are committing. We must understand that sinning gives us a certain power and happiness that is mostly caused by pride and self-centeredness.

Now here is why they are using their sinful nature to justify the actions of their sins. Now if we know that committing a sin or sins is wrong in the eyes of God, why do we commit such a sin or sins? Here is why, and it is simple: because it is also the free will of mankind's nature that gives mankind the opportunity to sin. We must also understand that still does not give mankind the right to sin in the eyes of God. This is the point where mankind starts to develop his consciousness as a spiritual being to stay constantly in tune with God's righteousness in order to prevent mankind from sinning.

When someone mentions it is the nature of mankind to sin, what are they actually referring to? It is not just an academic perspective; it is also a reality of mankind. It is rooted in mankind that took on his own to sin; the other is mankind, by nature, is prone to sin genetically to sin. Mankind should always take the opportunity to master their free will through the disciplining of God's divine Word. The discipline that is in God's Word is what also develops and enhances mankind's free will and nature to become the spiritual lighthouse of mankind's soul and spirit

Because it is in mankind's biological makeup for him to sin, that is what gives mankind the right, by nature, to sin.

Again, there is still no excuse for mankind to continue to sin in the eyes of God. Here is why: because mankind has the same free will to sin or not to sin toward God. Now the action of mankind's right to sin is challenged by mankind's free will.

The idea and concept of mankind's free will opens up mankind to all types of opportunity to sin. There has to be something in mankind's nature that is able to prevent mankind from sinning, and it's simple: it is the Word of God. Here is how the Word of God is able to prevent mankind from sinning.

When mankind is able to embrace the Word of God into their heart and consciousness, and when God's Word is able to resonate itself in the hearts and minds of mankind, that is what gives mankind the support and strength that mankind needs to stop sinning.

Again, mankind has to have something that gives mankind the discipline that mankind needs in order to prevent mankind from sinning, and that is God's divine Word. Now the Word of God sets the tone for mankind to develop a spiritual consciousness. That spiritual consciousness is what places mankind in the divine state of life that keeps mankind in tune with God's righteousness and faithfulness.

One of the problems with sin is it is not the act itself but the person or people's actions. The person's action toward sin is best determined by their true consciousness and their faith in God.

While we are committing our sins, it is the actions of our sins that makes us feel comfortable. The question someone should ask is if we feel comfortable in committing our sins, what causes us to feel that comfortable where we deprive ourselves and God of His faith and righteousness?

I already know that the act that is causing us to sin is going against God's Word, not only to commit the sin but just to feel comfortable in committing any sin, and it makes sin itself worse and places the Christian or Christians in a dangerousness position with their salvation and faith in God.

Now this is what I mean when I mentioned that some people feel so comfortable in their sins. Although what they are doing is wrong in the eyes of God, the emphasis here is to let us understand that sometimes we feel so comfortable in our sins that the sins we are committing do not feel like we are doing wrong in the eyes of God. let me repeat that the emphasis here is to let us understand that sometimes, we feel so comfortable in our sins that the sins we are committing do not feel like we are doing wrong in the eyes of God.

Sometimes when we sin, our mess, we think it does not smell or go unnoticed. But if we let the truth be told, it does smell, and our sins never go unnoticed.

I am saying all of this just to say, and let me reiterate, if a person or people commit the same sins or sin that we have already committed, we can never recognize that same sin in our own lives. We can only recognize sin in other people's lives. The honesty of sin is when a person or people is able to admit their sins to themselves and God, if we think that through our sin that we are judging others and not ourselves, then we are in a dangerous place with ourselves and God. It becomes easier to blame others than for us to stop committing the same sins that other people are doing.

The reason why David became successful in his sin with God is David had enough consciousness in him sinning to focus his sin on himself and ask God for forgiveness, and God forgave David. David created opportunities for himself to take advantage of people in order that his free will to sin would be exercised a lot easier. But through it all, David became submissive and repented to God for the wrong and injustices that he had caused others and to himself.

When we realize the righteousness of God in the midst of our sins, The true reality that we have to face in the midst of our sins is when our consciousness teaches us that we serve an awesome God, and in God's awesomeness and righteousness is where mankind wrestles with themselves and God to determine and try to understand what is keeping them enslaved to their sins. Now at that point is when we realize the awesomeness of God, not through His blessings but through our sins. Here is what I mean. We have a tendency to appreciate God during the good times in our lives. Then when the bad times come, where we get to become a challenge or be challenged by our adversities and adversaries, which exist in our life to challenge us every day in life. The only thing that protects us and gives us the courage we need to overcome our adversaries and adversities is understanding God's true nature of love, compassion, forgiveness, grace, and mercy.

This is given to us when we become submissive and obedient to God. Even in mankind's sinful nature and imperfections, God is still willing to forgive us and bless us as well.

Now when I say that God has blessed us, what is it that I am referring to? When mankind thinks about God's heart of forgiveness, what is it in God's heart that allows God to exercise such an unexplainable state of forgiveness toward mankind and still be able to grant mankind their true salvation?

God does not judge mankind based on their status in society or degree of sin but gives mankind an open policy to ask for forgiveness of their sins, even when mankind is able to exercise their free will.

And the one thing that I have always wrestled with is how God is able to forgive us all because of His grace and mercy; and I know and understand that state of compassion can only come from someone like God, who is divine, who is the creator, and who has to be more patient with mankind than mankind is with themselves. God is that person who has to understand mankind more than mankind is able to understand. In other words, God knows the potential of mankind. God also understands mankind's deepest thoughts. God knows mankind so well that before mankind knew how they were created or existed, God already knew mankind even in mankind's sinful nature and imperfections. God already knows mankind's sinful nature and imperfections better than mankind knows themselves. God even knows the potential of mankind's spirituality before mankind was able to understand or comprehend their own spirituality. In other words, God knew mankind before mankind knew themselves.

That is why it's so important for me and kind to stay in touch and in tune with God either through prayer, through supplication, or through submissiveness because God is able to understand us before we can understand ourselves.

What I have come to experience is when God blesses mankind during the good times, to me it feels like when God blesses mankind in our good times. We have a tendency to develop a certain comfort zone within ourselves and the lifestyle that we have lived.

We feel it is like people finding and appreciating God, more in their good times and blessings, and they want God to bless them in a miraculous way. You know it takes a Christian that is mature in the spiritual consciousness to even recognize and appreciate God through the difficult times that they are facing. This is done through the discipline of our consciousness and how we are able to patiently and submissively humble ourselves toward God.

When we recognize God in the state of our sins what, is it saying to ourselves spiritually and consciously that we have reached a point in our lives where we recognize the sin itself does not justify God's awesomeness in our lives? It means that we have matured enough to recognize that we are living for God and not ourselves. We also recognize that in the midst of our wrongdoing, we serve a just and righteous God who is willing to give us a second chance in life based on the sins that we have committed as a Christian.

One of the things that interest me about God is that He can reveal all of our sins to anyone He can. God can even reveal our sins to our enemies. God can reveal our sins to our friends. He can reveal our sins to the churches that mankind themselves attends.

How many people would be embarrassed if God were to expose their sins to the world? That is why we should never expose people's sins, especially those people who trust others with their sins, trying to find encouragement to better understand their own sins that they are struggling with.

When people trust us with their sins, we keep should keep their sins confidential. We should, or I should, always remember that throughout our faith and consciousness in God.

We are all trying to reach the same spiritual potential of our own salvation. One person cannot achieve spiritual potential by themselves. It can only be supported through mankind's consciousness, which can only be achieved through hard work and determination and a lot of support that comes from our brothers and sisters in Jesus Christ. Yes, it is our responsibility to God and each other to support our Christian brothers and sisters and help reach their spiritual potential in God, developing their consciousness.

I think sometimes the reason why some Christians talk about people to embarrass them is that it gives us some type of power or empowerment when in actuality, we are destroying the spiritual growth of each other, and the people who talk about others in the congregation and out of the congregation is in a worse position than those who constantly sinning and is asking for help from the congregations.

I know that Christians are imperfect, and we are sinners by nature, but this should never be and is not a spiritual sign of love toward each other. We should always love each other beyond what we can comprehend, love to be, and understand the struggles and adversities that we are all facing in this world; and that is when we should embrace each other with love once again for us to become successful believers and Christians who are consciously believers of God's Word.

When I get to understand God's omnipotent power that is able to reveal my sin to anyone at any time, instead, God tries to give me an opportunity to repent of my sins. Here is what I mean: sometimes the sin itself can be enjoyable to us. It can make you happy, but if people know, it would be an embarrassment to them and others who respect you. Sometimes ministers, preachers, and deacons are in this mess all by themselves. Why? Because they don't have the spiritual consciousness of God. They know God. They understand God. But once again, they don't have the spiritual consciousness in order to recognize the true essence of God's love and compassion that God has for mankind.

But God, because of His mercy and grace, tries to give us a chance to repent instead of trying to use His omnipotent power to embrace us in the midst of us committing the act of our sins because we cannot hide from God, especially if we are doing wrong.

When we sin and others do the same sins that we are doing, here is what we are doing to ourselves. We are fooling ourselves, but most of all, we cannot see the same sins that we are committing, that we see others doing. We try to exhaust every means to justify why our sins are wrong to commit, and we cannot recognize the same sins that we are doing in our lives which is justified in the consciousness part of the person or people's mind.

One of the things that mankind does in the midst of their sinful nature is mankind gets so comfortable in committing their sins that sometimes mankind doesn't think that what they are doing is wrong.

They themselves do not want to recognize that they are committing the same sins or sins that the other people that they are passing judgment toward are also doing themselves.

Every sin that occurs in our lives is nothing more than an action that tries to destroy our sinful nature and at most times causes us to lose control of our own sinful nature. Every sin that mankind brings upon themselves destroys mankind's spiritual consciousness in God.

One of the main reasons that mankind sin is mankind recognizes that in the actions of their sins, sinning can be very pleasurable and comfortable. Sinning sometimes becomes more desirable than studying God's Word and doing what it is that God wants you to do.

Yes, don't get me wrong, sinning is pleasurable, and sinning is entertaining. It is the actual act of sinning that is very enjoyable and pleasurable, which makes your actions toward sin more enjoyable, challenging, and very profound in our nature.

A question one might ask is this: If we know that sinning is wrong, why do we still do it? We keep doing it because the system of sinning is what appeases mankind's appetite and mankind's sinful nature.

Just to let you know, sin itself challenges mankind's nature and mankind's imperfection. Sin itself sometimes exceeds the nature and imperfection of mankind. Sin is the biggest appetite, which fuels the fire that burns deep in the spirit and soul of mankind's pride, which causes mankind to become submissive to their own sinful nature and imperfection.

What are the only things that could make mankind become successful over their own sinful nature and imperfections? It is when mankind is able to hear and become submissive to his or her spiritual nature. The key to a successful relationship with God is the discipline that His Word teaches us to obey.

The major thing that allowed mankind to become successful over their sinful nature is the discipline that mankind has to establish to elevate themselves and their sinful nature while developing their spiritual consciousness that God has placed in mankind through His consciousness and His divine Word.

We need to ask this question. Why does mankind sin? Mankind sin because it elevates mankind's pride. Sinning sometimes indulges in lust for material possessions.

But if we are willing to wrestle with our sins, that is placing us in this type of a position to compromise our faith and consciousness in God.

This is where we experienced the essence and substance of God's grace and mercy working within our spiritual consciousness to overcome our sinful nature and our imperfection.

That is why when we sin and humble ourselves toward God, and we pray for forgiveness and repentance for the sin or sins that we have committed. What is that we are truly praying for to God.

We are praying for God to develop and increase our consciousness. That we can always have strength and power over the sin or sins that are controlling our life, I am not referring to the sin that we have committed. I am referring to those sins that really control our minds, bodies, and souls.

The only way that mankind can elevate themselves beyond their sinful nature and imperfection is by overcoming the entrapment of our sins, and it is through the meditation and discipline we develop through God's consciousness.

When we pray we are also asking God's forgiveness for our sin or sins, what is it that we are asking for once again? We are asking for God's forgiveness. So when we truly ask God's forgiveness, what are we actually asking God? We are asking God for His forgiveness, and what are we saying to God? Now that is when we start to recognize God's compassion, grace, and mercy.

In God's grace and mercy is the essence and substance of God's forgiveness for mankind. When we sin, we separate ourselves from God. So we are trying to elevate ourselves and bring ourselves back into fellowship, harmony, and peace with God and ourselves through God's compassion and forgiveness.

That only God is able to do to give mankind a chance once again to elevate mankind from their sinful nature and our imperfection and bring mankind back into peace and harmony with God and ourselves.

The act of forgiveness is like recognizing the sins that mankind has done in the actions of the sin or sins that mankind has committed. When we ask God's forgiveness for our sin or sins that need forgiveness, we are first acknowledging the mistakes we make, and we trying to clear our consciousness and faith in God.

So what are we actually saying when we sin? Here is what we are saying: We are saying, "God, I know I was wrong, but my sin or sins had more control over me than my faith and emotions did." The other thing we are saying is that our spiritual maturity did not have the strength we need for us to become successful overcome our sin or sins.

I could not say no to my sins, which was enough for me to disobey God. But if I had a second opportunity or a third opportunity, somehow I know that through God's grace and mercy and me staying in constant fellowship with God's Word, I am going to become successful over this sin or sins that keep defeating me all the time because it is a habit.

The only way that I'm going to become successful over my sins is to be in constant prayer and supplication or by asking God to develop and strengthen me more in God's consciousness and in God's faithfulness. Just like we want God to forgive us when sin, we must also forgive and respect each other in the faith and especially those people out of the faith.

Just like we want God to forgive us, we must be willing to forgive our brothers and sisters, friends and family. One of the most beautiful things mankind can ever achieve is the compassion and love that only God has in His heart, which God is able to forgive in their spiritual life is to be able to develop the character and integrity of forgiveness.

Now I think that forgiveness is the true characteristic that brings mankind's consciousness and faithfulness to become more in the image and likeness of God.

I strongly believe that when God said "Let us create mankind in the image and likeness of us," I think the characteristics of mankind's forgiveness help mankind implement their faithfulness in the consciousness of making mankind.

Here is what I mean: If we love God to the capacity that we say we do or, let me put it in this perspective, if we say we love God faithfully and consciously, why would mankind want to sin?

Know that what mankind does is wrong, the question that comes to mind is this: Why do we actually sin, why do we do it, and then ask God for forgiveness? Here is why sin is very enjoyable and loving: the actions of committing sin also and once again stroke the ego and pride of mankind.

That is why we cannot serve God on the egotistical level, that is why we cannot serve God on a prideful level, that is why we cannot serve God on the selfish level, that is why we cannot serve God on an emotional level, that is why we cannot serve God on an economic level, that is why we cannot serve God on a political level, and that is why we cannot serve God on a material level because those are sinful characteristics that separate mankind from God if mankind's consciousness is not in tune or is in fellowship with God.

All of these things contribute to mankind's downfall. As much as mankind enjoys the love and appreciation of sinning, somewhere deep within mankind's heart and consciousness, mankind still has a love for God although mankind is still able to struggle with their sins.

Mankind's consciousness helps mankind realize that sin goes against the will of God and as mankind is able to recognize the impact of their sins toward God's righteousness.

One of the biggest struggles that mankind is realizing is how mankind themselves overcome the impact of their sins. As mankind's sins relate to God's love, God's compassion, and God's grace for mankind, mankind already understands the forgiveness and compassion of God's grace and mercy.

Here's how mankind rationalizes their perspective on sin, especially when they know that they have to come to God and ask God's forgiveness for the sins that they have committed.

I already experience the evidence of God's grace and mercy, and this is where we struggle with sin. We struggle with sin because we want to stop sinning, but somehow sin still has a tendency to have some control over mankind.

Sin is not afraid of mankind's maturity in God, nor is sin afraid of mankind's relationship with God. Sin does not care how strong or how weak your consciousness is as long as sin is able to overtake your soul, spirit, and consciousness.

We must knowledge to ourselves that Satan does not care how strong you are, and once again, sin does not care how strong you are. The main goal of sin is to conquer and destroy mankind's mind, spirit, and consciousness to destroy mankind's spiritual love and compassion that mankind has in God.

Remember, it was sin that took, Jesus Christ to the mountaintop and challenged Jesus Christ's faith, love, and relationship with His Father. Sin reminds me of some human beings who don't care about whatever it takes for them to destroy your relationship and happiness with God. There are some people who want to bring distraction to your soul through sin all because of your relationship with God, which some people are. This happens because some people can't find the happiness and joy that they have found in God. Some people still want to destroy your love, your kindness, and the graciousness that you have established through the discipline of God's Word, even in their own relationship with God, because they are consistently taking God's forgiveness, grace, and mercy for granted.

We must remember that forgiveness does not mean that God is always going to forgive you for your sins because you asked for forgiveness. Hell is made up of a lot of people who thought God was going to forgive them of their sins.

The struggle and understanding remind me of the apostle Paul's struggle with sin. Just like any human being in this world, all of God's prophets, ministers, preachers, deacons, and bishops had to struggle with sin but none as eloquently explaining as the apostle Paul has done.

> I found that the very commandment that was intended to bring life actually brought death. For sin, seizing the oppor-

tunity afforded by the commandment, deceived me, and through the commandment put me to death. So then, the law is holy, and the commandment is holy, righteous and good. Did that which is good, then, become death to me? By no means! Nevertheless, in order that sin might be recognized as sin, it used what is good to bring about my death, so that through the commandment sin might become utterly sinful. We know that the law is spiritual; but I am unspiritual, sold as a slave to sin. I do not understand what I do. For what I want to do I do not do, but what I hate I do. And if I do what I do not want to do, I agree that the law is good. As it is, it is no longer I myself who do it, but it is sin living in me. For I know that good itself does not dwell in me, that is, in my sinful nature. For I have the desire to do what is good, but I cannot carry it out. For I do not do the good I want to do, but the evil I do not want to do—this I keep on doing. Now if I do what I do not want to do, it is no longer I who do it, but it is sin living in me that does it. So I find this law at work: Although I want to do good, evil is right there with me. For in my inner being I delight in God's law; but I see another law at work in me, waging war against the law of my mind and making me a prisoner of the law of sin at work within me. What a wretched man I am! Who will rescue me from this body that is subject to death? Thanks be to God, who delivers me through Jesus Christ our Lord! So then, I myself in my mind am a slave to God's law, but in my sinful nature a slave to the law of sin. (Romans 7:10–25 NIV; https://bible.com/bible/111/rom.7.10-25.NIV)

Sin is enjoyable. Sin is loving. Sin is entertaining, and it is very appealing to the heart. Sin is always manifested itself in our thoughts and our minds, And because sin has all these attributes, we continuously find ways to commit sin to the point where we used biblical passages to try to facilitate the many excuses we have to commit sin.

Here are the many reasons why we are committing sin. Sin is the primary concern why we are committing our sins and why God's Word is being misinterpreted. In other words, mankind misinterprets God's Word in order to make the burden of committing sin a lot stressful, and it is also mankind's way of not to feeling guilty or responsible for the sins which they have committed.

Do you know why we have so many religions, so many ideologies, so many theologies, so many misinterpretations of God's Word? It is to distract mankind from experiencing a true reality of the power of God's consciousness.

Satan knows and understands the true reality of the power of God's consciousness and what it can do and what it is capable of doing to mankind themselves. That is why it is important and is imperative for mankind to develop their spiritual consciousness in God's Word. That is why he would do anything to stop mankind from achieving and empowering themselves consciously and spiritually in God's Word.

Let me put it this way: all of mankind's sins that mankind is trying to find excuses for are implemented, transferred, and transformed into the threads of society's schools of thought.

Here is what I mean: I'm talking about philosophy, theology, theory, and sociology.

That is why it is very important for us to develop our consciousness, and faith in God. We serve consciously, faithfully, and spiritually. That is why it is imperative and important, for mankind to serve God on a conscious level.

That is why we should serve God on a spiritual level, that is why we should serve God on a level and degree of faith, that is why we should serve God graciously, that is why we should serve God mercifully, that is why we should never take God for granted.

These are the attributes, that contribute to mankind's consciousness and mankind's perspective, on who God is, and if we keep these things in mind, we will consciously and faithfully be successful in our walk with God.

Now this is very important to our consciousness in God. Because some sins become a habit, and some sins nurture mankind's emotions, some sins nurture mankind's pride, and those sins that are very difficult to get rid of, those are the sins we keep struggling with until one day, mankind is able to develop and mature in their spiritual consciousness that would give mankind the wisdom, experience, and understanding to successfully overcome those types of sins.

I think after we sin we realized what we did is wrong. We also recognize that when we sin, the sin itself is not worth committing because sin itself separates us from God.

That is when we realize that we are more secure in the spirit of God than in the sin itself. We also realized that we feel more comfortable being in fellowship and in tune with God, and that is why we ask for forgiveness because we know that sin separates us from God. So in order for us to stay in constant fellowship with God, this is what gives us the power and understanding of God's grace and mercy.

Once again, sin can only be experienced through mankind's physical existence, and it is at that point in mankind's physical existence and creation that mankind is able to rationalize in experiencing sin. All of this is done through mankind's nature. Remember, it is mankind's sinful nature and imperfection that causes mankind to sin, which challenges mankind's consciousness and faithfulness in God.

The instinct of mankind's free will is what causes mankind to become a subject to sin. If mankind doesn't embrace their spiritual consciousness, mankind would always become subject and desirable to sin itself. The attribute that controls mankind's sins itself is pride. Pride controls the desire of what mankind wants to do and what mankind wants to have, even if it goes against what God wants from us.

Now because of that attribute pride, mankind would do anything through the emotion of their pride to hurt kill or destroy other persons, even if it means destroying their integrity or character.

Sometimes with the sinful nature, many people's pride gets in the way of convincing people that what they are doing is spiritually God driven, and they have a right to destroy or damage other people's integrity and character all because those people who are damaging other members of the faith and outside the faith want what God has placed in those people's lives.

Such are consciousness, faith, strength, perseverance, favor, and compassion. Instead of people who pray for him and do selfish work on developing the spiritual consciousness, they prefer to destroy what God has placed in you, and they don't understand that God saying "Do not do anything to the people that he has anointed to do" is with pride and is a dangerous thing for mankind to have and own. Look at the world in today's society.

And the reason they become jealous and prideful of the other people whom God has anointed and ordained is that God is not using those prideful people in the same capacity that God is using those whom He has called and anointed.

When God was them their pride go in the way, and their consciousness was not focused on God but on their sinful desires and wants in life, which is to destroy other people. Once again, God called upon His anointed, and those are consciously ordained people.

When God called upon those people who were prideful, they were too busy being prideful, self-centered, and dying to create hate amount the congregation and other people. Prideful people prefer to do those things instead of listening and being submissive to the will of God, so God had to call on those people whom the prideful thought were helpless, whom the prideful criticized and made fun of and talked about. So that left room for God to use those people He has anointed and ordained to do His well.

The other is sexual morality, which mankind does that causes mankind to destroy their own family's life and career. It's all because of mankind's sexual morality. The only thing that places mankind back on track is when mankind acknowledges through their sins the power of God's grace and mercy and His forgiveness to even rebuild and restructure mankind's spiritual consciousness and place mankind back in a position of entitlement and in fellowship with God.

I think although mankind might enjoy sinning, the reason why mankind might enjoy the actual sin and enjoy the love of sinning and the pride that comes with sinning is that at some point in time in mankind's life, I think mankind feels obligated consciously and because mankind also recognized how good God has been to mankind themselves and how good God continuously has always been to develop our consciousness and enlighten our perspective on the sinful and negative relationship we have experienced in life.

Sinning is enjoyable and entertaining, and we all loved it because of how comfortable sin is. The convenience of sin makes us feel good; and they come to a point where God's grace, mercy, and forgiveness can only extend themselves into a limited period of time. Then God's patience runs out on mankind's sinful nature.

That is why one of the most important things for mankind to remember is that the spirit of God is not going to become everlasting in mankind's life. At some point in time in mankind's life, mankind must understand that the spirit of God is going to run out on mankind's sin, and God's love for mankind is going to take its course in mankind's life.

God is not always going to have the patience that He has right now with us. After a while, when God's forgiveness runs out on mankind, it means that there is no more room left for mankind's sins to be forgiven, and that is when mankind can no longer depend on God's grace and mercy.

That is why mankind should always allow their consciousness to keep maturing and growing and developing in God's consciousness. The more mankind's consciousness mature, the more mankind is able to develop their love, faith, and strength in God.

Mankind must realize that for mankind to overcome their adversities, adversaries, that cause them to sin toward God, mankind must stay constantly in maturing and developing their consciousness and faith in God.

That is why while we are sinning or trying to sin, we must always remember this: when we do wrong or sin, we're not always going to be forgiven for the sin or sins that we have committed.

I think sometimes that as long as we continuously embrace and understand God's love and compassion in the midst of our sins and imperfection, we should consciously always remember that when we do wrong, we should never ask for forgiveness but beg God for His forgiveness and love once again. When we beg for God's forgiveness, it allows us to understand the importance of God's compassion, love, and mercy and not take God's love, mercy, and grace for granted just because God is giving us at this time His grace, faith, compassion, mercy for the sins that we have committed.

I think sometimes our consciousness as we study God's Word, we get an understanding of God's character and manifesting itself through His Word, and then we realize whatever trials of adversities we had, God never took advantage of us in the midst of our trials and adversities.

God has always been there to secure us and protect us from whatever trials or tribulations or dilemmas that we are faced with. I think sometimes that acknowledges to us and lets us understand the significance of sin, and that is when we reached out to rationalize our own salvation in God.

You know God's love for mankind sometimes reminds me of a parent and child or children. It is like the parent or parents have given the child everything that the child needs and wants.

The actions of the parents have secured the child's or children's lives with everything that the child or children need, and the child or children get so comfortable that the child or children start to abuse the parent or parents.

That is why we should stay constantly in God's consciousness because it keeps us constantly in spiritual consciousness in God. Here is what I mean: God has given us everything from salvation to forgiveness to standing up to fight our battles. When we stumble and fall through the obstacles of life, it is God's grace, compassion, and mercy that has always been there for us. I think sometimes we take that for granted, and we end up feeling comfortable in our sins with the acknowledgment of knowing that God is constantly willing to forgive us. We must understand that God is always willing to forgive us, but God does not forget the things that mankind has done while reviving His grace, mercy, and salvation for granted.

Sometimes our sins make us feel guilty, but in the process of committing the sins or sin, it makes every sin that we commit feel so good and joyous and grateful. Sin makes us feel happy; it helps us to become better understanding, loving, and appreciating of God.

But at some times when we sit back and evaluate our salvation through God's Word and how He has inspired us through his Word to develop our consciousness, once again we realize that our sin or sins are not worth continuously doing.

That is why we are constantly trying to develop our consciousness and the discipline we need to exercise our faith and spirituality that we would become stronger spiritually and consciously in God.

In other words, the person or people have come up with this idea that the sins that they are committing are consciously right, and they are using every means to justify to themselves that the sins that they have been committing are not wrong or are not serious enough for them to ask for forgiveness. To God, sin is sin, and there is no level or degree of sin. This is when people start to become comfortable in their sins.

Let us look at sin or sins from another perspective. Let us assume that the person who is committing the sin begins to become comfortable in their sins. When I say comfortable in their sins, I am referring to the people who allow their sins to become a habit.

What I mean when mankind becomes comfortable in their sin is how we know consciously what we are doing is wrong and sinful, but we do not want to recognize that what we are doing is wrong and is a sin against God.

Here is where the comfort zone lies when we talk about sin itself. When we are doing the act that is causing us to sin, we don't recognize or don't want to recognize that what we are doing is wrong in the eyes of God. Sometimes we even take pride in our sins where we feel like we are the God of our own forgiveness of sin and where we can become the judge of ourselves, and everything we do that is wrong is right as long as we are doing it. Let us look at sin from this perspective: sin has a tendency to control mankind with this philosophical perspective, and that is when we find a good and comfortable reason for mankind to sin.

Mankind would use the comfortability of that act to commit the actual act of that sin. We sin because it is comfortable, and it feels right to do even if it goes against the principles of God's divine Word.

Here is another philosophical perspective: as long as we are sinning and that sin doesn't hurt other people or people don't know about the sin that we going to commit or we already have committed.

The one thing that we must always remember is that all sins hurt God. What we are not acknowledging is that all sin, regardless of the degree of sin or impact of sin, all hurt God.

Now because God is powerful, the only thing that hurt God is mankind's sins. What does it mean when people mention that God is too powerful to be conquered and powerful to be replaced? The only thing that hurt God and caused God's death in life is mankind's sin, which was the actions of mankind's sins.

Not gunshots, knives, weapons, and bullets but mankind's actions of sin and mankind indulging constantly and sin and trying to elevate themselves faithfully, spiritually, and consciously.

Because people might not see you committing the sin. It doesn't mean that the same sin or sins go unnoticed. Mankind must always remember that they are constantly at war. Remember that everything we do in the dark comes out in the light. It might not be at the present time that we commit the sin or at the time we want it to come out in the light, but it does come out.

But when our sins do come out in the dark or in the light, they can destroy your career, they can destroy your family, and they can cause you to lose your job. Your sins also cause people to lose respect for you, and your sins can also be an inconvenience toward you and other people as well.

We must also try to understand that the hands of God's forgiveness might not be able to extend their hands long enough to forgive you of the sins that you have committed or done wrong.

Here is something we should think about all the time: If people think that they can get away from sin, then Satan would have that same philosophy where you think that you can get away from sin. You are thinking about getting away from sin, but that is the same sin that Satan would use to destroy mankind's salvation.

Sometimes we are placed in these positions of sin because we love the sin more than we love our faith in God.

The other is we keep sinning because people cannot see us sinning. Those are the actions of our faith in God.

When it comes to sinning, people do not see what we are doing, but there is one person who always knows what we are doing, and that is God. We tried to fake and hide the actions of our sinful nature and our imperfections.

But others cannot do the wrong that we are doing because we would also be wrong. At this point, we do not feel like we are responsible spiritually for the sins that we have committed. This is when we feel like we are the God of our sins. Here is what I mean: As Christians, we should always remind ourselves constantly about our relationship with God, which means we should constantly keep God on our hearts, consciousness, and faith in God. We already know what is right and wrong already, which is explained in God's divine Word. Now that is a dangerous place to be in because this is where we forget to confess our sins, and it is because we forgot to ask God's forgiveness and feel like we are our own gods in the midst of our sins. When we forget to ask God's forgiveness, we forget to repent. When we forget to repent, we end up dying in the midst of our sins; our only path to everlasting life is hell.

When we love the sin more than we love God, we forget to ask God for forgiveness. When we forget to ask God for forgiveness and we die in the midst of our own sins, we open up hell's door to capture our souls in hell or Hades and our sins become the lock, that locks closes the door to mankind when mankind goes to hell. But you know what becomes the key to opening up the doors to hell for mankind is God's divine Word and mankind's own faith in God.

So it is God's divine Word that also develops our consciousness in God. It is God's compassion, God's love, and God's grace that become the true key that unlocks the doors that prevent mankind from going to hell.

It is that same compassion, love, and grace that also lock the doors in hell and lock the doors of hell in the spirit and soul of mankind. The truth that protects mankind from hell is the maturity of mankind's spiritual consciousness.

Here is what I am trying to prove. Let us assume that you have become so comfortable in the sins that you have committed, and tomorrow, God does not open up your eyes. Now you have a one-way ticket to hell.

Here is what we should try to understand, and that is because we serve a loving God who is able to forgive us of our sins, it does not give us the right to continuously commit the same sin over and over again.

Many people get so caught up in their sins that they continuously commit sin. Please forgive me for reiterating this statement over and over again, but it may help someone today. We must also understand that if we are to commit the same sins over and over again because we know that God is going to forgive us and because we know that God is going to forgive us, and we keep sinning or committing the same sins over and over again.

We must also understand that we place ourselves in a dangerous position with God. It is like we are taking advantage of God's forgiveness. Here is what I mean when God forgives us of our sins.

What does this mean to us? It means that we have recognized that we serve an omnipotent God, but in God's omnipotence, He develops a state of forgiveness. In that state of forgiveness comes compassion, grace, mercy, and salvation. Now this is very important because we understand and know God's state of forgiveness, and we keep sinning, only because we know that God is going to forgive us.

When we sin because God is going to forgive us, we are actually taking advantage of God's righteousness, His compassion, His grace, His mercy. In order for us to get total fulfillment in God's forgiveness, we have to know the many facets that are in involved in the actions of just one sin, and that is how the consciousness of God works in the midst of mankind's sins.

When we know that and we continue to sin, all because we know God is going to forgive us, that though and the actions behind the though mean that we have already sinned again against God, it is because we are taking advantage of God's divine attributes and not God's actual state of forgiveness.

This is where I think that sometimes people have more confidence in their sins than in God's forgiving them of their sins. The true reality is that God is not always going to forgive mankind of their sins because there is a reason why we have heaven and hell.

Yes, God is going to forgive them of their sins. We must also recognize this is not true because we are thorough about heaven and hell.

But in a poetic world of poetry, the idea of God's forgiveness sounds good, but in a practical world where truth and reality exist and God's forgiveness depends on the security of mankind's salvation now because of heaven and hell, that tells me that God's judgment is certainly limited to the mankind's sins.

So in our world of practical reality and truth, God's patience is limited toward the sins of mankind. God's forgiveness and mankind's sins need to be explained more. Here is why: because God is always able to forgive mankind; and because of mankind's sins, where mankind's forgiveness cannot reach, it does not give us the right to keep sinning. We must always remember that sin also runs its course in the existence of life.

Now, my maturity in the midst of my sins comes when I have to face those same sins that keep defeating me. When I am able to overcome those same sins that keep challenging my faith in God or it's constantly breaking me down, the question should come to mind, how do I know that I have matured or that I am maturing in God's grace? That happens when I am able to use the spiritual consciousness that God has given me through His Word to become successful over my sins and my imperfections. Isn't it interesting to know that when we reflect back on our lifestyle sometimes, we can say that the things that once bothered us don't affect us anymore, especially when we start maturing in God's consciousness? It is our consciousness that gives the drive and motivation to constantly stay focused enough on God's consciousness, not to be distracted from His Word.

Once again, the things that once bothered us as we mature in God's consciousness do have the same impact and control over us. That means that we have matured in God's consciousness. This is a good place for any Christian or Christians to be.

It is good when Christians or people who believe in God can recognize the maturity and progress that they have made through Jesus Christ.

We have to thank God also for His forgiveness, grace, and mercy in order that we can regain our salvation through God's Son, Jesus Christ. Is it interesting that through mankind's sins, their bother sister, brother, aunt, uncle father, mother, cousins, friends, and so forth will give up on us; but God has understood mankind's imperfections and sinful nature better than mankind does.

But God keeps having enough patience with us to constantly forgive us. God's forgiveness, God's compassion, and God's love are what give us the ability to fight and develop enough courage for us to overcome our sinful nature and imperfections. That is what keeps us motivated consciously to continue to do God's will for our life in order for us to overcome our sins. One of the most important things that we need to acknowledge is that because God is so forgiving and because God has allowed us to develop ourselves spiritually in the state of His own consciousness does not make God naive to the conditions of mankind's sinful nature but more compassionate and loving to God. We should always remember that because God is so forgiving, it does not make God naïve to the sins of mankind.

Here's what I mean: Sometimes we use God's forgiveness as an excuse for the sins we have committed continuously. We can also use our sinful nature as a positive thing, especially when we look within our conscious state of mind to ask God for His forgiveness.

Now with our sins, we must also use God's forgiveness, which God has given to mankind, because of His love and compassion toward mankind. It is through God's love and compassion that God is able to forgive mankind of their sinful nature and imperfection.

Here is why I think God is able to forgive mankind. It is because God is allowing mankind through His forgiveness and mercy to mature and improve spiritually and consciousness in their sins and imperfections, all because of God's forgiveness and love toward mankind. Now I am also referring to pastors, preachers, ministers, deacons, and people of God's faith. God's forgiveness is proof that God has a deeper understanding and wisdom toward mankind's nature. It could be that God understands mankind's nature better than mankind are able to understand their own sinful nature. That is why Jesus Christ had to die for the sins of the world because Jesus's death it brought a greater understanding of how God is able to exercise perfect forgiveness toward mankind's sinful nature.

Now I don't want mankind to forget that God has sacrificed His Son not for mankind's goodness but for the evilness and imperfections that have been done and what mankind is going to do. I want us again to understand that God did not sacrifice His only begotten Son just for the goodness of mankind, his actions toward Him, but for the imperfection and sinful nature of mankind. In other words, one might need to ask the question why God would sacrifice His only begotten Son for mankind's sinful nature and imperfections of mankind.

One of the things that have puzzled me for years as I develop my spiritual consciousness and get to understand the Trinity of the Father, the Son, and the Holy Ghost is to experience through a spiritual consciousness is why would a God that is so omnipotent feel obligated to forgive me and mankind of their sins that mankind themselves has chosen all the goodness.

And God, through his compassion, even sacrificed His Son for the sins of the world or, in this case, for the sins of mankind. Now to me, that is a love that is on cannot be comprehended, understood, or even acknowledged by mankind.

That is why mankind has so much hate toward each other and on all levels of life—hate in the family, hate toward friends, which is jealousy. That is why the love of God cannot be comprehended or understood by mankind.

The only thing that allowed mankind to acknowledge and experience God's level of love for mankind is mankind's spiritual consciousness, which mankind gathers from God's Word. That is why it is important for us to study God's Word enough so that we would know God personally for ourselves.

I think that the only time that mankind can understand God is through mankind's maturity in God's grace and mercy. As much as mankind asks for God's love and forgiveness, mankind still cannot understand God's love and forgiveness enough to interpret and explain God's love. I think the only way that mankind can understand God's love and forgiveness is through experiencing the transcending knowledge that comes from God's divine Word, and it is through God's Word that teaches us who He is and how He loves us all.

Also, through God's faith, I get to understand the significance through studying God's divine Word the importance of His Son dying on the cross so mankind can continue the spreading and teaching God's Word.

How can God allow the sins of this world to be the primary cause of His Son's death? How can God who experience mankind's imperfections and sins, even from the beginning of creation, still have enough love and compassion for mankind to have the opportunity to be forgiven of the same sins and imperfections that caused God to sacrifice His Son for the imperfections and sins that mankind has committed? What is it about God that would cause Him to give mankind the time and effort to exercise His forgiveness toward mankind?

And then God is still able to return the favor of mankind's sinful nature and imperfections through His forgiveness and compassion for mankind. How can God who is omnipotent and omnipresent allow mankind to crucify His Son, Jesus Christ, although God has enough power to destroy the world in the blink of an eye? Why is it that God did not destroy mankind at the first sign of mankind's sins?

Now if mankind was in the same position as God, mankind would have destroyed the world. Just because mankind does not and cannot exercise the same forgiveness as God can, what we need to realize is that the nature and imperfections of mankind cannot comprehend or interpret God's forgiveness toward each other.

Although God allowed mankind to crucify His son, He did nothing to mankind or even save His Son's life on the cross. Here is what God did for mankind, although mankind killed His Son, Jesus Christ. God gave mankind the opportunity to repent and gain everlasting salvation. There are some characteristics and attributes of God that mankind cannot comprehend nor have the consciousness to understand. I know that I serve an awesome God, but even in God's awesomeness and love for mankind, I cannot understand God's characteristics and love for me and the people of this world, especially those people who took advantage of His Son's goodness and love and nailed Jesus, His Son, on the cross, just because they disliked the message that Jesus was preaching and teaching about love and goodness of the father. But it was that same message about love and goodness that stopped God from destroying this world. It is that same love that God's has given to us, even in His state of compassion and love for us, the same love and goodness that the world rejected in Jesus Christ, the same love that God uses to exercise His compassion and His love and goodness toward mankind, even when mankind killed God's Son, Jesus, and then nailed Him on the cross.

Do you also know that it is that same love and goodness that reconnects mankind back into righteousness and fellowship with God's consciousness? That same righteousness and fellowship is what allows God to exercise His compassion instead of His judgment upon mankind's sinful nature and imperfections. It is that same love and compassion that gives mankind, even in mankind's sinful nature, enough of God's love to grant mankind their salvation of righteousness.

Let me get back to my second perspective, which is acknowledging God consciousness through God's grace and mercy. The third thing is how God is able, even in the state of our imperfections, to grant us eternal life through

His salvation, and the fourth, which is most important, is how God is able to love mankind unconditionally.

Or let's look at it from this perspective, and that is, why would God want to embrace man's loves, knowing that man, by nature, is an imperfect being? But God still turns around and loves mankind based on His love, grace, and mercy. God is able to love mankind, even if mankind is not as perfect as God? Some people assume that God, through His consciousness, appreciates perfection more than imperfection, let me tell you.

Actually, God's appreciates man's imperfections more than mankind's perfection. Here is why: God can use His Word to develop mankind's consciousness and bring mankind into a more spiritual state of awareness, just as a means to shape man's imperfections.

Here is how: God has seen man's nature evolves throughout many centuries, civilizations, and cultures. So God knows the behavior and nature of mankind. God knows mankind better than mankind knows themselves, and one thing that I want to acknowledge is God has lived longer than mankind.

God even created mankind, so God has been in existence longer than mankind. So there is nothing that man cannot do in society that is surprising or new to God because God has already seen it happen. There is no sin in this world even as we advance in a technological society that God has not seen or experienced. There is no technology that is advanced even in today's world that God did not experience in His life.

That is why we make references and ideas saying that God is the Alpha and the Omega. He is the beginning and the end, and through Him developing and maintaining mankind's spiritual consciousness gave mankind the opportunity to become the Alpha and Omega of God's love and Mother Earth. God is always prepared for whatever mankind thinks. God has seen civilizations come and go. God even experienced strong nations falling because they had more faith in themselves than in God Himself.

There are some people who think that they are so bad or evil that if they go to church, the steeple might fall and hit them on their heads because they think that they have sinned so much that God does not have enough forgiveness in His heart and compassion for them. So why should they go to church? What they don't understand is that they are the same people that God's compassion extends His hands to and His love.

What these people who think that God cannot reach them both spiritually and physically is because they think they have sinned so much that God Himself cannot forgive them. Never experienced God's compassion and enough to understand that the power of God's love is able to extend its hands even to the people who think that God's love cannot reach them. If God's love and compassion reach me, then God's consciousness can also reach you as well.

Here is what I mean: The first sin is sin, just like forgiveness from God is forgiveness. God's forgiveness is extended in the hearts and minds of mankind. God does not use peripheral treatment or just judge mankind based on the degree of sins or level of sins.

What those people who think that they have so many sins in their life. Some of these people think that they are so sinful that God would not love them the same as He loves

His Son, and the people you believe and have faith in God. That is not the case. God loves us all the same; this love is expressed through God's compassion, love, and forgiveness for mankind.

God loves us all the same. It is a love that mankind cannot explain or justify or even comprehend or understand. Why do you think that mankind cannot understand God's love? Because mankind should develop their consciousness to the capacity in which they are willing and able to comprehend and understand.

God has omnipotent and omniscient love. What God has done for us through His love is for mankind to experience how God has used His Son, Jesus Christ, as an example to die on the cross for the sins of the world.

I mention that not as a biblical verse or statement but for mankind and those who think that they are so deep in sin or sins that God cannot help them. I would have told the people that it is through God's love. I would tell them that it is through the death of Jesus Christ, who is the Son of God.

God sacrificed His Son to assure mankind on all levels and in the capacity of their sins that God still loves mankind unconditionally, and that can be expressed through God's expression of His love through His Son, Jesus Christ.

What God you know that is going to kill His Son for the love of mankind's sins and not mankind's goodness. If you let your son die for someone, it means that you have loved them better than your son. I would say that God's love has its own reason and purpose to exist.

The essence and substance of mankind's love for God are dealt with through mankind's spiritual consciousness as mankind studied in depth, trying to understand the significance and importance of God's love for them. God loves mankind unconditionally even in the state of mankind in perfection and sinful nature.

Some people also do not want to be compared to church people, especially those Christians who go to church, and say that they believe in God, and their actions are no different than those people who don't go to church. So that is why the majority of the people would decide to stay home instead of going to church. The one thing that I like the world or people that is living in the world to understand is that because a person goes to church does not mean that they are spiritually equipped in God's eyes.

Spiritual equipment and spirituality come when someone is willing to develop their spiritual consciousness to the capacity in which God's Word has driven them to achieve such spiritual enlightenment and consciousness about themselves and God.

Once again, our spiritualness is developed through regular, constant studying in God's Word. That within itself is not enough to our faith in God and our spiritual maturity to develop mankind's faith in God.

As mankind develops in their faith, it is through mankind's faith that mankind's consciousness. It is through mankind's knowledge and wisdom from God's divine Word that causes mankind to express God's Word through mankind's integrity and character. Although this statement shows much honesty in those people hearts, it still does not excuse them from God's salvation. Let me put it in this perspective: although those people have shown much honesty and concern for how they are thinking, it doesn't excuse them from the hell.

This statement allows the person to show their honesty and make them feel that they are more honest than the people attending church. This school of thought has stolen many people's salvation. Now I can appreciate the honesty in that person or people's statements, but God's grace and mercy do not stop there just because man might be honest in his or her statement toward God by mentioning that they have sinned so much that steeple in the church might hit them in their heads for showing up in God's house. The statement is honest and funny, but it does not excuse mankind from their sin.

Instead, what God expects of us and wants us to know is God can sometimes use our simple and difficult conditions in life that we might be embarrassed about or ashamed about as a witness for other people to recognize that it doesn't matter the condition or conditions that you face or that you have done.

What matters is how you are able to accept those conditions that created your sinful conditions and still be able to elevate yourself through God's Word in order to develop and exercise your spiritual consciousness while exercising your consciousness through your faith.

Now your faith is the actions of your consciousness, and many people experienced their faith through their consciousness. Here is what I mean: our consciousness absorbs the wisdom and information that comes from God's divine Word. Now when we obey God's Word and make God's Word and the messages and information that we receive and exercise through our lifestyle, this helps develop our consciousness and the enlightenment of our faith.

And it is at that point where Christians can use their lifestyle, whether positive or negative, as a witness, where they can influence the masses of people's lives by transforming the masses of people's lives by the experiences the Christians have while being committed to God's divine Word.

All of this is done through transforming the Christians' lifestyle while the Christians are still developing themselves both spiritually and faithfully while being able to develop their consciousness through God's Word. It is through using their past life's experiences and future experiences as examples of not being afraid of where God has brought them from and now knowing where God is taking you to.

We misunderstand as Christians that our lifestyle, good or bad, even in the state of our sinful nature, can still be that example that God can use to elevate the hearts and minds of the masses of people to believe in Him. God can use them now and after our life to spiritually and consciously reach other people.

That is why we should never be ashamed of who we are as a person or people, but we must always remember to represent who we say we are; and in this case, I think men, women, and children can reconnect spiritually and consciously.

I mean, God's grace and mercy does not stop at a person or people trying not to be hypocritical. Although this statement shows much honesty in that person or people's hearts who do not want to be a hypocritical, just like the people who attend church do not obey God's Word, it still does not excuse them from God's salvation. Let me put it in this perspective: although those people have shown much honesty and concern for how they are thinking, it doesn't excuse them from the pit of hell that God is placing them in.

Although one might be honest if their honesty is not being challenged by God's consciousness than even in the state of their honesty, it does not mean that their honesty displays the true faith and salvation that God intended for us to have. In other words, mankind's purpose and reason is to serve God. It has nothing to do with what we think about, what we are thinking that is true or faithful or right in our eyes, and not in the eyes of God.

Let me simplify the statement of this text, and that is God will accept any man in the state that mankind is in, whether sinful or even in their imperfections. No man should feel ashamed of who they are in God's eyes. All of mankind is subject to sin because it is a part of our "free will." Our "free will" is also a part of our nature. Our nature is where mankind is able to exercise their "free will." Our "free will" can only be disciplined based on how well we mature in God's consciousness. Our maturity dictates to us how much control we have over our "free will" and also on how well we have matured in our faith through God's Word, and that is what develops mankind's state of consciousness in God.

I already know that because of my nature, I'm an imperfect human being and very vulnerable to sin. If I am vulnerable to sin, I cannot use sin as an excuse to continuously keep committing the actions of sin toward such a lovable God.

For example, just because I know that God is going to forgive me of my sins, it does not give me the right to continue to commit sin. If I have that attitude toward God, then that simply means that I am abusing God's grace and mercy to validate or accept my sinful desires toward Him, and that is not what the Christian life is about.

God wants us to understand that there are limitations in our actions, when we sin(s). That is why God, through His consciousness, teaches us the importance of heaven and hell. Because whatever choice we make, based on our free will, God already makes us responsible for our sins, based on our actions, and well, we are to exercise our "free will."

The "free will" of mankind gives man the opportunity to make his own choice in life and be responsible to the choices mankind makes. God being omnipotent as He is does not force mankind to obey Him. The concept of man's "free will" has challenged many philosophers and theologians for centuries.

Many library shelves are crowded with books on the philosophical and theological perspective on man's "free will" and God's existence. Many people have studied the theological and philosophical of God and mankind. Many people have studied theologically and philosophically God's Word, trying to prove the authenticity of God's divine Word, but from their perspective of God and mankind, and not from God's perspective. Read the book *The Theory of Theology* by James Grant.

That is why mankind's perspective comes with many ideologies of whether God exists to the capacity that God said He does exist to or even from. God even used mankind's free will to determine if mankind's free will was given to mankind by God or if mankind inherited their free will or was it God who created room in this world and universe for mankind to develop their own free will or was it God who created mankind's free will or was it mankind who develops God's free will.

Here is what the discussion entailed "Why did God create man with a free will?" Maybe people assume because God has given mankind the opportunity to embrace His knowledge, through His Word, while mankind is able to embrace God's Word, it is through God's divine Word that mankind is able to develops their consciousness. Through God's divine Word, mankind is able to comprehend and understand God from a spiritual level where mankind can elevate themselves into being a human being with a spiritual consciousness.

One of the privileges and opportunities that God has given to mankind is based on the word and understanding of choice. That choice and understanding that God has given mankind is mankind's free will.

Mankind's free will has placed him in a position where God has surrendered all of mankind's power, authority, and responsibilities to mankind himself. In other words, God has given mankind the privilege and the understanding to be in control of his own free will. But mankind's free will did not stop there. In order for mankind to have confidence in God and himself, mankind has to be in a position where he can exercise his own free will.

Also, mankind's free will comes with some great responsibilities. But the greatest responsibility of them all is the responsibility which challenges mankind's free will and his relationship with God. Mankind's free will is mankind's actions toward how he uses his free will to exist and live in this life with his fellow man and God.

Although God gave mankind a free will, it does not mean that mankind is more powerful or is as omnipotent as God. It only means that God is able to oversee everything, including mankind's free will and the things mankind has done and is about to do. Here is the truth about mankind's free will. In order for mankind to become a successful human being, mankind has to be in control of his own consciousness.

Here is what I mean when I say that mankind needs to be in control of his own consciousness. The question is how does mankind get in tune with his consciousness? By being submissive to God's teaching or His laws. In other words, submissiveness means that mankind needs to give up his free will to God and in turn let God redirect his lifestyle.

When God starts to redirect mankind's free will, that is when God is able to develop mankind's consciousness in Him. If I had to define consciousness, I have to say that consciousness is a state of mind that gives us confidence in the things that we believe in or want to do, and it is through our consciousness that we achieve greatness in the eyes of God.

Consciousness also means that we are trying to gather all of the information you need to compare and contrast our life experiences in this cause to God's divine Word in order to make sure if we should apply the Word of God to our hearts, in order for us to develop our consciousness, and in order that we can start to develop a spiritual relationship with God our father.

## THE POWER OF GOD'S CONSCIOUSNESS

Now when we embrace God's Word into our consciousness, it means that thing becomes a way of life. Why? Because we have embraced it also in our hearts and minds, and that is why it becomes a way of our life. Now that way of life is what starts to develop our character. Now when something has been embraced in our hearts, minds, and consciousness, it shows in our discipline. When something becomes a part of our discipline, now the discipline is manifested through our consciousness, and it is through the manifestation of our consciousness that produces and develops our faith in God.

When we are able to embrace God's divinity, and we are able to acknowledge God's Word in our consciousness, what comes after is a fear of God. Here is what I mean when I say fear God: when we recognize God's wisdom through His divine Word, it causes a certain fear in our hearts. When we study God's Word, we are acknowledging to ourselves the nature of God's presence in our lives and in the universe and how we can become secure in God's relationship with mankind.

Sometimes as a Christian, we might be fearful of the power we have being in tune with God's divine Word. I think fear distorts or tries to make us feel that we are powerless in our faith with God. I don't think that Christians who proclaim Jesus Christ as their Lord and Savior sometimes know how powerful they are. Sometimes Christians don't understand the power that they have just being a Christian and being faithfully and consciously to the Lord. The power of a Christian comes through transforming and transcending God's divine Word, "I tell you to truth anyone who has faith in me will do what I have been doing he will do even greater things than these because I am going to the Father" (John 14:12). The question is what does it mean when John mentioned that we should perform greater works than Jesus did.

I'll be better than Jesus Christ. I think what it means is that because we have been taught through God's Word the importance of Jesus Christ's life and the sacrifice that Jesus made along with mankind's salvation, we have the opportunity through our faith and consciousness to recognize that by believing in God's Word, we have the ability to do the same works as Jesus Christ. But it is interesting that God wants us to do better than His Son.

Now in most churches, they don't let God anointed people or people to do His will. The churches pick and choose whom God has not anointed to do His will for the masses of people. God did not choose a particular group of people to do His will.

Let me simplify the statement with the churches or church. The churches or church focused on the prestigious people with degrees, people with great academic status or political status, people who are highly rewarded by society measures. This has been the downfall of the churches.

Sometimes what happens is that these churches make these prestigious people with academic degrees, assuming that they are going to rebuild or even stay with the churches or church. But those people that churches or church place in authority need them for political and economic monetary gain, and they move on to a better position in life if the position is suitable for them.

The anointed people are the ones that God already prepared for the ministry. But those people that God has anointed are overlooked because the churches are looking at the status of people instead of people's hearts, minds, and beatitudes that are established through their consciousness and faith in God.

Now God chooses those who are His anointed. Do you remember the trails that we go through in life? Those trails that we go through in life are what prepare us for the purpose and reason that God has anointed us to carry out His ministry.

God, through our trials and tribulations, test our faith and consciousness and our actions as we go through our trials in life; and this is why our trials are very important as well as how we struggle and persevere in the midst of our trials because our trials help prepare us for God's anointing and calling that God has prepared upon our lives.

The church or churches must always remember that God understands the heart of mankind, and it is at this point. One of the biggest problems in the churches is that churches don't look at the heart or the spiritual development of the person but the status of the person. That is why the majority of the time, God's anointed people are not given the opportunity to spiritually work and get authority in the church when in actuality, God's people are not used in the churches. Even the people of God are not used in the churches of America. That is why the churches are so confusing about which direction to go in because God anointed people that He has prepared are being removed from the churches.

That is why when God calls his people, He calls the ones that He has anointed and the ones that He has anointed are the ones that He placed with much spiritual authority for others to appreciate their anointing.

We as Christians must recognize that we also have the same power that is in God. It is also within us. That power that God has transcended as the essence of our faith and our state of consciousness comes from God's divine Word.

It is through God's divine Word that the consciousness of mankind is able to transform itself from the mere physical into the spiritual existence of life. As our consciousness transforms itself from the mere physical into the spiritual existence of life, we are now taking God's transcending of power and bringing that power into our state of consciousness. That is where we get God's divine power from. That is the power that makes us aware of how much power we have consciously through God's divine Word.

The other thing that brings us in to God's divine power is the discipline we need to exercise how God's divine Word has transformed itself in our lives. When God's Word has transformed itself in our lives, it becomes the evidence, not because you told someone that you are a Christian but the true evidence of God's divine Word based on when someone can recognize God's divine Word and the presence being displayed in our character and integrity. That is evidence of a spiritually endowed man or woman.

Here is what I mean when I say we must have discipline: in order for us to execute God's divine Word, we must have discipline of God's Word. The question someone might ask is, what do we have to do in order to get God's divine power to become a part of our life? It is so simple. We have to be submissive to God's divine Word.

# THE POWER OF GOD'S CONSCIOUSNESS

Sometimes because we don't become submissive to God's divine Word, we lose focus of our own divine power that God has given to us in order that we can fight and overcome our own adversities and battles in life. We must become submissive to whatever God's will is for us to do.

I listen to many Christians speaking on how God has anointed them, but in reality, they are afraid to do the anointed work. Some of them have been Christians for so long but never develop their consciousness enough to let God anoint them to do the work that God has anointed them to do. There are some Christians who have not studied God's Word. I would say they have been in the Church for many years, but they have not grown or matured in God's Word. Their consciousness has not spiritually matured in God.

Here's why: those Christians who are not mature are not taking their Christian life seriously because they would take on the right precautions to develop their spiritual consciousness in God so that they can mature and grow spiritually in God's consciousness.

Instead, what those Christians who don't study God's Word in order for them to grow and mature in God's grace and consciousness do is that they preferred to talk about other people in the churches and implement bad ideas about the pastors and their congregation.

Sometimes we spend more time talking about others and creating disunity and hate in the churches instead of spending time trying to mature and develop our spiritual consciousness and faith in God.

Some of us are so busy complaining and talking about other people in the congregation, and that creates such a think cloud that prevents some of us from recognizing our true spiritual and consciousness and our own divine anointing for God.

We want to be anointed, but we do not have spiritual faith to accomplish our anointed. The reason why we are afraid is because we have not matured in our faith. So if we are not maturing in our faith, then we are maturing in our fears, and that is a dangerous place for any Christian to be in: to fear the fears of mankind. That prevents from us from doing God's anointed work.

Sometimes we are also afraid to exercise our anointed gifts because we cannot comprehend or understand if we have the spiritual power to achieve God's anointed that He has placed upon.

This is when we must understand that God is not going to give us anything that we cannot handle. This is where our fear comes from and to use them. That means that we have doubt in our faith. In other words, when we believe in our fear, we begin to doubt our faith in God. There is a statement that people mention about that has to do with fearing God. Here is the statement: I fear God. When people say that what they mean, first off, I think it is a spiritual perspective of fear. This is a very important state.

What are we referring to first? We fear people out of fear itself; we fear people out of intimidation; we even fear sicknesses, the emotion of love, and we even fear God. We even fear the responsibilities and the adversities that challenges our faith in God. We even fear the unknown. Here is why we fear the unknown: because we do not know what it is that we are facing that creates our fears in the state of the unknown.

# THE POWER OF GOD'S CONSCIOUSNESS

The question still needs to be answered: why do we fear God? If we already know that we serve a loving God, who is compassionate with His love and grace for mankind, there is a consciousness that comes with fearing God.

Here is what I mean when I say that there is a consciousness that comes with fearing God, and that fear is God has already been embraced in mankind's consciousness. That consciousness come with the ability to recognize our own fears in life. We all have an understanding that God helps us to understand and acknowledge within us His divine love.

With God's divine love comes God's compassion for mankind. That is why we have to understand God's true grace and mercy because through grace and mercy is a state of forgiveness.

Why do we actually fear God? We fear God out of His greatness. Now that is a statement that has always been made, but no one has been able to eloquently explain it in a way that we can get a better understanding and comprehension of God's greatness in our life.

I think we equate power with evilness. I think some of us don't equate power with greatness or goodness. So that is what distracts us from God's goodness and greatness. I also think that sometimes goodness and love are interpreted sometimes as a weakness, and sometimes we treat God's love and goodness as such until we are able to realize that we serve a God that is powerful only through His grace and mercy. And when we recognized the true and honest love, that is in God's power, that same love and goodness is designed and created for God's grace and mercy. That power that is in God's love is what develops the power that is in our consciousness through God's divine Word.

In other words, we fear power because of its evil nature, but we fear God's greatness because of the His power and goodness. Because somewhere in our lives, we have experienced how God's goodness had to conquer Satan's evilness in order to bring us out of the mess we were in.

So if God's goodness is more powerful than Satan's evilness, then that is the power in God's goodness which we do fear, and that is what makes us fear God out of love and greatness. I will elaborate more in the text. The fear of God is the first step in introducing God's greatness to mankind's consciousness and heart.

It is mankind conscious in God and not because mankind was placed in a position to fear God either spiritually or physically. Let me elaborate more on the concept of fear as it relates to God's consciousness.

Let me try to define what fear is from a spiritual perspective. Fear is recognizing the power we have in God's consciousness. Or let us look at it from this perspective: fearing God means to have knowledge of God's power through our faith that we have in God.

Fearing God also means that our faith, through regular studying of God's Word, allows us to recognize the power of God's truth enough to fear Him. Fearing God means that you have an understanding of God's knowledge, enough to become faithful to Him.

For example: Matthew17:14–20 says

> When they came to the crowd, a man approached Jesus and knelt before him.

"Lord, have mercy on my son," he said. "He has seizures and is suffering greatly. He often falls into the fire or into the water. I brought him to your disciples, but they could not heal him."

"You unbelieving and perverse generation," Jesus replied, "how long shall I stay with you? How long shall I put up with you? Bring the boy here to me." Jesus rebuked the demon, and it came out of the boy, and he was healed at that moment.

Then the disciples came to Jesus in private and asked, "Why couldn't we drive it out?"

He replied, "Because you have so little faith. Truly I tell you, if you have faith as small as a mustard seed, you can say to this mountain, 'Move from here to there,' and it will move. Nothing will be impossible for you."

The only way that we can move a mountain is through faith. How much faith do we need to move a mountain? We need as much, as a mustard seed. Now when we look at a mountain, what do we see? This land tarring, a huge piece of land mass we also call a terrain. A terrain has boulders and rocks with all sizes of rocks that are heavy.

Then we look at the construction machines, and we realize the power and time it takes to move a mountain. But the faith that we have received from God's divine Word that gives us a certain type of power. That power that mankind has can make the weakest man in the world move many mountains, even those mountains in their lives, faster than the machines that mankind has made, the faith that mankind has enough power where mankind can move the mountain faster than machinery. So there is nothing more powerful and faster than the working of faith.

But as a Christian, through God's consciousness, what we need to do is just have enough faith the size of a mustard seed to move many mountains in the universe. Weather it is with machinery or our faith in God, it requires us to have great power in God's Word. Man might require. machinery. God's way requires us to have just faith. The size of a mustard seed.

As much faith as a mustard seed. In other words, God's faith is only the size of a mustard seed to move the mountain while man's power deserves huge machines to move the same mountain.

So to fear God means that you recognize within yourself how powerful God is in his own right and might. Still and yet, with that same fear that we sometimes fear, God has enough power to destroy the whole world as fast as He can blink His eyes faster than I can blink my eyes. Now through God's consciousness, we recognize His power. It is in the state of God's consciousness that we recognize God's power as well as fear God's power.

Now what do you mean that within God's consciousness, we know His power? Here is what I mean: God's consciousness gives us the awareness to understand God's power and fear God out of love and understanding, and it is at that point in our faith that we become in tune with what God's true wisdom is in our lives where we have better understanding of God's fear. We recognize that God's fear is not out of intimidation but out of compassion and love.

Now as we get to strengthen our faith through God's compassion and love, our consciousness in God's power gives us great confidence in God knowing that God would not destroy us out of hate or pride but through the Word that becomes the main source. of our consciousness. We acknowledge the wisdom of God that we embrace from God's Word, that we have acknowledged through God's love that God will still love us, even in our state of imperfection and nature of our sins.

Now if mankind was given or had the same power or authority as God, let me look at from this perspective: if mankind was place in the same position as God to lead and rule mankind's life, just like God is doing now, what would happen to the world based on mankind's judgment and authority? Now we are talking about mankind being in the same position that God is in the universe.

Now what would happen to mankind if mankind was God and had the same authority and power that God has?

You see, I am not blaspheming God by asking such a question. We ask those question when we are faced with our trials and temptations in this life because it depends on our adversities and being challenged by our own adversaries. These are the thoughts that we have been faced with in life, depending on how severe our own circumstances are. Even when we look at the conditions of the world, we are glad that God is in charge instead of mankind being in charge.

Many people have thought about that same question or statement that brings control to the world. Many times, we ask the question of what the world would be like if mankind was in control and was the god of this world.

Now that would be a lot of power for mankind to have. Now think about that for moment. We already know that because of God's love and compassion for mankind, we prefer God to have the power that He has instead of mankind.

Here is why: because of mankind's sinful nature, we already know that mankind, because of his pride and self-centeredness would have destroyed the world already.

Here is why: mankind already takes pride on trying to be God or trying to be like God or sometimes mankind is trying to replace everything that God has done for the goodness of mankind. Sometimes we even try to judge each other, like we are God ourselves. Now that is very interesting in that we have a God who is a God to mankind and who is in control of this world instead of mankind themselves.

I mean a God that loves and understand mankind better than mankind can understand themselves. I mean a God that is able to judge mankind based on His compassion and love He has for mankind. I mean a God that is able to take the time out to understand and love mankind through mankind's sinful nature and imperfections and is able to grant mankind salvation, even in the midst of mankind's sinful nature and imperfections. Here is why: because of mankind's submissiveness and humbleness toward God's will in his or her life, God is still able to love us and give the opportunity to have everlasting life.

All because we understand God based on our consciousness and love we have for Him, we already developed with in our own consciousness the faith and the confidence to acknowledge God's love and compassion for mankind. We appreciate how much power God has, and in appreciating how much power God has, we fear God's power.

Here is why: because with God's power comes compassion and love, a love that surpasses mankind's comprehension and interpretation of what mankind has come to understand what love truly is because of God's authentic love for mankind.

Now because of God's unconditional love for mankind, we prefer God to be the one with the power instead of mankind. Because through our faith and consciousness in God, it gives us an in-depth appreciation why we prefer God being the one with the power instead of mankind.

My main focus is to try to bring some clarity to the theological perspective of why I prefer God to have all of the power instead of mankind. Here is why: because of God's love and God's compassion for mankind, God's omnipotent power if I look at God's power from the perspective of being omnipotent.

I think within the word *omnipotent* comes a true spiritual undertone that is never mentioned in the word *omnipotent* that many theologians might never think exists within the word itself, but it has a tendency to support the theological ideology of why God has the right to have all the power instead of relinquishing that same power to mankind.

Here is why: God's love for mankind is made up of compassion. Compassion produces a state of forgiveness where the nature of mankind would not allow mankind to reach the potential of such a divine love that is unconditional. Here is why: because mankind is a created being from the authentic hand of God, and God is the ultimate creator of mankind. The nature and "free will" of mankind can never reach the potential of God's unconditional love for mankind.

As a matter of fact, mankind cannot love God the same way that God loves mankind. If that were true, God would have never used the prophets to show us the way or even used the prophets to deliver and cherish His Word. Mankind's consciousness in God would be on a level where every decision mankind makes, mankind would be able to implement and seek the wisdom and spirituality of God's guidance in their lives.

Also, if mankind's love was as unconditional as God's love, God would not need prophets. Our love in God would have developed to the potential where God would not need prophets. God compassion gives mankind the opportunity to seek God's grace, compassion, and most of all, God's salvation. Just a reminder: mankind's love can never reach the same potential as God's love.

We must also understand that through God's compassion and love for mankind, God's power is able to protect us from any demonic forces that we are about to face in the world. It is through God's power that we are healed. Even in our state of sickness, we know that we have a powerful and awesome. That is able to heal us of our sickness if it is His will.

It is through God's power that we feel secure, even in the midst of our storms, that we have enough confidence to stand up and stand firm for God.

When other people might not think so or even have the courage to stand up for Him, even in some of the most dangerous situations and some of the most uncomfortable circumstances in our lives, especially those circumstances and situations that, when we represent God, do not make us popular or famous with the masses of people in the world but allows God to know our names for His sake.

It is through God's consciousness that we have the courage and strength to stand firm in our belief for God, just like God stands firm for us when God crucified His Son, Jesus Christ, for us. We should also stand firm for God, just like God stands firm for us when Satan tries to destroy our faith that we have in God.

God stands up firm for all of mankind's temptations and proves Satan wrong when mankind is able to overcome their adversities and adversaries. God even challenges Satan by saying to Satan, "You can destroy mankind's body, but you cannot do anything with mankind's soul."

When Satan tries to destroy our souls, God stands firm and face-to-face with Satan not to destroy mankind. Now if God is able to stand up for us face-to-face with Satan, then we should be able to stand up for God all of the time, even if we are not placed in a popular situation to do so. We must always let our faith and consciousness represent God at all times.

We should also recognize that because we have embraced God's consciousness through His Word, we have the same power that God has. Here is how it happens: when we embrace God's consciousness through His Word, there is a certain power that comes with just studying and embracing God's Word faithfully and righteously.

Now that same power has transcended to transform our minds into a spiritual state of consciousness, and it is that same state of spiritual consciousness that gives us the same power that God has. That is why everything that we do. we must call upon God's name; it is in God's name that we get the strength to heal and cast demonic forces out of people. It is through that strength that we get the power within ourselves to cast out the demons. There is power in just calling and praying in God's name.

It is that same power I have in God that gives me the power to fight the battles that I know I would have never won. It is through my consciousness that gives enough faith to understand God's love and power, but more importantly, I have enough confidence and courage to give up and give in to my "free will" and follow the direction of where God's grace and mercy is leading us.

Let me get back to the topic of mankind's free will. Why is it that God does not force mankind through extreme violence to obey Him because God wants mankind to enjoy and exercise the essences of their "free will?" God wants mankind to exercise their own free will based on their own accord which allows God not to be responsible for mankind's actions toward their own free will.

God, as He created mankind, gave mankind the opportunity to exercise the decision on his own "free will"; we must also understand that mankind's free will is based on God's salvation. God's salvation gives mankind the opportunity to be judged as well as reconciled through their salvation, based on mankind's "free will." Because of mankind's free will, it does not mean that because mankind has been given a free will by God that mankind would not be judged because of it. God still allows mankind to be responsible for their own judgment based on the decisions that mankind makes under their free will.

No man or woman is guaranteed salvation, although every human being has the potential to receive it from God, but salvation is a choice that every human being has to decide on, based on mankind's free will, life conditions, and state of his or her spiritual consciousness in God.

The only way all human beings can reach their salvation is through embracing God's consciousness. That consciousness comes through God's divine Word. The only way people can become in tune with God's consciousness is by reading, studying, and most of all living God's Word.

We must understand that salvation is a gift from God, but it is a choice that we make. We must also recognize that within those choices, there are consequences and our spiritual consciousness, based on how we exercise our "free will," is why we make the decision of whether we are going to heaven or hell.

Our actions dictate what position in life we choose either evil or good. We make the decisions on whether we are going to hell based on our state of consciousness and understanding in the interpretation of God's Word and most of all living by God's Word.

We are going to heaven or hell, which is based on the power of our consciousness and our faith in God.

# Understanding the Conditions of Our Sins

Sin has been one of the most challenging behaviors that have challenged mankind's faith and consciousness in God. One of the greatest challenges that mankind has in their lives is being able to wrestle with sin itself.

What mankind wrestles with are the challenges, which challenge mankind's choice to do what is evil versus what is good. The challenging part comes because mankind knows that sin is wrong. Yet mankind cannot escape sin, although sin is constantly knocking at mankind's door.

Sin is always waiting and becoming that weight that can break the backs of mankind's faith and consciousness and mankind's belief in God. Sin is constantly knocking at mankind's hearts for mankind to open the doors to their heart.

In order for mankind to embrace sin in their own hearts and minds, that is why we should constantly use our consciousness in God as a weapon to defeat our sinful nature and imperfections in order for us to grow in the likeness and image of God.

Sin has been one of the most misunderstood characteristics or acts that mankind cannot comprehend, except God. Again, let me look at sin from this perspective: God might not have compassion or forgiveness toward sin. In other words, because God does not tolerate sin, what I can never understand or even comprehend is the why and how in the actions of mankind's sin as it pertains to the love, grace, and most of all, God's forgiveness.

Here is what I mean when I say the how and why: I am making reference to the attributes of God's grace, love, and forgiveness. Again, here is why: first of all, God does not tolerate sin on any level, yet God has within His spirit the compassion, love, and understanding to forgive mankind of their sins. To be honest with you, the problem of why I can't understand why and how we sin, and when I say why mankind sins, God is able to forgive mankind's sin. Once again, how God is able to forgive mankind's sin. This is where our spiritual consciousness manifests itself even through sin.

Every time we sin, there is a harsh reality that has a painful lesson that God has already tried to prevent us from experiencing. So the only way for us to experience and have knowledge of the lesson is through the pain and suffering that comes with the lessons, which causes the sins in God's eyes.

This means having the knowledge through our consciousness to recognize God's grace and mercy that comes with mankind's faith, which is the actual act of understanding God's forgiveness for mankind.

We know through the readings and studying and reading the doctrine of God's divine Word that we serve a God that knows how to forgive and why He forgives me and mankind and gives me and mankind a second chance in this life. I really don't know why God is so forgiving. The one thing we do know is that God really does whatever He says He is going to do, and that includes God's forgiveness.

The reality of God's forgiveness sometimes has to do with how mankind approaches or understands God's Word in the state of mankind's forgiveness. Now God's forgiveness is expressed through God's grace and mercy, and that is how mankind is able to develop its spiritual consciousness through God's Word.

When we become spiritually in tune with God's divine Word, we are able to recognize God's anointing, we're able to recognize what it is God wants us to do for Him, and we are also able to recognize our purpose and reason for living. When we are spiritually and consciously aware of God's divine Word, that is what keeps us in tune and in focus in our consciousness with God.

That is very important because even in the state of our spiritual consciousness, we cannot recognize the things that God recognizes, see or understand the things that God

## THE POWER OF GOD'S CONSCIOUSNESS

understands. No one is that spiritually driven or motivated enough to have that spiritual insight to even compete with God's wisdom.

Mankind does not have God's wisdom or consciousness to even know what God knows or understands that is done through the beginning of our life and the ending of all creation.

Mankind only knows what God has revealed to them from the spiritual realm of God's existence in signs or revelation or a message other than what mankind has no recollection or knowledge of the spiritual realm. In order for mankind to experience the spiritual world, mankind has to be in tune and in fellowship with God's Word. When mankind stay in tune and in fellowship with God's Word, this is when mankind is able to experience God's messages and revaluations coming from the spiritual realm.

Nor do we know what time or place we are going to die; even our faith cannot tell us what time or place we are going to die. It is not even in our spiritual consciousness to know what God is going to do or how God does what He does. So when we try to rationalize God's forgiveness consciously, sometimes we don't know if God has forgiven the sins that we have committed.

We realized that we cannot comprehend or understand how and why, but we know that the reality of the how and why does exist because that's why we have heaven and hell to separate what is good from that which is evil.

See, we will always know the wisdom of God, and we will always embrace the wisdom of God through our consciousness, but we will never know how God does some things and why God does what He does, and that is why

God will always have the authority and power to forgive and not forget mankind for their sins.

We must always remember that sin is a convenience that is very enjoyable and loving to mankind. Although mankind enjoys the action of sins, God is still just and forgiving to mankind as mankind exercises its sinful nature and imperfections. The problem is mankind sometimes does not know why they sin. It makes mankind feel as powerful as God or more powerful than God or just as powerful as God.

With that comes with why mankind sin once again, the only reason that mankind sin is based on mankind's convenience. That convenience is what gives mankind the free will, the option, or the opportunity to choose rather than to commit sin or not. God gave mankind free will. So when mankind exercise their free will, mankind is responsible for the actions of their sins and free will, and that is what gives God the freedom to judge mankind's sinful nature and imperfection.

I think sometimes mankind have a tendency to place themselves in the position or situation of sin. Here is why: mankind wants material possessions to impress others, mankind wants political power to impress others, mankind wants monetary gifts to impress others. The satisfaction that comes with impressing others is what causes mankind to sin.

These material possessions, pride, envy, hate, ignorance, and when people do not see the same things in themselves that they are judging others of, that is a dangerous place to be in spiritually and physically. It is this disposition and mindset, which causes mankind to sin tremendously and sometimes end up losing their faith and consciousness in God.

Sometimes when we evaluate our sinful nature, we enjoy the sin itself. It brings us great joy, happiness, and pleasure. Here is what I mean: We enjoy the material possession, power, authority, and pride that come with sin itself. Sin is enjoyable, sometimes more than sitting in church or reading the Bible. It is our consciousness and love that we have in God, which reminds us of the truth we have in God that develops our faith or commitment with God. Our faith in God is not to enjoy life, where we lose focus of who and what God is to mankind but use our faith as a means to prepare us for life itself and the struggles, adversaties, and tribulations, which come with life itself.

Sin helps mankind reexamine themselves through their faith in God's consciousness.

God is able to forgive mankind's sin. The one thing I want man to understand is that God's forgiveness does not make Him weak. God's forgiveness is an example of strength that comes with mankind's spirituality that embraces God's own power of forgiveness.

I mean, God is able to forgive mankind's sin without any malice or making mankind accountable or responsible for their previous sins that mankind has committed, although God Himself has placed limitations on the actions of sin.

What becomes very difficult for me to understand is how can God, who dislikes the actions of sin, be able to forgive mankind of their sinful actions when it was the sins of mankind that killed God's Son, Jesus Christ?

In other words, how could a God who dislikes sin have enough compassion to forgive mankind of their sins and still reward mankind the gift of salvation? Now the sins of mankind are what caused the crucifixion of God's Son, Jesus. Because of mankind's sins, God's Son, Jesus Christ, died on the cross. His death was one of the most brutal deaths in the history of civilization and throughout the ages.

Still and yet this same God is able to display an honest expression of compassion, love, and forgiveness through His grace and mercy toward those same men who killed His Son.

That is why we must recognize that mankind's sins are a delicate action and behavior toward God. Still and yet although mankind's sins are not tolerated, by God, He still has enough compassion and love for mankind. Yet God is still able to favor mankind enough to bless, love, and forgive mankind of their sins.

God even gave mankind a consciousness to understand their imperfections enough where mankind is able to recognize the presence of God, even in the midst of their imperfections and sins. That is why mankind is able to understand God's consciousness to the point of where mankind can acknowledge the manifestation of God's true compassion; that is, embrace His love, honesty, and forgiveness.

That is also why mankind is able to love God's omnipotent power and character out of love instead of fear. One of things that I would like to know is how is it that God is able to use the same compassion to forgive mankind and use that same emotion of compassion to send mankind to hell?

This is a very important perspective because even in God's state of compassion of forgiveness, He is still able to allow mankind to decide their fate with God through and based on mankind's free will.

The question someone should ask is how is God able to let mankind decide his fate and future under mankind's free will? Now that is simple. When mankind separates themselves from God, they are exercising their own "free will." That is what gives mankind the opportunity to be responsible for their own actions under their own "free will" toward God.

So the masses of people cannot say, "How could a God who is all loving also enjoy sending people to hell?" Some people would admit that God places people in hell when in actuality, it is not left up to God to place people in hell. It is mankind's own decision that he make under his free will that places mankind in his own hell.

Here is why mankind choose hell for themselves: it is made through mankind's free will. Mankind's "free will" places them in the hell, yet they are blaming God for placing them there when in actuality, it is mankind's actions and love for sin that places them in their own hell. However, some people feel that it is God's position to place mankind in Hell because of mankind's sins.

What some forget to realize is that God still has the potential to prevent mankind from going to Hell. You see, God is acknowledging to mankind through His forgiveness that God is not in the business of sending mankind to hell.

But through mankind's sins, God shows mankind that He is able and competent to resuscitate mankind from the sins of the world and bring mankind into a spiritual consciousness of reviving themselves both physically, spiritually, and most of all consciously in the character and integrity of God's consciousness, spirituality, compassion, and love. It is mankind's own free will and imperfections that cause mankind to choose the destiny of their own Hell.

Through mankind's imperfections and sinful nature, God is still able to give mankind the opportunity to be granted salvation. All of that is determined by mankind's "free will." What God does in His judgment is to make mankind responsible for their sins under their own free will. What makes God as such is that God does not control the actions of mankind. Mankind controls his own free will based on his choices that mankind makes, and that is what makes mankind responsible for his own actions.

I would like to ask this question, and that is, at what point in our lives do we think that God is able to forgive mankind of their sins? Knowing how much God dislikes sin, I would say when mankind is able to mature in their sins.

Here are some of the reasons that God is able to forgive mankind of their sins when a person or people knows that they are maturing in their sins. One is when a person dislikes their sin just as much as God. Second is when we have matured in God's love, and we love God more than we love our sins.

I mean those actions or temptations that have caused us to sin and keep placing us deeper into sin, especially those sins that almost destroy our faith and relationship with God and start to love God more than our sins that we have committed. Third is when we recognize our actions that lead us to our sins is not worth the sins that we keep doing. Fourth is when you have realized that your sins are not able to influence your "free will" anymore that has been causing you to sin.

Also, here is the point because even in the midst of your sins, you are able to recognize God's true love and compassion that He has for you, and that is when we begin to mature in our sin toward God. This is very important because that is when we start to stop our sins, not out of fear but out love. That is when we use all of our discipline to overcome our sins. Fifth is when a person or people realize that their family is more important than their sin. That the children and family are more important than their sin, because of our sins in life, it predicts the sins of the family structure and how those sins are being broken down or have already been broken down, and they are trying to rebuild their sins through prayer and fasting and staying in order to stay in tune with God's Word.

Our spiritual consciousness is mankind's safety precaution when it comes to God's forgiving mankind of their sins. Mankind's consciousness is what allows God to exercise His forgiveness of mankind's sins.

Last is when you realized within yourself that your sins are becoming more distractive to you and the people that you love and those that are around you. This is when you realize that even if God was not in the business of forgiving, you have come to realize through your sins that it is not worth committing anymore.

This is the most important perspective out of all them. Here is why: because you have reached the point where you have experienced that your faith and consciousness is constantly maturing everyday, but it is also being tested everyday during our trials and temptation. God's Word would only strengthen us and protect us in the midst of our trials and temptations. In other words, you have taken it upon yourself to look at your sins right in their face and not run from them but face them head on, realizing you have matured in God's grace.

When you don't need to constantly act out that sin or those sins anymore, it means that you overcome your sins. It also means that your "free will" that God has given you through yourself discipline. You have also mastered your own free will, and now you have the courage to become successful enough to overcome your sins, all because of your faith in God, and that is the maturity that we all are trying to achieve and experience through our consciousness and experience in God's faith.

That is why when I mentioned how a person who is maturing in their sins is constantly struggling with their sins, I am making reference to the idea of how well we wrestled with our sins determined on how well rooted we are in God's consciousness, especially when our sins become our way of life and a habit. When I mentioned you have mastered your own free will, what I'm trying to say is that you no longer allow your free will to control you, and you have also realized that you cannot allow your free will to become influenced by how the masses of people's in society view or talk about God. It means that you have known God beyond what other people or the masses of people can either comprehend or is able to understand who God actually is.

And that is because you study God's Word enough to convince yourself to embrace the message, which comes from God's Word. That would help develop and support your relationship with God, through God's Word that helps mankind develop their own spiritual consciousness and maturity in God.

Now do you know because of your consciousness, or may I rephrase the question and say because of your spiritual consciousness and enlightenment in God? To master your consciousness based on your responsibilities and commitment, along with your faith in God, is what gave you the discipline that you need to overcome your free will.

That is one of the most powerful things a Christian can do. Is give up their free will for God's faith and consciousness. That also shows the stage in maturity because you are no longer depending upon or letting your free will influence your experience of your sinful nature.

That means you already understand what type of commitment, determination, and hard work it takes for mankind to develop their spiritual consciousness.

Now the development of mankind's consciousness comes only from God Himself. One of the things, which mankind already acknowledges, is embracing God's consciousness, which means that mankind is giving up their own free will in order to embrace God's consciousness and righteousness.

You no longer allow your free will to dominate the sinful decisions that you make, especially those sinful decisions that constantly cause us to sin. Now is the time that we recognize the importance of developing our spiritual consciousness.

As a weapon to defeat the sins, the choices that we choose that are evil and sinful can only be defeated by the power of God's consciousness that God transcends within mankind's spirit and soul, which can only transcend into mankind's consciousness through God's divine Word.

When our sins that we have developed become a way of life and a habit, the sinful habit and way of life that we have developed through our sins have taken control over who we are as a person or people of God. Now, to me, there are two types of sins, although to God, sin is sin.

Now stay with me for moment. Let me bring some clarity to this statement. Now to God, sin has no status, sin has no care sin, and sin has no favorites. But sin itself does not care whom it destroys as long it is destroying God's people and the masses of people. Just like Satan doesn't care about whom he destroys, sin itself doesn't care whom it destroys.

Sin is the action of Satan. That is why when mankind embraces God's consciousness in their spirit and soul; that is when mankind can recognize and be comfortable to face any sin that Satan places before them. Some people could say "Lead me into temptation," but it is in the temptations that test the strength of mankind's consciousness and faith in God.

The only way for me to win this battle with sin is to embrace and study God's Word so that all of mankind can develop a strong, courageous, and conscious spirit in order to overcome any sin that is placed by Satan to challenge them. Once again, God does not look at the degree of sin.

For example, God does look at sin for what sin is and what sin represents. Mankind looks at sin in degrees. Here is why mankind looks at sin in degrees: in order to rationalize and label the level of seriousness of our sins.

Some crimes, which is also another name for sin, are punishable based on the degree of crime. The question is why do sins have degrees to its name, of sins. So mankind decides to sin and still not break God's heart. What I mean by that is God already set the stage for sin by letting us know that all sin is sin.

I think the reason why mankind give sin a label is that mankind I think wanted to categorize it to make it not as serious as it is, but what God already wants us to know once again is to let us know that sin is sin. Because all sin weather the degree is all sin is sin.

Then with mankind, each degree of sin is punishable by mankind, or in this case, people in society with authority judge the masses of people. God is letting us know sin is sin, it is wrong, and they should be no levels of degrees of sin at all. Sin is sin; and they should be no level, no degree, no status for sin itself.

There is only one cure for sin: the knowledge and wisdom mankind embraces through the knowledge and wisdom of God's Word, which develops mankind's consciousness when mankind's consciousness begins to mature spiritually.

Through mankind's consciousness is where the strength and protection to overcome sin exists. Our faith is the actions of our consciousness, and our consciousness shapes our beliefs in order that mankind would recognize sin, even in its state of principalities and things unseen.

The only protection that mankind has toward sin is developing their own spiritual consciousness, where mankind can become anointed and be able to have the capacity to develop their spiritual gifts of discernment of sin itself. This also is done through the Holy Spirit.

As the Holy Spirit transcends into mankind's consciousness, developing mankind's heart and consciousness, that is when mankind can recognize sin or sin before it happens or try to destroy mankind's relationship with God. It is through mankind's consciousness that prevents mankind to mature in his or her spiritual state of consciousness.

At what point and time would mankind become vulnerable to sin? I think when mankind is facing adversities of life and when mankind is going through their trials and tribulations. The venerability that comes with sin is when the weight of mankind's trials and tribulations becomes so heavy that mankind can feel the weight of their sins becoming a burden, which comes with the intensity of mankind's pain and suffering. I mean the pain and suffering that is able to break the spirit and soul of mankind's faith and consciousness in God.

Now here is the truth, which answered the question about what point and times mankind become vulnerable to sin. Once again sin is enjoyable, makes us happy, feels good about ourselves, sometimes sin makes us feel better than the Holy Spirit.

Through our state of consciousness, we learn that the Christian life is not a life of emotionalism but of sacrifice. We also learn that our consciousness teaches us that we must have enough spiritual insight to recognize that we don't live by our emotions but by our faith in God.

## THE POWER OF GOD'S CONSCIOUSNESS

It is our consciousness that makes us embrace God's wisdom and knowledge that let us know our lives as Christians don't define or depend on mankind's vulnerability and emotions but on the understanding of knowing that through God's consciousness we are able to recognize that our Christian life depends on our faith in God's decision that impacts mankind salvation with God.

And sin is so enjoyable and loving and it serves and has a way of appealing to the sensitivity of mankind's nature. It is sin which pacifies the wounds of mankind's pain and suffering.

Now when mankind focuses more on the enjoyment, love, and happiness that comes with sin, that mankind is going through, even in the midst of mankind's pain and suffering, the only refuge mankind has is the happiness and joy mankind find themselves in when they are sinning.

Sometimes mankind gives everything to sin. And that is what becomes the downfall in the corruption of mankind's spiritual consciousness in God. Sin does not ease mankind's bird; it increases mankind's burden. Sin can also destroy mankind's consciousness and spiritual awareness in God.

And we use the excuse which is we feel that God is not listening to us, and because God is not listening to us, we have a right to sin. And sometimes we feel that we are alone fighting our battles in life. We feel like God has abandoned us and left us alone to fight and fend for ourselves. Sometimes we feel like He does not care. We feel like God is not in the midst of our sins. Sometimes we feel like God does not care about us, so why should we sit here and continuously serve a God that does not care about us.

We misunderstand this lifestyle that we live as Christians. It is not our home; our life is given to God through our confession to God. Not only that, through God's ability to create life and create within us, it seems that we only like God and worship God during the good times of our lives; but when we are challenged by the adversities and by our own adversaries that stand in the way of our successful relationship with God, it seems that we prefer to throw in the towel instead of fight for our spiritual consciousness and faith in God.

We must realize that our salvation is determined by God. God is the author and finisher of our lives, and when I mentioned our lives, it includes our salvation with God. That is why we should constantly stay with God.

When we think God has abandoned us, has left us, and forget about us, and when we think that God has no usages for us when we think that God does not care about us, that is when we began to use our sinful nature to dictate to us our own spiritual agenda.

It seems that that mankind is using their sins as an excuse to justify their own sins. It seems to me that mankind is using their sins as a means to pay God back for the sins that they have committed. That is the biggest trick Satan has played on mankind. That is how our actions of sins would steal mankind's joy in the midst of our suffering. That is why it is very important that mankind stays in God's Word.

In order that mankind would continue to develop their spiritual consciousness and faith in God. That is why it is imperative to study God's Word and, most of all, develop our consciousness in the midst of our adversity, pain, and suffering that mankind would experience their own conscious state of mind and faith in God. In God's consciousness, sin is sin, and we as Christians should treat sin as sin, just like God does because we are an example of God's consciousness. Our character dictates that through the spiritual lifestyle that we have lived. We must recognize that we are a manifestation of God's consciousness, and that is based on our faith and submissiveness to God.

We must always reflect God in our character, even in our sins. We must even try to reflect God in our sinful nature. If we sin, our character in the midst of our sins reflects our consciousness and actions of how we define God to be in our lifestyle, especially when we embrace God's consciousness. Embracing God's consciousness keeps us tuned to God. We become one with the Almighty God as we embrace His consciousness through God's Word with our hearts and souls. There is a true statement that said that some pastors and preachers know God's Word well enough to mislead the masses of people. The pastors, ministers, preachers, deacons, and bishops are very well at misleading the masses of people. That is why it is imperative that we study God's Word. Here is why: because of the discipline and wisdom that God transcends through us sometimes by the Holy Spirt to develop our spirituality and consciousness in God Himself.

Where mankind can recognize as well as discern, the true reality of false teachers. God through His Word keeps telling us to show how to approve we are in knowing and consciously studying God's Word to show how to approve we are to embrace God's grace, mercy, and love through God's divine Word.

Here is a prime example of the action of deception that we have pastors and ministers, deacons, and bishops that are teaching people more about emotionalism than spiritualism. Yes, we do we have pastors, preachers, and ministers teach us about emotionalism and not spiritualism.

We must recognize that God is not emotional, although He is a God that exercises compassion, grace, forgiveness, and love. All of those things have a direction and purpose in shaping God's emotions toward mankind. But they do not replace mankind's sinful, nature, and imperfections.

God has compassion, grace, forgiveness, and love; but God doesn't depend on mankind's emotions to serve Him. What God's depends on from mankind's faith and consciousness is for mankind to acknowledge their true sinful nature and imperfection and be able not to be influenced by sin itself. I don't think that we should control be influenced by sin. Our emotionalism can also be a sin if that we are not being led by God Himself.

But emotionalism is a thing that is physical; it is not spiritual. Every time mankind depends on their emotions; life itself goes wrong. That is when mankind starts to fall short of God's Word and consciousness. It is easy to deceive mankind spiritually because Christians try to feel more about the Holy Spirit than trying to embrace God's divine Word for themselves.

Christians become emotional more than they do trying to study God's divine Word and developing the state of our consciousness so that they can experience God's divine Word through the act of discipline. The discipline of God's Word keeps us informed about what is good and evil.

So much about the emotionalism of people worshiping God that we can tell if a person or ourselves is being emotional or being led by the Holy Spirit of God in order to do God's will for our lives.

Here is why the important thing for mankind to do is keep maturing in God's Word: God's Word created spiritual wisdom that is only given to mankind by God, which is called discernment. *Discernment* means that your mind is similar to the physical eye.

In other words, discernment is the eye of mankind's consciousness and mankind's soul. Discernment is to the soul what the physical eye is to mankind's physical existence. In other words, mankind's physical eye is used to see things that relate to the physical realm of mankind's existence.

Everything that exists in the physical world, our eyes can see. Everything that exists in the spiritual realm, we experienced through the eyes of our discernment. If I had to define discernment, I would have to say that discernment is to the soul of mankind what mankind's physical eye is to the body.

Whatever mankind's eyes experience with their physical eyes is what mankind experiences with discernment, the spiral realm of mankind's physical existence. Discernment sees everything in the spiritual realm and allows mankind to comprehend and experience everything that exists in the spiritual realm, and it is true that mankind's discernment transcends the information from the spiritual realm so mankind can experience everything in the spiritual realm to be transcended and transformed into the physical realm to become the true reality of mankind's consciousness, love, and faith in God.

Discernment is the spiritual realm that brings both the spiritual world and physical realm together in order to bring insight and enlightenment into the physical world for mankind to embrace the message and wisdom that comes with God's consciousness through intense studying for mankind.

Discernment is the window that reflects the existence and view of God's spiritual realm, and it is at that point of discernment that brings mankind's existence and physical life into allowing into a spiritual relationship with God.

What discernment also does to befit the consciousness and spiritualness of mankind is to see and experience everything that exists in the physical world. Here, mankind can become in tune and in touch with all of the gifts that God has anointed mankind to experience. That experience is built upon the beauty, compassion, and love of God's Word.

Now discernment only exists in the state of mankind's consciousness. We must remember that discernment is driven and motivated by mankind's consciousness and his or her faith in God. Now here is another point: discernment exists in the spiritual realm but is exercised through mankind's anointing in the physical realm and reality of mankind's existence, sometimes in the form of messages, signs, or symbols.

Now let me be more transparent. Discernment is also driven and motivated by mankind's consciousness and faith in God. Now discernment is the spiritual eyes of mankind's existence while our physical eyes help us experience the reality of mankind's existence.

Discernment also helps us experience the reality that exists in the spiritual world, which impacts mankind's spiritual and physical existence. This could only be seen through the eyes of mankind's discernment and not mankind's physical eyes.

Mankind has two eyes—one physical, which relates to everything that exists with mankind's physical creation, and one spiritual, which are the eyes of discernment. Discernment is the key that unlocks the door to mankind's spiritual reality, and mankind's spiritual vision, and most of all mankind's consciousness through God.

Discernment has the same function that the spiritual eyes have for mankind's consciousness and faith. play the same exact role that the physical eyes play for the human body.

I guess the physical realm and the spiritual realm have experienced the same relationship of teaching each other to help develop, and support mankind's consciousness and faith in God.

Although they are in different realms of mankind's existence. Discernment is the spiritual eyes, while human eyes are physical. We misunderstand that God created discernment, and God also created the physical existence of mankind's eyes as well.

But we understand that both realms, which one is the spiritual realm. That I referred to as discernment, and the other is the physical realm, which I mentioned to you. But both, realms spiritual and physical, complement each other in order to develop mankind's consciousness and faith in

God and bring mankind even closer in fellowship with God.

Both realms, physical and spiritual, give mankind the experience of both realms. Yet they both bring mankind's consciousness into the spiritual realm and physical realm, where mankind is able to experience both realms of existence.

Both worlds or realms teach mankind how to complement, adjust, and respect both realms because both realms interact with mankind's consciousness; and both realms are here to appreciate each other faithfully and consciously.

What pastors and ministers want to do is keep people misinformed about God's consciousness while manipulating them for the benefit of the pastors and preachers financially. This is when a preacher's and minister's pride begins to overrule their faith in God. This is when mankind's consciousness is more focused on materialism than God's divine Word.

This is when the pastors and preachers love materialism more than God's Word. We appreciate those pastors and ministers that speak well still, and yet we get more caught up in their speaking ability more than to ask ourselves this question: are they living a spiritual life for God? Or are their entertaining the souls of mankind instead of entertaining the truth that is in God's Word.

Now some people get judging mixed up with reconciliation. Reconciliation is taking God's Word and applying God's Word to the situation and circumstances that the pastors and ministers are sinfully involved in. We are in no position to pass judgment upon each other, but God's divine Word gives us the opportunity to develop a consciousness of love just to show a brother or a sister, that what they are doing is wrong.

This love of reconciliation goes from the pulpit to the congregation, pastors, ministers, bishops, deacons, and sometimes the head of the churches. When these men do something wrong, this brings shame to the congregation, especially when these men and women use their God-given authority as an excuse to manipulate the minds and hearts of the people and masses of people. Yes, they need to be sat down if they are not doing or applying God's Word to their lives or to the scriptures that they are preaching and teaching to God's people every Sunday. That is right to bring judgment toward the pastors, ministers, and their actions.

Pastors and ministers are more vulnerable to sin. In this case, I would say that pastors, preachers, and ministers are more vulnerable to sin, and their sins have more impact on the people and masses of people's lives than any member or members of a congregation.

I think pastors, ministers, bishops, or anyone that is an authority of the Gospel must always, remember every second, they must remember the impact that they, can have on people's lives if they sin.

For example, A person that attends church and is faithful to God is very venerable to sin because, of the lifestyle, and image of God that they represent.

That image that they represent to the masses of people is a true manifestation of God's consciousness. When mankind is able to worship God in the state of body, mind, soul, and consciousness. That is when Satan does not want other people to see, or experience that lifestyle because they will follow the consciousness that God has implemented in the minds and hearts of the masses of people to follow God. When mankind embraces God's consciousness, it is at that point, in mankind's life, that weakens Satan's power and people's desire not to do what is wrong, and sin. Pastors and ministers are as vulnerable to sin, just like any member or visitor of their congregation. I think I have a better understanding of sin. Let us assume that we are being challenged by sin. When I say challenge by sin I mean, being tempted by sin. What can mankind do to prevent the temptations of sin?

We must never allow sin to resonate in the minds and hearts of mankind for too long. The longer we remember what we should do, especially when sin starts to challenge us, we have to always remember never to let sin resonate or stay in our minds or consciousness for too long.

The longer we focus on the challenges of sin, and the longer it resonates in our minds. What we are doing to our spiritual life, we are allowing ourselves, spiritually to become submissive to sin itself.

When we wrestle with sin for a long time, sin itself begins to distort our faith and consciousness in God. That is what forces us to continue to commit the sin or sins we are wrestling with. We must never allow sent to conjugate in our minds our hearts and in our consciousness, we must always keep our minds focused on God's divine Word to strengthen mankind's consciousness in God.

The other thing we must do is never underestimate, the power of evil, also never underestimate the power of Satan. We must remember that sin itself cannot be forgiving. The only time that sin becomes sin is when we think and carry the actual act of sin itself.

And also the only time that sin becomes sin is when mankind both physically and spiritually carries out the act of sin. The only time that sin has control over mankind is when we become submissive and become the subject of sin.

That is when sin is able to control mankind is when mankind constantly let that same act of sin resonate in their minds too long because that is when sin finds room to influence the masses of people to sin. Satan even make you fight, with consciousness every day remind you of the sin or sins you have been committing, and that is what sin or your sins want to do, and that is to haunt you and cause you to destroy your spiritual relationship, consciousness, and faith that you have in God.

Also, from this perspective, if we think of something that is a thought that causes us to sin, that thought alone is a sin. Here is why: because that thought alone is what creates the awareness which causes us to commit the actual act of our sins. So in order for us not to continue committing the act that causes us to sin, it is better for us not to think about sin. That thought alone can manipulate the mind of mankind to carry out the physical actions which would cause mankind to sin toward God. Now if we think of a thought, and that thought alone is a sinful one, although we did not officially carry out the physical act of that sin, we have already sinned.

The main focus is for mankind to keep himself motivated and focused on those things that are spiritually motivated. In order for mankind to be successful in their Christian life, mankind needs to stay focused on those things that are spiritual and righteous. Here is why: if mankind does not stay focused and constantly staying and learning about God's authentic Word, We must always keep recharging our conscious state of mind in order that we would not become vulnerable to sin itself.

We must always adopt one principle of mine if anything else we can't remember that our lifestyle is an example and it also manifests who God really is and truthfully is to us as believers in God's faith and righteousness. And this is what would keep mankind focused on spiritual things instead of being focused on things that are sinful and damaging to our faith also in God.

One of the things that sin does for us is to let us experience how spiritually equipped we are in God. Sin does not discriminate. What sin does for us is teach us how to recreate ourselves spiritually. Even in the midst of our sins, we still recreate who we are spiritually.

In other words, sin teaches us how to recreate and redirect ourselves spiritually. Here's what I mean: when we give up on our sins and they are able to control us whatever the situation is or circumstances are, that is when our sins take control over our spiritual consciousness.

But let's say for some strange reason, which we all can identify with, is that sin itself took control over us; and we still have the consciousness date in mind to develop enough power and courage to try to wrestle in order to overcome sin itself how do we go about doing that and that is simple we stay in constant prayer, and supplication reading and studying and achieving the discipline that it takes for us through our conscious state of mind to overcome that sin that is constantly beating us down and taking over our spiritual consciousness remember.

That is when we experience, even in the mist of our imperfection and sinful nature, God is still not looking for perfection in mankind's life. Because God already knows that mankind has a sinful nature, and is already imperfect.

The question someone might ask is why would God create mankind with a sinful nature. The other question is why would God create mankind with a sinful nature, along with mankind being imperfect. We must understand that God created mankind with a perfect nature, mankind made the choice to choose what was wrong.

In other words, mankind had a choice and that choice is an exercise through mankind's free will God did not create mankind to be enslaved by him just because he was God an all powerful God created mankind with a free will to make the choice to choose good over evil or evil or good God did not create mankind just because God is submissive.

God did not create mankind to be continuously submissive to Him. God created mankind to become one with Him through God's faith, grace, and mercy; and it is through God's consciousness, grace, mercy, and faith that elevates mankind to become like the image and likeness of God Himself.

Now that image and likeness that we speak about and mankind has experienced the fashioning of God's creation. It is through God's fashioning of mankind that God even introduce mankind to something called free will. That free will is a decision that mankind receives from God during the creation of his or her existence.

Once again, it is mankind's free will that allows mankind to become like God but not God or to give mankind the opportunity to become like God but not God, or as some would say, mankind has the potential to be God but not God Himself.

A prime example of a person being God is mankind having the potential to make their own decisions in life. Whether it affects mankind or impacts mankind's life in a positive manner or negative manner. The one thing that mankind's decisions are based on is this powerful God, who created mankind and gave mankind free will.

I think when we talk about mankind's free will, or mankind having the potential, to exercise their free will. It is through mankind's free will that develops mankind's consciousness.

Here is what I mean: mankind's free will is what gives mankind the opportunity to serve God or not to serve God. That is what you call mankind's free will; it is based on mankind's own choices that mankind only decides on, which are mankind's choices.

It is through mankind's free will that gives mankind the potential to be in the image and lightness of God. Here is what I am referring to: just because mankind can think for themselves, it puts them in the position to be in the image and like of God but not to become God.

Now here is another perspective: just because mankind is able to serve a powerful God. The God of mankind is a God of compassion, not a God of control. I think most people come up with a philosophical, theological, and theoretical perspective on how can this powerful God create mankind with free will.

And this same God who is all powerful does not exercise dominance, power, and control over mankind's decisions. And what mankind is able to do, and most of all how come mankind does not feel enslaved to the creation of God.

Now that is the thought that spark so much curiosity about God and mankind—that same thought of mankind having free will and God not being willing to control mankind. It's where we developed so many theological, philosophical, and theoretical schools of thought.

That is the school of thought that developed the premise about the ideology about if God exists or even if mankind is their God without the creator or without the God who actually created mankind.

We must understand that we serve a God whose nature is compassionate and not a God where His nature is to control, dominate, and destroy mankind by killing them because mankind disobeyed God. God's nature is to exercise compassion, grace, mercy, and forgiveness toward mankind; and with God's nature, He protects those people who believe in God and those people who don't believe in God. Why, all of this is embedded in God's consciousness, compassion, love, and faith.

Here is something I think that we are familiar with. This is when we speak of a God that is powerful. We make reference to a God that is powerful. I think the reason why mankind cannot comprehend God's power is not being in control or abusive. I think we experienced some from God when it comes to the discussion of power, which is based on what we experienced from people in society who actually become abusive with their power.

Here is what I mean: we experienced people politically, economically, socially, and religiously who have power abusing the power that God has blessed them with.

We must understand that mankind's free will is once again based on mankind's consciousness in God. The people who experienced, from people in their society would be trying to expect that same behavior from God when in actuality, God is compassion. God does not compete with anyone to become God.

Almost every position that mankind has managed, or has been in an authority has been compromised and abused by mankind. Here is why: it's because of how we displayed mankind's own perspective and view of how mankind displayed their own power and authority.

I know that in order for mankind to exercise their political authority, economic authority, and social authority where we can experience God's compassion in the midst of one's power and authority, we must be people who have to believe in God's consciousness and a people who have experienced God compassion being exercise through mankind's authority. Mankind would have to embrace God's consciousness.

Everything that we do and achieve, we should always give thanks to God Almighty. That is why when we read and study God's Word, mankind's experienced how God's Word is able to develop and transform mankind's consciousness into becoming spiritual enlightenment for mankind's consciousness to develop and give God all of the prayers and anointing that mankind needs to become that spiritual beacon and enlightenment for God. Mankind can only become that beacon of light. Through studying and living in the consciousness state of God's Word. Sin teaches us how recreate ourselves, even incur state of our spiritual consciousness. Our sins also let us experience how well we mature in God's faith and grace. Although sin is a state of thought and action, sin still leaves room for us to experience how our own sins have controlled our thoughts and minds, and our sins still leave room in our lives for us to mature and recreate who we are spiritually for God.

It is also interesting to know that sin itself is a thought with or without the actions that goes against God's divine will and that God has for mankind, but it is the place where mankind is able to develop and mature in God's grace. Sin is the breaking point of mankind's spiritual consciousness, but sin is also the spirituality of God's compassion toward mankind's sins, and it is at this point that God is able through his compassion to exercise complete grace and mercy toward mankind's sins.

Sin is also the experience that mankind needs to know where God has brought mankind from and where God is taking mankind to; and most of all, sin is where mankind is able to recreate his lifestyle all over again, just because of God's compassion and love for mankind.

# MINISTER'S PERSPECTIVE ON SIN

We must also understand that the ministers, deacons, preachers, and pastors are no closer to God than we are. We are all subject to sin, just like the ministers, deacons, and pastors. To be honest, some ministers and pastors are in worse conditions than the people in their own congregation.

In the book that I wrote, *The Theory of Theology*, I strongly address this issue, which talks about how we have allowed the philosophers, theorists, and theologians to practically destroy and recreate a certain image of God in the scriptures in some cases some of thinking that God needs us or God cannot be God if don't believe in God. The truth of the matter is we do need God, sometimes more than we think, especially during our trials, adversities, and adversaries.

I think some of the churches want so much to become megachurches, but God has to prepare that churches' consciousness to become recognized as a megachurch, with about one thousand or three thousand members or more. But the success of the large churches depends on the consciousness of the congregation. The churches' consciousness has to be that of God.

If we are afraid of teaching or preaching God's Word, why are we so afraid of teaching God's Word? That we want to fit into a society that wants us to compromise or dictate to the churches how the churches should be teaching and they should compromise God's Word to a changing society? Could it be that we want new members to gain some type of political or economic status? Instead, we should be trying to gain spiritual status. God's Word is authentic. It is not to be changed and to accommodate the masses of society. We are supposed to teach the truth and preach the truth about God's Word, not compromise.

God's consciousness is not in some of the pastors. In other words, some pastors do not embrace God's Word like the people of their congregation. Sometimes you would experience that the people of the congregation are more faithful to God than their pastors, ministers, and deacons are. The reason why the churches are not growing is simple: it is because the people who are placed in certain positions in the churches are not living up to their expectations that God wants them to live up to, and that is what is affecting those people who are seeking to get to know God like the new members of their in the churches' congregation. We are supposed to develop the consciousness of God spiritually, and that is what brought me to this perspective and that is which I referred to as the power of God's consciousness.

I think sometimes the people in the congregation are more dedicated to the consciousness of God than a lot of pastors, preachers, and ministers, all because God's consciousness is not about what the world thinks or wants God's churches to want to do but instead about what God wants them to do. Here is what happened to the churches that are following the world. Sometimes churches are looking more at their security than their salvation.

We might not want to admit this, although it is true, and the problem with the churches is not the people in the world; it is the people who are placed in the positions of authority who preach and teach God's Word but act differently in their private lifestyles. Pastors must acknowledge that your status as a pastor impacts the lives of the people who depend on your lifestyle to be that reflection of Jesus Christ.

People also have a tendency to see God's spiritual consciousness reflecting in the past life and pastors. When a person is developing in God's consciousness, they are basically experiencing God through His own manifestation and love for mankind. And that is how God has resonated and manifests Himself in mankind's lives.

When God manifests Himself in the consciousness of mankind through His Word, that is when people are able to recognize the true essence and substance of transformation in that person's life. When God's transformation takes place in a human being there is a certain essence and substance, about God's consciousness, which that person or people displayed which is God's consciousness.

It is through God's consciousness. The best sermon that a preacher preaches is the sermon that the preacher doesn't preach that reflects the image and likeness of God's consciousness.

The best way to determine if a preacher, reverend, deacon, or bishop is authentic in their sinful nature and imperfection is based on how they manifest God's Word in their life, their integrity, how they treat their own family and others, and how they exercise their faith and consciousness that represents God. So when the pastor sins, it impacts the lives of the masses of people he is supposed to support and their relationship with God.

Now there are some people who might think that their pastor is perfect. Now that is a dangerous place for a congregation to be in. Because if any congregation thinks that because a man preaching and teaching the Gospel, that is what makes that man or woman perfect in the eyes of God, that is a dangerous place for that congregation to be in also. That means that the congregation has just placed the pastor on the same level as God and His Son, Jesus Christ.

When a congregation does not have a consciousness of God's divine Word, they allow the pastor's position to dictate the agenda for the church instead of allowing God's anointing of that pastor to set the church's agenda.

First of all, when we think that our pastor is perfect, we must first try to understand that pastors are human beings, just like everyone else. Because of mankind's free will and the nature of his free will, mankind, including the pastors, are also subject to the nature of sin and their imperfection, just like everyone else.

Now the people of the congregation contribute to the pastor's actions of sin. Here is how we treat the pastor like he is God and cannot make a mistake. For some strange reason, we want to see God so quickly and so soon that we have a tendency to treat the pastors like they are gods. We buy to buy them things on their birthday, yet we try to make sure that they are okay. We do certain things for the pastors that we should probably do for the senior citizens in the churches or the people who need it the most in the churches. We accept the sins that he is doing instead of seating the pastor down and teaching the pastor under reconciliation to reexamine his relationship with God before coming back into the pulpit.

The question someone should ask is what makes a pastor great in God's eyes? First, that pastor has to have a spiritual consciousness that is developed through God's divine Word. Also, that pastor has to be anointed by God for the pastoral position that God has anointed pastors to do.

What the churches should focus on is trying to develop a divine consciousness which would allow people to become more spiritually motivated to preach and teach God's doctrine.

We must also generate this question, and that is, why are the churches not growing? Why are the churches losing their members? Because people are losing respect for the Gospel. Because the pastors are not teaching on the things that might be edifying to the consciousness state of the people's hearts.

Some pastors and preachers have become so comfortable in their sins that they have committed and are still committing that their sins have become a comfort zone.

In other words, the pastors have no shame for their sins that they have committed because they have used their authority as a pastor or minister to find a biblical base or reasoning for the sins that they have committed.

I am not saying that the pastor and preacher need to be perfect, just like Jesus Christ. What I am referring to is that pastors and ministers must realize that people expected more from them because of their status and authority, and their title represents to the masses of people.

This is to stand up and represent God and not try to destroy God's image, character, integrity, and consciousness. This happens because of the pastors, reverends, bishops, and ministers' sinful lifestyles.

I am referring to those pastors, reverends, and ministers who act in this manner. They should also recognize that there is a word called *reconciliation*, which gives people the right to judge those people who are in spiritual authority. It also includes the members of their congregation as well.

As a pastor or preacher, you should be more in tune and in more in fellowship with God than your congregation. Yet some of the people in the congregation are more in tune and are more in a state of spiritual consciousness than the pastors, bishops, and ministers.

This happens because the pastors and ministers are not mature enough in God's consciousness if they are constantly in sin or directing God. Some pastors, reverends, and ministers should act more like they have developed and mature and is in control of their faith and God's consciousness.

It is the pastors, ministers, reverends. Their faith and consciousness should be a lot stronger than the people in their congregation and more of an example than the members of their congregation.

I think that sometimes pastors, ministers, and reverends have more pride and lust for material possession than the members do. I am also, saying that I myself fall short of God's Word so I am not perfect, but I am not using my imperfections and my sinful nature as excuses to sin. What I am doing is recognizing who I am as a child of God. Do I use my spiritual consciousness as an exhortation and a manifestation to continue in constant fellowship with God when I fall short of God's Word?

You would see that some ministers, pastors, bishops, and deacons will use that as a tool or example to pick themselves up and become stronger than they ever were before their sin and not use their sinful nature as an excuse to constantly stay in sin and disrespect God our Father.

What I am referring to is that as a minister, reverend, pastor, deacon, or bishop, we are the people that need to act upon the discipline and maturity of God's consciousness that our preaching love becomes the example of who God really is to us.

We people hold authority and represent God first, not our pride, not our selfish behavior. We can have excuses for why we sin and why we do wrong, but what we are doing is using our sinful nature and imperfections as an embarrassment to God. We are supposed to believe in righteousness and the consciousness of God.

It also means that the revenue, ministers, pastors, and bishops are also destroying the words of God by their actions and not being examples of what God's faith should be manifesting their lifestyle. When a pastor sins, we must comfort the pastors of their sins. We should not try to judge the pastor but talk to the pastor, preacher, ministers, and bishops in a subliminal manner that is able to leave enough room for reconciliation.

Reconciliation is using the Bible or God's divine Word to correct the wrongs or sins that a person or people have committed. We should never try to destroy our pastors, especially the people in the congregation.

If someone approached the pastor or a person in authority trying to beat them up and trying to prove to the people in the congregation how awful, dirty, nasty, and promiscuous that minister or person in authority is.

If the congregation has this type of attitude, then that congregation is not inspired by God's consciousness and forgiveness. It also means that the people in the congregation are as guilty as the person that they are bringing sinful charges against. Reconciliation is a spiritual act. Reconciliation, for me, is the spiritual act of mankind to be able to forgive each other for whatever the consequences are or whatever the person is being challenged by with each other.

Reconciliation is the act that brings about mankind's consciousness, compassion, faith, and love all together in as one attribute for each other. Reconciliation is the action of forgiveness, which allows mankind to display the same image and likeness of God through mankind's actions of forgiveness.

Now the one thing that we must try to understand is that, the pastor, ministers, reverends, bishops, deacons, and deaconess. These men and women are like spiritual psychologists; for some strange reason, they don't get the credit that they deserve because they take on everyone's problems, situations, and circumstances. Also, they have to produce a sermon on Sunday.

This leaves room for the pastor, preacher, or minister to be burnt out or become short tempered. The congregation must recognize and understand that pastors, ministers, and bishops are a job that takes the men and women of God from their immediate families.

It seems that sometimes the men and women of God such as pastors, bishops, ministers, are more of a family to other people's families in the congregation than being a parent to their own family. All these men and women of God have a spiritual Consciousness that keeps them motivated and honest to the responsibilities of the father.

So we must also have the same patients and forgiveness that we want God to have for us we must exercise that same divine forgiveness, which God has for us. We to should have that same spirituality, consciousness, and love that God also has for us, we should also have for each other. Even in the state of our reconciliation toward God.

Even in the state of mankind's sins, the actions of mankind's sins, we can still find compassion as human beings to forgive that pastor because of the nature and condition of his sin.

Here is what I mean: a pastor or pastors should not allow their sins to become a habit or continually use the congregation's forgiveness and God's forgiveness as an excuse to constantly sin.

Any pastor that has used and abused God's forgiveness and the people of their congregation's forgiveness, his pastoral authority is questionable and can also be a disgrace to the charter of God's righteousness and forgiveness. Although we are to forgive people such as pastors of their sins, the weight of a pastor's actions becomes questionable in the eyes of God. That is why pastors have to be anointed by God because of the responsibilities which come with being a pastor.

We must all remember that even Jesus was tempted, but Jesus did not allow greed, pride, lust, and love for materialism to overpower His love and judgment for the Father. Jesus did not worship any of those things. That is why he was respected so much by the Father.

Some pastors, evangelists, and ministers have a tendency to abuse God's Word by manipulating the masses of people for their own financial benefit rather than teaching the true essence and spirituality of God's divine Word.

For example, this is what some of them would do: they used God's Word as a tool to manipulate the masses of people, including their congregation. When a pastor, minister, evangelist, or preacher surrounds themselves with material possessions, when a pastor or minister tries to compete with the entertainers or entertainment world, that is when they lose faith in God's consciousness and go back into a world of sin. Trust me, that is when you become what you worship. It is even displayed in our behavior and character. If we worship God, it will show in our character. If we worship material possessions, it will show in our character.

Those pastors, preachers, and ministers, for example, develop also a love for materialistic possessions, just like everyone else. They are people whose authority sometimes manipulates their love for God and makes them compromise God's Word instead of enhancing their faith in God.

The love that ministers have for God can sometimes be replaced with their love for material possessions. We must understand that with pride and self-centeredness, it challenges mankind's relationship with God. The pride and self-centeredness that comes with the love of material possessions is the first stage of what causes a person's fall from God's grace, including pastors, ministers, and preachers as well.

When pastors and ministers begin to worship God out of convenience instead of worshipping God out of love, faith, righteousness, understanding, and spiritual maturity, that is when we can say that a pastor, preacher, or minister begins to worship material possessions more than God; that is when their life conditions that they created for themselves because of their sins begins to destroy the integrity of the church and their integrity, which is a representation of God.

Pastors and ministers must always remember that the Christian lifestyle is not about them nor is it about Christians; it is about Jesus Christ and it is about the Father. That is why Jesus teaches us through His life for us to stay in the complete consciousness of God's grace and fellowship. We must always remember that the Christian lifestyle is about what God's will is for our lives and not what our will is for ourselves. What we try to understand is that our free will and the choice that we make are no longer ours to make. We must understand that through God's consciousness, we no longer think for ourselves.

We no longer belong to ourselves, we no longer do what is best for us, we no longer think for ourselves, we no longer know what is best for us or what is best for me, it is what is best for God, and what God's Word has allowed us to experience, through God's consciousness and faith.

It is through our consciousness and faith in God that manifested itself in me through God's consciousness, which dwells in me, all of that is experienced through God's divine experiences.

The Christian lifestyle is defined in our consciousness toward God. It is express in our character and our life conditions that we are faced with every day toward God. It is not about how faithful you are to God but rather how submissive and humble you are to God's will for your life.

That is why in today's society, the churches are challenged by their own ignorance and their faith and fellowship of God. Here's what I mean; let me bring some clarity to what is happening in today's society. First, the churches are not living up to the spiritual expectations that God wants the churches to live up to. So the church is being challenged, by their own ignorance, an ignorance that is allowing society to dictate the rules and laws of God's churches when in actuality, we should be dictating the rules and regulations of this world to the masses of people in the world. But the world is dictating to the churches God's agenda.

People, there is something wrong with some of the churches in today's society. Where are the strength and faith of some of the churches today? The people in the churches are letting the university and colleges or some places in the universe who are letting the universities and colleges dictate God's agenda for mankind's life.

When in actuality those academic institutions such as colleges and universities, cannot teach God's Word. We must always remember that God's Word is though with compassion, grace, mercy, love, forgiveness, and all of those things have the knowledge and wisdom needed for mankind to develop their own spiritual consciousness while strengthening their love and appreciation for God's wisdom, faith, and love. We are even letting universities and colleges dictate God's agenda to the churches in our communities. Again, that is why the church is having a difficult time convincing the world about the authenticity and spiritualism of God's Word. The church is diminishing in numbers and faith.

Let me say this again, but from my perspective, some church members are leaving the churches because there is no substance in the teaching of the Gospel in some of the churches, and most of all, because of the lifestyle that some of these pastors and preachers have been living, for some strange reason, we think that we are not supposed to pass judgment on pastors; but again, pastors are not God, so we have the privilege to pass judgment under reconciliation.

I agree with that we do have a spiritual and divine right to pass judgment based on reconciliation, a term that is used for correcting the wrongs of mankind, as long as we are able to use God's divine Word as the true basis and meaning, as the deterring factor of reconciling our differences with God's divine Word. We don't have a right to judge but we have a right to use God's Word to allow a brother or a sister in Jesus Christ to reconcile their differences or the act that is causing them to continuously sin toward God.

Yes, we can compare God's Word against people those people are spiritually faithful in God's Word, especially those people who are Christians. In other words, who says they have faith when they are falling short? We're supposed to use God's Word within the constraints of love to let people look at their lifestyles and compare it to the Word of God.

It lets us acknowledge whether or not what we are doing is either right or wrong, and for some strange reason, most pastors don't want to be held accountable by the flocks or the people that they serving to become disciplined, or be removed from a position in the church.

You see, Jesus Christ was a prime example of showing us the responsibilities and setting the example of looking out for the people that pastors serve, for example. Let me say this again, for example, tell me if you know any pastors or ministers who have these characteristics. For example, tell me, how can a God sit down and wash the feet of men instead of letting these men who are His disciples wash His own feet?

Jesus over and over again has shown what a submissive character He still has. The submissive character of Jesus Christ is a lesson that pastors and preachers should have and need to display more by teaching their congregations how to become more submissive to the masses of people God has asked to become a pastor or minister to serve.

Second, what Jesus did also is to let the people know that "because I am a God, I still have to humble myself to the people of this world and to the people I am serving. Also, because I am a God, I am no better than a human being because God created us all in the image and likeness of Himself. I am as important to the Father as you are."

In other words, no preacher, minister, nor deacon lets the people serve them; they are to serve the people. Jesus is to let us know that "because I am His Son, mankind is also His sons and daughters, and I am no better than you are nor am I greater than you are." Jesus is saying to mankind that "My death on the cross was made evident for the sins of the world, and through My death, the compassion of the Father still is able to grant mankind salvation," even in that moment of Jesus's death on the cross.

We must recognize as believers of God that men and women who hold a position of authority and integrity should be responsible to the person or people that their positions serve, which means a person or people in authority for God, their lifestyles should reflect an example and reflection of God's consciousness.

For example, what would happen if Abraham, Moses, Jacob, and Job—just to name a few—did not take the position that God placed them in seriously enough to let their character reflect the integrity of God's true consciousness? Everything that manifested God's consciousness in their lives should reflect God's divine character in our lifestyles, and that is what helps express our spiritual consciousness in God.

We must remember that God sets standards for the responsibilities that God has given us. For example, the Levites were a group of chosen people sent by God to be pastors or ministers to God's people. God showed other people how serious he was about the people that he anointed to be in these positions. The covenant of the Ark could not be touched by anyone except the Levite priests.

There is an example in the Scriptures where a person who wasn't a Levite priest tried to stop the ark from falling on the floor, and I guess if it fell on the floor, it would bring shame to God. But because the person who touched the Ark of the Covenant was not authorized by God to even touch the Ark God, God killed him. That within itself tells you how God takes preachers and ministers and pastors in authoritative positions which He has allocated to be very serious.

When a pastor or minister have more pride for materialistic possessions than trying to do what God has anointed the pastor to do, that is when the pastor's perspective on God has changed. First of all, we must understand that being a pastor or minister is a difficult job because no one knows who pastors the pastor when the pastor needs pastoral counseling or just help.

It has nothing to do with one's college degrees or academics. It has nothing to do with how equipped we feel that person is to become a pastor or minister. It has to do with if God called that person to do His will as a pastor to the people of God.

It has nothing to do with how we feel about that person as a pastor. The one thing that it has to do is if that pastor is anointed to serve God in a ministerial capacity and be compassionate to people. The pastor should always be submissive to serve as well as be submissive to God's divine will for his life.

If a person is called by God that person must be anointed by God, not just a counselor of men. That means that God has chosen that pastor or minister for a particular purpose in His ministry which is to preach and teach God's Word.

The problem with the churches today is that the churches want to be entertained by the pastors and ministers instead of being responsible to the knowledge that is in God's Word so that we can develop our consciousness in God.

What I have come to understand is that there is more entertainment in some of the churches than those pastors and ministers preaching the Word of God. The only way that a person or a people is able to reach God's consciousness is by reading and studying God's Word. It is through the Word of God that allows people to reach the potential of their divine consciousness through the teachings of God's Word.

Now let us keep that thought in our minds for a minute about God's Word. When God calls a person to represent Him in any authoritative capacity, that person becomes anointed by God for that particular position or task, especially if those people of God have been called to be pastors or ministers.

Let me stress this point: when God anoints or is even in the state of your anointing, what do you think God is looking for in that person He has anointed? I am not going to give you a long drawn-out explanation, but I will keep it simple. God is looking, even in the state of our anointing.

God is still looking at our imperfections. It is mankind who looks for perfection in each other in order to best determine where that person's fit in God's righteousness while God looks at the inner heart and faith of mankind's imperfection to determine those who are anointed and what positions they should be placed in as God's anointed people.

As a pastor or minister, God has never said He wanted perfection in all of us; our imperfection gives us the motivation to humble ourselves toward what God's will is for us. So it is not up to mankind to choose who we should be in the position of a pastoral or ministerial position.

How do we know that God has called a particular person that we might think is competent for the position, with our own humanist instincts, of pastor or minister? We must always pray and ask for God's guidance in the relationship. Also, we must look for God's divine character and integrity in that person. In other words, it is all based on the person's divine integrity and how well that person's character becomes the image and integrity of God's divine consciousness.

We cannot accept a person to be called to be a pastor because of the authority that person's parents have in the church. In God's divine Word, that person has to be anointed by God. Whoever is called for both of these ministries, pastor or minister, should never be influenced by mankind's favoritism but by God's anointing because God has put them through the trials and temptations in order to develop their discipline and integrity where they proved themselves worthy for positions that God has placed them in as a pastor or minister.

There should be something in a man's heart that carries more weight than his college or university degrees or his parents' authority in the church or even his status; and that something that carries more weight than a man's status or authority in society has to do with God's consciousness.

In other words, man's consciousness should always stay in tune with God's divine Word. If that person is constantly in tune with God's Word, his consciousness will display the essence of God's true divine character in his life. When a pastor is able to embrace the essence of God's consciousness, that is when that pastor begins to mature spiritually in their walk with God.

Now if that pastor continues to stays in tune with God's divine Word, it does mean that pastor is in a good place spiritually, and that is expressed also through the consciousness of the pastor's congregation. That is when the pastor's congregation begins to grow and manifest itself in God's righteousness and faithfulness.

When a person is called into a pastoral position by God, that person is called into that position based on God's anointing. What does it mean to be anointed? It means that God has called you to do a particular task which God has not chosen anyone else for that task. It also means that God has called you for a particular task that no one else is competent to do but you.

Here is another question: why would God call you for that particular task? Because that is how God is preparing you. First of all, God has prepared you through many challenges, like our adversities and adversaries, also through our trials and temptations so that we can develop our divine consciousness in order that God can better equip the pastor through his adversities; to better equip the pastor to become spiritually discipline in order that the pastor might develop a God-fearing consciousness and character.

That is when the pastor has become anointed through God's grace and mercy. Now that is when the pastor is able to comprehend things beyond his physical and spiritual realm because of how God has developed his consciousness and awareness in order for him to become spiritually enhanced in order for him to develop and mature in God's faith. When a pastor is able to understand the physical and spiritual realms, that is when that pastor has become spiritually endowed. As that pastor becomes spiritually endowed, he focuses on what God's will is for his life; that is when the pastor begins to know his reason and purpose for his life, especially in this life.

One of the things that I have a difficult time understanding is how God is able to use our broken spirit to achieve greatness in Him through Him. When we become submissive to God's divine Word, through our submissiveness to God, our state of consciousness is what transforms us into becoming spiritual beings. When this happens, our perspective in life even changes. That is when we become human beings with a spiritual experience.

Although God is not looking for perfection in us to achieve His greatness, God can used mankind's imperfection to still achieve his greatness within this world. What I think God is looking for is a person who is broken, and in the state of that person's brokenness, God is able through His divine eyes to see that pastor's spiritual ambitions before that pastor is able to recognize or notice God's anointing with in him.

The pastor is able to recognize his anointing through his adversities in life and learn how people you trust can become your adversaries when a pastor experiences how edifying his adversities and adversaries are to his spiritual maturity. Also, it happens when pastors recognize through their adversities and adversaries how vulnerable they can become to life of sin. But the solution to the problem is simple. Through God's anointing, pastors can rebuild their state of consciousness to the point where pastors can still find enough grace in God to rebuild and restructure, within their divine consciousness, the inspiration of their spiritual exaltation and manifestation that exists with their own lives. That comes through the authenticity of God's divine Word.

# Looking at Our Trials and Temptations

Our trials and temptations give us the strength and faith we need in order to make the decisions surrounding our ideas about whether we are going to follow or not follow God.

God prepares people before He places them in positions of authority. Here is what God does before He places people or a person in a position of spiritual authority. God already places people through many trials and temptations. God does this to develop our spiritual awareness. This is even done for pastors as well because pastors also need to have the same discipline and sermons, preaching and teaching in their own congregations.

Now some pastors bring a lot of problems on themselves because they don't develop a good networking system to help them through their crisis of life or their conditions.

Some pastors turn to drugs. A matter of fact, some of the drug dealers are members of the pastor's congregation. The other reason is some pastors and ministers place themselves on a pedestal where they don't have enough discipline to maintain the pedestal that they have placed themselves on and not the pedestal that God has been preparing for them.

That is why being a pastor has its difficulties. Here is why: a pastor's life condition can become a weight, pouring heavy problems upon the pastor. A pastor can sometimes have to leave their families to save a young man that has been shot or killed in the community where he serves, especially in the middle of the night, when pastors have to leave their families to help others, and sometimes it makes them feel that they are alone in this world; to be honest, some pastors are very lonely.

I know some people would say, "How can some pastors become lonely?" You see, pastors are human beings as well, and they are subject to the same flaws as any other human being. Some people would make the statement that if a pastor has God in his life, they should never be lonely. You see, pastors might be okay spiritually, but physically, they could be struggle with situation and circumstances in their lives that affect the people in their congregations, and most of all, their spiritual relationship with God.

Sometimes our own life conditions are more of a burden to us than the spiritual things that we are faced with in life. I mean those life conditions that can break more than the camel's back but can break the spirit of mankind's salvation so bad that it makes mankind feel that he is lonely and serve a God that does not care about us; or we serve a God that sometimes makes us feel that He does not care about us, especially when we are going through some difficult times. Difficulties are the most challenging part of the Christians, and pastor's life because it brings the best out of us, but it is also used to sharpen our consciousness and faith in God.

When life has been breaking our backs with trials and the tribulations in life, that is when life is able to become the last straw that is able to weigh you down, and if you're not prepared for whatever those challenges are in life as a pastor, life itself can break your spirit and your back as well.

If the pastor is not anointed, the congregation is not spiritually driven or motivated by God. The anointing of God produces and prepares the pastor for his spiritual journey, for his leadership role. When I say anointed by God, I mean a person who has been directed, authored, and anointed by God's divine wisdom to teach and preach His Word.

Here is what I mean: first, that pastor has to be prepared for that pastoral position. The only person that can prepare a pastor for his leadership role is God. When God prepares a pastor for his pastoral role, it is very important that we recognize the importance of God's anointing. Now the other thing that we need to keep in mind is that the consciousness of the pastor develops into a spiritual consciousness where his awareness in God is driven and motivated by his faith in God. The pastor's faith gives the pastor the courage and strength not to compromise God's divine Word but to teach and preach God's divine Word without fear and with boldness.

The pastor must always be recognized because God has placed him there in the position as a pastor, so if we disrespect the pastor, then we disrespect God. He is God's anointed person for the leadership position that God has placed him in.

That is why it is very important that the pastor has a spiritual life that consists of discipline. Most pastors are good at orating, but their lifestyles and consciousness have no spiritual discipline, and that is a very dangerous place for a person to be in. Many pastors who are orators, their sinful behavior is overlooked by their congregation because they might be eloquent speakers. It does not mean that he is an eloquent pastor, but in God's eyes, that pastor can be replaced for abusing their anointing with God. Because of a pastor's ability to orate a sermon, it does not make that different than anyone else when it comes to sins. Sometimes they have to be replaced until God replaces them with someone else because the pastor's lifestyle impacts the life of his congregation and other people on a more severe level. We must understand that the pastor is not God; the pastor is a representation of God, although many worship the pastors like they are Jesus Christ in the flesh.

Some of the sins that I have been experiencing from some of the pastors or bishops have been a disgraced to the body of believers and God Himself and also to the masses of people in the world. The devil is using the sins of the pastors' and bishops' lifestyles to make them compromise God's divine Word. You do not have to believe me, but look at what is going on our society today. The Word of God has been compromised, and the body of believers are trying to get a grasp on what the truth is and that God wants us to understand and live by.

It is not the people who are disgracing God's faith; it is the some of the pastors who are not anointed, that are preaching without His anointing. And those people might not be anointed by God to become a pastor of the church. If our consciousness and faith are not focused on God, then the decision that we make not be the right decision. That is needed for a spiritual position such as looking for a pastor. We are not embracing the faith that we need to make a conscious decision that would influence a spiritual position in our lives for God. Here is what I mean: Jesus Christ had brothers, but Jesus Christ was anointed; it does not mean that His brother was also anointed. Many of the prophets had children and brothers and sisters, but they were not anointed by God.

I think sometimes one of the biggest problems with some of the congregations of the world is that they try to replace the pastor with someone who fit into the congregation's agenda and not God's agenda. The congregation sometimes thinks about whom they think is equipped to do God's work.

Instead of the congregation praying and asking God to send them someone who has already developed their spiritual consciousness and faith in God. We must always develop a consciousness of praying and fasting for everything that we ask God for, even as a church because we needed someone with anointed consciousness of God to lead the church.

One of the things that the churches do is to have a family that has more influence in the church than the pastor, bishop, minister, deacon. This happens because the congregation looks at the family's thieving than the family's spiritual consciousness.

One of the biggest mistakes is when the pastors are retiring. We want to replace the pastor with his son or his daughter. Now if the pastor's son doesn't have a spiritual consciousness or the pastor's son might not be anointed for that position as pastor, and then put the pastor's whom God did not anoint for that position, then the church is leading itself straight to Hell, and it's destroying the lives and the member of the people in their congregation's salvation. Sometimes, we treat the Gospel like it is a monarch. Here is what I mean: we think that because a son's or daughter's parents have been at the churches for over forty years, their children should be given the pastoral position because it is open. Sometimes we even try to groom people for those positions, but if God is not grooming them, then the position is not for them, and because God did not prepare them for that position, they can destroy that church because of the lack of the person's spiritual discipline. A person might not be spiritually conscious or even spiritually equipped to have a position as a pastor. Even though that person might have the credentials from a college or university or their family might be very popular in the church, and community, that still does not give them the right to pastor a church. That is one of the dangers that some of the churches are in today.

But that does not make them spiritually equipped. It does not make them spiritually conscious of who God really is. It does not make that person a spiritually endowed person to be a pastor. This is why because God did choose or anoint them to be a pastor only to mankind.

Some people in the churches are placed in positions because of their family privileges in the churches. They are not placed in the positions of authority because of their spiritual consciousness. Here is what I mean: family privileges could mean my father was a deacon or minister or my family has more than fifty years been a member in the church. If that person is not anointed by God, and the congregation placed the pastor in position, that is when we give the heart and soul of the congregation to the devil that is in sheep's clothing.

We are looking for people who are institutionalized and not spiritualized. We must also understand a pastor has to have a spiritual consciousness, not an academic education because the pastor's character and integrity is what helps shape God's divine Word in the lives of other people. This is the pastor's own reality of life. The pastors must always recognize that our lifestyle is a reflection of God's divine Word. Pastors are always under scrutiny, even in their state of weakness.

One of the most dangerous places that I am experiencing is the churches or congregations using academics as an anointing qualification to qualify a person as a pastor. This is a very dangerous place to be for any congregation. The one thing that we should recognize is that God, is not looking, for ministers to be educated. God's through our trials and temptations are looking for people who are willing to give up their free will, God wants ministers and pastors, who are also looking to give up the things of this world, God is looking for people to become submissive to His will. God is also looking for people who want to develop their spiritual consciousness and faith in Him. The Sadducees and Pharisees stress education, and it is true their education that they never develop their spiritual consciousness and faith in God.

The Sadducees and the Pharisees dressed up the religion they focus on. The religion they did not focus on, the integrity and the development of the spiritual consciousness that needed to embrace God's divine Word in order to experience God's revelation and salvation, all of that was lost because they focused and had their perspective on things of this world and not things of the spiritual world.

We want people who have a master's degree in order for them to be qualified, to become a pastor, and this is a dangerous place for any congregation to be. We must always remember Jesus's relationship with the Sadducees and Pharisees. The educated people were the politicians, theologians, academics of Jesus's time and were the ones that crucified Him. So those pastors who have been academically institutionalized are conditioned not to teach and preach the truth of God's Word. Most of the time, they have been conditioned through academics not to teach and preach the true message of God. This is where the compromising starts to take root in God's divine Word. God's Word start to take route. It takes route when one becomes educated in these academic institutions that don't implement the teachings that develops the integrity and spirituality of God's divine Word. Many of these universities and colleges removed the spiritualism of God's Word from their academic institutions and replaced it with a lot of theories and theologies. Stop rewarding the pastor's academic achievements and start to reward the pastor's consciousness.

In other words, if God did not call you to be a pastor, and you decided to portray that image as a pastor or minister, that means that you begin to bring danger and embarrassment to God's faith. Here is why if you are not prepared by God: you will face the obstacles that He has placed before as a pastor to help the pastor develop spiritually in their walk and discipline with God.

Let me just say this: I know we all are far from being perfect, but that's not what I'm talking about because if you are a pastor or minister, you're not going to be perfect, but there's a certain discipline that is required of you because of your position and authority as a pastor.

Some pastors and ministers change their attitudes toward their congregations because they are focusing more on the material possessions of this world, and also they are focusing more on themselves, and not God.

Now there are some pastors who think that they are the protagonist of God's divine Word. God should always be the main character and has the character and integrity in His own hands to be God. No pastors or preachers have that authority.

Some pastors want to be the main protagonist of the gospel, but honestly, they are not equipped, spiritually or even consciously to carry that responsibility. Once again only God has that responsibility to be God, just because He is God.

Let me put it in another way: most pastors and ministers are focusing on material possessions of this world, and that is distracting them from God's divine Word. Instead, the majority of the pastors are not focusing on God's divine Word.

One of the things that I've come to notice is that the pastors looking for the same material possessions like the movie stars, the actors, the entertainers. It seems that God's Word is being taken out of the church and is being placed on shelves as an entertainment tool to produce represent the world of entertainment than the spiritual world of God. The churches need to go back to the basics and bring God's spirit back to His house.

It seems that the churches are not trying to rebuild the communities. The pastors have a very strong impact in our communities, but God wants the churches to contribute widows, the old generation, the sick, and the younger generation. Old men are to teach the younger men; older women are to teach the younger women.

This is how the Word of God stays pure in the hearts of the younger generation. When we teach our children about the Word of God, they would never be able to depart from God's divine Word.

The children who know God's Word might leave God's Word for a season, but the children would come back to God within the fourth season. Our children who leave God's Word for a season are trying to place God's Word and its position.

What I have come to experience with the younger generation is God's Word would never make sense them. Here is why: if they could not compare what they have learned from God's Word, then God's Word has no sufficiency, meaning unless it is challenged by the reality of life's adversities.

The Word of God holds its true authenticity, even during our adversities, and when we come face-to-face with our adversaries. This is the point where the younger generation starts to develop a consciousness.

That consciousness gives the younger generation experiences needed for the younger to face the reality of what is good and evil and how God's Word is able to enhance their own consciousness.

God's divine Word allows the younger generation to make better decisions even in their state of adversities. Here is why: because the Word of God gives the younger generation something to compare with the evilness of this world.

We are challenged by the adversities of life and our adversaries that we constantly face in life. This is where the younger generation is able to experience God's Word for its true reality and how they are able to use God's Word to challenge the adversities of life that they are faced with.

When the younger generation is faced with their adversities, the reason that they experience the pain and suffering in their adversities is that the younger generation does not have the life experiences to understand that their adversities cause them so much pain and suffering. They must also understand that life experiences give you the wisdom that you need to become successful over all your trials, tribulations, adversities, and your adversaries.

We must understand that life experiences will always be the tool that we need to use every day. Here is why, because what we experience in life is our own reality of our life. Nothing can substitute that mankind's true reality.

Mankind's true reality is experienced and defined through mankind's consciousness. A person who has struggled in life seems to have a better chance of surviving on the streets, and someone that is not knowledgeable of the streets or never grows up in the streets.

Now I am not saying that people who are academically educated versus those people who are not academically an educator. It doesn't make the people who have experienced street life smarter than those people who have to survive on the street better and those people who have never experienced the streets.

But what it does is show us that experience is what sharpens and develops a person's consciousness in God. The more mankind develops their consciousness in God or the more that mankind develops their spiritual insights in God, that enlightenment is what develops mankind's faith in God, and that is the experiences people have to face in order for them, to become better Christians in the eyes of God.

So when we bring the younger generation in the churches, and they hear the Word of God, we are giving them a lifetimes of experience before they become adults. Or may I say we are giving them a lifetime of experience just to secure their futures in life.

When we give our children God's wisdom, we are reinforcing information that places our children in a position that would prepare them to face the true reality of life, and that is what gives them the consciousness they need to become more successful in life.

The younger generation develops a spiritual consciousness that is able to develop their awareness about who God is and the importance of their life with God.

Let me get back to my point. It is like as soon as the pastors get approval and are comfortable with their congregation, it seems that is the time the pastors use the Word of God to manipulate the congregation and the masses of people and spend time developing people's minds to become spiritually conscious and driven for God.

Here is why sometimes, some pastors take advantage of the love and authority they have if they are not disciplined by the anointing of God: because some pastors decide that they want to keep up with the entertainment world or they want to keep up with the entertainers of this world.

Some of pastors want the same lifestyle and materialistic things that the entertainers want. We are to be in this world but not of this world. Pastor and ministers have the responsibility of preaching, teaching, and living the lifestyle that complements and is based on God's divine Word, not trying to compete with the entertainment world. If a pastor is not anointed, then he is not disciplined to understand the true reason and purpose of God's divine Word because that is what makes it easier for any pastor to worship the material things of this world and be compared or be competitive with the things of this world.

In other words, pastors cannot use God's Word as a means to have the same love, lust, pride, and self-centeredness as some of the people in the world. In other words, because we sing and give praises to God, it does not make us entertainers of this world. We are not entertainers, pastors, and preachers. Those are the people who should be giving praises and be in constant fellowship with God, so through your consciousness, you are to better lead God's people. Pastors and ministers need to stop trying to become entertainers of this world. I am not saying that you should not earn money for your family. God is still going to bless you according to your works and faith in Him.

Ministering and pastoring depends seriously on how that pastors preach and how ministers embrace God's consciousness. When we make reference to God's consciousness, we are trying to determine how God thinks and the direction in which God is trying to lead us in and also what is God's will for our lives.

Although we acknowledge God's consciousness, it does not mean we know how God thinks or we know God's mind enough to know what God is going to do in the future; no one knows that except God Himself. Not even the angels or mankind have that mental capacity to think like God or even know what God is going to do in the future.

When we become submissive to God's will, it allows God's consciousness to shape our integrity and allow the consciousness of God to resonate in our hearts and minds so we can embrace God's true consciousness in order for us to become more submissive to God's will.

In other words, when we talk about being submissive to God's consciousness, what are we making reference to? We are making reference to the idea that we are giving up our free will in order to accept whatever God's will in our lives is because when we decide on handing over our free will to God, we are recognizing that somewhere in this life, the roads that we have traveled have created some difficult crossroads in our lives which we have traveled where we realize that the roads that we were traveling lead to nowhere but our own pain and suffering in our lives here on earth.

When we reach this point in our lives, we realize that we need to make a change or changes in our lives because the roads that we have been traveling lead us to a spiritual and physical death, and that is when we realize that we need God's consciousness in our lives; that is what makes us give up our free will and become submissive to God's righteousness and consciousness.

Now at this point in our lives, we realized the importance of God's consciousness in our lives, and whatever we do as we keep coming to intersections and crossroads of this life, we can now recognize the importance of God's consciousness in our life.

This is when we recognize that we, too, have to make a detour in our lives, and that detour that we have to make has to include God's divine plan for our lives.

When we talk about detouring toward whatever God's divine plan is for our lives, we must also recognize that we are giving up our free will.

Now the question that should come to mind is why would mankind want to give up his free will or freedom? Because mankind's freedom has been compromised and challenged by God's consciousness. So when we give up our free will, we are giving up our nature as human beings totally to God, and in doing so, we are allowing God's divine inspiration to direct our lives, and this becomes a spiritual and physical battle between mankind and their free will as mankind embraces God's consciousness. This also is when we understand God's consciousness is best defined in this manner, which applies to God's Word. The consciousness is the wisdom we gather from God's Word in order for us to get a better perspective and understanding about life and what God wants us to do for Him.

When we give up our free will, here is what we give up: first, we give up our human nature while trying to replace it with our divine nature. Second, we give up our self-pride. We become submissive to God's will instead of our own will. We are even giving up our material possessions. We learn how to differentiate between our love for material possessions and what we really need to survive on a day-to-day basis without the love or lust for material possessions. We learn how to live and appreciate the material possessions of life and not to lust over them. Why? Because our state of mind has changed due to God's consciousness.

Because our material possessions become a part of our enslavement and bondage, some people love their material possessions more than they love themselves. Third, we have to give up our pride, especially the part where we think we are better than others because of our status or career in society.

So when mankind gives up their free will, we are really giving up our human and sinful nature. We are giving up our free will, the physical existence of life; but when we embrace God's consciousness, we are elevating ourselves into the spiritual realm of what God's will is for our lives. People must understand that when we give up our free will and embrace God's consciousness, we are giving up our free will not out of fear in God but out of love and faith in God, and that is where we develop our own spiritual consciousness and faith that we understand through reading and studying God's divine Word.

# THE STATE OF LEADERSHIP AND AUTHORITY

One of the things that I have come to realize is to see how people in our society today and previous years have used their leadership abilities as well as their authority to take advantage of other people who are less fortunate.

Whether through sexual, social, or economic abuse, people in power have used their power of authority to hurt or destroy the weaker people in society.

Now what would happen if God, though like toward, mankind? I mean, if God was to use His power and authority to destroy mankind. What God uses His power for is to revitalize and empower mankind, even in the state of mankind's sinful nature and imperfection.

The reason why God blesses people with power and authority is simple: it is to bring joy and love to others in the midst of their poverty, pain, and suffering.

People who have power are able to make changes that affect people's lives and their families; that is why people even with their power and authority must humble themselves to the people that they are leading, just like Jesus Christ did when He washed the disciples' feet. The people who are in a position of power and authority must have a divine consciousness that leads and is directed by God in order for them to make the right decisions that impact and affect people's lives.

Power and authority become a problem when the person or people who have the power and authority cannot separate themselves from their own power and authority especially when it is time for them to humble themselves toward God. Let me bring some clarity to the statement we must always have a conscious mind, and if God places people in positions of power to impact the world, which God himself created. Whether it is political, economic, or social, we must understand that God has places in these positions as Christians to help and support each other.

We must always help people just like we want God to help us. We as men and women should never abuse our position of power to hurt or cause people to lose their jobs. God places us in those positions to help others, and support others. We constantly every day remember that we are men and women who have embraced the power of God's consciousness. Once again we must not be allowed the power, and authority that we have from these positions, that we are serving to take control over all of our minds, and we must always remember that we serve a God of compassion, of love, of forgiveness, and consciousness, and faith.

We must always maintain as men and women of God that spiritual consciousness, and discernment that we may need to make decisions, to help and love others. That not only make us look good but decisions that people bring to us that challenge our relationship with God.

That is when we must let people that we stand strong with God. We must at all times stay in constant love and compassion that God has for us, we must exercise that same love and compassion to do so, even when it is not famous or popular to do so in the midst of the masses of people.

We cannot go to a job and treat people like they are dirt, or that they are beneath us, we are all created equally. Because it will come a point and times when you need the position to support your family. That God will remove you from that position all because you have abused His name, and by abusing God's name you have destroyed many people's families' lives as well.

We must also remember everything that we have is a gift from God. Even the careers, and positions that we get from God. All the jobs that we have, the children we have, the family that we have, and the friends that we have are all gifts from God; and if we abuse them, God will take them away from us at the time that we are in need to let us know what we had in these people in these things that God has blessed us with.

Because what would happen if God decided to exercise the same behavior and treatment that you are doing to those people knowing, that you are a Christian, knowing that you should be an example of who God is through your in your life and how God has developed and mature you in God's spiritual consciousness.

Christians who are in authority who have supervisory positions should always exercise that same love and consciousness, that God exercises toward us. Christians who are in a position of authority economically and politically should always remember that no one holds more authority in this universe, earth than God.

But isn't it amazing that God does not judge mankind the same way mankind that mankind judges each other? We already know that God has more power than mankind. Mankind already knows the power that mankind has. Being the creator of it all.

Still, this same God has enough compassion to forgive mankind for the sins that mankind has done to others but still allow mankind to be responsible for consequences that have caused mankind to sin. While in some cases mankind, themselves, cannot even find a drop of forgiveness to forgive each other. like God has forgiven us.

Of the things that we have done for God, our main goal that we should never forget is to develop a deeper consciousness, which would enhance our spiritual consciousness, which would give us the authority and strength and courage to produce the actions which would strengthen our faith in God.

Even in the state of our authority in the positions that we hold as Christians, whether in the church, career, politics, or society, we should always reflect the spiritual enlightenment that God has placed in mankind's consciousness.

If people allow the power and authority especially those people that are in corporate America, who are politically active, people who are socially active, allow their power and authority to get in the way of how they conduct themselves spiritually.

Now if they cannot do that, it means that the political power, it also means that the economic power, it also means that the social power, and the authority that comes with them exercising their power and authority.

If a person has a career and they are able to exercise power and authority and they cannot see God in the power in authority that there are exercising, because they are taking advantage, and abusing their power, and authority. Then how could they say that they are men and women of God?

That means that they are no longer interested in God's divine Word. I was studying God's Word to develop a more discipline that they would no longer be a part of or allow their power in authority to enslave them in sin. which allows them to carry out the power or regulate the power to other people, like God regulates His power, and authority to us, in the state of our compassion, and love for God.

That is when the power of authority begins to enslave and entrap their consciousness. That is why most people who lose their power and authority end up committing suicide. You see the consciousness of God once again is to keep us in tune and in fellowship with Him. If you notice it as much, some people in the world hate to admit it when we stay close to God in everything that we do and everything that we control in every position that we are responsible for, we can successfully achieve it.

Material possessions power and authority is an allusion that becomes a figment of mankind's imagination to even the power, and authority that mankind acquire, is not a true reality of mankind spiritual consciousness. The true reality of mankind's consciousness is God's divine Word. That is all of mankind's state of spirituality and God's reality of mankind.

That is why most people acquire a lot of material possessions in this life and use the material possessions that they acquire and use their materials possessions, to gain people's respect and love.

Those material possessions are like a time clock, which causes people to commit suicide and turn to drugs. That is why mankind needs to develop their consciousness and love in God, here is why because that's conscious god's love gods compassion God's mercy and God's grace is everlasting and it is the key to mankind salvation.

These are the attributes that God portrays in order to give mankind everlasting life, and these my friend are the same attributes and characteristics. That we should display in love, and with each other as Christians, especially those Christian's that is consciously and spiritually equipped in God's Word, toward each other.

Here is why: because they worship the authority and power more than God. If mankind gives me and you power or places you or me in a position of power and authority, he or she can take it from us.

When God gives you power and authority, you can be guaranteed that position is for life. Now having power and authority is good when you have it, but when you lose it, always remember that the same people you step on are the same people you are going to see on the way down.

That same power and authority when a person loses it is not prepared to lose the power and authority that they have, but when they do lose it, it causes them to destroy themselves.

One thing with life, it has something in it called the Law of Returns, which means whatever you do to people, it will come back to you and your children.

There's a good feeling when you can use the power and authority that God has given you and use God's consciousness as a means to execute your power and authority. I know that mankind feels it was his effort that placed him in that position, but it was God.

It seems that if God places you in a position, we would have to accept the position based on God's responsibilities and expectations for you. If we feel like we've got the position based on our own merits, then whatever injustices that we afflicted upon others because we had to power in the authority to do so, and we do it without even having any form of spiritual discernment or spiritual consciousness.

Then we end up threatening our salvation with God, and when we think that we are so powerful that we have the authority to destroy people's lives, and we have no remorse toward what we have done to others some of us think that because we have so much power and authority.

You do not develop the conscious mind that you need to have the discipline, it takes to exercise the authority that means that God is going to take that position away from you, and the same people that you hurt, you going to feel very shame, to ask them for their help but he or she would recognize.

That the only help that God is going to allow you to have is from the people that you cause so much hurt and pain to.

Because God always puts us in a position where when we don't use our spiritual consciousness, and gifts in the right manner, especially if it is not pleasing to God. God is going to place those same people that we hurt and make fun of in our lives.

That is when we realize at that particular time that everyone that we hurt, at some point in time, God is going to put them in your life to teach you the lesson of compassion, patience, love, grace, and mercy.

But if we know that God has been the reason and purpose behind our position of power, then we have to uphold it in a spiritual manner so we might help people more. Even if we are in corporate America, we have to follow the same spiritual principles because we have been anointed and have developed God's consciousness in our hearts and minds.

God places us in positions to help other people so they can come to experience God's consciousness through the way we live, and with how we execute our power and authority, even in corporate America, we should show God's love and divine consciousness toward others, even when we have authority and power.

That is the only way that you can see or experience God's divine power and authority within yourself. Instead, some people use their power and authority to destroy the lives of other people's families or other people in general, and we should also understand that life also has a reciprocation for those people who have destroyed other people's lives, just because they have the power and authority to do it.

But when God's judgment comes upon them, they have a tendency to feel the fire of judgment a hundred times hotter than the fire that they have placed others people in while they have destroyed their lives and families.

Some people in our society have a tendency to misinterpret love and kindness as a strength. We experience the qualities that God has given us to share with one another, and it is through that quality of love that people have a tendency to abuse as a weakness. God who is loving and caring gave us these attributes for us to help and support each other, not for love and kindness to become a weakness.

We are to take good care of those who are in need of help, not those who are abusing the authority of mankind. Let us look at the book of First Timothy for moment. In the book, it says:

> Do not rebuke an older man harshly, but exhort him as if he were your father. Treat younger men as brothers, older women as mothers, and younger women as sisters, with absolute purity. Give proper recognition to those widows who are really in need. But if a widow has children or grandchildren, these should learn first of all to put their religion into practice by caring for their own family and so repaying their parents and grandparents, for this is pleasing to God. The widow who

is really in need and left all alone puts her hope in God and continues night and day to pray and to ask God for help. But the widow who lives for pleasure is dead even while she lives. Give the people these instructions, so that no one may be open to blame. Anyone who does not provide for their relatives, and especially for their own household, has denied the faith and is worse than an unbeliever. No widow may be put on the list of widows unless she is over sixty, has been faithful to her husband, and is well known for her good deeds, such as bringing up children, showing hospitality, washing the feet of the Lord's people, helping those in trouble and devoting herself to all kinds of good deeds. As for younger widows, do not put them on such a list. For when their sensual desires overcome their dedication to Christ, they want to marry. Thus they bring judgment on themselves, because they have broken their first pledge. Besides, they get into the habit of being idle and going about from house to house. And not only do they become idlers, but also busybodies who talk nonsense, saying things they ought not to. So I counsel younger widows to marry, to have children, to manage their homes and to give the enemy no opportunity for

> slander. Some have in fact already turned away to follow Satan. If any woman who is a believer has widows in her care, she should continue to help them and not let the church be burdened with them, so that the church can help those widows who are really in need. (1 Timothy 5:1–16 NIV)

This is the true manifestation of what people want to see: God's manifestation transforming itself self in the lives and consciousness of people's lives, especially those people that are in leadership positions, which also has great authority in leadership.

You see there's a certain perspective and position that God wants us to have that comes through the consciousness of His word, which develops mankind's consciousness, in order that mankind would understand the importance of forgiveness and most of the love.

It is God's Word that is able to develop mankind's consciousness. To the point, where mankind's consciousness, can achieve the same compassion, which God has displayed toward mankind themselves. All human beings have that same spiritual consciousness, and compassion, that God has for we have to have that same compassion for each other, and the masses of people. Even those people who have done us wrong. One of the things that the church has to do is to confess the sins that the church has committed. That have impacted the masses of people's life. The question someone might ask is the churches have to confess their sins?

Pastors, bishops, ministers, deacons, and any authorized person or people from the pulpit to the congregation that use their authority and church status to destroy or abuse God's Word by using God's Word and their authority in the church to manipulate the masses of people in their congregation and throughout the world.

Because the churches have come together and confessed their sin to the masses of people and members of their congregation, those people whom the churches have abused and destroyed their faith love for God. We are experiencing the repercussions of the church's sinful nature and imperfection through the decrease in membership and how people have lost interest in the Word, and God Himself. All of the hate that the churches have caused toward people, in their congregation, and the masses of people in society.

That same love that the churches are speaking about, is the same love that the churches need to be an example of that same that they are teaching and praying about.

The churches are becoming the devil's playhouse. What I mean by that is the devil's house is using the churches as his playhouse. The pastors, the bishops, the deacons, the deaconess, the ushers, and people from the pulpit to the congregations exist in God's congregations.

What I mean by that is the sinners are becoming confused because the church people are in competition, with the sinner, and the masses of people are confused, because they cannot tell who the Christians are, and who the sinners are.

The churches need to confess their sins toward the masses of people that they have hurt and destroy the perspective and love for God. The churches can no longer sit back and blame the sinners for the trouble, chaos that they have caused.

The churches have to look internally and go directly to the head of the congregation to confess their sins to the world that the churches have used to destroy the innocent hearts and minds of the masses of people.

That is why the truth and love that the churches teach is the same love and truth that the churches need to teach themselves, internally.

I would like one day to experience the churches going to Washington, DC, or a place that is filled with a lot of spiritual serenity or in a place that is full of nothing but serenity, love, and understanding. Now the whole place should be televised. With the experience to exercise more love and forgiveness toward each other. so that it can be televised so that the masses of people would experience, and exercise the true honesty of faith and love.

With the assumption of confessing their sins to the world and the injustices that the churches have done to the masses of people as well. Those injustices and sins that the churches have caused the masses of people.

The church has to use once again the same teachings that they have taught to others in their congregation, and in the masses of people's that is in the church themselves, and throughout the world. The churches need to be able to confess their sins, of what they have done wrong over the years to the masses of people.

So that the church can teach the truth about, God's divine Word to the masses of people in order to revitalize and correct the mistakes and the damages that the churches have done to mankind and masses, of people's spirit and soul.

I know when the church stands up proud asking the masses of the people in the world to forgive the churches for the sins, that they have committed and how they have caused them to stray away from God's Word.

When the churches are to confess their sins to the world, that is when the world can experience the miraculous consciousness of the churches. What is miraculous about the church's consciousness is when the churches confess their sins to the masses of the people. That is when the masses of people can experience that miraculous consciousness, that the churches preach and teaches about.

We must recognize that when the churches ask for forgiveness from the masses of the people. That is when the masses of people are able to experience, the true compassion of what the churches teach about God.

God's Word teaches about the confession that mankind should have toward God. But because the churches have destroyed and hurt the masses of people's relationship with God. It is time for the churches to become submissive to God's divine Word where the churches can acknowledge the wrongs that they have done to the minds and hearts of the masses of people.

In order that the churches through their confession will enlighten and reunite that spark that the churches need to bring the masses of people, in masses and large groups and numbers, back into the house of the Lord. I can tell you I don't consider myself a prophet, I considered myself a child of God.

But the one thing I can tell you is that will and act of compassion that the churches will exercise and display toward the masses of people that the churches have hurt and abused.

It will show the unconditional love and compassion that only the consciousness of the churches teaches. It is compassion and love, and it is the teaching of God's compassion and love that the churches teach that develops the churches' spiritual consciousness of the churches.

Now that is when the churches are now able to put their teachings into actions by first being an example of their teaching, on love, compassion, repentance, and forgiveness where they can express, that spiritual love toward the masses of people. That the churches have destroyed and abused, and been teaching about.

Now if the masses of people can sit back and forgive the church for the wrongs and injustices, along with the character assassinations, which the churches have exercised toward the masses of people, and the masses of people, are supposed to be sinful by nature and imperfect.

The question that comes to mind is if the masses of people forgave the churches for the wrongs, and injustice that the churches have caused the masses of people. That the churches have caused so much hurt and pain, and that hurt and pain that the churches have caused the masses of people.

Now the pain, suffering, and abuse that the churches have caused the masses of people. And the masses of people in the world were able to forgive the churches for hurt, pain, and suffering. And those people started coming back to the church, gracefully, and respectively, honoring the Word of God.

Now the question that comes to mind is who are the better people, the church people or the masses of people who have a sinful nature and are imperfect? Now think about this for a moment.

I would say from my perspective the people who have a sinful nature and is imperfect, by church's perspective have more of a spiritual perspective understanding and enlightenment. Sometimes better than the people who are in church.

That spark of faith, which comes from those people who, are Jude by the people in the churches. Seems sometimes to have a better relationship with God, than people who are in the church. Here is why their consciousness seems to develop more than the people who have rejected them from the church. Those are the people who have developed their bodies to be the edifice of the church. The physical bodies become a church or temple without walls.

Although the churches try to discourage them. The people who were discouraged by the churches became the true men and women of God. God uses us in different capacities of life. Even in the state of our rejections in life.

We can still be used and sharpen our spirituality through our own consciousness that brings us into atonement, fellowship, and in tune with God's consciousness, and it is through God's consciousness that those people who became edifice without walls use the discipline of their actions in order to produce their faith, in God.

That is why the people that the churches have abused have grown to acknowledge and understand the importance of consciousness, love, forgiveness, and compassion. These are the attributes that spiritual men and women should always have but in some cases could be a difficult time with people who attend church and are always referred to as church folks.

That love and compassion, which becomes the spark that is needed to resuscitate, revitalize, the spiritual consciousness, of the churches can only be achieved by the churches confession, to the masses of people, for the abuse that the churches have caused the masses of people. Now each person that is a member of a church that has caused so much abuse, to masses of people, needs to confess their sins to masses of people.

I mean the sins and confessions that the churches teach about, those same confessions that the churches teach about are the same confessions and sins that the churches themselves need to repent of because some of the churches are committing the same sins as the masses of the people are committing.

The same confession that the people in the churches teach needs to be activated in the same actions, in which the churches teach and express toward the people that the churches abuse and hurt. those lessons of forgiveness and compassion need to be practiced and exercised toward the masses of people that the churches have abused, and even destroyed their faith in God.

What is going is that people who go to church seem, to act like they are the best thing that ever happened to Christianity, since Jesus Christ. The majority of the time, some Christian people try to judge people, based on their standards, and not God's standards.

What church people need to do is judge people based on God's perspective, call reconciliation. Reconciliation is judging people based on the spiritual consciousness of the scriptures.

Here is what I mean. It judges people based on the awareness of the scriptures. It is using the awareness of the scriptures, in order to consciously and rightfully judge mankind, under the umbrella of the scriptures.

Not under what the people in church's own selfishness, of what they, think or feel is right or wrong. That power of judgment is only given to those people who are spiritually and consciously and faithfully develop their consciousness through God's divine Word. Mankind did not create each other in order for mankind to judge each other.

That is why mankind having the knowledge of God's consciousness can judge on under reconciliations. This is the statement that still holds true, about mankind's judgment toward each other, and that is when you judge each other, always remember. That you also have to remove the thorn, from your eyes as well, and stop trying to remove it from other people's eyes.

These are the same people who are constantly trying to break you down, now I am not talking to those people who are in the world. I am talking about churches folks, who have to confess their sin and beatitude to the masses of people, that they themselves have hurt, abuse, and destroyed.

You have a lot of actors in churches. Some dress the part every Sunday, smile on your face, but talk evil of you. I am talking about church folks. Those are the people who would sit down and as time goes destroy, the spiritual consciousness and faith in the church.

Some of those people are great performers in the church, you know like actors. They dress the part on

Sunday, but when people are not around those are the people that become the worst of the worse, disguise like the devil himself.

Trying to convince people that you are the most spiritual human being since Jesus Christ. That is not a God-fearing attitude or beatitudes or a Christian that is consciousness spiritually equipped, as a Christian. That is not projecting the consciousness of God in your life.

Some Christians people, try to convince others, how spiritual they are or other people that they have this powerful revelation from God. When in actuality, they are speaking in tongues. In actuality you can speak in tongues, you can heal the sick, but if you have no love that means that whatever you do for God, is in vain, or worthless. In other word whatever you are doing it is not done through faith, compassion or love. But pride and selfish desires and behavior. You have the belief of God, but your faith is not driven or motivated.

> If I speak in the tongues of men or of angels, but do not have love, I am only a resounding gong or a clanging cymbal. If I have the gift of prophecy and can fathom all mysteries and all knowledge, and if I have a faith that can move mountains, but do not have love, I am nothing. If I give all I possess to the poor and give over my body to hardship that I may boast, but do not have love, I gain nothing. Love is patient, love is kind. It does not envy, it does not boast, it is not proud. It does not

dishonor others, it is not self-seeking, it is not easily angered, it keeps no record of wrongs. Love does not delight in evil but rejoices with the truth. It always protects, always trusts, always hopes, always perseveres. Love never fails. But where there are prophecies, they will cease; where there are tongues, they will be stilled; where there is knowledge, it will pass away. For we know in part and we prophesy in part, but when completeness comes, what is in part disappears. When I was a child, I talked like a child, I thought like a child, I reasoned like a child. When I became a man, I put the ways of childhood behind me. For now we see only a reflection as in a mirror; then we shall see face to face. Now I know in part; then I shall know fully, even as I am fully known. And now these three remain: faith, hope and love. But the greatest of these is love. (1 Corinthians 13:1–13 NIV https://bible.com/bible/111/1co.13.1-13.NIV)

You can even heal the sick and have no love. God does not work through those types of vessels. Those vessels are ordained by Satan himself. The emotions that come with the power of love are what destroy the vessels of satan's evilness, and Satan Himself.

I say all of this is to bring us to this point, and that is. People are not looking for sermons anymore, although sermons are stimulating they bring joy and happiness to the masses of people.

What people do expect from the churches is consciousness and faith, which gives mankind the discipline mankind needs to be successful. Pastor, preachers, deacons, and bishops and their lifestyles should be reflected in the heart and minds.

As they express their spiritual consciousness. of the people in the congregation from the pulpit to the pews. In reality, many churches are destroying the image and likeness of God's consciousness and faith. At the expense of their greed and pride, people would destroy the house of the Lord for it.

In other words, people don't want the pastor to preach to them anymore because the majority of the pastors do not live up to God's Words or God's expectations of a pastor. Some pastors are preaching from God's Word, but they are not living up to God's expectations a pastor because God's consciousness is not in their minds and hearts anymore.

God's Word, it seems, is becoming nothing more than ritual and not a consciousness of power and authority that is driven by God's faith throughout His Word.

What people are looking for from pastors and ministers is to let their lifestyles manifest the words that they use to produce the messages from God and that they preach and teach to others but allow the words that they use to reflect the true reality of their faith in God and lifestyles that they live.

Pastors and ministers cannot preach the Word of God without doing what the Word of God is asking of them. The pastors and ministers can be very arrogant where they assume that no one can tell them what to do or what they are doing wrong. Some pastors and ministers would say to the congregation, "Do as I say and not do as I do," and this is when the pastors and ministers come into their comfort zone; that is the most dangerous place for pastors or ministers to be, especially when it comes to their faith in God.

The people worship pastors and ministers like they were the God that the same pastors and ministers should be worshipping. Now people are worshipping their pastors and ministers like they are God. They are giving them a false illusion. That is when the pride of the pastor or minister starts to become their own downfall.

Also, when people start to worship and praise their pastors or ministers, that worship and praising is what brings the pastors and ministers into mental state delusion that starts nurturing their pride, and we all know what comes before the fall: pride. That illusion can only be created by how much people have worshipped their pastor and how their pastors accepted the compliment rather than to give their praises to God.

The truth of the matter is when that pastor or minister starts to develop their own delusions that they are the people's god instead of God Himself, that is when their own delusions become their own reality, and when a pastor or minister allows their illusions to become their reality, that is a bad place for all pastors and ministers to be in, and that sometimes causes them sometimes to deviate from God's consciousness and forget their own relationship with God.

We must always remember that being a pastor or minister creates a different mission that comes with different perspectives. If most pastors or ministers adopt this perspective, they would be all right because I would say if you can teach it and you can preach it, then you should live it. So if pastors and ministers preach it, then you say it and you should do it; you should also live and lead by example to develop God's character that you have been preaching about and not letting this world influence the god that is in your hearts, especially the messages that they are preaching to the masses of people. Always remember when we compromise God's Word, when we manipulate God's Word for the convenience of the pastor's agenda and not God's agenda, the true essence of the manipulation of God's Word ends up manipulating the pastor's and minister's lifestyle, and that is what causes them to sin when they are trying to reach their own agenda.

The more the pastor or minister tries to manipulate God's Word, the more that pastor or minister deviates from God's consciousness, and when the minister or pastor deviates from God's consciousness, he loses the essence of his own spirituality; or may I say that is when mankind loses their own spiritual direction.

This, to me, is a bad place for any pastor or minister to be, especially in the grace of God. Here is what happens: the pastor loses the ability to think clearly, and that is what distracts the pastor or minister from focusing on God's Word, and this is when he or she starts to distort God's doctrine for their selfish gain.

The preacher's or minister's pride becomes his first stage of destruction to him or her in the faith of God. One of the things that I have come to realize is that there's a place that exists within all of us, some place where we cannot ever escape the reality of the thing that we have done that is wrong in this life, even if we are not a believer of God because it is unnatural and inhuman for us to do wrong. You see, it is not mankind's nature to hurt each other; it is mankind's nature to love and appreciate each other.

This is especially true with those wrong things that we have done to our fellow man and God. That place lies deep within our subconscious thoughts where mankind cannot escape the wrongs and injustices they have done to others, but it reminds the pastors and preachers of what they are doing that is wrong.

It becomes more prominent when mankind is struggling with a disease, such as cancer or other health issues. It seems this is the time where mankind is searching for answers of when they die where am I going to heaven or hell. That is when we begin to question life or death, and the more we question life and death, the more we realize it could only be defined, through the power of God's consciousness. Do you ever hear this question, "If you are a Christian and believe in God, heaven, and hell, then you should be able to die right now and go to heaven"?

What we need to acknowledge is the question of what heaven and hell have to do with, the consciousness of the person or people's faith in God. It is mankind's consciousness and belief that helps support God's truth. Now that belief and consciousness that mankind supports and believe, in should take mankind directly to heaven. The question with that statement is Heaven and Hell depends on how many times you begin to live life, through the spiritual consciousness and faith in God.

Heaven and hell is not a decision, it is not a philosophy, it is not a theology or It is not even a theory it is the reality of the choices mankind makes based on their consciousness and faith. Hell and heaven are places that mankind chooses based on their free will, or as some people would say, it is a choice mankind's consciousness makes.

That is when I would say and that is why I would say that heaven and hell are based on a person's state of consciousness.

God knows how to reach mankind's deepest thoughts because God created us in His image and likeness. Some people do not respect the idea that there is a heaven or hell. Pastors and ministers, I have noticed, do not preach and teach about heaven and hell. When I was child coming up, my mother sure taught me about heaven and hell, especially when I did what was wrong in life. And now I am writing those same things in life that my mother had taught me not to do as a child of God because of the teaching of heaven and hell. My mother chastised me when I did the things that were wrong.

Our subconscious is a quiet place in our minds that takes us away from the reality and the spirituality of life and lets us experience who we are, even when we sit there with deep thoughts, trying to rationalize who we are and the things that we have faced and the things that we are about to face in life where we are looking for a certain peace to resonate in our hearts and our minds and in our souls. It becomes one of the most dangerous places in the hearts, minds, and souls of Christians. It is deep, in our subconscious; most people refer to it as our inner self or where we find our true state of inner peace.

The inner self of the Christian is the true gateway to our soul that is more destructive to the Christian than anything that the Christian has to face in their life. I refer to it as a silent, destructive, dangerous, and deadly weapon that is related to the Christian faith. For example, our inner self is not a place where you can walk and escape from it. It is not a place where you can walk with friends and family; it's not a place where you can dictate what you should do; it's not even a place where you can touch it and feel it to know that it's there or has the pain and suffering you are going through.

Although your inner self does exist, it is a psychological perspective that has destroyed a lot of spiritual people's faith in God. Here is why: because if you're walking in your subconscious as a Christian or even a pastor or minister, you have to always take God with you.

It is a place where you can't touch it or feel it, but you do know that it does exists. It puts us in a position where we don't want to look into the eyes of reality and face our true presence of our own reality. Our inner self is the true reality that becomes the window of our hearts and souls.

Mankind has always felt intimidated by their true reality of life. The only thing that can cause mankind to defeat the reality of life and have enough confidence to face the reality of life is through the power of God's consciousness, which is able to transform our inner self into becoming that faith that we need to strengthen our commitment with God our father.

When a Christian is able to use God's consciousness in order to develop his awareness and knowledge of God's Word, he or she recognizes that it is through God's consciousness that allows that Christian to develop enough faith where he or she is able to come face-to-face with their own realities of life.

Mankind's faith becomes a problem when they become comfortable in their commitment with God. When men and women who are in a position of authority become comfortable in their faith with God, this has always been a dangerous place for lots of Christians. It creates a comfort zone that has stolen a lot of Christians' faith and salvation, including ministers and pastors, truth be told.

The question many people might ask is, what causes pastors or ministers to start to lose control over their faith in God? I would have to admit that the pastor's or minister's job is very difficult. Their challenges start with this one statement, and that is when they start competing with the world, wanting to have the same materialistic possession as those in the world or when the pastors or preachers start to act like the people in the world.

That is why we should always remember what God has warned us, and that is, "Be in the world but not of the world."

Here is another statement that feeds into the hunger of mankind's greed, and that is, "Let me see what I can get now before I die." Here is what sparks that pride in some pastors and ministers: it is when they appreciate the authority that comes with them trying to be a pastor.

For example, people might appreciate me for my ministerial authority that was given to me by God. But I want them to also experience how God has blessed materialistically. Now that mentality has shaped a lot of ministers' and pastors' characters to continuously have a good enough excuse to dwell in the sins of the world.

Yes, a lot of pastors and ministers have sold their souls to the devil or may I say that they are better massagers for the devil than for God. Here is why: because they are trying to convince themselves that they need material things to witness to the world about God when in actuality, they don't. What they need is only God's Word. God's Word is enough to witness to the masses of the people along with the pastor's character. The pastor's character is as important as a salesperson who is marketing a product for corporate America. But in this case, God's Word is the gift of salvation, and we are the marketers of God's faith, righteousness, and salvation to the masses of people.

Do you know why pastors arrive at this lifestyle? It's simple. This is when some of the pastors begin to compete with the material possessions of the entertainers, such as the movie stars, music entertainers, etc. This is when the some pastors, not all pastors but some pastors, are using excuses to get material possessions in order to keep up with the entertainers of this world. It also has to do with their pride and materialism that creates the greed that is in the pastors' or ministers' hearts.

Some pastors or ministers get very comfortable with their status as a pastor or minister. When this happens, that is when that pastor or minister needs to develop their spiritual consciousness to protect themselves from falling and when a pastor or minister does not fear God's Word anymore.

Here is why: because God did not reveal their sins to the world yet, so when the pastor or minister feels comfortable in their sins, that is when the pastor or minister does not fear God.

When I say fear of God's Word, I am making reference to the idea that the pastors and ministers have become so comfortable in their mess or their sins and what they are doing and what they want to do and not what they are being led to do by God.

When I make reference in the text about God's consciousness, I am acknowledging the idea that if a person or people reads God's Word, that person or people gains a certain type of wisdom that is transformed into knowledge. When that knowledge becomes the experience of a person's life, that experience is now matured into wisdom. That wisdom comes directly from God and is transformed into that person or people as knowledge. When I mentioned a certain type of knowledge, I am talking about a knowledge that teaches us about our spiritual self and how to deal with our physical nature and imperfections even as we pursue God's divine consciousness in our lives.

We learned about the burning desire of our physical nature, which we must also learn that mankind are spiritual beings experiencing a physical existence of life that is waiting for us to develop our spiritual consciousness in the image of God our creator.

We must also learn that our spiritual or spiritualism that we embraced has more of an impact on our salvation than our physical existence does. In other words, our souls are preserved through our spiritual existence with God. In other words, how faithful we are in the physical existence, trying to live a spiritual life, this is where our faith becomes so important to our spiritual experience in life.

For example, when we die, I was told that our souls are removed from our bodies, and God makes the final judgment on where we go, either to heaven or to hell.

It is through God's consciousness that we are able to extend our life beyond the mere physical existence of this life or even what we experience life to be, all because we stay in tune with God's Word. Staying in tune with God's Word is where we mature spiritually in God's grace through prayer and meditation and supplication.

Our spiritual existence redefines our nature while giving us a reason and purpose to live. The true nature of mankind is to live a life that would give mankind the opportunity to live in heaven with God. We must also remember that we live in our physical bodies, but our physical existence is limited in this world through God's consciousness.

God's consciousness transcends in our mind from the biblical knowledge that we read and through our hearts and minds. But it is through our souls that our spiritual essence of life becomes the energy of who we are as human beings. The soul of mankind is everlasting; it is the soul that is the energy source of mankind's existence, and that is what gives mankind everlasting life.

Here is why: when we die, we move into a more spiritual realm of existence. That spiritual realms allows us to experience God's Word in a more divine perspective because when the body is removed, the soul of mankind is in its true state of spiritualism.

When we are able to experience God through reading His Word and embracing His Word in our consciousness, that is when our faith causes us to experience God as our reality and not a figment of our imagination. It's interesting to know that faith helps determine our spiritual destiny and our existence with God, but it is our consciousness that secures our faith in God. Now when we submit to God's divine will for our lives, that is when we become physical beings with a spiritual consciousness to serve and please God.

# God's Consciousness in Our Lives

When we read and study God's Word and apply it to our lives, that is when God's consciousness becomes our reality of life, but as we progress in our physical life, we must understand that our ultimate understanding and comprehension of God's consciousness is based on our faith in God, which means that God is going to challenge our faith through our good and bad times. What I mean by that is, how is God going to challenge our faith? For example, many people asked this question: how do we know the prophets—like

Moses, Abraham, Joshua, David, Samuel, and the Apostle Paul—did not tamper with God's doctrine?

This is the question that many atheists ask Christians, especially when the atheists want to disprove the existence of God and God's message, especially the message that develops our consciousness. When God's consciousness exists in the hearts of mankind, it resonates the character and integrity of who God is in our lives.

The other is when the atheist is trying to prove to Christians if God's Word is relevant to our society today or if God's consciousness is still present in our society today. This is what I mean when I say that the atheist is trying to degrade God's consciousness within the hearts and minds of God's people or even assumes that God is not intelligent or God's Word cannot tell our future. Let get back to point about God placing man in the state of trials.

Trials strengthen our faith in God. They allow us to recognize who God is in our lives. Here is why: trials even allow us to recognize if we truly want to follow God or not.

For example, if you or me gave up on our trials, especially those difficult trials that are able to knock the wind out of our sails or those trials that are able to rock our entire world, then we were never serious about our commitment with God. We spend time speaking about how much faith we have in God until we come up against some tough trials.

We would testify and try to convince our congregation about how strong our faith is in God. We must always remember that the strengthening of our faith comes from our trials and how we handle them and how we use God's consciousness as a means to strengthen our faith in God, even in the midst of our trials. Sometimes what we say might sound good until our faith is tested and challenged by the evil desires of this world.

Instead of spending time developing our faith in God through reading and studying God's Word, we spend more time trying to impress people about how faithful we are in God's consciousness than spending time maturing in God's consciousness. When we spend time developing our consciousness, we are embracing the knowledge and wisdom of God where we can become submissive to the will of God through our state of consciousness and faith.

In actuality, their faith is shallow, and what they are trying to do is convince people that they are strong and truthful Christians that everything they say I want you to do is manifested in them through God, but in actuality what they want to do is impress other people and make them feel that they are the most spiritual person on earth. Some people might think that they are more spiritual than Jesus Christ Himself.

And those are the same people who are willing to take all the praises that Jesus Christ has done, but they don't want to take the crucifixion and the pain and suffering that Jesus went through on the cross to be Jesus Christ.

But we want to take Jesus His praises like we were the ones that actually did the work I mean the work that Jesus has done for the Father. Those are the people that resemble the Sadducees the Pharisees and the scribes who always want to impress people but never live in their own spiritual consciousness, and faith in God. They are like the Pharisees and Sadducees who always want to impress the public more than God. Here is why it makes people think that they are strong in God's faith while in actuality they are weak spiritually. The only thing that can bring them alive spiritually is if they become submissive to the will of God and try to develop their spiritual consciousness more, and spend more time studying God's divine Word. The key to a successful Christian relationship with God is constantly spending time in God's Word, trying to develop and mature in God's consciousness.

The people that we are trying to impress and make them feel like we are strong when the tough trials come and stagnate or disturb our faith in God, they are the people who are able to recognize the ignorance that those faking their faith was built upon which is nothing but sand, so when God places us through our trials, our integrity is developed through them. Our trials are the pain and suffering of our purity that exists within God's faith. Now if we prolong our trials, and if we are able to overcome our trials, if we are able to make up in our minds that we are going to overcome all of our adversities and adversaries, and if we are willing to wrestle with our trials in order for us to preserve our salvation with God, then we understand our spiritual potential that we are developing through God's, consciousness. Now that will satisfy the integrity that surrounds the true existence of God's consciousness that leads to God's salvation which exists in the transcending reality of mankind and God's divine essence.

Now if we adopt the attitude or beatitude that we are willing to wrestle with our trials, in wrestling with all the trials, we are going to give God the glory in the midst of our trials; now that is when we start to develop God's consciousness within our hearts and minds.

Now if we give up on God during our trials, it means that we were never serious about our commitment and relationship with God. Here is how trials strengthen our faith in God. It challenges our free will that God has given us. Your free will would allow you to make the choices you need to decide whether we can become successful in our trials or not.

For example, when God places certain obstacles in our lives, we have to be willing to use God's Word as the source to guide, instruct, and reinforce our free will, and in doing so, we have become submissive to God and to whatever God's will is for our lives. Do you think that God is using your trails as a message to minister to others?

One of the most important things about our trials is that there exists in our lives the opportunity to prove our loyalty to God. We can also look at it from this perspective, and that is we have trials in order to develop our potential so that we can improve and perfect our faith in God's consciousness.

It is very important for us to recognize that our trials have to do with our spiritual choices in our lives. Our trials also teach us the discipline we need to become aware of the choices that God has placed before us. Now that decision can only be decided on and based on how mature that person is in God's consciousness.

# The Consciousness of Our Faith

As we read God's Word and develop in His consciousness, we recognize and feel confident in God's Word. We begin to develop something called faith. Now faith is the spiritual trust that we develop from reading and studying God's Word.

That trust is transformed into something called faith. Faith is using God's consciousness to achieve both spiritual and physical goals in our lives that are able to transform our physical ability into the spiritual realms of God's consciousness. Let me define both faith and God's consciousness. First of all, it is a five-letter word that is powerful enough to transform any person's life to its fullest potential and spiritual existence in God.

I have faith because I know when we get into God's consciousness, I already understand that our Christian life is not just about reading and studying God's Word but placing the information that we learned from reading and studying God's Word into actions. Through our actions, we actually define our faith in God and our maturity in God's righteousness.

God's Word becomes the ammunition we need to fight the wars, battles, and obstacles that we are faced with every day, especially those wars that we fight in the state of principalities. There is a reason why God sends us through some trials. What would that reason be? That is a question that is asked by every Christian who has faith in God. I hope I can give a more clear answer.

First, we must understand that every trial that we are faced with develops our character and progress of our faith, and it is through our trials that we mature in God's consciousness. When God puts us through a trial or trials, He prepares us to develop the skills we need to advance with our spiritual walk with God.

Here is how you advance in your spiritual walk with God: one is through being submissive to God's will during the times of our trials. God uses trials as a means to prepare us for the next stages or phase in our spiritual lives.

Here is something we learn in the state of our trials, the true essence of God's grace and mercy, even in the midst of our trials. The one thing that you learn is how to handle your emotions in the midst of the storms that cause the trials.

Emotions are very deceiving because it is our nature to depend on emotion, but our wisdom comes when we are able to make decisions based on our faith in God, even in the midst of our trials. Every trial or trials that we encounter, we must always remember that it challenges our human nature. Our human nature appeals to our senses; our senses relate to our emotions.

Here is the point that I am trying to make. Our human nature and senses can only be disciplined through our trials. The information we need to overcome our sins is in the midst of our trials which come through God's Word.

God's Word gives us the wisdom and knowledge we need to overcome our obstacles in mist of our trials in order for us to become successful over trials; in other words, we can achieve success in our trials through God's consciousness.

What God wants to teach us in the process of our trials is that we need to let go of our human nature and free will and hold onto our faith in God while struggling with our trials. Someone would ask, why is it important to learn how to handle our emotions in the process of our trials? Because trials create a lot of pain and suffering that affect our emotions, but our emotions become a part of our human nature, just like our senses. When we are able to lean more on our faith in God and not our human instinct or human nature, we are rewarded through our spiritual growth and our salvation in God's consciousness.

We must understand that trial are like a burning flame that is hot enough to bend any piece of metal or gold, but they can still purify the subconscious of mankind's soul.

Our faith comes through our trials. For example, God shapes our character in the midst of our trials. Here is how God does it: God bends us, shapes us, molds us in His image by transforming us into what God Himself wants us to be.

So we can be strong and courageous. It's God who is able to bend us and shape us and transform us in the image and likeness that He would like us to be in, just because it is easier for God to use us and bring us close into our state of salvation. That is why when we are bent, broken, and damaged, God is still able to shape us in His image.

Here is why: it is God trying to let us experience how faithful we are to Him and not to the nature of ourselves.

God, who is all-knowing, already knows our spiritual limits better than we do. We don't know ours limits unless we are tested. What God is trying to do is let us experience within ourselves what our own spiritual limits are so we can better enhance our spiritual consciousness in God.

Please let me reiterate. Every trial that we go through is a shaping and bending of our integrity and character, just because God wants us to understand the importance of what true faith is in God. True faith is being able to bend, shape, or even try to develop an elasticity of faith in God.

Elasticity is the bending and shaping and stretching of our faith in order for us to become like Jesus Christ or manifest a faith-like attitude, just like Jesus Christ. Now let me be honest for a minute about trials, and I'm not writing this book to let you think that I am perfect when in actuality, I know that I am not, especially when it comes to my own trials.

Yes, God has put me through some devastating trials in my life, where I felt like crying, and some made me cry like a baby, but I have become victorious in my trials because I recognized that in the state of my patience is where I have gained the strength to become victorious over my trials.

There's an old saying that experience is man's best teacher, and the reason why I can identify with that statement is because I have experienced a lot of devastating trials that almost knocked me off my feet to the point where the trials have challenged my faith in God tremendously and where I felt like giving it all up. But for some strange reason, God has a way of allowing us to reflect on our past to let us experience where God has brought us from, and prepare in our minds how God wants to use us in the future to do great things for Him.

So when I mentioned and talked about trials, tribulations, and the crossroads of life, I am writing from my own experiences. This is when we try to figure out why God put us through so many trials, tribulations, and crossroads of life.

Sometimes our self-pity causes us to lose our faith in God. Here's why: we feel that God has put us through our trials and tribulations and the crossroads of life because He does not love us or we are not living up to God's expectations of what God's will is for our lives. Or sometimes we feel that we have fallen short of what God's will is for our lives.

Sometimes we feel that somewhere in our life that although we are living a godly life, somehow, we feel that we have embarrassed God so much that God is using our trials, tribulations, and the crossroads of our lives as punishment for our sins that we have committed toward God.

It is easy for us to think that way, but did we look at it from this perspective? Have we ever thought that there is beauty in our trials? Have we ever thought that there is a life lesson in the midst of our trial? Have we ever though that there is a form of maturity in our faith through our trials in God? Do you ever think that God is using your trials as a lesson for you to teach others through your trials? Do you think that God is using your trials a message to minister to others in the midst of your own trials?

God put us through trials for us to mature in our faith in God. I think God put us through trials to give us a light bulb moment in our lives. God does not have to use your sins as an excuse to put you through our trials. We are to constantly mature in God's consciousness through reading and studying God's Word.

Although our trials are painful, it seems that is what challenges our faith as well as our maturity spiritually in God's grace. Trials are stages of our growth and maturity. Our trials, tribulations, and crossroads of life are the most powerful lessons in our lives. We must also understand that trials and temptations are nothing more than spiritual obstacles. I mean those obstacles that are placed before us to challenge every ounce of your faith in God.

Trials are very sensitive and emotional. They bring out the strongest emotions in us as human beings. Our emotions can allow us to have confidence in God's consciousness than in our faith with God. I think the Apostle Paul so eloquently stated in Philippians when he said, "The things that I don't want to do I keep doing, and the things that I am supposed to do, those things I do not do."

You see, Paul is allowing us to recognize that sometimes our human nature takes precedent over what God's will is for us to do, and our biggest battle is trying to give up our emotions in the midst of our most difficult trials that we are facing.

So what God wants us to do is in the midst of all of our trials. He wants us to learn how to let go of our emotions and hold strong and steadfast to our faith because our faith is the foundation of God's consciousness. Our faith is the foundation of our salvation in God. Our faith is where we grow and mature in God's grace, mercy, and His consciousness.

But when we learn how to separate our emotions from our faith, this is when we start to overcome our trials, and we learn the importance of depending on faith. In this case, God is trying to teach us how to humble ourselves during our trials and does not let our emotions take control and take advantage of us in the midst of our trials.

Our emotions are part of our nature, but although our emotions are a part of our nature, it still does not give us the right to make decisions based on our emotions. How do we separate our emotions to make the right decisions according to what God wants us to do? Our faith in this case becomes the key component to how we are able to separate our emotions in life from our own true reality of what God has called us to do or make the decisions that we need in order to become submissive to whatever God's will is for us to do.

We can only make the right decisions that God wants us to make based on our faith in God, if we have faith in God's consciousness. One of the things that God wants us to experience as we progress in His grace is not to depend on our emotions but depend on our faith in Him.

So in this case, God is trying to teach us, even in our trials, to let go of all of our emotions and hold steadfast to our faith. In other words, God is not asking mankind to get rid of their emotions but to learn how to separate their emotions, so that we can fit in a consciousness state of mind, in order for mankind to reach their spiritual potential in God. What God is trying to get mankind to understand and experience is that your emotions exist based on your feelings.

Our feelings are where we understand and feel the presence of God and the Holy Spirit interacting with us through our spiritual consciousness and allowing us to use our faith as the action to overcome our adversities, trials, and tribulations in life. The other thing that God wants us to recognize is that feelings can be deceptive, depending on the trial or trials that we are going through at that time. Our emotions are a part of who we are. We learn about our emotions from the times that we come out of our mother's womb, especially when the doctor slaps us while faith is what we have to learn through God's consciousness. So it's more difficult for us to accept and try to develop and progress in the state of faith than for us to give up totally on our emotions.

This is when we need to recognize when God talks about us decreasing in our selfish ways, when God talks about us letting go of our selfish desires to embrace God's Word faithfully. This is when we start developing our state of consciousness in order to develop confidence. That we need to let go of all of our emotions and allow God's consciousness to increase in our heart, mind, body, and soul; and this is how we deal with how well we are maturing in our faith within God.

What God wants us to do as Christians is to develop our emotions in a sense of compassion, but not in a sense of deception. Later on, I will focus on the concept of deception and compassion as it relates to how we perceive God's consciousness.

What God wants us to do is hold on to our emotions and control them but hold on to His faith. We must use our emotions as a sense of compassion because during our trials, our emotions can make us feel sensitive, and it is our sensitivity that can sometimes distract us from what God is trying to teach us, even in the midst of our trials.

The weakness of all trials come because of our human nature instinct. If we depend more on our human nature, then we would become vulnerable to our sins. But if we are to focus more on our main goal, which is being submissive to God's consciousness during our trials, we would always become successful and victorious in our most difficult trials.

The question one would ask is, what is our main goal during our trials? Our main goal during our trial is to be able to use God's Word as the sword which cuts and pierces through our trials, giving us victory over our trials. That is why we must always keep God's Word close to our hearts and our minds because God's Word is the protector and armor that gives us the strength and is the foundation and strength of our spirituality and the development of our consciousness through God's divine Word.

# THE EMOTION OF OUR CONSCIOUSNESS

Some people worship God out of their emotional feeling than out of their faith in God. That is why we must understand God's consciousness well enough to know if we are making a decision based on our faith or based on our emotions.

All of our decisions when we embrace God's consciousness should become faithful decisions of God. Each trial or trials we go through is teaching us how to implement God's Word in our lives during our trials that we are faced with than us constantly depending on our emotions to make the decision that we are going through.

## *Trying to recognize our comfort zone*

In this race that we are running with God, we must always remember that we cannot become comfortable as Christians. We cannot create within ourselves or within our consciousness a comfort zone where we can relax and become secure in our commitment with God.

The only place where we can feel comfortable, even in our state of consciousness where we can develop a comfort zone that is spiritually secure, is when we embrace the faithfulness and righteousness of God through His divine Word. When we embrace God's Word in our hearts and minds, that is what truly shapes our faith in God. This is when we get to know who we are through God's divine Word, and this is where we even develop our true state of our divine consciousness. Our consciousness is developed through God's divine Word.

We cannot even become secure in our faith because we are constantly being challenged by the devil. Even those people who are not Christians can become comfortable. Here is why: the main goal of a Christian lifestyle is to study God's Word to develop your consciousness and act upon your faith to face your trials and adversities while developing your spiritual consciousness in God and, most of all, to mature in God's grace and His mercy in order for God to have compassion for others and decide on giving us the joy and peace and understanding of what salvation is to mankind

What does that mean? What does maturing in God's grace mean? It means that God don't want us to stay on the same level of faith that we started out with when we became Christians. We must constantly try to do the things which are needed of us to mature in our faith with God. These are the areas God wants us to mature in. First of all, God wants us to mature in our faith. God wants us to mature in our consciousness. God wants us to mature in our discernment. God wants us to mature in our character. And God wants us to mature in our spirituality.

The Christian life is not a life of convenience or personal choice. If anyone told you that the Christian is a life of convenience or personal choice, they did not get that information from Jesus Christ's lifestyle. He died on Calvary for the sins of the world.

Jesus Christ's life is a prime example of not living a life of choice and convenience. That is why Jesus died on the cross for our sins, and Jesus's death is the prime example that God, through His mercy and grace, even grants us salvation. If someone told you that the Christian life if full of choices and convenience, tell them to talk to Jesus Christ first because I know they did not hear it from Jesus Christ because Jesus Himself said, "Father, if this cup could pass."

The Christian life is the life where we must recognize that we have to stay in constant prayer and supplication to God. The Christian life is a life of submissiveness, and love toward God. The Christian life is a life where mankind has to stay focused, and in harmony, and fellowship with God.

In order for mankind to develop their own spiritual consciousness and awareness of the reality of who they truly are, in the scheme of God's creation, mankind has to stay consciously faithful in fellowship with God, and most of all, mankind must stay in constant prayer and supplication with God.

The Christian life is a life where we cannot take it for granted. The Christian life is a life that we have to live by example and by faith. Jesus Christ died for the Christian life. The Christian life is a life that reflects and becomes the example of Jesus Christ.

Jesus Christ's death let me repeat that the Christian life is a life with the example of Jesus Christ's lifestyle reinforces the spiritual essence and substance of Jesus Christ death we should live our lives like Jesus Christ live hits we read become martyrs of the gospel of Jesus Christ. Being Christlike means going back into the image that God has created us in. For example, it is going back into the image when God said, "Let us create mankind in our image and likeness of us."

It also means being Christlike and being submissive to God's consciousness, and whatever God's will is for our life, we should do it. I have heard this statement from the atheist's perspective and also from many theologians about trying to define how knowledgeable God is.

This is the same God, which also created every human being that exists upon the face of the earth male and female, from the essence and substance of the woman's womb, and it is through the woman's womb that the consciousness and spirituality were able to join the creation of mankind use the knowledge and wisdom of God to place organs in its particular or in its right place and consciously and to place a heart in the right place to place or mine's in the head of our creation.

It is the woman that God has used to be the key component of mankind's creation, and she is also the key to all of mankind's decisions that God has to make for mankind. The woman is the most powerful vessel and component in the world. Here is why: it is true her womb becomes the hands of God.

And every profit that God has created and set forth in His name came through the woman's womb. Read the book Women are God's by James Grant. It speaks about how the woman is the spiritual essence and substance of God's creation and mankind. This is the same God that created even the world that we live in; this is the same God that gives us life. This is the same God that we questioned His authenticity of predicting the future and our futures.

Here is the question: why does God put us through trials? Now to me, that is an honest and a true question. Many atheists would argue the fact that if God has to put me through trials in order to find out if I am worthy of His grace, then God does not know everything. What God does know is that in order for mankind to develop his spiritual potential to the full, mankind has to know his potential spiritually in order for mankind to recognize his own potential and for mankind to understand who he really is in the eyes of His own creator who is God. Then mankind would have the confidence to develop his faith in God. In other words, mankind has to know his own potential spiritually in order that mankind would be able to know how strong he is in God's faith.

Here is something we need to understand: when God puts us through trials, it has nothing to do with God not knowing who we are. In this case, when God puts us through our trials, what God wants us to do is to use our trials as the key to unlock the doors to our faith and our consciousness in order to get to know Him better. Trials also determine our commitment to God's faith.

We must also understand that our relationship with God is personal and with our personality that we develop from reading and studying God's authentic word, our character in God must be developed in our subconscious in order to let us know where we are in our faith with God.

When it comes to our trials, our trials are not trying to prove to God who we are and how strong our faith is in God or what we can be or what we want to be. You see, our trials are given to us by God based on our level of maturity and spirituality in God's faith. Here is why we go through trials: we go through trials to recognize where we are subconsciously in our faith with God and also to let us know how we are developing spiritually and faithfully and how we are constantly in fellowship and prayer with God.

Trials allow mankind to recognize where they are weak in their faith with God and to develop those areas that we are weak in in order that we can become better and stronger in our faith with God and work on the things that we need in order to enhance and strengthen our faith in God.

If I had to define trials, I would say that trials are our spiritual obstacles in life that we have to face in order to strengthen as well as develop our faith in God. The other perspective is we must realize that our relationship with God is personal. We must also recognize that because we have a personal relationship with God, it does not mean that we shouldn't be faced with some of the most difficult trials in our lives.

What is so interesting about trials is that God is using trials as a means to help prepare us to be used by Him. Let me also look at it from this perspective: trials also mean that God has recognized our presence and loyalty to him by letting us know that it is time for us to strengthen our faith and mature in God's grace, so each trial is a stage of spiritual growth in God.

# Understanding the Power of God's Consciousness

The one thing that I have come to realize is when we are discussing God's consciousness, we are trying to acknowledge God's transcending presence in our lives, which leads us to a serious state of submissiveness, a state that is submissive enough for us to understand what God's will is for our lives.

Before I move on further, let me bring some clarity and understanding to what I mean when I say God's consciousness. I am referring to being able to read God's divine Word and embrace His Word in our hearts, minds, and souls. But not only embrace God's Word but also try to put God's Word into action, allowing the actions of God's Word to become our true character and integrity and reality of our lives.

This is how we mature in God's grace by putting what we read into our consciousness and bringing God's Word to life through our character and integrity. When we read and apply God's Word in our lives, that is when we mature in God's grace.

As we mature in God's grace, we are constantly staying in tune with God's consciousness. Now because you are able to embrace the consciousness of God through His Word, this does not mean that you know God's mind. For example, in the book of 1 Corinthians:

> These are the things God has revealed to us by his Spirit. The Spirit searches all things, even the deep things of God. For who knows a person's thoughts except their own spirit within them? In the same way no one knows the thoughts of God except the Spirit of God. What we have received is not the spirit of the world, but the Spirit who is from God, so that we may understand what God has freely given us. This is what we speak, not in words taught us by human wisdom but in words taught by the Spirit, explaining spiritual realities with Spirit-taught words. The person without the Spirit does not accept the things that come from the Spirit of

> God but considers them foolishness, and cannot understand them because they are discerned only through the Spirit. The person with the Spirit makes judgments about all things, but such a person is not subject to merely human judgments, for, "Who has known the mind of the Lord so as to instruct him?" But we have the mind of Christ. (1 Corinthians 2:10–16 NIV)

The key that really unlocks the doors to God's consciousness is the person or people who are being submissive to God's will in their lives.

Please let me clarify something. Being in the state of God's consciousness does not mean that person or people actually know who or what God is thinking or can read God's mind.

What God's consciousness simply means is God has placed you in a position to elevate yourself from the mere physical existence of life into the spiritual realm of one's life existence. Now that sounds theologically correct. Here is what I mean: we exist on three dimensions—the physical, the spiritual, and also in the state of energy.

We as Christians, for some strange reason, we don't look at these three dimensions of our life existence. We think that there is only one, which is the physical existence, but we have the spiritual existence as well. The physical existence is where mankind has more control because mankind is able to control his free will in his physical existence of life. "We wrestle not against flesh and blood but against principalities and things unseen" (Ephesians 6:12).

Now the spiritual realm is where mankind has no control, when mankind gives his free will to God; that means that mankind is beginning to experience God's consciousness. That is where mankind is able to experience the spiritual existence of life.

Now the energy of our spirit is what reconnects us back to the Holy Spirit. We are all made up of substances which are blood, matter which is our tissue which are "from dust to dust we will return," and form is what determines who we are in life; for example, either male or female. Now our consciousness as human beings explains to us which road we should travel in life. Our trials and experiences in life determine which crossroads we are going to travel in life.

Now the Holy Spirit is that energy that transcends into our bodies and connects to the energy of our soul as the Holy Spirit and human soul connects. That is where God is able to work in us and through us. It is also at this point in our lives that we become submissive to God's will for our lives and start to develop our consciousness in God. That is why when we get the knowledge of God's consciousness, we are automatically connected to the Holy Spirit.

The transforming of Jesus Christ into the physical realm is how God the father has created us from substance, matter, and then forms us into a complete human being. This is what connects mankind's spiritual essence to God's consciousness. What I'm simply saying also is the wisdom that mankind embraces from God's consciousness is what psychologically and spiritually elevates mankind from a mere physical existence of life and places mankind into the spiritual realm, just because of God's consciousness.

## THE POWER OF GOD'S CONSCIOUSNESS

One of the only ways that mankind is able to know God is through God's Word. God's Word is what develops man's divine consciousness. As mankind's develops in God's divine consciousness and is able to mature, his faith increases rapidly in God's consciousness.

When we embrace God's consciousness through His Word, it does not mean that we know the mind and thoughts of God. It means that we are able to respect God's perspective. We are able to understand God's nature as it relates to God's creation and the discipline that comes with mankind being submissive to God's will through God's consciousness, and most of all, God's authentic power. And when I say God's authentic power, I am referring to the God who is powerful enough to destroy the world without fighting in a nuclear war but has enough grace and compassion in His omnipotent power to forgive mankind even of their sins; or may I say even when mankind himself sins against God.

Now being in tune with God's consciousness does not mean that you know the thoughts and mind of God. God's consciousness means that a person or people have been elevated into the spiritual wisdom of God.

Now here is the answer to that question because you have been elevated in the spiritual realms of God's wisdom. It does not mean that you know the thoughts and mind of God. What it does mean is that you are privileged as well as favored to embrace the consciousness of God because we have a more divine essence; it means that our life has a more divine purpose and reason for us to exist through God's divine presence.

Our consciousness of faith exists through our discipline in God. The one thing that I want to clear up is to let people know that mankind, with all of social, economic, social, philosophical, and religious issues, can never reach God's consciousness if mankind does not learn and study God's Word.

The question one might ask is, how does someone learn about God's consciousness? We learn about God's consciousness through the information that we gain knowledge from while reading and studying God's Word, which is the sixty-six books of the Bible.

Through studying and understanding God's Word, we are able to grasp God's character. We see God's compassion in His love for us and through our sins. We also take a look at God's mercy, and then we are able to experience God's grace. We are able through God's Word to get an awareness of who God is.

We also recognized how much of man's nature God would tolerate before mankind's action becomes a sin. Now if we are able to get an awareness of who God is, then that is the simplest way of defining God's consciousness to ourselves. We must also remember that our relationship with God is personal. Here is what is very interesting about God's consciousness.

God's consciousness gives us the ability to think like Him, be submissive to Him, but not to know the thoughts of His wisdom. God's consciousness gives us the security to develop and mature in our faith with God, have faith in Him, walk like Him, and be able to speak like Him.

God's consciousness is also able to give us the ability to heal the blind, make the cripple walk again, make the dead rise, even in their state of death. God's consciousness can give us the power we need to bring the dead back to life.

What makes the Bible different than any other book is that the Bible has a certain spiritual essence of wisdom that is not found in any other books. It is also God's authentic Word. Now an atheist might assume that is not the case because an atheist might assume that a book is a book because they don't understand God's salvation, God's mercy, and most of all, God's grace. And if we as Christians depend on the atheists and the people in the world to define the Bible through God's consciousness, then the Christians themselves have missed the whole concept of God's divine message for their life.

In actuality, the atheists are the ones that already miss the whole concept—or as some would assume, Christians are a group of naïve people, especially those who believe in God—because the atheist does not believe that this Bible is more than just a simple book. From my experience, I can tell you that the Bible is more than just some ordinary book that people read.

The Bible is a book of God's wisdom. The Bible is a book that talks about what it is that God loves and dislikes. It is a book of elevating one's self to become better within one's self awareness of God. The Bible is a book where mankind has the potential to elevate himself or herself to reach the potential of God or even seek the "why" in God's will for mankind to do.

The Bible is the only book that is inspired by God. The Bible is a book that can develop the consciousness of mankind and transform mankind's mind into a spiritual state of one's divine consciousness and existence. Mankind's consciousness does not stop there. It evolves into giving mankind a reason and being. That reason and being needs to become submissive to the will of God, and because we become submissive to God's will, we start progressing to a state of God's spiritual presence.

Also, the Bible puts us in a spiritual perspective and gives us an understanding of what life is all about with the intention to recognize that we are more of a divine being than just a people with a physical existence.

The Bible is a book which give us the ability to recognize that there is more to life than our present existence here on earth. Personally, from my spiritual experience, that is how I experience the Bible to be. When we embrace God's doctrine, we become in tune with God's consciousness.

When we talk about God's consciousness, we are referring to a divine awareness that God has instilled in our hearts and mind, and that is what gives us the privilege to better understand God's grace and God's mercy. All of that comes with a package, and that packaging is to understand God's wisdom enough for a person or people to consciously develop enough of themselves to be rewarded the gift of salvation through their salvation in God's grace.

Salvation is the divine reward that God has promised us. That is why we must always remember that God's Word cannot be compromised nor manipulated to satisfy any person or people's religious agenda. What is God's doctrine? God's doctrine is the sixty-six books of the Bible. I would say because of God's consciousness; it is God's consciousness that brings the awareness of mankind's beliefs into a transcending power that reflects the consciousness of mankind's faith and wisdom in God in his life.

The question one should ask is how does one achieve God's wisdom? It is not something that you see nor is it something that you hear nor is it something that you do nor is it something that you can achieve by yourself. It is something that can be attained through the rigorous studying of God's doctrine that we are able to gain God's consciousness through His doctrine.

But what do you mean, Brother James Grant?

This is what I am referring to: the Apostle Paul told Timothy in the episcopal, "Do your best to present yourself to God as one approved, a worker who does not need to be ashamed and who correctly handles the word of truth" (2 Timothy 2:15).

Here, Paul is telling Timothy to do his best. God is not looking for perfection in us. God just wants our best, and your best is enough, even in your state of imperfections. God can take our imperfection and make our imperfection our greatest aspirations for Him, and that is defined through our consciousness and faith in God.

What God is trying do is get the best from us, even in our state of imperfection.

That is why we cannot judge our brothers or sisters, even in their state of imperfections or their sinful nature because we don't know what God's potential is for that person. We don't know what God's will is for that person. That person can become more submissive to God than those people who are judging him or her. What God can do is bring us from any state or condition of life and elevate the consciousness of mankind into becoming a spiritual being.

This paragraph seems to be my life story. It seems that you have been overlooked because people might be afraid of what you have to say, although what you have to say edifies God's kingdom. People are looking for a passive people. As much as people want to hear the truth, it seems that they don't want to be reminded of the truth itself. Here is why the truth itself makes people responsible to the Word of God.

Yes, the best that we can give at that time so we can mature in God's grace is we should recognize that whatever we do, we should give God the glory. God wants us to do our best, and when we fall short of God's Word, just like everyone does, including myself, this is what God wants us to do. He wants us to have enough of a consciousness to accept the wrong that we have done and ask Him forgiveness. It is through God's grace and mercy that we are forgiven of our sins.

One of the most beautiful things mankind has is how God is able to understand our sins enough, where God is able to exercise His grace and mercy toward us, putting us in the state of forgiveness. It does not matter the degree of the sin or (sins) nor the degree of God's forgiveness.

If we have enough faith in God's consciousness, we can look the devil in his eyes and have the power through our faith in God's consciousness to defeat and acknowledge every move and decision the devil makes. The knowledge of God's consciousness is the power that would always defeat the devil at all measures of our life. Even when the devil is at his greatest moment in our lives or even when the devil is impacting our lives, even when the devil is at his greatest moment, we can defeat the devil if God's consciousness is in our hearts and minds.

The reason why many Christians lose their battles with Satan is we are not prepared. Here is why we are not prepared: because we are not putting on the whole armor of God, just some of the armor, and the some of the armor that we have put on is not enough to protect us in this day and time from Satan's attacks on us.

Now with God's consciousness, we can give the devil enough of the hell Satan wants to place us in, and by using God's consciousness, we can put Satan in the hell that Satan has been preparing for us and the people of the world all of our lives. When Christians stay in constant fellowship with God or in tune with God's consciousness, the Christian faith can become very strong that you can become the devil to Satan.

Many pastors, theologians, and biblical students would wrestle with this statement, whether this statement is true or not true. This is a rhetorical statement, and that should be when do Christians become the devil to Satan? When Christians are able to stand firm in their belief and when a Christian becomes the devil to Satan, that is when the Christians are able to use God's divine Word and their faith in God to overcome their trials and temptations that the devil has placed upon the men and women of God.

Here is what I mean when I ask the question, When does a Christian become the devil to Satan, not God? Or when do God make mankind the devil to Satan? When the faith of mankind become strong, faithful, and righteous enough, where the evil desires of Satan cannot penetrate or even shake or destroy mankind's belief in God all because of mankind's confidence, belief, and love for God?

Also when Satan's temptations cannot penetrate or distract the Christians' belief that he or she has in God. That is why it is very imperative that the Christians stay focused on God's divine Word. When the Christians study God's divine Word, that Christian is able to become the devil to Satan.

The Christians become the devil to Satan when that Christian becomes the angel to God. Here is why, if the Christian is able to use God's divine Word as a tool to work through they sinful nature and imperfections to overcome Satan's attacks and his trickery, that is when the Christian becomes Satan to the devil.

That is when we all can say that the Christian has become the devil to Satan, just like Satan is the devil to mankind. The Christians become the devil to Satan when Satan does not have any control over the Christians' belief in God.

First of all, we acknowledge that Satan uses evil; we must also acknowledge that Satan is the devil and the devil we refer to is Satan. Satan did not get the name Satan or the devil because the evilness that causes mankind is wrong but yet challenging to mankind's faith in God.

All of that is referred to as the evilness sinfulness of Satan. Satan strives off evilness. Some people refer to Satan the devil or as the creator of all evilness. The devil hates all the goodness, love, compassion, and God's forgiveness of mankind that God has bestowed upon mankind.

Anything that contradict God's Word such as theology, theory, and philosophy, satan is always willing to exercise his sinful nature toward God and mankind.

When the devil cannot use his sinful nature to entice mankind's imperfection and sinful nature, that is when mankind is able to reflect on Satan who mankind also referred to as the devil and has something we call a devilish's spirit nature.

Now when Satan becomes frustrated and deviant with God's people, who are being submissive to Satan's desires and temptations, that is when mankind is becoming the devil to Satan himself.

All because the Christian brothers or sisters prefer not to become subjective to Satan's temptations or attack on them, that is when the Christians acknowledge to Satan that they are the devil to Satan himself.

It is like becoming Satan to the devil himself while rejoicing and acknowledging God's divine Word as the tool which works its way through all the pain and suffering that Satan is trying to cause you because you are spiritually endowed. We must also remember that Satan do not challenge those people who are not spiritually in endowed.

When Satan realized that his evilness and satanic deception is not able to penetrate or destroy the Christians' belief and faith in God, especially those Christians who have strong enough faith in God, they can withstand Satan's attacks.

It is like giving Satan the same hell that he is trying put you into and is the same hell that you are putting Satan in. So that is when I say when a Christian is able to withstand Satan's temptations, that is when a Christian becomes the devil to Satan especially when Satan cannot shake the foundation or faith of the Christian's faith.

When a Christian overcome the adversities in the principalities of Satan, that is when the Christian's spiritual consciousness is giving the devil back the hell that he is trying to put you in and is the same hell you have put him in when you keep your consciousness focused and discipline on God. That is what I also referred to as the power of God's consciousness.

Every time that you overcome a trial that Satan is trying to tempt you with, that is when you are giving Satan the hell that he is trying to give you, and that is when you are putting Satan through the same hell he is trying to put you through. Once again, that is what I referred to as the the power of God's consciousness.

When the Christian is able to use their faith as a weapon to stand firm in their belief in order to protect themselves against Satan's attacks and influences, it is not a theological theory or even a philosophical belief. It is an exaltation of the power of the Christians' consciousness in and through God's Word.

This is when a Christian becomes the devil to Satan when the Christians are also able to use their faith and God's Word to defeat and defend themselves against Satan's attacks.

What we are accustomed to is Satan being the devil. But the Christians become like Satan while using and uplifting themselves spiritually in God's Word and defending themselves toward God.

Some people would call this statement a reverse psychology; we have a Christian who is so strong in the belief that when Satan tries to tempt him or her, they can withstand Satan, look Satan, and let him know that they are stronger than Satan himself.

Just like when Satan starts to tempt us, we don't want Satan to tempt us; we don't want Satan to win overall temptation or trials when you're strong in your faith. You can turn around and say to Satan, because I was not submissive to your will or what you wanted of me to do in the mitts of your temptations, Satan I still disobeyed you. I was not a subject nor a product. Satan becomes submissive to your will during my time of temptations.

So that is when we make the statement that we are giving Satan the same hell he is trying give us, and Satan is also trying to lock us away in. So that is when I would say we are giving Satan the same hell that he is trying to give us and all of God's people in. And that is when a Christian becomes the devil to Satan. When that person's consciousness and faith is so strong, the evilness of Satan cannot penetrate the the Christians's spiritual life.

Here is why because mankind study and develop their consciousness state of mind, which becomes the strength of mankind's faith. When mankind believes in God's faith and is able to apply God's divine Word to their lifestyle and when mankind is able to define their character and integrity through God's consciousness and walk the talk of God's consciousness in their lives.

Any Christian that walks with such power and authority is giving Satan back the same hell that he is trying to give them and place them in. That is when the Christian or Christians become the devil to Satan himself.

When mankind develops their consciousness their wisdom, understanding, and knowledge of their true faith in

God, it develops the power and strength of mankind's faith and spirituality, and it is that position that all Christians men and women can say to Satan that they are the devil to Satan.

It is like when someone or some people are trying to manipulate or control, you to do the wrong thing. It is because you already know that it is wrong.

The question you ask yourself is if you don't want to do something because it is wrong, why are the people who are asking you to do wrong is getting upset and frustrated?

They even start swearing and trying to manipulate you especially out of their selfish desires. Just like Satan does, it is the same here when Satan is trying to tempt mankind.

When mankind's consciousness is rooted in God's faith, mankind is letting Satan know that they can be the devil to Satan and that is when mankind is able to be the devil to Satan.

# THERE'S POWER IN GOD'S CONSCIOUSNESS AND CREATION

One of the things I think many Christians take for granted is the power we have through God's consciousness. Through God's consciousness, we can achieve anything that is granted to us by God. We serve a God that created (Hebrew: *Bara*) the world, placed the moon and stars in skies, created the waters of the world, like the oceans and the lakes. I think sometimes we forget about the power of our God and the resources God has placed before us for us to be comfortable in this life.

The reason that we do not recognize the power we have in God is because we take God's power for granted. Here is what I mean: because we have taken God's Word for granted, sometimes it could be that we have not had enough trials in our lives in order that we would recognize through our trials how powerful God is in our lives. The most important thing that Christians need to recognize is that in order for mankind to develop their confidence and faith in God, mankind has to be determined to study God's divine Word. When mankind studies God's Word, the studying of God's Word keep mankind in tune and in fellowship with God. When mankind stays in tune and in fellowship with God's divine Word, that is when mankind is able to develop the potential of their faith in God. If Christians do not have faith in God, then that Christian(s) does not understand the strength of their faith in God. Or could it be that we reached a point in our faith with God where we don't value God's love anymore? Instead, we value the love for material possessions?

The material possessions that we value are the same material possessions God has created. We should never forget that God made mankind responsible for everything that He created, including mankind. Everything that exists within the human experience comes into existence because of God's authentic creation.

The creation that God created, mankind duplicated it. In other words, mankind can never be created. Mankind is the imitation of God's creation. Everything that mankind does is nothing more than an imitation of what God has already done. For example, let us look at the process that mankind has to go through in order to procreate. It takes mankind nine months to achieve what God has done in less than a blink of an eye.

There is a statement that people have a tendency to acknowledge, and that is why would God create mankind in His image? The question can be answered based on us trying to look at it from a spiritual perspective rather than a physical one. When mankind was being created in the likenesses and image of God, this set the tone for a particular interest of God's consciousness as it relates directly to mankind's creation. We are created in the image of God, but our soul and spirit is embraced in substance, matter, and form, which is our physical body.

So let me reiterate this statement, and that is we are all physical beings with a spiritual potential to develop our inner selves and characters in the spiritual image and likeness as God. This helps validate that God knew us and gave us a purpose and a reason to exist way before we were created here on earth in order for us to better identify with our reason and purpose to exist through God's consciousness. Here is why: "Before I formed you in your mother's womb, I knew you before you were born I set you apart; I appointed you as my prophet to the nations" (Jeremiah 1:5).

The consciousness is where we are able to comprehend what is God's purpose and reason for our existence. The key that unlocks the secrets to our purpose and reason lies in the doorway of the pages of the Bible. Our purpose and reason are manifested in what God's will is for our lives.

This is why we asked the question, what is God's will for our lives? That is our spiritual consciousness that develops our reason and purpose to exist. When we ask that question—What is God's will for our lives?—we recognize that there is a maturing process that one has to achieve in the presence of God.

That spiritual maturity is what allows us to stay in tune with God's consciousness as we embrace God's will in our lives through His consciousness. As we reach that point in our lives, we are acknowledging our spiritual existence through God's grace. Our spiritual existence defines who we are in the image and likeness of Jesus Christ.

When we speak of God's will for our lives, what are we making reference to? First, we are making reference to recognize that we must give ourselves totally to God. We have to give up our will in order for us to achieve perfection within God's consciousness. One of the most difficult things in our lives is trying to give up our will. We must develop enough consciousness to accept God's will for our lives.

Even in relationships, even our children struggle with parent discipline versus their own free will. We know as children how difficult it is at a certain age for us to give up our free will. We all were once children. We had a difficult time listening to our parents. Marriages are broken up because someone in the relationship feels vulnerable if they give up their free will to the other person. I think in American society, with laws governing our lives, we have morals and we are deep rooted in our culture.

Still we struggle with giving up our free will. When a person gives up their free will, we must also remember that their free will that they are giving up must become discipline in order for mankind to become successful in their spiritual walk and growth with God's consciousness.

## THE POWER OF GOD'S CONSCIOUSNESS

A person has to love God enough for them to give up their free will and appreciate the discipline it takes for them to give up their free will and follow God. Here is a very interesting question. How does one give their free will to God? And why would anyone want to give up their free will to God when they have never seen God nor even have enough knowledge of God's divine presence in their life?

To me, that is a very honest question that deserves an honest answer. Those questions bring clarity to God's Word, and it shows honesty in that person's character to even have the courage to step out and ask such a question.

Now here is my response to that question: we have a tendency to find God in the midst of our struggles or problems in life. When we find God in our trials or difficult times, are we using God as our pacifier? Or are we seeking God out of our desperation because we want the pain and suffering of our problems to end? Or are we truly seeking God's love?

That answer can only be answered based on our trials, temptations, and how well we handle our trials and temptations, if our trials or temptations defeat us, and we return back to our sinful ways. Those were the people who were using God as a pacifier and crutch. The people who were using God were never interested in serving God as their personal Lord and Savior. They thought they were using God just to overcome their problems for that particular time that they were in their state of pain and suffering, and then we go back to our normal way of life again, repeating the same thing over and over again. Every time we have problems, we use God as our pacifier, and not to develop ourselves spiritually. God knows how honest our hearts are;

that is why God allows us to go through our trials and be tested through our temptations.

It's interesting to me sometimes how an atheist can find God even in the midst of his or her struggles. They sometimes meet God at the end of their intersections of life with God being at the intersection of their crossroads in life.

Many people act like they don't know God but wait until they are faced with some serious trials, especially when our loved ones are involved in some of the trials and tribulations that they are facing in life or even when our relatives or close friends have died.

That is when God's compassion, grace, and mercy is challenged and questioned by the reality and conditions that truly affect man's existence and his or her perception toward God. In other words, we find God sometimes through the chaos of this world, through the trials of this world, through the struggles of this world, and through the reality and adversities of this world.

I think Christians have a tendency to have a more disciplined relationship with God. I am not making reference to a more faithful relationship with God. When I say discipline, I am making reference to the idea that they pray only when they are going through trials because sometimes, trials have a tendency to make us give up our free will, including the atheist. Between an atheist and Christian who experience pain and suffering during their trials, the Christian becomes more disciplined and faithful to God while going through their trials.

Here is the simplicity of defining God's will: the will of God means acknowledging that there is a direction that we want to achieve with our lifestyle. Now that direction comes with a process of how one is able to mature and grow in their discipline with God.

Discipline is a state of submissiveness that is expected of us through our divine consciousness that we have in God. Our consciousness develops our integrity and character of how we actually define God or perceive God to be. Our discipline is a reflection of our behavior as well as our personality toward how we define God by our actions. When we become submissive to God's will, we are actually embracing God's consciousness.

We must understand that although we embrace God's consciousness, how do we know how strong our faith is in God? How do we know that we are striving to develop the discipline we need to follow and stay strong in God in faith? How do we know how secure we are in our relationship and fellowship with God? We can only achieve this based on how successful we are in our trials through our faith and discipline toward God.

# THE DIFFERENCE BETWEEN OUR TRIALS AND OUR SINS

In this chapter, one of the things I would try to do is define the difference between a sin and a trail. Now the other question is why God would put us through trials. Second, our trials become a sin when we lose focus of God's consciousness while we are going through our trials. Now let me bring some clarity to the statement about differences between trials and sin.

If we are serious about our commitment with God, it does not matter about the outcome of our situation while we are going through our trials. Let me phrase it in this manner: if we are very serious about our relationship with God, then let us assume we are not successful in our trials. This might be a good place for me to interject this statement that makes reference to the difference between being tempted and being faced with many difficult trials while we are going through our trials and being faced with our temptations.

We must always remember during our temptations that the success of any trial deals with our temptations. We must always remember that our sins and trials are temptations.

But in the mist of our temptations, we are once again strengthening our own spiritual consciousness, so we can take the right action and responsibilities that we need to exercise through our faith in God that we have embraced from God's divine Word.

Now stay with me for moment. It's a very interesting position here, but let me bring some clarity to the question about what is the difference between being tempted and going through a trial. Temptation comes from Satan, and a trial is from God. Temptation is a convincing act or thing that Satan wants you to do. Anytime that you do something against God's Word or you do something to disgrace God's divine Word, that, my friend, is the temptation from Satan. Satan always influenced mankind to sin, and it mankind's sins that Satan uses to challenge whatever God's will is for mankind.

So whatever good and spiritual thing that God has placed in the consciousness of mankind, it's mankind's responsibility to use every available resource that God has given to mankind, for mankind to become spiritually equipped to do battle with, Satan and his angels.

Here are some of our spiritual resources. Like prayer, submissiveness, obedience, love, compassion, these are the things we need to do in order to stay in constant fellowship with God. Even in our own state of adversities, and trials.

Mankind's consciousness is developed not only by the Word of God but the experiences that mankind goes through even in the mitts of the pain and suffering mankind, that mankind receives from experiencing their own trials and adversities in life.

Mankind's maturities do not only come from the good things of God. Mankind's developmental stages of growth and maturity come also from the bad experiences mankind has experienced, received, while in the midst of mankind's trials, and tribulations.

It is our consciousness that lets us know that because God might not come on time, that God is still time friendly. Here is what I mean. To mankind, that means that God might be late, on answering mankind's prayers. I think sometimes the people of God forget whom they are serving. Sometimes the people of God lose confidence, in them having confidence in God's consciousness. In other words, we serve a God that owns and control the universe and everything that is in the universe.

It is God who controls the air from now until infinity, everything that exists in the universe comes through God and is around Him, God controls and can change the disposition of the universe to fit into your prayers. This is the power of God's grace and mercy that mankind sometimes forgets they have.

If you are not staying God's Word, if you are not studying and meditating and not in constant fellowship with God at some point in your life, you are going to forget the power your Father has manifested in you and through you.

If mankind does not study God's Word once again, it is easy for mankind to forget the power, that mankind has inherited, from God your father. That is your inheritance that Jesus Christ has died on the cross just for you to have, the love, and compassion, and mercy, that God's mercy, grace, and forgiveness of the father who is God Almighty have in stored for us as his children.

We must also remember that Satan's job is to destroy mankind's salvation. Let me say that again, Satan's job is to destroy mankind's salvation. Satan's biggest weapon is to challenge, mankind in the state of principalities, and things unseen to the physical world in which mankind exist.

The question someone might ask is why would Satan use principalities and things on seen in order to challenge mankind's faith and consciousness in God. Here's why: mankind's spirit and soul are embraced in mankind's physical body.

So 99.5 percent of mankind's realities exist in the physical reality of mankind's life. Everything that mankind does is physical. What mankind comprehends or understands is all physical to mankind's reality.

Now the only way that mankind is able to unlock the doors of the spiritual world is, through embracing and studying constantly God's divine Word. The key to unlocking the doors to the spiritual world is in the essence and substance of mankind's consciousness. It is not in mankind's faith. Here is why faith is the actions of mankind's consciousness being displayed from the knowledge, and wisdom that is in God's Word.

But the principalities and things that are unseen to the evilness that mankind faces is in the spiritual world, which surrounds mankind's physical existence. But still, mankind cannot comprehend or understand, anything that exists in the spiritual world.

It is the spiritual world in which Satan is able to manipulate mankind very easily, but the only thing that gives mankind its true reality of Satan, in the spiritual world. Where mankind can comprehend and understand the spiritual world, is the consciousness, that mankind gets from God's divine Word. That consciousness which mankind gets from God's divine Word is what helped shape and carve mankind's consciousness to become the true reality of mankind's faith.

That is why it is very important for mankind to constantly stay in tune, and in focus, and in fellowship, with God's Word. Here is why, because it's mankind stay in focus and in fellowship with God's Word being in mankind's heart, and consciousness, mankind is able to discern, the evilness that exists in the state of mankind's principalities, and things that are unseen to mankind's physical existence.

The weapon to a successful Christian life is studying God's divine work constantly praying for God's will to be done in your life and walking faithfully every day in the eyes of God this is the key weapon. That would destroy all of Satan's evil desires to destroy mankind's Satan attacks and trickery, which Satan uses to destroy mankind's salvation in God.

God's Word is what elevates mankind into becoming a being. That is why mankind has to always keep their consciousness, sharp intact, and allow their consciousness of God to become the true shield, and weapon that Satan uses to destroy mankind's salvation in God.

That is what strengthens our consciousness and our faith in God. That is why it is very important that we stay constantly in tune with God's divine Word and in fellowship with God. That is the only thing that mankind has once again to overcome Satan's attacks and temptations.

But the outcome of both the trials and temptation is that you use every ounce of your faith and discipline that God has given you to overcome your trials and temptations. One position is that you are being tempted, and the other is you are being tested. But the outcome is that you have to use every ounce of your spiritual consciousness to overcome your trials or temptations.

I think sometimes we try to place titles on people. We view people based on their status. We have a tendency to appreciate people more based on their economic status, which brings me to this point about what is the difference between a trial and a temptation. Now a trial means that God has placed the obstacles or adversities and sometimes our adversaries in our lives, just to challenge our faith in Him. We must also understand that we are tempted in the same manner, just like Job has been tempted.

As Christians, our job in the midst of our trials or temptation is to become successful in both our trials and our temptations. Some people would assume that both trials and temptations are the same. Some people also feel that trials come from God while temptations come from the devil.

Whatever we think about our trials and temptations, our major emphasis, even in our trials and temptations, is to use God's Word as the sword to fight and defend ourselves against our trials and temptations. And as we gather knowledge from God's Word, we must embrace God's Word to become our consciousness where we can strengthen our faith and spiritual consciousness in order for us to withstand our trials and temptations and in order for us not to become vulnerable to our temptations or trials.

The success of our trials depends on how strong our faith is in God. Let us assume you are in a difficult trial or temptation, and your trials and temptations got the best of you, and you did not become successful in your trial or temptation.

Your trials and temptations, they have defeated you. You were obedient to God's Word. Your discipline toward God's authentic Word was well-structured. When I say structured, I mean you get up early in the morning about 3:30 or 4:30 and pray.

You participated in all of the church activities; you made sure that everyone that was sick, you attended to them, even in the state of their sickness. You even sent cards out to those who visited the church that Sunday and those who were sick. You ended up doing your due diligence as a member of God.

All of a sudden, one tough trial or temptation comes and knocks you off your feet, causing so much pain and suffering. This is when you realize how important it is for you to still have the courage to stay consistent in God's consciousness. Yes, even when you sin in the eyes of God, you still have victory over Satan. As long as your sins do not take you into the grave before you repent, God's grace will forgive you of your sins.

Let me elaborate for a moment. In other words, you have many opportunities to be forgiven of your sins, but you only have one life. You have many opportunities to be forgiven and mature in the sins that you have committed, but you only have one life.

I need to make an explanation when I say mature and grow in your sins or sin. I am not making reference to a person becoming better at their sins to ask God of His forgiveness. What I am making reference to is that we have come to a point in our spiritual maturity where we recognize that we can no longer continue to keep drowning and committing the same old sin(s) because when we start using excuses for our sins, we will never ask for God's forgiveness, and even if we ask God's forgiveness, we are not serious enough to change our sinful ways. That means that we love to sin more than we love God's actions of forgiveness. Is there any sin in this life that is worth more than God's forgiveness and consciousness? That is the question I need to ask. Please let me reiterate again that it means that we love the sin more than we love God's forgiveness it also means that we love to send more than we love our salvation. When our salvation is in the state of our forgiveness, it is sin that some people still prefer over their forgiveness. That means that we choose hell over the forgiveness of our sin.

Two of the most important things that God has for us, because we stay steadfast in God's consciousness, is His grace and mercy. God's grace and mercy adds up to one of the most divine and spiritual essences that shapes the characteristics of mankind, which is God's compassion and His love for mankind, even when we fall short in our walk with God.

Mankind tries to look for perfection in each other while God, who created us, looks for our imperfections. Again, let me remind you God is not looking for perfection in a person. God is looking for those who are faithful to Him. The idea is to admit that you recognize that you have sinned against God and you actually have done wrong and you have sin, acknowledge that you have sin, and want God's forgiveness, and you want to become in tune with God's consciousness.

Your first step after acknowledging that you have done wrong is to pray and ask God's forgiveness while praying and asking God to give you the faith and strength to endure in case the same situation or circumstances arise again that cause you to sin.

It means that you would have enough experience from your previous sin not to consistently commit the same sin or sins again, and when you sin, you should stop worrying about your sin and pray while using every ounce of your faith to pick yourself up and focus your energy on trying to ask God's forgiveness and move onward with your life.

Through repentance, that is God's character that displays His compassion, grace, and mercy toward mankind. As a human being, I can never comprehend God's understanding of repentance. How can the I in me define repentance? What is repentance?

Repentance simply means that I recognize that I have done wrong, I recognize my sin, but we (I) want to get back in fellowship with God. The first stage of forgiveness is to acknowledge it, is to acknowledge that I have done wrong, and allow God's grace and mercy to place me back into fellowship with God's consciousness.

Now the question that one might ask is, how do we know that God is going to forgive us of our sins? The answer to the question is that we don't know if God is going to forgive us of our sins.

What we do know is there is a process through God's consciousness that all the people who have sin have to go through in order that we can recognize that we serve a forgiving God, a God that is true to His Word and uses love and compassion toward mankind to stay honest to His Word. In other words, God is more honest to His Word than mankind is to their word toward God.

The other thing that we do know as powerful as God is, is we know that God is true to His grace, His mercy, and His compassion. That is what gives us the security that God is going to forgive us. But that might not be enough to capture your attention about God's forgiveness toward mankind.

What actually puts everything in perspective spiritually is mankind's faith toward God. Faith is mankind's consciousness in understanding God's compassion toward mankind's unworthiness, mankind's weakness, mankind's sinful nature, and imperfections toward God.

Some people have come to realize that it is better for them to ask for forgiveness than to continuously dwell in their sins. Now let me reiterate my point about how we know that God is going to forgive us. We know that through our faith in God. Our faith in God has placed us in a position where our God-driven consciousness makes us recognize that God has always been authentic in His Word, even though we might not know whether God has forgiven us of our sins or not. Our consciousness guides us through our trials and sins. Now, at this time, let me try to define the difference between a trial and a sin.

We still develop enough courage and understanding that gives us enough security to know that God has forgiven us of our sins. We should continue in sin, but through my faith and through God's consciousness, we have come to realize that God will forgive us as we continuously mature in our sins with God as long as we learn from our sins and try to continue in fellowship with God. We know that God has forgiven us of our sins when we commit the sins, that we know that is wrong, and we have been puzzled and tried to figure out how can you ask for forgiveness.

The key is that God already knows that you have committed the sin, but because you ask forgiveness, you really don't know if God's mind, and heart, enough to figure out whether or not God has forgiven us or you of that particular sin.

I strongly believe because I have fallen short of the Word of God that when I sin and I pray to God, asking Him for my forgiveness, it seems that there's a presence that appears in my heart that allows my consciousness to have enough faith that would spark enough curiosity in my life, which would spark my belief in God that resonates a certain feeling that manifests God's presence of forgiveness.

## THE POWER OF GOD'S CONSCIOUSNESS

The situation, circumstances, trials, tribulations, temptations that I was just faced with, and the presence of God resonates in me. Then that gives me the feeling to acknowledge consciously that God has forgiven me of the sins, that I have fallen short of.

In other words, faith gives us the confidence and the substance that we need to know whether or not God is going to forgive us of our sins. We must also recognize that we again serve a God of forgiveness. Even in the midst of God's forgiveness toward our sins, we need to acknowledge that our sins do not stop there. We are still responsible for the consequences of our sins that we have committed.

But our sins have messages and lessons instilled in them for us to learn from them. Yes, we do learn from our sins as sometimes, as painful and longsuffering as they are, we are still able to learn from our sins. We must also recognize that our sins have messages and lessons in them. As we learn from them, we must mature in our sins, and as we mature in our sins, we must also remember to stay in constant fellowship with God through our faith and consciousness that we have in Him.

When I repent, I am acknowledging to myself that I have done wrong. I am not allowing myself to recognize that my sins are not going to become a weight and burden in my life. I am not going to stop praying. I am going to pick myself up. and keep focusing on God's salvation and what God's will is for my life.

Here is something that is very important to the Christian that applies to their sins. It is easier for a Christian to sin than to allow his sins to become their weight or burden to the person or people who commit the sin. If you do not repent, here is how your sins will destroy your faith and relationship with God.

You begin to feel guilty and complacent about your sins. Sometimes, when you are not giving up on your faith, while trying to hold onto your sins, your sins would send you into a state of confusion and disbelief, and it also distorts your faith in God. Sometimes our sins cause an uncomfortable, disoriented, and emotional feeling in our hearts toward God.

Those people are superficial Christians. I mean those making people think that they are the most faithful person or people to God since Jesus Christ. What we need to realize is being a superficial Christian is not going to get you into heaven. It makes you look impressive to others who truly don't know your story, but God already knows and wrote your story.

A superficial Christian is a person or people who thinks they are the best thing that has ever happened to Christianity since Jesus Christ. What is going to get faithful Christians to heaven is being able to embrace God's consciousness and acting according to what God's consciousness tells you to do.

We must also understand that through God's consciousness, we should never try to underestimate or take advantage of God's grace and mercy. Here is why many Christians take advantage of God's grace and mercy. Here is how: because they continuously keep committing the same sins over and over again.

When you do not become successful in your trials, it does not mean that you have failed in your life, commitment, or your relationship with God. I am not pacifying

God's Word to satisfy anyone or tell anyone that it's okay for them to sin. This is a very intricate part of man's free will. Man is given the opportunity to exercise his will, even if it goes against God's salvation, Word, and God's consciousness. Some Christians use excuses to compromise or give reason to continue in their sins.

# People's Word Is Their Bond

What are the most disappointing things that I have come to understand is that we don't make people responsible for their spirituality, especially the things that they say they should do. Our success and the development of our consciousness is a commitment that we can only achieve through constantly being focused on God's consciousness. That makes us responsible for us to become successful.

It seems that we are living in a world where we don't make people responsible for the things people say they are going to do rather consciously or through their consciousness or for them being conscious.

Even we are meeting people for lunch, movies, business for the commitment all the things they say that they are going to do.

The integrity and the spiritual consciousness of mankind are determined by how well mankind is able to keep his or her word. People judge you based on what you say you are going to do.

It showed how responsible we are for the things that we say we are going to do. People, we need to develop the consciousness that helps us develop the discipline we need to understand the importance of keeping our word.

It shows the honesty of our commitment to God as well and others, and it also shows our integrity of ourselves. I am not saying that you can't be late, but always be considerate and have the same compassion that God has for you. You should always have for others.

The only person I know that is able to show up late, even several days, late and still be on time is God. When we pray to ask to stop our trials or temptations and become struggling with our trials, sometimes we think God has forgotten us. Why? Because He was always late, but my consciousness has developed enough faith in God to recognize that God still comes on time.

Why is always time even when God is late? In other words, God is always on time even when mankind thinks that God is late. Why is God always late but He is still on time? Because God is letting mankind know that we have not humbled ourselves enough to become submissive in God's consciousness and grace to recognize that they are a message in the patience of waiting for an answer from God. The waiting comes from in order to develop mankind's patience. Whatever mankind is going through and thinking, God is not listening or heard them. The waiting and the patience is to let mankind know that the reason why their prayers are not answered is simple: mankind has not listened to God enough in order for mankind to get the answer, which mankind has sought in order for mankind to better understanding and comprehend the message from in order to give mankind answer to their problems or trials.

Once again, in order for mankind to get answers to their problems, trials, adversities, and adversaries, when we become submissive enough to stop listening to others and when we stop allowing our problems to distract us from the message that God is trying to teach us or want mankind to learn, that is when God revealed His message to mankind. The reason why is able to reveal His message to mankind when God wants to is that God is always in control of mankind's existence and decisions.

It is because God is always in control of everything, which means that God wants to have enough confidence in Him to know that He is always there for you and me, and also God's time is not our time.

We must understand that we do not have that power of consciousness as God does. That is why God is God because God controls all the power of consciousness, which exercises and exists in the universe.

I know that mostly atheist is something else it's just like people want to reach spiritualism without, first seeking God who created and give us enough room to exercise or spiritualness through our conscious state of mind.

Sometimes we need to hold people responsible for what they say and do. To me, if a person breaks their promise to you or does something different than what they say, it is as bad as someone lying.

For example, lying is wrong, but we become so accustomed to people lying that we give it different categories of lying. We call some lies a white lie. We try comparing the lie to the culture of a people who are popular at lying. Some people do not care if you have to lie to make it in the world or in corporate America. No one takes pride in allowing their words to become their bond or the character they live by.

First of all, when we study God's Word, we must realize that we are becoming aware of God's divine Word. It is through that awareness that comes from God's Word. It is through God's Word that mankind gets the opportunity and privilege to embrace the power of God's consciousness.

Through mankind's study of God's Word, mankind is able to embrace the message that is in God's Word. It is God's Word that mankind is able to receive with their true spiritual enlightenment of mankind's consciousness in God.

When we study God's Word and we receive the messages and knowledge that is in God's Word, what is it within God's Word that brings mankind's awareness into God's consciousness?

It is this point that gives us the wisdom that mankind needs in order for mankind to become conscious and faithful to God. As we study God's Word it keeps mankind in constant fellowship and intonement with God's grace, mercy, and most of all, salvation.

The key to God's consciousness is to let God's consciousness resonate in the heart and mind of mankind and is where the awareness of how mankind is able, to develop. The true identity, the character of who God is to them, is experienced and exercised in the integrity and character of the Christians.

Now we must remember that there is a responsibility that comes with acknowledging God's consciousness in the lives of the people who have acquired God's consciousness in their life. This is what God has acquired of us, and that is what gives us the opportunity to also recognize that there is a heaven and hell.

We live in a society that does not respect God's Word, God's people, and God's consciousness. We have a society that rewards bad behavior over good behavior. It also means that society prefers to destroy itself than to become submissive to God's Word and consciousness. I mean any society that does not respect God's consciousness. That is when that society is destined to fall into its own sinful nature and imperfections.

You would get to realize that the more any society withdraws and denies the power of God's consciousness within that society, the society will constantly be in a state of chaos such as crime and families turning against each other.

Husbands and wives would not see or experience the importance of being committed to each other and their families. Families will kill and destroy each other, and would not be committed to each other. People in that society would constantly be fighting, each other.

When people in society refuse God's consciousness and compassion that society is destined to feel destroyed self and bring destruction to its citizens. If that society does not take want to build and develop its morals and ethics in God's consciousness.

That is when that society spends more time trying to defend the wrongs that are being committed in that society when God's conscience does not take root or is not spiritually driven by society.

Where people appreciate a lie, to become the truth, and the truth into a lie. That society is leading itself into a devastating trap of entrapment, which would destroy, and kill the nature and spirit of that particular society is not being influenced by God's divine consciousness.

Here's why because we live in a society that does not respect honesty, love, and compassion. Those types of attributes are taken as weaknesses.

A person who keeps their word knows that it magnifies their integrity. When a person lies or adopt the ways of the world, they have a tendency not to be highly appreciated by others. I have a question that we need to ask ourselves: If we know that a person lies and looks at lies or the people who lie, why do we think that people who lie are stronger than people who don't lie? Once again, people in society don't accept God's consciousness to become implemented into their society. It seems that we live in a society that appreciates people who lie than those who tell the truth—our political system, our government officials, our academic institutions have even destroyed the truth of who God is. What is happening is the Christians who know God's Word is still confused about who God is. Even when we pretend that we love someone, we are still lying to them.

The only time that God's Word becomes a lie is when the pastors, bishops, deacons, and it seems that we have no commitment to the truth. The only commitment to the truth that mankind has is the power of God's consciousness.

When mankind does not live up to God's expectations or consciousness, that is when God's Word becomes a lie. Here is what I mean. We suppose to live in the truth of God's consciousness.

When the people who are supposed to believe in God's Word deviate from the truth, that is when God's Word becomes a lie. Because we are not living the truth of God's divine Word.

You know the only true truth this world has is God's authentic Word, and that truth of God's consciousness can only be expressed and interpreted through mankind's faith in God. When mankind cannot live up to God's expectations, because mankind prefers to live the lie. It means that mankind's example of God becomes a lie.

Now if mankind starts to sin unexpectedly and ask for God's forgiveness, then I think that God is willing to forgive mankind; but to sit and take God's grace and mercy for granted means that your lifestyle becomes that lie, which is constantly destroying society's perspective of what God's Word is to the masses of people.

If the people who believe in God's consciousness cannot give God's consciousness its true meaning based on their lifestyle as Christians. It tells the masses of people that their lifestyle is a lie to God's Word and to God's consciousness as well.

That is why people in the church is losing hope, and confidence in the church, because the people that they trust, to teach God's Word, are the ones who are not living up to the expectations of God's Word and they are the ones that are destroying God's Word from the pulpit to the congregation.

We need to take a look at ourselves as Christians, especially the Christians who believe in God's consciousness. The Christians who are supposed to believe in God's consciousness that is sinning should stop using the masses of people's lifestyle as an excuse of them, denying and destroying their own faith in God. In actuality, it is the people in the church that are destroying God's consciousness to the masses of people's faith and belief in.

Here is why: Christians already accepted the fact and responsibility to follow God's Word. And the people who confess that they are not living up to God's consciousness are the truth behind the masses of people not believing in God's Word. Christians are the ones that are destroying the masses of people's perception and love toward God's divine Word

I'm not making a statement to say that you have to be perfect to follow God, but what I'm actually saying is if you believe in God, act as you believe in God because the masses of people are judging you based on your integrity in God.

I am making a statement to say that we are responsible for the truth of God in our lives, even as we embrace God's consciousness through His Word.

So the lie becomes the truth, and the truth becomes the lie. And because of the lie that most Christians are living in today's society, nobody is able to define what is the true reality of the truth is itself, about God, in our society.

So now God's Word is becoming more of a lie than God's Word becoming a lie than the truth within itself. The

Word of God is been watered down through the believers' actions of how they identify God through the actions of their faith toward God and their consciousness and belief in God.

People who are truthful are known as being weak and vulnerable. Those people who tell the truth are never respected as being strong and honest people. I am glad that through God's consciousness, we have faith in being truthful to God. Being truthful to God is where the true truth is rewarded and appreciated, regardless of what the world thinks or what people think of us.

We must understand that honesty and truthfulness actually develop who we are as a person. Our integrity is based on our word. Your word tells me something about you. It does not stop there. My word is also my bond. Your word lets me know that you are a trustworthy person before I ask you about yourself or even get to know who you are as a person.

The problem in life is everyone wants to lie. It seems that no one has the courage anymore to admit when something is wrong or even if God's consciousness says it is wrong. Where is our faith and our strength as it pertains to God's consciousness in our life?

Even the Christian community is simply falling apart because some of us have lost our courage and faith to stand up and represent God's consciousness. We are losing serious ground and we are losing faith. We are even losing God's consciousness of heart. We are losing. God needs strong people to revitalize as well transform His Word to the masses of people. With boldness, stand up and represent His faith and His Word.

One of the things that has become very interesting to me, like a double-edged sword, is how many Christians talk about how God has blessed them. They talk about the many good things that God has done in their lives, but for some strange reason, when it comes time to represent God, we have a tendency to lose control, hope, and our faith. One of the challenging things that cause us to lose control over God's faith and consciousness is when we value material possession over God's divine Word. Here's why because when we start focusing on material possessions.

It seems it seems that if we are not focused on God. That is when we begin to love the pride and status that comes with material possession in our lives and sometimes if we are not focused on God's consciousness. Then the material possessions, become the love of mankind's consciousness, and it is that love for material possession that destroys the spiritual consciousness of mankind.

Sometimes our material possessions, make people worship us like we are God. Now that is what places mankind's consciousness in a very dangerous position in life. Anytime mankind tries to embrace the position of God, that is when mankind begins to fall in life.

Now that status that mankind has been given, or rewarded by the masses of people, to be God. It makes mankind feel that they are God. Now that is a very dangerous place, for anyone to be in.

Especially in our consciousness, where mankind feels like he or she is God. We should always keep focused on God's consciousness because it keeps focusing on God's consciousness and faith in God.

Once again, that is why it's very important that we begin to develop our spiritual consciousness in God. So that we can constantly stand firm and recognize Satan's attacks, even in the midst of our pride, lust, and material possessions, that has caused us to stray away from God's divine Word. We must learn how to stand firm in God's consciousness.

Many Christians today do not have the courage and commitment to stand up for God's Word. God's Word is our consciousness that develops our faith. God's Word is the essence of our spiritual development of our consciousness in God.

We cannot soften the blow of God's Word by compromising His Word, just because we feel that if we soften God's Word, it would give us better privileges in a society. I mean a society that has already reject God's Word or we try to compromise God's Word because we want God's Word to be accepted more by society.

It is not up to mankind to set God's agenda or compromise God's Word. It is not up to any man to compromise God's Word because God's Word is consistent as well as faithful to all men. God has kept His Word. Let the truth be told, the problem is we are not keeping or being faithful to God's Word.

We must also realize that society does not guarantee us salvation, but even if God's Word did not guarantee us salvation the theological question and philosophical question that arises with this statement is, would I still serve God? Would I still serve God as I am now? Would I still serve God as being fearful of Him? Would I still serve God as an authentic God? Would I serve God as an omnipotent God?

## THE POWER OF GOD'S CONSCIOUSNESS

And the answer to that question is yes. Here is why God's Word provides a certain consciousness of stature and structure, and any social or moral society needs to govern the masses of people in a more disciplined manner. There is a certain message in God's Word that teaches love and allows us to respect each other's position in life, even with our faults.

God's Word is also able to transform people's lives from the mere physical existence into the spiritual manifestation of God's consciousness. Even if salvation was not offered, God's Word still gives us the confidence and security we need to embrace His consciousness so we can have confidence and security in God's Word, even if our salvation was not offered.

Without God's Word, we would have chaos in any society that does not want to embrace God's Word in it. Look at the society that does not embrace God's Word, their culture, or even their laws. These are the societies that are still constantly destroying themselves.

The pride of a society that does not have preferred to destroy itself, to embrace God's consciousness, and righteousness in it. All because of the lies of that society continuously, assume, and portray, to their citizens or the masses of people that God does not exist to the capacity, in which the Scriptures say that God does exist.

The structure of this world has denied that his true existence and presence in the world that God has created. This is where you get so much philosophy, theory, theologians all trying to argue God's position in the existence of the world's creation.

I think the question that comes to mind when people have doubt about God is that they use mankind sinful nature and imperfections to try to judge God's perfection toward life and toward creation; but we misunderstand as human beings that the nature of mankind it's not the nature, understanding, and perspective of God.

I think sometimes mankind displayed a harsh judgment, on each other all because when they judge each other, they think they have the authority of God to judge each other; in reality, mankind does not have the authority or the spiritual consciousness of God to judge each other.

What mankind has to judge each other it's reconciliation. all judgment is done by God through mankind's reconciliation. So mankind always feels empowered to be God, but mankind does not have the mental capacity or the spiritual consciousness to judge each other.

That authority was never given to mankind, because mankind might feel like they are empowered to do so, and that is a bad place for Christians to be. Here's why: sometimes the people in the church who feel empowered use their power of authority to feel like they are the God that the congregation should be worshipping instead of God themselves.

Let's assume that the atheist is right about how God does not exist, but let us also assume the idea that God's divine Word, exists but not God himself. Now The people who have authority in the churches, still want to use God's Word to judge other people but not to judge themselves. Because if their will experienced that they are worse, off than the people that they are judging. Even if salvation was not offered to us through God's consciousness, we would still have a better world.

If we use God's Word to develop the structure of morals and ethics, that should govern our society, and we should be committed as a people or society in order for us to live by those same moral ethics. All of the laws that governs our society have come from the Bible.

Now just think for moment with all of the chaos, the wars, the hate that comes with the color of a man's skin. What really holds this world together? Sometimes we feel like God has left us alone, but it is through our faith in God that makes our faith, a very intriguing thing. It is the action of mankind's spiritual consciousness. The difference is mankind's spiritual consciousness, which is what becomes the foundation of our faith. Here is why: as a person or people think and act on what they think or believe in, that is what they become.

That belief is manifested in our hearts and minds but once again what we believe in can only be determined and recognized through our state of consciousness. What puzzles me about faith and what is intriguing to me about faith is when you're going through many difficult trials.

Do you know that your belief and how you think become part of your consciousness in God? Everything you believe in is challenged by your consciousness and faith in God.

Sometimes your pain and suffering can become so heavy, that it can make you lose your faith and righteousness in God. Here is what I mean, the pain and suffering which we are going through, could also challenge your belief in God, and make you think that God Himself forgot about you, and don't care.

What is happening is that because we cannot see or touch our faith or even recognize faith, our faith is developed based on our strength, consciousness, and the enlightenment of how our knowledge, comprehends, interprets, and understand what God's Word is to us as human beings. And that is how God's consciousness is experienced through His Word to mankind. And when mankind reached that level of comprehension, interpretation, and spiritualism of the scriptures, that is when mankind's faith become the love and inspiration of God's consciousness.

Please let me remind the atheist about God's divine and authentic word. If we did not have God's Word, what type of condition would this world would be in? The world is held together based on God Word and His compassion for mankind's true existence.

That is why we should never try to compromise God's authentic Word or try to let God's Word fit into society's agenda because God's Word is the glue that is still holding the whole world together. Although society is trying to ostracize the Word of God, it's interesting to know that it is God's Word that is the strength and foundation of our society.

We must always remember that we are in the world, but our consciousness should never be a part of this world, so we should never compromise God's Word in order to fit into society's agenda.

Sometimes people who are spiritually conscious and those that are not spiritually conscious have a tendency to think or do things when it is convenient for them.

So loyalty to the gospel or to some people to ethics and morals of life it seems does not have the value, significance, respect, and discipline that it once had.

When you look at a society that teaches ethics morals and a way of life, especially that society that embraces God's divine Word. The Word of God set the stage for that society to develop the consciousness needed to bring peace and harmony to that society. We must recognize that the key to better living spiritually is being able to acknowledge God's Word in your life and being able to implement God's Word in our society. For example, the ethics and morals of life have no more value anymore. The respect and loyalty have no more significance. Christians must always remember that we do things base on God's Word and will for our lives, and our consciousness is the wisdom of our faith in God.

For example, in order for you to have faith, one must have knowledge of the things that they are learning about in order to have an understanding of that thing that we are learning about where it generates enough of a consciousness to create a strong enough of a belief of that thing causing you to develop enough faith in it.

Having knowledge of a thing gives one confidence of that thing, enough confidence that would generate a belief in that thing; in this case, it would be God's Word. The knowledge that one has of that thing generates within their mind a school of thought. That school of thought brings one into a mental state of consciousness.

In this case, those people who are reading God's Word for knowledge and direction are actually acknowledging God's presence in their everyday life. The knowledge that we get from God's Word acknowledges how we should live our life as faithful believers in God's grace.

That knowledge develops our consciousness. That consciousness is what develops our faith in God.

Our faith is strengthened by the many obstacles, trials, and temptations that we encounter as believers of God's faith. When we develop in God's faith, we are making progress in God's grace and mercy, and with God's grace and mercy come God's compassion for mankind. There is an essence or a certain flavor of love that comes with God's compassion, and that is God's salvation.

The salvation of God is earned through our faith that we are able to earn God's salvation. People say it is a gift based on what God has done for us through Jesus Christ, and now to offer mankind salvation based on God allowing His Son to be sacrificed for the sins of the world, knowing that God has given His only Son to be sacrificed for the sins of the world. I can say based on my experience of God's salvation it is a gift, but to me, it is more than gift. I would say it is an earned gift that is given to mankind based on our faith and consciousness in God.

The one thing that I always remind people of is that God's Word has always kept its promise to the world and people who have faith in God. Even in the state of controversy, chaos, and adversity, God's Word has kept His promise to mankind, but mankind has not kept their word to God or their promise to God.

So we do not need to compromise God's Word just to fit into a society what the majority of people do is that they do not respect God's Word but still ostracize God's Word as well. We must remember that people's positions in life and consciousness change people's thoughts, challenges in life, and people's lifestyle. People's consciousness changes their commitment to each other, but God's Word has always stayed the same.

When we study God's Word and get a better understanding of God's wisdom, it develops in us a consciousness. That consciousness becomes the foundation of our righteousness, and it does not change. God's consciousness is able to transform the mindset of mankind into a spiritual beacon of light, a light that reflects our spiritual character and faith through our consciousness.

God's Word does not change. It has existed for centuries and centuries and has surpassed its time. God's Word has been challenged over and over again. It stands strong. Here is why: because it does not change. God's Word is the consciousness of transformation. God's Word can take the smartest man in the world and transform him to be God's apostle.

God can take a man who has ostracized His Word and his people and transform him to be an apostle of righteousness. God can take a man with little self-esteem and bring him to a point where he can become a prophet that can lead millions and millions of people into a foreign land and give them the freedom He promised them. God always keeps His Word.

# Transformation of Saul's Consciousness into Paul

For example, let us look at the Apostle Paul's life. He was placed in a situation where he had to listen to God. There is nothing wrong with being humble, especially to God. Now let us look at the story of Saul being transformed into Paul. For example, here is the story of Saul's transformation to Paul (Acts 9:1–20). Now in chapter one, Saul was still making murderous threats and slaughtering God's people, especially those people who worship God. Now we can recognize from Saul's transformation to Paul, how Saul wanted to bring the Christians back to Jerusalem to prove his loyalty to the high priest who ruled Jerusalem, probably by making this statement, "This is how many of the Christians that I (Saul) have captured." Then some of the Christians were made a mockery because of their faith in God; others were killed in public to prove to the masses of people that God had no power. So why would anyone want to serve a God like that?

In this case, we had the apostle Paul killing and slaughtering Christians and murdering Christians based on what he believed was the truth. I remember the apostle Paul asked this question and that is. How can people serve a God that does not come out and support them, or even save them from the dead?

We must remember that the apostle Paul was in authority of the government he might assume that the God, that they were serving is a human being. Who function and do things just like mankind. Paul might assume that God himself had a sinful nature and that God is imperfect. Just like the people Paul has persecuted and killed.

Suddenly through this experience, the apostle Paul realized that God was more powerful than the Roman government, that God was more powerful than Paul's swords, and then the question which sparked Paul's curiosity was that if these people were willing to die for God, in what capacity does God exist or even influence their life enough where they would be willing to die for God.

God was still able to manifest Himself through Paul's life and not only manifest Himself through Paul's life, but Paul became one of the most prominent apostles that God had after the twelve disciples that basically lived and travel with Jesus the Christ. Paul never experienced meeting Jesus Christ.

And this is why Paul was puzzled with this statement why does he allow me to keep persecuting Christians and killing them, and God is a coward and that is when decided to transform Saul into Paul. What people need to know is that God had a personal relationship with Apostle Paul. God was able to transform Saul into Paul.

And Saul was able to be transformed as Paul to become one of his most prominent disciples of Jesus Christ. Paul believe in God so much that he became a model of the gospel of Jesus Christ and God's divine Word. This could be Saul's attitude: we kill God's people, but we never experience His presence coming to save them.

Then the main question comes to mind, does a God who is supposed to have Christians believe in Him never left a finger to save the people who worship Him when they are in trouble? What type of a God is this who does not avenge His people's life that is being killed?

God, if he does not fight or destroy those people who are trying to destroy His people? What type of a God do Christians believe in, who is supposed to be so omnipotent and omnipresent, but at the same time, this same God does not even save his Son or His people who have faith in Him while they are being persecuted by the hands of other people who do not believe in God?

Sometimes God's actions can be misinterpreted by mankind's judgment toward God. This is when we experience how important our faith in God is when it comes to how we interpret God's Word in order to develop our consciousness and discipline in God's faith.

## THE POWER OF GOD'S CONSCIOUSNESS

To the physical eyes, mankind's nature cannot comprehend God's divine consciousness. Mankind's nature cannot experience or have knowledge of God's wisdom, so what they experience as God's wisdom might not be God's interpretation of what mankind's nature interprets it to be.

Now those people who have a consciousness of faith already know that God has always been there for them and brought them out of many difficult situations in their lives; that is why we serve an awesome God, regardless of life or death.

We must understand that our interpretation of God's faith does not help those Christians who have faith in Him. Sometimes we feel that way when we are going through our personal trials. We feel like God has left us alone. I think sometimes we think that God has removed Himself from the situation or problems that we are faced with, but let me tell you, God is constantly in the midst of everything in our lives, trying to bring justices to those that want to hurt His people and bring damnation to His people.

What the king did not know was the tide was about to change. The God that we serve is so patient that we think that God does not exist sometimes. The God we serve, we might think that He is not listening. The God serve, we might think He does not care. The God serve, we might think that He does not have enough compassion for his followers. So why do we serve Him as faithful followers of God's divine faith?

Then the question that should come to mind is why we are worshipping a God if He is not faithful to us and is not answering the praise of His people. In the essence of God's patience, He is waiting for mankind to understand their own ignorance that has caused mankind to sin, and sometimes God is waiting for mankind to acknowledge the wrongness of their sins.

Christians have a central resource in their lives that would help them solve any problems, and that is faith and prayer. Those are the two most powerful weapons in a Christian life that combat any evil desire that Satan has placed before mankind. Those two weapons can be used to solve anything this world has placed before the believers of God.

Most of the time, the problems that we face, whether or not we notice we have the physical ability to solve them ourselves, we bring a lot of problems on ourselves because we think that we are gods all by ourselves. So we start trying to solve everyone's problems in life, and the majority of the time, we cannot even solve our own problems. This is when we start to venture onto other people's territories or I would say their private lives.

Sometimes it is best to let them seek God out. We can give each other support, but we cannot take God's responsibilities away from Him while trying to support our brothers and sisters in Christ. We must always let God do His work, so whatever situation you are faced with, you would come out right. We let go and let God do His work.

Let me get back to my point: Saul got close to Jerusalem. Saul noticed a round light or a light in the shape of a circle. The presence of the light from heaven made Saul fall to his feet in a submissive position to God. That experience with the light was the beginning of Paul's transformation of Saul to Paul, and it was Paul's consciousness that caused Paul to fall to his feet and change his name to Paul.

## THE POWER OF GOD'S CONSCIOUSNESS

He heard a voice say, "Saul, Saul, why persecute thou me?"

Saul asked, "Who are you?"

And the voice said, "I am the God who you persecuted."

Saul actually was trembling to the point where Saul himself was astonished by how God was able to transform man's ignorance, such as Saul into the spiritual experience that transformed Saul into Paul. This is the God Saul thought never existed and gave up on His people who believed in God.

This became one of the most miraculous revelations that has transformed the consciousness of a man's life, and through God's consciousness that was transcended through Saul, this in itself is one of the most that was done that God's consciousness had transformed such a man like Saul to Paul.

Now that is enough evidence to let all Christians know that they serve an awesome God. When God brings man into the His spiritual consciousness, it allows that man to develop his divine consciousness spiritually, just like an Apostle of God, just like Saul's transformation into the Apostle Paul.

This is how God did that. Then Saul asked God a question, and that is, "What do you want me to do, Lord? I know through your spiritual awareness and inspiration. God, I know with your conviction that you are God, and you are the living God as well." Saul asked the Lord, "What will thou have me to do?"

Now the question one needs to ask is, why was Saul going to Damascus? We must remember that Saul was going to Damascus to kill Christians. The men (soldiers) who were with Saul had quite a spiritual and physical experience. Here is why they saw God's consciousness being displayed upon Paul. God used His authentic words as a means to witness also to the soldiers that were with Saul. Let us focus more on the soldiers' experience.

God gave them a spiritual experience that they had never experience before God while taking the Apostle Paul through his spiritual experience which again God was able to transformation him from Saul to Paul.

I think some of the soldiers might have also become saved during the Apostle Paul's transformation, just like the thief who was on the cross with Jesus Christ. The men were speechless after hearing the voice and realizing that the voice was communicating in the same language that they were accustom to speaking in. Remember these soldiers had killed Christians, and now God decided to take a stand for His people, like He always does in order to proclaim His Word.

When Saul arose from the earth, he was blind for three days. During those three days, Saul was led into the city of Damascus where Ananias was. Ananias was also a disciple of God, but God told Ananias in a vision to go to Judas's home, and Ananias said to God, "Behold, I am here, Lord."

When God told Ananias to go to Judas's home for a person called Saul of Tarsus, he had seen him in a vision while Saul was praying about his physical transformation with God. God humbled Saul enough where he began to experience his own physical blindness.

Saul was stilled, given a spiritual enlightenment in a vision, like the image of Ananias. So when God gave Saul back his vision, he would know that his physical and spir-

## THE POWER OF GOD'S CONSCIOUSNESS

itual transformation of God's consciousness had a divine purpose and essence with God. That divine purpose was to change Saul's name to Paul. We must also remember that they are vowels in the Geek language. We must also remember consonants and vowels are interchangeable. So to change the S to the P was okay in the English grammar and in the Greek language.

Now in verse 13, Ananias tried to let God know that Saul had brought much evil upon the Christians, even those saints in Jerusalem. "And now, Lord, you want me to go and bring him (Saul) to meet the same men and women that he has killed for many years."

Here is God's plan: it is never mankind's plans. Mankind, even in his state of consciousness, cannot comprehend the thoughts and decisions of God. No person knows the plan or thoughts of God but God Himself.

This is especially true about those men and women who became the forerunners of your faith. "God, for many years, Lord, this man has persecuted people in your name. Remember, Lord, Saul has granted all authority by the chief priest to bring or kill the Christians of Jerusalem."

I can experience this statement coming from Ananias saying, "God, I love you. God, I have faith in you. God, I would do anything for you, but are you my Lord? Are you sure about Saul and his transformation?" I feel that Ananias might have thought the same way that I am thinking, and that is, *God, are you sure that your words have impacted Saul's heart enough to transform him to Paul?*

Now here is the question I would ask because I have experienced how mankind has used their pride, selflessness, hate to kill others, just because they have the authority to do so. People like that never want to change because it makes them feel empowered.

God's consciousness has a way of changing any man's heart that even thinks that he is both man and god. That is why faith becomes important to mankind, even when mankind's consciousness cannot comprehend God's wisdom. God's consciousness is the only thing that is able to humble man through his faith. It takes a lot of courage to have faith like Ananias.

I can experience God saying to Ananias, "I am sure. Let My will be done through you, My son, because Saul has become a changed man in the faith of the Lord."

I could still feel a sense of uncertainty coming from Ananias, saying, "God, are you sure? Okay, God, if that is what you want me to do, then I will do it. Still, anything you want me to do, I will do." What happened was Ananias did not know that God already took care of all this doubt that Ananias had during Saul's transformation to Paul.

That is why God told Ananias that Saul had a vision of him in the spiritual manifestation of life. Now Saul's experience has become a spiritual experience as Paul's power.

So God told Ananias, "Go your way." God is trying to let Ananias know that He is competent for the job. "That is why I choose you, Ananias, so let My will be done through you so My work can be accomplished through the Apostle Paul who became an apostle of the brotherhood of God. Saul is a chosen vessel unto Me, bearing My name, witnessing to the masses of people.

"He (Saul) will stand up as the Apostle Paul in the synagogue, between the pillows of Rome, and the world proclaiming God's name to the Gentiles, to the kings, queens, and to the children that I am the Lord, his God, for whom I am pleased with, and he will spend all of life serving me as Lord. Just like I know Paul would say let every knee bow and let every voice confess that I am God, your Lord."

Just like God has made mankind become submissive to the His power, God will let mankind submit to Him the almighty God. Now at the time that Saul became filled with the Holy Spirit, remember, Paul's eyes had scales on them that God had placed. I think Paul, because of his divine consciousness, would go on to say, "The God I serve is not a seasonable God. He provides stability in our lives."

He does not change based on your race. He does not let mankind manipulate His Word. God changes us because of His grace and mercy and because of His compassion for mankind. God's Word has always been constant. God's Word, faith, loyalty, and most all, God's love toward mankind has never changed, but people toward God change.

It is through God's consciousness, through his grace, and through God's mercy and compassion that takes us into a future beyond what our physical existence can comprehend. What would that be? It would be nothing but man's salvation through Jesus Christ. God's consciousness brings about some form of knowledge and wisdom to mankind, especially those people who are in constant fellowship with God.

# THE CONSCIOUSNESS OF GOD'S DISCERNMENT

Here is what I know: when we live in the spirit of God, we can better discern God's messages through our consciousness and faith in God. Our faith in God is the window to our consciousness toward God. We need the window of our consciousness as Christians to be able to discern God's messages.

In order that we would know if the messages that we are to discern are from God and not from man or Satan, this can be achieved based on God's consciousness. In order for us to understand God's messages as it pertains to God's discernment, we have to stay constantly in God's presence and in tune with God throughout His Word.

In order to get a better understanding of God's discernment, our ability to interpret God's discernment is done based on our faith in God. Our faith is the key when it comes to interpreting the messages of God through all of His discernments.

That is why we must work hard to achieve maturity in our faith that we would become more responsible to God's kingdom and become more enthusiastic about teaching God's Word and salvation to the masses of people.

We have to make sure that we know who, how, when, and where these messages are coming from. So that is why we always have to stay consciously aware of God's Word. That's the only way that we can achieve greatness in our faith in God by constantly staying in God's Word and meditating in the realms of God's consciousness.

This is the challenging part of one's commitment with God, and that is staying focused on God's Word. How else are we able to recognize the signs of discernment being comforted to us from God? Here is why our spirit should become so in tune with God's consciousness that we should be able to acknowledge His thoughts transcending in our hearts and minds.

Also, we should know that the messages we receive are actually coming from God only and not of Satan or man—just from God's consciousness. The discernment of God and the messages that are being sent to us from God, the Christians that are given the gift of discernment have to be in tune with God's faith and consciousness.

The gift of discernment takes a mature consciousness. It is a spiritual gift from God; it is a serious matter. Here is why: look at John. If John did not have the gift of being in tune with God's consciousness, John would not have been able to complete the book of Revelation. For example, if we read the book of Revelation, we would experience God's consciousness transcending through God's faith.

All of this can be accomplished through God's consciousness that has to be translated through the state of God's discernment. Now the person that God is going to use to interpret His Word has to be inspired by God in order for that person to interpret God's discern messages to the masses of people.

We must understand the importance of discernment. Discernment is best expressed in this manner: it is most expressed in the book of Revelation because the majority of the book of Revelation was written in the signs of God's discernment, and it is acknowledged in man's divine consciousness.

If I had to clarify discernment, I would say it is a message that is wrapped up in signs and symbolism for the interpretation of the people or masses of people. Discernment is a transcending message that comes from God to be translated to mankind through a particular incident or message. Many people might disagree with me, but it depends on the person's spiritual maturity.

For example, how do we interpret the messages of discernment that come from God. Also, how does God discern His messages toward mankind? God transcends His messages through the consciousness of mankind. We can achieve this by being in tune with God's consciousness.

# THE POWER OF GOD'S CONSCIOUSNESS

The consciousness of God is the spiritual power and enlightenment of man's wisdom and knowledge of what God is willing for mankind to do or say to the people of God for a particular time as now.

We must also understand how God brings man to the level of His consciousness to recognize the signs and messages of His discernment. Now discernment is very important to the body of believers.

Here is why: it depends on the social challenges the churches are faced with in this century which present some difficult questions and answers. Now the person that God chooses to interpret His messages of discernment has to be faithful and submissive to God's consciousness.

A person who is able to receive the message of discernment has to stay in tune with God's consciousness all the time because you don't want to misinterpret God's message of discernment. Now discernment is not a gift that is given to everyone. Discernment is given to God's anointed people and people who are mature in God's faith.

If our consciousness is not focus on God, as it should be, and we give out the wrong information, we can cause damnation to others, especially those people who respect our gifts of discernment. If we lose focus and tell others about a message we think comes from God, when in actuality it is not of God, that, my friend, can sometimes lead to the death of many Christians in the world. We must recognize that it is through our faith in Him and consciousness in God that we are given the ability to become discerners of His Word. We will define discernment further on in the text.

# Mankind's Purpose and Reason to Exist

Before man is able to acknowledge his own existence as well as his purpose and being in life, God is able to define mankind's purpose and reason in life.

Our nature determines our character as human beings, but our true essence for existing is to stay in tune with God's consciousness. The more we stay in tune with God's consciousness and be submissive to whatever God's will is for our life, as we stay in tune with God's consciousness, we are staying more in tune with our purpose and reason to exist. And when we stay in tune with God's consciousness, this is where and how our true purpose and reason for living become clear to us.

The question one might ask is, how can God define our reason and purpose in life before we can define or even know who we are in life? Here is why God knew us before we entered our mother's womb, but through our spiritual experience, that is what brings us into a closer relationship with God.

If God knew us before we were born, how come we don't recognize Him in our physical state of existence when we are born? To be honest with you, we don't even know anything about our previous existence or even being alive.

We are living in our physical existence, but we are not aware of anything, including our own human nature. Now that we are born, what is our purpose and reason to exist in this world? It becomes very simple: we are here to serve God. That is our purpose and reason to exist. How do we get the opportunity to know God? First of all, let me put it in this perspective: God created us to love Him.

God is not caught up in the emotionalism of mankind but the spiritualism of mankind. Let me elaborate more: there are two things that exist here. One is mankind's nature breed, more of an intellectual and philosophical perspective than a spiritually driven perspective by God because the only time that mankind is able to experience spiritualism is through the experience of God's faith and fellowship. That is why mankind is so philosophical and leans more on their intellectual abilities than on God's spirituality. Mankind uses his intellectual ability in order to rationalize God's existence and His reason for created mankind.

The reason is that mankind never existed in the spiritual realm long enough to understand that they are another dimension of creation which consists of heaven and hell. Mankind has never existed in the spiritual realm, and in order to consciously understand the spiritual realm well enough to comprehend the idea, that is where their souls transcended from before mankind's soul was originally place into their own physical bodies. That is why God told Jeremiah, "I knew you before you entered your mother's womb."

Mankind has no experience of compassion and love. So mankind's nature leans more on their physical existence than their spiritual existence. That is why God said that the physical man can never understand the spiritual man. Here is why: because they have a different state of consciousness.

Let's assume I wanted to get involved in serving God. What would be my approach? The question one should ask is how we get to know God. We get to know God through the difficulties in our lives when we hit the crossroads of life. Mankind, for some strange reason, makes it easy for himself to get to know God. When things are going good in our lives, we have a tendency to forget about God.

This is very important to mankind. In other words, God gives us many opportunities to serve Him and love Him, but in the midst of our lives, the last thing that mankind wants to do is serve God.

That is why the only being that created man was God because of God's patience and compassion. That is why if we recognize our true purpose in life, we would have to give that credit to God. For example, the one thing that God actually did for man was to allow mankind to have a free will. That free will which God created in man has to become man's choice of consciousness and awareness. Man's state of consciousness and awareness can lead mankind into a state of discernment. When God created man, he gave man the opportunity to be created in His own image and likeness.

For example, in the book of Genesis 1:26, "Then God said, 'Let us make mankind in our image, in our likeness, so that they may rule over the fish in the sea and the birds in the sky, over the livestock and all the wild animals, and over all the creatures that move along the ground.'"

Man knew that he could not comprehend his existence nor even create himself. The creator Himself in the book of Genesis 1:1–5 it states:

> In the beginning God created the heavens and the earth. Now the earth was formless and empty, darkness was over the surface of the deep, and the Spirit of God was hovering over the waters. And God said, "Let there be light," and there was light. God saw that the light was good, and he separated the light from the darkness. God called the light "day," and the darkness he called "night." And there was evening, and there was morning—the first day. This was not all that God has done.

Let me get back to man's state of consciousness and reasoning. We know that God created the heaven and the earth. Also based on the Scriptures, we have knowledge that the earth was formless. God uses his wisdom and takes the substance of a formless world and uses it to create a beauty of a world and the nature of it.

God did that by transcending the substance of a formless world into the matter of this world. Then the matter God use based on his wisdom transformed that same matter into a solid mass that we now recognize as Mother Earth. That same light that God used to create the world became the soul of mankind.

He did not stop there. God even used darkness as a means to separate the light, giving light and darkness its own nature and reason to exist in order to help accommodate man's existence and comfort of living.

# THE LIGHT AND ENERGY OF GOD

Let's define the concept of the light that God used to help create the world from my perspective. The light itself that God transformed Himself is an energy force that does not restrict God's existence. God being God has no limitations in His creation.

That force is the light of all creations of life. Nothing in our existence that is able to transcend into matter or creation escapes the authentic hands of God's creation, not even man. Matter is determined based on its ability to move and create motion. The other question is why we think God's Word is physical but is transferred to us in a state of energy.

God's Word is a very powerful force that only transcends to us in a powerful manner. It is God's Word that transforms and transcends into the hearts and minds of mankind, developing mankind's consciousness. It is that same power that puts us in a position to have the same power that God has and Jesus has, which gives us the same power and privileges to heal the sick, make the blind see, and raise the dead back to life. When we embrace God's Word physically, we can do miraculous works spiritually.

Now motion is where God placed all of His energy into creating everything that walks upon the earth. We know that God created everything, but in everything, we are all connected to one divine source of life, which is God. This is when people try to define spiritualism without recognizing or implementing God's energy in the process of creation. In other words, people misrepresent God by implementing other definitions of what God has already created. No man or woman can read or define spiritualism without going through God's consciousness.

What they try to acknowledge to themselves is the transcending energy of God but not God Himself. This is a very important point again about what mankind tries to do, and it is to define their spiritualism without implementing God in it. We must always remember that it was God who actually created the reality of mankind's spiritualism, but mankind tries to do so but does not give God the glory.

This is when some people would say, "I don't believe in God, but I believe in spiritualism. I am a spiritualist, but I do not believe in God." We must understand that the light of energy is what God used to embrace matter, that light is what gives matter motion to move, and that is what God uses to bring creation into the manifestation of life.

That movement of matter is transformed into all of God's creation. That same energy has taken on many different dimensions in the theological doctrine, even as God is able to use words and his image in the form of a light, bringing that light into the creation of life. Moses experienced that same light as the burning bush that was never hot. That same light is the burning light of every man's soul creation, and it becomes the light of his salvation. That light is the consciousness of mankind's soul.

The light of God has never been explained to the depth it should be. We must let God's Word be the light of the world. We must let God's Word be the light of our souls. We must let God's Word be the light of the world. We must let God's light be the consciousness of our souls. We must let God's Word become the energy that God used to create the world and every human being in the world.

Now how could that be? That is simple. We Christians must remember that God is able to take on any type of transformation and transcend His energy of transformation into motion and transform that motion into creation of life, and that is what God's uses to transform the existence of life.

The human existence is nothing more than a consciousness of substance, matter, form, and energy. That energy transforms into whatever creation God's consciousness wants that thing to be. Whatever God has created, it all has to have a nature, a purpose, and reason to exist in this life.

Now we know that the atheists believe that God does not exist. In this case, I know that God does exist. Here is why: the bright light is the energy of God's transformation and creation of our physical life. Our physical existence means that God has created us with a purpose and reason to exist.

The Bible has always referred to God as a source of energy in the form of a vision, prophecy, fire, bright light, cloud, and sometimes as an inspiration of energy transforming into itself into the images and likeness of man in order for God to tap into consciousness of mankind or even try to reach the consciousness of mankind. That same energy or bright light has transformed the dry dead bones into life.

Many people ask this question: do I believe that message that God has taken dry bones and brought them to life? I tell them, yes, if God is able to create the world and us in it, then I do believe every drop of God's Word because I have faith in God's consciousness. As Christians, we need to stop selling God short and start letting people recognize God's presence in our souls. Yes, I have no shame in believing everything that God says and wants me to do. This means that I am still maturing in God's grace.

We must remember that anything that God created, He is also able to take on that same image of life and likeness of anything that God Himself has created. Sometimes God does that based on what message He is trying to reveal to man and how he trying to reveal His message to mankind. That light is the Alpha and Omega of all of God's creation and existence.

## THE POWER OF GOD'S CONSCIOUSNESS

Now that same power that God uses to create the light is the same power that God uses when it comes to creating a formless world into a solid world for mankind to live in and enjoy. As Christians, we have a certain power and connection to God's consciousness because of that light which is the same power that is in me and you and which comes from God.

# DEFINING THE STATE OF GOD'S CONSCIOUSNESS

Let's define the act of consciousness and how it relates to God, man, and sin. Consciousness, as we know, is the act of free choice that God has allowed every human being the privilege to have and act upon.

Within every human being, there is the ability to act on their own behalf in order that they can exercise their free will. Now if a person has faith in God, the choices that person exercises are based on the consciousness of their faith in God which allows them within the realms of their own faith to choose their free will. Now when a person exercises their free will, that person or people must also understand that there is a responsibility that comes with one exercising their free will.

In other words, the act of our free will is free, but to exercise our free will without a consciousness, we must understand that having a free will means that there are consequences and responsibilities that come with it.

That sometimes leads to our sins, and when our free will leads to our sins, that means that we have some consequences and responsibilities that we must address with God. This is where mankind's free will ends and God's authority and judgment begin toward mankind.

When a person has knowledge on what is right and wrong, that is called discernment. Discernment is also a term used to for people to recognize thing what is right and wrong before these things happen. It is also a term used to define spiritual wisdom. This is when we must realize that God never limits mankind's actions or choices with mankind's free will which allows man to act upon his consciousness based on his knowledge of God and man's understanding of life. Now here is why man uses his consciousness as a tool: to exercise his free will. Yes, man's consciousness is somehow influenced by his physical characteristics, although it is developed more on a spiritual level.

For example, when we walk into a room and listen to someone speaking, we can determine a person's intellect by their mannerisms and knowledge. The depth of their wisdom and knowledge determines their level of consciousness. We are who we are based on our consciousness and how we respect people.

The mannerism of a man is determined also by his confidence and spirituality in God's consciousness which sometimes leads to man's countenance and submissiveness to God because of the concept of knowing what is right and wrong; for instance, Adam's consciousness of knowing right and wrong led him into serious state countenance.

If I was to define *countenance,* I would say that it has to do with one's facial features or just a person's physical appearance and expression. I would say it allows your expressions to show on your face, such as how you feel about a particular thing. For example, we repent because of our consciousness of knowing that what we do or have done that is wrong in the eyes of God.

Do you know how stressful it was when Adam did what was wrong and had to face God for the sin that he had committed? It seems in the text that Adam knew God would appear, but he did not know when God was going to appear again. Now to me, that could have created much stress. Adam was like a child who did wrong but could not hide from the wrong God told him not to do.

That is when God and Adam had a conversation about Adam's countenance:

> When the woman saw that the fruit of the tree was good for food and pleasing to the eye, and also desirable for gaining wisdom, she took some and ate it. She also gave some to her husband, who was with her, and he ate it. Then the eyes of both of them were opened, and they realized they were naked; so they sewed fig leaves

together and made coverings for themselves. Then the man and his wife heard the sound of the Lord God as he was walking in the garden in the cool of the day, and they hid from the Lord God among the trees of the garden. But the Lord God called to the man, "Where are you?" He answered, "I heard you in the garden, and I was afraid because I was naked; so I hid." And he said, "Who told you that you were naked? Have you eaten from the tree that I commanded you not to eat from?" The man said, "The woman you put here with me—she gave me some fruit from the tree, and I ate it." (Genesis 3:6–12 NIV)

When God came into the garden, walking, he noticed that Adam's physical characteristics had changed. It was because God knew that Adam's consciousness had changed in a position where Adam and Eve's physical mannerisms were reflecting a different character, a character of disconnection. They were disconnected from God's divine presence because of their sins. We must always remember that our consciousness is a reflection of our integrity and character.

Now remember the reason that God recognized Adam's countenance? I believe that when God created mankind, the emotions that God created mankind with were to connect mankind through our consciousness to stay in tune with God. First of all, the human spirit is nothing more than energy, that energy that transcends but it is in control in our human bodies. Now that energy we refer to as the spirit of mankind. When we are going through our trials, temptations, or pain and suffering, it is detected in our senses and is expressed through our emotions. Our senses are an expression of how we feel.

We radiate the emotions of our senses through our feeling and our consciousness. Our senses control our emotions; our emotions are disciplined through our consciousness. In the state of our consciousness is where God can sense our countenance to know what we are doing that is wrong. That is how God knew that Adam and Eve had sinned.

God exists as spirit that transcends beyond all human existence. When we pray, our prayers are answered by God in the state of energy which is our souls. That is why it is the soul of mankind that we are trying to save. We can only save our souls through God's Word, and it is through God's Word that we embrace His consciousness. In other words, we need God's Word to save our souls.

God is also able to tell or explain through mankind emotions of what is wrong with mankind. That is why when we stay in tune with God's consciousness, God is able to recognize our pain and suffering through our emotions that God created within each and every one of us. That emotion is the spiritual connection mankind has with God.

That connection is spiritual. I am saying we have a tendency to do this all the time, especially when we have developed a relationship with a person that you can tell how they feel, how their emotions feel by their voices, or how they look. That is why God felt a negative energy in

Adam's character when He came into the garden. That is why he said, "Did you eat of the tree of good and evil?"

When Adam and Eve ate of the fruit, it allowed Adam and Eve to have a consciousness of discernment. They were able to know what was right from wrong. They did not want to constantly depend on God's Word for guidance. They wanted the ability to have the knowledge to distinguish what is right and wrong. Because of them eating the apple, it placed them in a position of discernment. I am not going to get into a theological argument about whether it was a fruit or even an apple. Now the truth of matter is that God gave mankind a choice and direction that would cause them to live in perfect peace and harmony with God and themselves.

At the point that Adam and Eve were able to get a better understanding of what was right and wrong, they came into an understanding of what was right and wrong, which I refer to as the understanding of discernment; or let me put it this way: when a person is able to discern what is right and what is wrong, this is where mankind's consciousness becomes very important to his free will because if we know that something is right and wrong, we are responsible for our own actions because we already know that what we are getting ready to do or not do is wrong, and it is God who makes us responsible for our sins toward Him.

Although Adam sinned, it was not the act of the sin that God recognized but Adam's mannerism that caused God to know that Adam did something wrong. Our mannerisms are also a reflection of our consciousness.

Adam and Eve now knew that they had a price to pay about their free will and the responsibilities that come with

God's free will. When you are conscious of the truth of right and wrong, just because man is able to exercise his free will does not mean that man is able to challenge God's authentic power or wisdom. The state of all consciousness is best defined in its own state of development which has its own character of action.

For example, the conscience is a person who developed a sense of quality of one's character and conduct, adherence to moral principles of life while in fellowship with God, and a consideration of fairness of one's own submissiveness.

When we look at the spiritual views of consciousness, especially from my perspective, I would say that it is knowledge that is spiritually motivated by mankind's faith toward God. It is spiritually a transcending sense of knowledge that creates discernment in a person's character. It is a miraculous sense of knowledge and power based on man's experience of life, which brings man into some type of a realm of thought that causes man to exercise his spiritual and divine power toward God.

# THE CONSCIOUSNESS OF GOOD AND EVIL

Now the serpent was craftier than any of the wild animals the Lord God had made. The woman said, "The serpent deceived me, and I ate." Now in the state of man's ability to reason is the question that comes to mind, who gave man the knowledge, wisdom, and the ability to reason? Who was it? It was God. This is when man actually realized that he had no control over life or death. Death is in man's state of reasoning.

Man realized he could not prevent life from existing or death from becoming a part of his nature. That alone puzzled man because life and death are part of man's nature, but how could something like life, which is so precious, rob man of controlling it? And death, which is a part of man's nature, still robs man from controlling his true death as well as mankind's destiny?

Let me remind you, God gave man the authority over the birds of the air and beasts of the field. God did not give man control over the complete existence of life and death. Man must remember that authority (dominion) was given to him by God. Power and control have always belonged to God.

Let me repeat that again: power and control have always belonged to God. From the time that man through his concept of reasoning thinks that he should be God or has the potential to be God or even think that he is God, that is where all of the hate and destruction of the world starts, and evilness starts to take root and becomes a true reality to many people in the world.

At this point, we have to understand the importance of why mankind should develop a spiritual consciousness and stay in tune with developing our spiritual consciousness through God's divine Word.

Now, again, the time that man through his concept of reasoning thinks that he should be God or has the potential to be God or even thinks that he is God, this is what starts many religious doctrines and schools of thought, such as philosophical thought, theological thought, and most of all, theoretical thought and the atheist school of thought where mankind thinks that he is God and he created himself and would even agree that God does not exist in the capacity that the Bible say God does. Please read the book *The Theory of Theology* by James Grant.

This is what we refer to as existentialism philosophers. This is the school of thought that gave birth to many religions in the world that do not teach God's divine doctrine. Here is why: because mankind wants to take God's place, but mankind does not have the potential, the discipline, and the power it takes to be God.

Remember that it is mankind's spirituality that keeps him connected to God through prayer and fasting. The idea that a person knows that God exists creates a spiritual awareness in that person mind, but it is the commitment of faith that keeps us in tune with God's righteousness and God's grace.

It is up to mankind to develop their spiritual awareness in God. Our spiritual awareness is strength and development of our faith in God. That is why it is not in man's authority to control the existence and creation of life and death, but again, it is in the power and control of God to do so. But if mankind does not know or has control over his birth or his death, what gives mankind the audacity to want to be God?

This alone allowed man within his physical existence to recognize that he is seriously limited in the physical manifestation of his existence. Man should question his limitations, especially when man is limited in the realms of his own physical creation that God has prepared before mankind. As man progresses in the essence of his consciousness, both spiritually and physically, he should somehow recognize that God's power is beyond mankind's control or is a power that mankind cannot control.

Again, just like mankind does now, when he is going to die, mankind still doesn't know even know how he was created. Mankind should have already understood that there is a power which is more powerful than what mankind can imagine. That omnipotent power is God's power that exists in the world, which actually surpasses man's understanding and comprehension of the true existence of life and creation.

Man has always asked the question, what is God's purpose for my life? How do we as human beings get to define our purpose in God, what is required of us? And how do we reach our potential as Christians to actually know what God's purpose is for our lives?

When we speak about how we define our purpose in life through God's omnipotent power, when we look into the book of Genesis, we get an understanding about God's potential for all men and women. Genesis 1:26–27 says:

> Then God said, "Let us make mankind in our image, in our likeness, so that they may rule over the fish in the sea and the birds in the shy, over all livestock the creatures that move along the ground. So God created mankind in his own image of God he created them; male and female he created them.

To me, this is one of the most powerful as well as most profound verses in the Bible where God has shown His love for mankind before man was created or even acknowledged themselves as human beings. We get a better understanding of God's spiritual essence and divine omnipotent power that transcended as well as transformed His power into the creation of mankind's existence.

If God created man in the image and likeness of Him, wouldn't it be obvious that God wanted men to be like Him, where man can enjoy life and become more spiritually motivated and have a better understanding of each other, reaching the many spiritual levels that God has bestowed upon us as human beings always allowing God to magnify His purpose and presence in our lives as human beings?

Now when we look at verse 27 of the same book, Genesis, we recognize that God gave man and woman the authority over everything that moves upon the face of the earth. In some verses, the word *dominion* is strongly expressed to give man more authority to maintain order in the authority that God has given to mankind throughout the world.

For example, when we speak of the word *dominion*, what is God making reference to? He places man in a position of authority, and that authority is the order of how things should be. For example, *dominion* means to maintain order, and that order God gave man; that authority to exercise over every living creature on earth. He did not mean that man should exercise dominion over each other. We must remember that dominion was first given to Adam and Eve.

Dominion was also taken from Adam and his wife because of the sin they committed. Adam and Eve were to pass the dominion of God's authority on to their offspring. That consciousness of dominion was that of a spiritual purpose and reason for mankind to be given such a privilege over God's creation.

Now the question we need to ask is, if God gave man dominion over the birds of the air and over the animals of the earth, then every man and woman is given a purpose by God, right? Because all authority, especially from God, is given mankind. So because of mankind's existence, it comes with a purpose from God, and only God can reveal that purpose to man. Why did God give man this type of authority over the animals and everything that crept upon the face of the earth?

Because of man's being (existences) placed in the image and likeness of God. God was able to give man and woman more of a consciousness to rationalize their meaning and being in life through whatever choices mankind chose.

Most people want to define their purpose through their children. Now having children is our nature, and in having children, we begin to prioritize our lives not losing control of our focus on God. It is not God's purpose for our lives to have children because it is more of a gift. God's purpose is determined and based on our direction in life and how submissive we are to God's will.

Here is what happened. We can admit that we serve an awesome God. He is so awesome that He knew us before we were even created in our mother's womb. In the book of Jeremiah 1:5, God emphasizes on the idea that, "Before I formed you in your mother's womb, I knew you; before you were born, I set you apart; I appointed you as a prophet to the nation."

Man's nature is not determined by his purpose. It is determined by his process of life. Man's purpose is determined by God's reason for his life. That person's purpose and responsibility in life are governed by their actual faith in God.

There is a statement that God acknowledges to us in His Word, and that is before we entered our mother's womb, God knew who we were. God knew who we were before we entered our mother's womb. That means that God created every man with a purpose and reason to exist.

Does that mean that God is going to give each man a purpose and reason to exist? Or does that mean that our lives are defined through our purpose and reason in life by God?

What people need to understand is when we accept God as our personal Lord and Savior, we are given a special introduction to God's faith. This introduction consists of a very important privilege which is salvation. This is when we get a better understanding of God's grace and mercy.

Here is something that we must recognize, and that is from the very first time that we accept God as our personal Savior, we embraced God's faith. Remember when we accept God, we accepted God not knowing what His faith, mercy, and salvation actually means.

This is why our faith becomes very important to God. It is through our devotional time—personal time with God—that we begin to understand and develop our own spiritual awareness, and that is what helps us shape our Godlike consciousness and integrity.

The consciousness is the state of mind. It is how we think and how we develop our thoughts. It also has to do with our understanding of God's Word. But our character is a reflection of our integrity. Our integrity determines our faith in God's consciousness, and we live our lives determined to develop our consciousness in God's grace and mercy.

Our faith is our belief in God's consciousness, and whatever we believe in, it is developed in our character and mannerisms, and that is how we develop our Godlike consciousness which relates to God's authentic love for mankind.

# EXISTENTIALIST PHILOSOPHERS BELIEVE?

One of the most interesting things about mankind's free will is it makes mankind responsible for their own actions, even if mankind's actions go against God's will. This simplifies and brings clarity to why mankind is responsible for their own sins.

In other words, mankind can do what he or she wants, even if it goes against God's will. Remember mankind has something called free will. We can also look at mankind's free will and God's compassion in this sense that God is saying to mankind, "I love you so much that I still have enough compassion through my grace and mercy to forgive you, even when your free will goes against My will that I have called you to do."

Even when mankind's free will goes against God's consciousness and faith, God's grace and mercy have developed enough compassion to forgive us of our actions that go against God's will for our lives.

Let us look at it from this perspective: it seems that in the essence of mankind's free will, God gave mankind free will to disappoint Him or maybe to let mankind know that they have to be responsible for the actions of their own free will.

What God is trying to acknowledge to mankind is, even in your state of your free will, you are responsible for your own actions. It also means that God never wanted to control mankind enough where he couldn't be responsible for their own existence, especially when mankind's free will goes against God's consciousness and God's faith. Whatever the outcome of mankind's free will is, God still has enough compassion to forgive mankind beyond what mankind cannot comprehend as the true state of God's forgiveness.

It is like God creating mankind to be free; free enough to even dispute or disagree whether God Himself exists or whether God is the God that God says He is. Now that is a powerful state for mankind to be in when we begin to implement mankind's nature in the state of mankind's nature.

In the state of mankind's nature, mankind has no limits in what mankind can achieve. Where mankind has no limits in their thoughts or even in his nature. Because of mankind's free will, mankind is able to exercise his free will, and this is the price that even Jesus Christ paid for mankind's free will on the cross.

In other words, mankind's free will was created by God, but it still cost the death of His Son, Jesus Christ. When mankind's free will goes against God's will, that is when mankind's free will becomes a sin toward God. Mankind's action of their free will becomes the sin that mankind has committed toward God.

The question one might ask is, why would God give mankind such a freedom of a free will? With mankind's free will comes a certain state of consciousness, a consciousness to understand what is right and what is wrong under the free will of man. There comes a consciousness that is able to direct mankind's free will to travel in a path of spiritual righteousness toward God.

It has always been interesting to see how God is able to give mankind a "free will," and in the process of man's "free will," God is still able to give enough compassion to forgive mankind, even when our thoughts go against whatever God's will is for our lives.

Mankind even came up with a philosophical ideology that is known as existentialist philosophy which acknowledges that mankind also believes that there is God Himself, and mankind is also able to define their own existence without God being their Creator.

When we become a part of God's consciousness, we become like God, just like we were made in the image and likeness of God. We become one with God in mind, body, and soul. It's interesting how people use God's Word to satisfy their agenda.

Now many people want to be God in their own right, but they don't have the compassion and the love and the discipline it takes to be God. What happens if God dies and leaves you in charge of the world? Would you have the same compassion and love to rule the world? Or would you destroy the world because you are so tired of mankind complaining and fighting that you decide, "I am going to end this world?"

God already knows that it takes love, compassion, mercy, and most of all grace to still love mankind beyond the actions of mankind's free will and nature. When people want to take God out of the equation as God, they use this verse, but here's a verse that is always use by the philosophers and those people who are atheists who are trying to build on a false premise that God does not exist, and it's interesting that they don't read the Bible, but what they end up doing is going directly to this verse to say that we are all gods and that God does not exist:

> The "gods" know nothing, they understand nothing. They walk about in darkness; all the foundations of the earth are shaken. "I said, 'You are 'gods;' you are all sons of the Most High. But you will die like mere mortals; you will fall like every other ruler." (Psalm 82:5–7 NIV)

Let me elaborate. The existentialist philosophers also believe that man is his own God. The existentialist philosophers believe that if you want to give meaning to your life, it is left up to you; for example, you determine your own meaning and being in life. Now with that type of mentality creates this type of character in a person or people, and that is, "I am my own God," and when we think like that, we become self-centered, heartless, and most of all damaging to others. This is when we try to conquer others. This attitude of conquering others creates many wars, mass killings, and causes many societies to neglect the poor and the widows. This attitude comes when a person or people does not want to be responsible for their own free will or be affiliated with understanding God's consciousness.

Here is one person or people who does not respect God's consciousness: these are the people who do wrong to others in order to gain material possessions. People who think that God does not exist and exercise their "free will" have this sense of an attitude: "I do not have to answer to anybody, not even God."

This statement becomes foolish of the prideful man who thinks that God does not exist. Here is why: because they have satisfied themselves enough with so much doubt about how God does not exist that their consciousness actually tricks them into believing that they are gods and that God truly does not exist.

Now when we believe in God's consciousness, we have a spiritual responsibility to mankind. One is to teach and preach God's Word; second is to have compassion for the rich, poor, and widows of the world because I am my own god. Now that's great. That same mentality sometimes exists because of man's free will. Sometimes because man is given the opportunity to exercise his free will. Man somehow exercises his free will enough that mankind sometimes feels that he is a god all by himself and everything that mankind does is all right.

This is the mentality of the world as it relates to God's teaching along with man's free will. God mentioned in His inspirational writings that we are all gods. This is what it says. So does that make the existentialist philosopher right about their statement toward who God actually is? Let us look at God's Word where he actually mentioned that men are gods.

> God presides in the great assembly he renders judgment among the gods. How long will you defend the unjust and show partiality to the wicked? Defend the weak and the fatherless uphold the cause of the poor and oppressed. Rescue the weak and the needy; deliver them from the hand of the wicked. The gods know nothing they walk about in darkness; all the foundations of the earth are shaken. I said you are gods you are all sons of the most high. But you will die like mere mortals, you will fall like every other ruler. (Psalm 82:1–7 NIV)

First of all, the more we remove ourselves from God, the more chaos and the more disoriented the world is becoming. Right now, the world is losing it structure, values, morals, and direction. When Satan is saying he wants to be like God, what was he making reference to? I want to be my own God. That became the fall of Satan. Then, when I look at the existentialist who mentions to people that they are their own gods, first of all, almost everyone wants to be their own god. Sometimes we feel that sense of responsibility. But men do not have the potential to be God. Now that should not conflict with the idea that man wants to hold himself responsible and have the same standards as God. That is not blasphemy Because God did say, "I created man in My image."

Now we do admit that we should be Christlike. We do admit that we want to be examples of Christ. We do admit that we want to be constantly staying in tune with God's Word which is also making reference to God's consciousness. We do admit that we have faith in God. We do admit we believe in God. Then there is nothing wrong with wanting to be responsible for being your own god.

That is why it is very important for us to become submissive to God's will because he can use us like the gods we want to become. For example, He want us to be faithful. God wants us to have faith in Him. God wants us to be dedicated builders and believers of his faith. God wants to grant us His salvation. God wants us to be a teacher of His Word. God wants us to be doers of His Word. God even wants us to be lovers of our enemies.

Before man can comprehend or even think about the idea or thought that he is his own god, man has to come into his own understanding that he is the existence and being of God's creation. Man has to realize that he was created, and he is not the creator of his own creation. Man must also understand that he is not in control of his destiny, like he thinks the Creator of creation is in control of His own destiny. And God is the substance, matter, and form of all existence. We are privileged to even embrace God's consciousness and become a part of God's creation.

Man must realize that he did not create himself. God created man. For example, it takes a lot of discipline and responsibility to achieve God's success as it relates to the creation and free will of mankind's nature, but only God can achieve those things. Here is why: because He is God Almighty. I know I could not be God.

I do not have the compassion, the extended love it takes for me to achieve the forgiveness that God has for me. I know that I do not have that same love for others like God does for me. Because if you try to kill one of my family members or my children, I cannot be like God and Abraham, although that same God has given me the potential to become like Him and Abraham in my faith and consciousness.

That is what I am striving to become. I do not have the love that my God has for me and mankind. I do not have the patience that my God has for mankind's needs. I only have the potential to be like God.

Always remember that you might think that you are gods, but you will die like mortals and you will fall like every other ruler. The mortals we know are like men who will die, but God will live on forever. These were men that were ruling, but remember that God does not die.

While in the physical manifestation of life, we are limited. We are limited because our matter is the form of our physical body that houses the soul of mankind until eternity, so that is why we are limited.

Even the rulers of the world are limited. Our energy is placed into matter, and that limits our ability in life. Now we must remember that God is a spirit, and in His state of energy, He transcends in the essence of power. No man, no king can amount to God's compassion, power, and righteousness.

First of all, God's state of existence is transcendental. It exists in the spiritual realm, yet it is a power of energy that transcends into substance, matter, and form. Let us look at the energy of God and how it pertains to God actually being a spirit. That is what we refer to as the spirit of God or God's spirit.

That spirit is the energy that God uses to transcend into substance that substance could be water, liquid, or even the blood of life that Jesus Christ shed on the cross for the sins of the world. The blood that Jesus shed for me and you has a certain power in it, and within that power, God created mankind. That energy we are talking about creates the state of substance.

Now substance is determined by its own nature or the makeup that is in the substance that is being transformed into its own physical existence. That substance takes on the nature of motion. Motion is the movement of creation, especially when that motion is in the state of creation. We need the motion of movement in order to create life. In this case, we need God's movement in order to bring the creation of life into existence. Nothing exists or is created without motion and God's authority.

Motion is determined by God, but it also depends on the nature of a thing as God moves substance into its motion. What causes motion, even in the state of our existence? Motion comes from the gravity of the universe that holds the energy that God transcended into substance, and everything that is being held by gravity is all controlled by God.

While the gravity of the universe slows the substance down, it gives substance a chance to become matter. As matter changes, it creates the nature of the thing that comes into existence. As matter slows down, it holds the substance of life together. That is when matter takes on the created process of form. Now what we are to be reminded of is that everything that exists comes into existence because of God's consciousness. As that thing comes into existence because of its form, God gives that thing that is in its own form a nature.

How do we define nature? I would define nature from this perspective, and that is the purpose and reason of why we exist is really our nature. Our nature defines our reason and purpose of why we exist. Our reason and purpose are best defined through what God's consciousness and will is for our lives.

The reason why God created mankind had to do with God's consciousness. God's consciousness is what gives mankind a purpose and reason to exist. Each person exists with a purpose and a reason.

God created us with those two things in mind. Our reason and purpose is why God created us, hoping that through our trials, through our adversities, and through trying to battle on a day-to-day basis with our adversaries, in the midst of it all, we would recognize our reason and purpose to exist through God's consciousness.

The only way that we can give our lives true meaning and being in life is through God's consciousness. It is in God's consciousness that mankind's existence has a purpose and reason to exist and serve God as his ultimate creator in life.

When mankind becomes submissive to whatever God's will is for his life, that is when mankind is able to define his reason and purpose to exist. In order for us to define what God's will is for life, it is for us to be submissive to God's will. Being submissive to God's will is how mankind can actually define their true purpose and reason to exist.

We use our reason and purpose to support and enhance the kingdom of God. It is up to us to give our lives true meaning and being. It is our meaning and being that define who we are through God's consciousness. We exist as human beings because we have a nature that exists also within us. Our path in life is determined by our choices. Each choice we make determines what path we are going to travel in life.

The question is, are we going to walk the traveling path that leads to God's conscience? Or are we getting ready to prepare ourselves for the path that leads to hell? That is why in order for us to better enhance our relationship with God and others, we have to stay consistently in tune with God consciousness so that we can actually give our life its true meaning and being to exist.

The problem with that is only God has control over a person's meaning and being in this life, whether we agree or not. We must also remember that although mankind has his free will, God is still in control of mankind's existence, nature, and destiny. It is all control by God's consciousness. It is just a matter of time before mankind dies, that mankind allows his free will to reconnect him to God's will and also God's divine consciousness. When mankind is able to reconnect to God's divine will, that is when mankind is rewarded the gift of salvation.

For example, everything that has a nature has a purpose to exist. That is why God says, "I knew you before you even came into your mother's womb." Because first of all, the energy that we have that we call life is a transcending energy of God's creation. So God knew us before we were actually given a nature and purpose to exist. How can we become a god when in actuality, we did not create our own nature of existence, and we don't have the consciousness to define our own meaning and being in life? How many of us are working in the field that we majored in while in college?

# THE MEANING AND BEING OF OUR LIVES

Here is what I mean when I say, "The meaning and being of God in our lives." We cannot give ourselves a purpose or reason to exist because we don't know what our purpose and reason are in life.

That is why people would go through life trying to find why they are here on earth. Some would go through life trying to make sense out of the nonsense which exists in this world while trying to define what their true purpose and reason in life is. They miss the mark because they never submit to God's consciousness.

Our creation was not left up to us. It was placed in God's hand. Our purpose is determined by God who is the creator of all of the human existence. Think about it. If we created ourselves through evolution, why would we want to choose a lesser means of creation or status in life for ourselves?

Our consciousness of God gives us enough knowledge and experience to know that human beings don't have enough wisdom to create themselves. If we did, we would create ourselves to be superhuman beings who don't die. We are not God. We are the creations of God. The world is a true product of God's creation and existence.

Now let us look at evolution based on the laws. I'd love to create myself as an eagle flying high enough where I can look down at the ignorance of mankind's evilness instead of being a part of mankind's corruption, self-centeredness, and the pain and suffering that we put each other through. I could not make that choice because I had no control of creation and existence.

I might not want to be a human being. Just because I would not want to be a human being, I have no control over my existence and my purpose and reason because of what God wanted me to be, and that is a human being with a nature and purpose to exist in life. Now that decision was decided on through God's consciousness.

The only thing I have control over is to gather enough knowledge and wisdom where I can actually define my purpose in life and try to use my free will as a means to consistently stay in fellowship with God.

Why not choose the responsibility that evolution gave me to be a God? Or why not put a crown on my head to be a king? Why not a God, like the one I serve? And the reason why I cannot do that is simple. That same God created me in the likeness and image of Him. So, yes, I can be like God. I can have a Godlike integrity, but I can never have the omnipresence and omnipotence of God.

Just like I can be God, as long as I recognize my place in the laws of creation—and that is first—I can never be God because I am the created vessel, not the creator of the human vessels, and I am also staying in tune with God's consciousness that makes me in the likeness and image of God.

Whatever position of creation God places me in, I am willing to accept the conditions. Now here is the most serious point in my life, and that is, whatever God wants me to be, I have to stop wrestling with the idea and do it and listen to His Word in order that I might achieve God's purpose and reason for my life to its fullest potential.

I have no control over my complete existence. I have the potential to be a king of this world, but I am not the king of the world. I have the potential to be anything I want based on my free will, but as long as I have given my life to God, I have to be submissive to God's will that he has bestowed upon my life.

Let me reiterate I have the potential to be anything I want based on God's purpose for my life but not a God. Because it was through the authentic hands of God that fashioned me into the image and likeness of Himself. It was through God's consciousness that brought mankind's existence into life and again gave mankind a reason and purpose to exist.

I do not even have the potential to be God, but I do have the potential to be a servant of God. Anything that has any type societal status, man is attracted to it; for example, like a lawyer, doctor, businessperson—all because of the "free will" that has been granted to them by God. Only God knows, and He tries to let us recognize it, even when we go through our trials and tribulations in life. See, when we are faced with our trials and we are going through our trials and adversities, it is the elasticity of our trials that has stretched us so thin that we are getting ready to break. It is in that state and moment in time that God is able to define within us all our reasons purpose and reason.

You see, what happens is you are wrestling so much with your problems and your spiritual consciousness that you have to make a decision, but all the time because you paid more attention to your trials and the blessings that God has given you and you also pray more, sometimes when our trials have manifested themselves in our lives, we also have a tendency to pray more for the adversities that we are facing. And it is through those adversities and trials that create many conditions that God is able to define mankind through mankind's adversities and adversaries the purpose and a reason for to live.

# WHY DID GOD CREATE MANKIND?

One of the most intriguing questions is that why did God created mankind or even take the position just to say let us create mankind. God took His creation of mankind further by saying, "Let us create mankind in our image and likeness."

I think the image and likeness of God mean—remember, this is from my perspective—when God said, "Let us create mankind," He means to think consciously and be able for mankind to depend on and make decisions based on their own free will. That is when God gave mankind the opportunity to be like Him but not the power to be God.

Now the potential that mankind has to exercise the power of God comes from the knowledge and wisdom mankind has of God's Word, which brings mankind into the power of God's consciousness. Even when God gave mankind dominion over everything that is upon, and on this earth.

The knowledge of God—some people ask the question if God is all-knowing, why does He continue to create man? If God is all knowing, God should realize that mankind has a sinful nature and is imperfect. That is why we need to stay in constant fellowship and unity with God. Here is why because mankind is constantly vulnerable to sin, and will do wrong and create injustice acts toward each other.

The question still remains: Why does God continue to create mankind? Some people would say to give mankind an opportunity to be forgiven of their sins. God gives mankind the opportunity to repent.

Even in the state of mankind's repentance, that gives mankind an opportunity to develop their spiritual consciousness, in the state of mankind's awareness of who God is. The problem is no one knows the heart and mind of God. We all can have a question of an opinion, but no one knows the mind, or heart, of God.

The one thing we do know is that God is so compassionate that His compassion is sometimes taken as a weakness by the people who believe in God. I think sometimes we don't struggle enough to prevent ourselves sometimes, from sinning.

I think we sin because we know that God is going to forgive us. To me, that is abusing God's grace and mercy and putting your salvation in jeopardy. Sometimes we need to realize that God might not forgive us for the sins that we have committed because God already knows that you have committed voluntarily and you were not under any pressure. You just committed sin or sins because you know that God, through His love, grace, and mercy, is going to forgive you.

You sin not because you were being tested or challenged by the adversities and principalities and things unseen but because you know God is going to forgive you. I think for someone to have that type of mentality in any type of relationship is abusive to the relationship, and it is abusive to God's grace and His mercy.

That is why we should constantly develop enhance and mature in God's consciousness that these little things have significance and we know the significance of God's true grace and mercy.

For example, if God is all-knowing, why create man? God should know that the next person He creates is going to sin, so why continue to allow man to waste his time committed to sin and allowing mankind to die because of it?

First of all, man should be privileged that God created them in the image and likeness of God Himself and still gave man the dominion over everything that God had created. When God created man, He created one man which was Adam. Adam determined the future and the outcome of all human beings.

For example, when God created Adam, he created Adam based on love. God had an appreciation for mankind. God placed man in a stress-free environment. The other question is that because God created man, does it not give man the opportunity or privilege to think that God created him and then gave him power other His creation and the world? Mankind needs to be reminded that we all exist because of God's consciousness.

Sometimes I think that mankind thinks that he is doing God a favor by trying to be God and taking God's responsibilities away. Although mankind wants to be God, mankind does not have the mental capacity to be God or even comprehend his own responsibilities.

From my perspective, God does not need us. We need God. We will always need Him because our physical existence is limited while God is omnipotent. His existence has no limits, and God is constantly creating the existence of life. Man in his own physical existence should never feel that he is doing God a favor. Instead, we need God's favor upon us so that we can be grounded firm in our salvation through God's consciousness, which God has already implemented in our minds and in our hearts.

For example, when God created man, it was not like man was one of God's first creations. It was not that man was God's first form of creation. So why do some men give themselves so much credit and pride, assuming that God could never be God if He did not create them from their mother's womb? Some people have the audacity to believe in that manner.

I cannot understand why these men would ask God a question like this, and that is if God is knowledgeable of all things, "Why is it that man assumes that God should end the world because He knows which of the men on Earth are going to heaven and which are going to hell? So why prolong human life?" Well to help that person out if God did end human life, the same people who ask that question would be going to hell. God created everything in order, including mankind, but only God knows the time when life will end.

First of all, the Bible begins without making man God's first creation. The Bible begins with the creation of the universe; it does not mention man was the first creation. It states in Genesis 1:1, "In the beginning, God created the heavens and the earth." This single verse describes the actual transformation of God's creation. Now let us look at the second form creation

Now the second creation was influence by a thick mass that was over the earth. This was long after the universe. Genesis 1:2, "Now the earth was [or became] formless and empty, darkness was over the surface of the deep, and The Spirit of God was hovering over the waters."

The first recorded words of God that we have was creating the light of the world. Now let us look at the book of Genesis. Let us look at the whole chapter for a minute and what we observe as a young child coming up in church sometimes because of our life's experiences as we mature. It seems that some of the things in the Bible have changed.

In reality, as a child, we did not have the life experience to confirm the true evidence of God's Word. We must understand that God's Word has repositioned itself based on the life experience we have matured into as adults.

God's Word does not change. It validates our faith and commitment as well as our purpose and reason for living with God. As we grow older in life, our reality changes because our experiences in life causes us to mature into whatever our own state of reality is. Our experiences in life are what shapes and develop our true reality in life. As mankind embraces their experiences in life, subliminally, those experiences shapes who we are as a person.

Whatever experiences we face in life good or bad, it is those experiences, which shapes who we are as an individual, or person in life. Now when we embrace God's Word, everything that we have experienced once again shapes our integrity and character.

Our integrity and character create and produce our reality. Our reality is what we have learned about who we are the things that we want to achieve, the things that we want to do all of this is in our conscious state of mind.

Where we can only experience everything that is physical, that we experienced in the physical realm of our existence is physical. Now as we try to define what our true reality in life is, or what we try to comprehend, what our true existence is, is when we try to define our true purpose, and reason for life.

Now once again everything that we have experienced can only be defined through our own conscious state of mind. That consciousness state of mind brings makes us seek our own spirituality of whom we are embracing God's consciousness and salvation.

That is what makes us who we are, but it is not for us to stay in a state of seeking out who we are because everything that we experience in life is in the physical realm of our existence.

Our physical experience, whether good or bad, is what drives us and motivate us to seek more of who we are, what we want to become, and what we can become and use our experiences, to start to seek more in death, for ourselves of who we actually are in the consciousness of God's existence.

The more we seek, we realize that there is a spiritual realm that we need to conquer, understand, comprehend, and live by in order for us to develop who we are and comprehend who we are and understand who we really are as a person who has believed in God's Word; and it is through our own spiritual consciousness that exists within ourselves that we can develop the reason and purpose why God allows us to exist.

We must ask the question what is it in our lives at a certain time, that drives us to become motivated, and driven just to be like God.

With all of the good and the bad things that we have experienced in life.

It seems that there is something in life that drives us and motivates us, where we want to become like God. Some people ask the magic question, and that is. This all to life is our existence, or there is more to this physical life that we exist in.

But then we get a light-bulb moment that gives us the determination and motivation to want to seek God in the image and likeness of who God really is and the image and likeness in which God says that He has created mankind.

That is when we start to challenge the idea of what it is like to be in the image and likeness of whom God said that we created us in, which is the image and likeness of what God said when God mentioned, "I created mankind in the image and likeness of who God is," which I think is mankind's free will.

We start to say "I want to want to seek what is it about that image of likeness greatness that God has created me in that I want to seek and talk about for mankind to become consciously aware of that statement the image and likeness of God." What is it that exists within ourselves that drives and motivates us to become spiritually enlightened by God's essence and the substance, which I referred to as God's Word and which from a spiritual perspective and not from a philosophical or theoretical perspective of where mankind wants to control the world, that mankind did even create? But from a spiritual perspective, this embraces and allows us to exercise the love that God is talking about. Our free will give us the opportunity to exercise God's love, compassion, grace, and mercy. Mankind has that opportunity based on mankind's free will. That is what I think the image and likeness of God mean to mankind.

I'm not referring to greed or people being self-centered; it is about having that thirst, motivation, drive, and ambition, to try to place themselves in the image and likeness of God.

What mankind doesn't want to realize is that it is in the Bible when God said let make man in our own image, and likeness.

> Then God said, "Let us make mankind in our image, in our likeness, so that they may rule over the fish in the sea and the

birds in the sky, over the livestock and all the wild animals, and over all the creatures that move along the ground." So God created mankind in his own image, in the image of God he created them; male and female he created them. God blessed them and said to them, "But fruitful and increase in number; fill the earth and subdue it. Rule over the fish in the sea and the birds in the sky and over every living creature that moves on the ground." Then God said, "I give you every seed-bearing plant on the face of the whole earth and every tree that has fruit with seed in it. They will be yours for food. And to all the beasts of the earth and all the birds in the sky and all the creatures that move along the ground—everything that has the breath of life in it—I give every green plant for food." And it was so. God saw all that he had made, and it was very good. And there was evening, and there was morning—the sixth day. (Genesis 1:26–31 NIV; https://bible.com/bible/111/gen.1.26-31.NIV)

The reason to seek, and want to become created, in the image and likeness of God, is because God has already, created that trend of thought, in our DNA. while creating mankind to exist in His own consciousness and creation. That thought has been made up in mankind's biological makeup.

As we travel through life experiencing so many things, there is that one experience out of many, which sparks that curiosity, that this cannot be the only thing that exists in our life. This is when we become thirsty and develop a hunger to seek and become in the image, that likeness of God.

This is when we realize that there is more to life than just what we see on a day-to-day basis, there is a spiritual element that is hidden from us. That we can only tap into, through the spiritual consciousness of God.

Our spiritual purpose and reason to live are really defined through the image and likeness of God's consciousness. Which exist within mankind's heart and soul.

Now that is the thought that drives and motivates people to change their way of life and transform their lives. Whatever their conditions are in life, wherever you are right now in your life, and what your conditions are in life. That is when the transformation of mankind from the physical reality of life, becomes the enlightenment of God's consciousness.

In other words, when we deny who we are, and let God's love increases, in our life. That is what ignites the flame, that begins set off the spark, which mankind uses to transform themselves, from a physical being, into becoming a spiritually, consciously, faithfully person that is needed to use God's Word, as their knowledge base to develop their spiritual consciousness, to become in tune, and in fellowship with God's grace and mercy.

That is what allows us to tap into our spirit and soul, and that is what gives us the motivation and determination, to seek our path, through God's righteousness, which we used to better develops our own consciousness in God.

## THE POWER OF GOD'S CONSCIOUSNESS

The things that bring us into our own spiritual existence in life, which are able to transform us from the physical existence of life into the spiritual existence of life. And the only way that we can do this and achieve this is true mankind's consciousness that only he or she had got the opportunity to develop and acknowledge from God's divine, and authentic Word.

First of all, as we mature and understand life more, our life experience also grows. Let us look at this from a realistic perspective. For example, let us look at the hermeneutic interpretation of Genesis:

> In the beginning God created the heavens and the earth. Now the earth was formless and empty, darkness was over the surface of the deep, and the Spirit of God was hovering over the waters. And God said, "Let there be light," and there was light. God saw that the light was good, and he separated the light from the darkness. God called the light "day," and the darkness he called "night." And there was evening, and there was morning—the first day. And God said, "Let there be an expanse between the waters to separate water from water." So God made the expanse and separated the water under the expanse from the water above it. And it was so. God called the expanse "sky." And there was evening, and there was morning—the second day. And God said, "Let the water

under the sky be gathered to one place, and let dry ground appear." And it was so. God called the dry ground "land," and the gathered waters he called "seas." And God saw that it was good. Then God said, "Let the land produce vegetation: seed-bearing plants and trees on the land that bear fruit with seed in it, according to their various kinds." And it was so. The land produced vegetation: plants bearing seed according to their kinds and trees bearing fruit with seed in it according to their kinds. And God saw that it was good. And there was evening, and there was morning—the third day. And God said, "Let there be lights in the expanse of the sky to separate the day from the night, and let them serve as signs to mark seasons and days and years, and let them be lights in the expanse of the sky to give light on the earth." And it was so. God made two great lights—the greater light to govern the day and the lesser light to govern the night. He also made the stars. God set them in the expanse of the sky to give light on the earth, to govern the day and the night, and to separate light from darkness. And God saw that it was good. And there was evening, and there was morning—the fourth day. And God said, "Let the water teem with living creatures, and let birds fly above the earth across the expanse of the sky." So God created the great creatures of the sea and every living and moving thing with which the water teems, according to their kinds, and every winged bird according to its kind. And God saw that it was good. God blessed them and said, "Be fruitful and increase in number and fill the water in the seas, and let the birds increase on the earth." And there was evening, and there was morning—the fifth day. And God said, "Let the land produce living creatures according to their kinds: livestock, creatures that move along the ground, and wild animals, each according to its kind." And it was so. God made the wild animals according to their kinds, the livestock according to their kinds, and all the creatures that move along the ground according to their kinds. And God saw that it was good. Then God said, "Let us make man in our image, in our likeness, and let them rule over the fish of the sea and the birds of the air, over the livestock, over all the earth, and over all the creatures that move along the ground." So God created man in his own image, in the image of God he created him; male and female he created them. God blessed them and said to them, "Be fruitful and increase in number; fill the earth and subdue it. Rule over the fish of the sea and the birds of the air and over every living creature that moves on the ground." Then God said, "I give you every seed-bearing plant on the face of the whole earth and every tree that has fruit with seed in it. They will be yours for food. And to all the beasts of the earth and all the birds of the air and all the creatures that move on the ground—everything that has the breath of life in it—I give every green plant for food." And it was so. God saw all that he had made, and it was very good. And there was evening, and there was morning—the sixth day. (Genesis 1:1–31)

When a person experiences the harmony of God's power, is it true that God needs mankind? Or is it true that mankind needs God? The truth of the matter is man needs the presence of God in their lives. Here is why, and in our need for God, our purpose and reason is manifested and revealed to us.

In the beginning, God created the heavens and earth. Let's move on. God let there be light, and there was light. He even separated the waters to bring order to the land in Genesis 1:27.

I think when we take an in-depth look at God's creation, we must look at the root word of creation. The atheist has used God's creation to try to disapprove the existence of God. People used time as means to disapprove

God. They would say, "How long did it take God to create a rock? How long did it take God to create water?"

The question I ask is, how long did it take Jesus Christ to turn water into wine? So God created the world in seven days. This is the truth. I also think that God could have finished the world sooner. The question I have asked most atheists that ask me that question is, how long did it take Jesus to turn water into wine? How long did it take Jesus to heal the crippled person? How long did it take Jesus to heal the people? How long did it take Jesus to heal the blind? Because of the power of Jesus, the blind man was able to see in seconds; not years or mounts, but seconds. God's consciousness is developed through reading and studying God's Word; but the significance or, may I say, the essence and substance of God's Word come and are manifested in mankind's consciousness.

When mankind is able to embrace God's Word and recognize that through God's Word mankind is living a lifestyle, which reflects the studying, and consciousness of God's Word.

The faith of God's Word comes through the studying of God's Word, and it in the midst of studying God's Word is the technique that brings mankind into spiritual awareness, and it is that state of mankind awareness that develops mankind's consciousness, in God's Word.

It is God's Word, which teaches mankind about the faith, and discipline which comes through God's Word. It is through God's Word that mankind is able to develop and transform their consciousness, through God's Word.

Faith becomes mankind's true reality when mankind is able to use God's Word as a discipline mechanism to manifest God's Word through mankind's physical life, which reflects the discipline of God's Word.

We must act upon God's Word. You see God's Word is a true disciplinary tool that gives mankind a more profound perspective where mankind can sharpen mankind's character and integrity of life. This is what God expects from His believers.

God does not calculate time like man. Then, in regard to what the atheist says, God gave man the opportunity to be created in His image and likeness. Now could man do all this and create the order that the world is in today as the same time as God?

When we look at creation, we should define it from this perspective, and that is *Bara*, which is the Hebrew term that means "God creating something from nothing and bringing it into existence," like mankind. The second Hebrew term is "ex nihilo" and "asah," making a thing or something that already exists in the form of creation, the materials to make something that already exists. But bring that thing to the realization and comprehension that relates to mankind's senses. That comprehension acknowledges the thing that is being created by man's intellectual ability. To recognize the thing is being created by man is being able to recognize its existence for what it is when people create something or manufacture something out of nothing.

For example, when a husband and wife create a child, they are the creators of something that already exists. God through His consciousness already made the process for procreation to exist. So when we think we create something, we are only a process of God's creation. *Bara* is manufacturing something out nothing. In other words, it takes males and females to do what God has done by Himself and in seconds.

Man is in charge of the political, economic, and financial systems of the world, and look at the chaos the world is in, all because man is trying to replace God. There is an imperfection in mankind where mankind cannot govern himself; that is why the more mankind tries control the world, the more chaos the world is in.

The more mankind deviates from God's Word, the more distraction comes into the world. Look at the world's condition now; it is in chaotic state. Whenever a country might be in the process of trying to destroy the world, it seems that there is a spiritual intervention that comes and saves this world. That spiritual intervention is enough where people who are not spiritual cannot recognize and be convinced that God does exist; but those people who are faithful to God can still recognize and experience God's hands in the midst of mankind's chaos.

God's consciousness is His Word. Mankind is able to embrace God's consciousness through learning and understanding God's Word. Truth be told, mankind is able to learn and understand the consciousness of God. But mankind would not understand the mind of God. I know it is God's consciousness. We need God's compassion and consciousness to bring order and peace to this world. The Word of God brings order to this world. How does the Word of God brings order to man's life?

First of all, the Word of God's consciousness sets standards for man to follow. It discusses how man should live. It teaches about the quality of life we have in God's salvation, especially when we die. The Word of God teaches us about the importance of the family structure. It teaches us about our life. It teaches us about how to develop our relationship with God. It also teaches us how to develop our relationships with each other. The Word of God teaches us how to love each other. Even in spite of how people treat you, the Word of God teaches us how to be humble. Even when people dislike you and hate you, for whatever their reason is, even when people think that you are incompetent, even when people think that God is blessing you, more than them, or because God has blessed you more than them.

Also, God who is all knowing is blessing you, and they think that God should not be blessing you or giving you the blessings, that He has been, and is doing to you. Keep focusing and praying to God and giving him all the praises he needs to be the God, that He is in your life

In this case, the one thing that people don't recognize is the hard work and dedication that you have done for God, and that is why God Himself is blessing you. He also knows of the dedication and love that you have acquired and love in doing God's Work.

That is why God, has been blessing you, and the reason that God has been blessing you is simply to but difficult for others. Here is why, because you were in constant praying, and supplication with God, and because of that you, not arguing and quarreling with God, because the work that God has blessed you through, and bless you with has become a burden.

Instead, you flip the script on those same people who have complained and find excuses not to do what God has called them to do. People, you cannot fool God because God created you, men and women, that God refers to as mankind. As a man, you cannot fool a woman because your mother created you from her womb.

And the reason why God is blessing you is that you are doing the things that God has anointed you to do, and this is what brings jealousy amounts the believers of God. What they don't understand is that your relationship with God is what God wanted from them, but they were too self-centered for God to use them or even work through for the positions that God has chosen you and anointed you do.

People still don't know that it is your hard, and determination, to serve God, comes because of your consciousness, and faith in God. It is also your state of mind that God has developed spiritually and manifested spirituality.

The thing is that people have already experienced God's manifestation in you, and they are willing to destroy God's manifestation and happiness. Which God has given you, and placed in your heart and mind. Even in the times of your adversities, trials, tribulations, and temptations and even when you have to face your adversities and your adversaries.

So the question is, does man need God? Or does God need man? In order for mankind to have a divine purpose, he must recognize the existence of God. In order for man to become successful in his salvation, he must first acknowledge the presence in God's faith. God's faith is determined through God's consciousness, and the knowledge and wisdom that a person receives from God's consciousness are the steps that mankind needs to embrace God as his personal Lord and Savior.

If God is able to create the world in the magnitude that God has created the world in, then God is the only one that is able to control the chaos and distraction in the world. Also, He is able to grant mankind his true purpose in life and give man His salvation. To me, that shows the awesomeness of God's relationship working in harmony with mankind's consciousness.

Now here's the thing: when we talk about consciousness, what are we referring to? We are referring to a belief. When a person or people is able to accept that belief, and that belief transcends in their hearts and minds, they love for that belief to become a part of their mind. When the person's or people's mind embraces that belief to become a part of their consciousness, that is when it achieves the essence of faith.

Faith means that you are applying your belief to become a part of your lifestyle. When you embrace your belief to become a part of your lifestyle, that is when you have experienced enough about your belief that you want it to become your reality of life. Now that is with anything, but in this case, this is how God's wisdom becomes the faith and consciousness of mankind's life.

Now we have to look at what is a belief. A belief is nothing more than faith. Then what is faith? Faith is nothing more than a than a belief. How do we know about the difference between faith and a belief? The one thing that faith and belief has is shown in the person's character and mannerisms, or faith and belief becomes the true reality of who we are. That true reality is manifested by our divine consciousness in God.

# WHY THERE WAS A NEED FOR THE HOLY SPIRIT?

I could never understand why God allowed the Holy Spirit to become a part of the godhead or become a part of the Trinity, especially after Jesus's death, the relationship that Jesus brought to man teaching the inspired Word of God.

I think that God knew that after mankind had killed His Son, Jesus Christ, the evilness of man would stop at nothing to destroy God's anointing and His word that God has placed in you in order to elevate your spirituality and your confidence in God.

One of the major things, that God has done for mankind, after the death of His Son Jesus Christ, was to introduce mankind to the Holy Spirit. It is through God's anointing that He gives to mankind and the essence and substance of God's goodness toward mankind that God created something that is more powerful than mankind and more powerful than anything on earth.

What was it that God created that more powerful than mankind themselves or is a powerful force, which dwells in mankind's hearts, mind, and consciousness that gives mankind the power and confidence to serve God? It is called the Holy Spirit.

The Holy Spirit cannot be touched, comprehended, or be understood by a normal person's mind, also the Holy Spirit. The Holy Spirit can only be experienced through people who have are faithful and have a spiritual consciousness.

Our spiritual consciousness comes when a person or people are consciously inspired by God's divine Word or by God. The Holy Spirit cannot be touched, felt, or be experienced by mankind unless God wanted it to happen.

Now the Holy Spirit can only be defined through mankind's consciousness. Mankind's consciousness brings the Holy Spirit into awareness with God, and it is that awareness that exists in mankind's consciousness.

This brings mankind into communication and in tune with God. The Holy Spirit exists, although mankind cannot see, touch, or feel the Holy Spirit. The Holy Spirit is only experienced through mankind's spiritual consciousness.

Mankind also can experience, the Holy Spirit through, God's divine Word. The key to having the Holy Spirit constantly in your life is to protect mankind from their sinful nature and imperfection, especially when mankind is challenged by adversities and adversaries in life. I mean those things that exist in the principalities and things unseen to the human eyes and the human experience that exist in the spiritual realm of mankind's existence.

Someone asks the question, "If mankind can only experience the Holy Spirit in its own nature, what is the nature of the Holy Spirit?" The nature of the Holy Spirit is to lead mankind into all righteousness. But in order for the Holy Spirit to lead mankind has to be in a certain state of consciousness.

Which is the presence, of the Holy Spirit can only take a rest in the house of mankind's body, which is in constant fellowship, and the Holy Spirit is also exercised in mankind's consciousness and faith in God. The Holy Spirit is exercised through mankind's faith in God.

The Holy Spirit is a power that cannot be seen by the physical eye, but it can be experienced by mankind's physical existence. The Holy Spirit can only be seen and recognized through the spiritual eye of mankind's consciousness.

The one thing I want to acknowledge and distinguish is it through mankind's spiritual consciousness. God's Word teaches us about the trinity. God existed for us to correct mankind's sinful nature in imperfections. Then Jesus Christ came also to correct mankind's sinful nature and imperfections. Then the Holy Spirit came and we are living in the time of the Holy Spirit and it is through the Holy Spirit that mankind is able to get some type of clarity of the power of God through the Holy Spirit.

What I'm trying to bring to your attention or emphasize is that the Trinity does exist, to the capacity in which the Bible says it does. I know that there's a lot of theological perspectives and philosophical perspectives that argue against the Trinity.

Each person in the Trinity serves a certain purpose and reason to exist at a certain time of mankind's existence. Who always with for mankind, the intercession of the Holy Spirit comes to mankind through mankind's consciousness.

We must always remember that in the book of Ephesians 6:12, "For we wrestle not against flesh and blood, but against principalities, against powers, against the rulers of the darkness of this world, against spiritual wickedness in high places."

God knew that during the time of Jesus's life on earth, man had the inspiration of Jesus to protect them from the evil men of the world while bringing life to the men and women of the world through God's miraculous Word. This is how we experience the physical manifestation of God's existence. We experience God's manifestation through Jesus Christ's lifestyle and Jesus's relationship toward the father.

Now we must also remember that when we embrace God's consciousness, we are placing ourselves into our own spiritual realm of knowledge and understanding that comes only from God. When we put ourselves in a position of knowledge and understanding, we are becoming in tune with God's fellowship. Our knowledge and understanding of God is what produces the birth of mankind's faith in God.

We must remember that when we live by faith, and our faith is activated, based on the Holy Spirit, the Holy Spirit is the comforter that brings us and keeps us in perfect harmony with God to fight our temptations and trials we have to face. That is why Jesus says in the book of John 14:26, "If you love me, keep my commandments. And I will pray to the Father, and He will give you another comforter."

The Holy Spirit recognizes that mankind already exists in the physical realm of life. Our physical existence is full with much pain and suffering and a little joy if needed or if lucky. If you don't believe me, ask Jesus Christ about pain and suffering. No one has been through as much pain and suffering like Jesus has.

I say that to say this: now we progress into the spiritual realm where man is faced with principalities and things unseen. Now if mankind is not in complete fellowship with God, how can mankind overcome the principalities that he is faced with in this world?

The spiritual realm takes man into a different dimension of life where man is fighting more of his physical battles in the spiritual world. When Jesus spread God's Word, He was giving mankind the spiritual knowledge to fight their physical battles.

Now when Jesus died, Jesus brought mankind closer to God because mankind, through Jesus's death, can identify with God both spiritually and physically. Through Jesus's death, mankind was able to receive salvation. He brought the essence and substance of faith to mankind through Jesus's death He allowed mankind to embrace God's consciousness through the Father's word.

Through Jesus's death, mankind was given another comforter, which is the Holy Spirit, to give mankind the direction needed after Jesus Christ's death, and that is to reconnect back into God's grace. This is a very important point that relates to the Holy Spirit. Jesus knew that when He died, He was going back to the Father in heaven.

Jesus knew from His experience here on earth and while living among the nature of mankind that mankind would do anything they could do to destroy the works of the father.

Jesus and His Father already knew of this time that mankind needed something that could not be touched by mankind or even be manipulated or even be in a position to compromise God's Word or be held by the hands of mankind or even be prisoned or be confined by mankind.

But it had to be something that was still able to allow mankind's consciousness to be spiritually driven and motivated by God's Word. Mankind's faith and spiritual consciousness in God. That is no other than the Holy Spirit.

In other words, something that is in the spiritual realm that mankind cannot touch nor hold long enough to kill or destroy, just like mankind did when they killed Jesus Christ. It has to be something that understands mankind's nature, imperfection on good and evil, but is not absorbed enough to be influenced or controlled by mankind's nature and still be able to understand and have enough knowledge of mankind's nature in order to interact with mankind's nature.

The only one that can do this for mankind is the Holy Spirit. But also, He is spiritual enough to lead mankind in the same direction that God the Father want mankind to walk in and still allow mankind through his free will to experience God's divine purpose and reason for themselves and give mankind enough freedom to exercise his free will, even if it means going against God's divine Word. Now that we have the Holy Spirit, that is what makes the Holy Spirit the true intercessor for mankind.

Now let us view the nature of God's spirit which I referred as similar to the Holy Spirit. When I look into the book of Genesis 1:1–2, "In the beginning God created the heavens and the earth. Now the earth was formless and empty, darkness was over the surface of the deep, and the Spirit of God was hovering over the waters." What I experience from that chapter and verse is how the nature of God's Spirit exists, just like the Holy Spirit. In this verse, I am focusing on the state or sentence that relates more to the Spirit.

We gathered that God's Spirit is a spirit that transcends. When I say *transcend*, I mean that something is in motion. It can move from one place to another. While the spirit of God is in motion, it is not limited like mankind is in the physical existence.

The spirit is not embraced in matter, so it has no limitations of its existence. Because the spirit is energy. It can transcend and transform into anything that is material or has matter, and everything that God transcends into has a nature.

Because God is the Creator, He is also able to become transcendent and transcend into the transformation of the nature of that thing, but when God wants to transcend into anything, although mankind might able to transcend into something, God is able to use the nature of that thing and change it to reach the consciousness of mankind. For example, let us look at Exodus 3:1–17:

> Now Moses was tending the flock of Jethro
> his father-in-law, the priest of Midian,

and he led the flock to the far side of the wilderness and came to Horeb, the mountain of God. There the angel of the Lord appeared to him in flames of fire from within a bush. Moses saw that though the bush was on fire it did not burn up. So Moses thought, "I will go over and see this strange sight—why the bush does not burn up." When the Lord saw that he had gone over to look, God called to him from within the bush, "Moses! Moses!" And Moses said, "Here I am." "Do not come any closer," God said. "Take off your sandals, for the place where you are standing is holy ground." Then he said, "I am the God of your father, the God of Abraham, the God of Isaac and the God of Jacob." At this, Moses hid his face, because he was afraid to look at God. The Lord said, "I have indeed seen the misery of my people in Egypt. I have heard them crying out because of their slave drivers, and I am concerned about their suffering. So I have come down to rescue them from the hand of the Egyptians and to bring them up out of that land into a good and spacious land, a land flowing with milk and honey—the home of the Canaanites, Hittites, Amorites, Perizzites, Hivites and Jebusites. And now the cry of the Israelites has reached me, and I have seen the way

## THE POWER OF GOD'S CONSCIOUSNESS

the Egyptians are oppressing them. So now, go. I am sending you to Pharaoh to bring my people the Israelites out of Egypt." But Moses said to God, "Who am I that I should go to Pharaoh and bring the Israelites out of Egypt?" And God said, "I will be with you. And this will be the sign to you that it is I who have sent you: When you have brought the people out of Egypt, you will worship God on this mountain." Moses said to God, "Suppose I go to the Israelites and say to them, 'The God of your fathers has sent me to you,' and they ask me, 'What is his name?' Then what shall I tell them?" God said to Moses, "I am who I am. This is what you are to say to the Israelites: "I am has sent me to you."' God also said to Moses, "Say to the Israelites, 'The Lord, the God of your fathers—the God of Abraham, the God of Isaac and the God of Jacob—has sent me to you.' "This is my name forever, the name you shall call me from generation to generation. "Go, assemble the elders of Israel and say to them, 'The Lord, the God of your fathers—the God of Abraham, Isaac and Jacob—appeared to me and said: I have watched over you and have seen what has been done to you in Egypt. And I have promised to bring you up out of your misery in Egypt into the land of the Canaanites, Hittites, Amorites, Perizzites, Hivites and Jebusites—a land flowing with milk and honey." (Exodus 3:1–17)

The bush appeared to be burning. Both the angel and the Lord's presence were able to capture Moses' attention, just enough to make Moses inquisitive enough to go over to the bush because the bush was not on fire. Moses wanted to experience that bush burning, although there were flames coming from the bush, and the bush was not hot enough to burn the leaves of the bush, which the flames were coming from. But God spoke to Moses from a bush that was burning yet not hot enough to scorch the bush. That is how God is able to change the nature of a thing in order to capture the attention of mankind if something is acting out of its nature. Then that thing that is acting out of its nature, God can use it to capture mankind's nature.

Please pay attention. It is God trying to transform your consciousness in order that you might be submissive to your free will so that you can do God's will. Now this is also very important to know, and that is why mankind needs to be taught about the principalities and things unseen, especially those things that mankind has no control over, such as the principalities and things unseen to mankind. This is why Jesus let us know that we are going to have a comforter, and Jesus listed the position that the comforter was going to be responsible for toward God and mankind.

Jesus is letting us know about the spiritual integrity and relationship of the Holy Spirit. In order for man to fight against the principalities and things unseen, man has to have something or someone who understands the nature of these things that Jesus refers to as principalities and things unseen and that man is going to be faced with.

The thing that we must recognize as Christians is to keep mankind in a spiritual position to spread God's Word. When Jesus died, it started a spiritual battle for mankind's souls. That is why we need the Holy Spirit to support us in better combating with the principalities and thing unseen.

Here is why: because mankind exists in the physical manifestation of life. Mankind is still limited in their existence. Now because our spirit is an energy that is able to transcend as well as transform mankind into matter, our physical existence is limited.

What the Holy Spirit does is allow us to recognize the strategies and evil desires of Satan's relationship with mankind so we can prepare ourselves through God's consciousness and so we can recognize the unseen evil of Satan that exists around us that we cannot recognize within our own physical existence.

For example, have you ever woken up with the intention to get to work on time, but for some strange reason, things are not falling in place, like you cannot find your keys? That is when you say it is one of those days, and now for whatever reason, you leave late.

Now that morning, you got a phone call from someone, telling you that the road you travel, many people die on that road. At this point, that is when we recognize the importance of the Holy Spirit's protection upon us from God. Now because you were late going to work, you were protected by the Holy Spirit. That is when we experience the true intercessor, the Holy Spirit.

We did not understand the outcome of the situation or even the adversities that we might have faced at that time that would have caused our deaths. So this would allow man to recognize the evilness that he is surrounded with on a spiritual level.

Man exists in the physical manifestation of life. So how would man know what goes on in the many different dimensions of life, even on a spiritual level? Matter exists in the physical plane of life. Mankind's existence is physical. Man needs the Holy Spirit to intercede for him, even in a different dimension of life, especially the spiritual dimension. We think that all we do is read the Scriptures, and everything is all right. No, we are always struggling with principalities and things unseen. That struggle will never stop as long as we are living.

That is why mankind needs a divine consciousness. That divine consciousness is what keeps us aware and cognitive of the Holy Spirit. The Holy Spirit is mankind's eyesight and wisdom into the spiritual world of good and evil. Also, the Holy Spirit is the vision of mankind's eyes in the world of darkness and the eyes of mankind spiritually. What happens in the spiritual world affects mankind physical existence.

Now if mankind does not have the Holy Spirit, then mankind does not have any vision in the spiritual world. So that's makes mankind vulnerable and exposed to all evil desires in the world. We are living in a society where we have Hollywood producing so many movies on satanic powers, and we are feeling like satanic movies are comfortable to watch, and the behavior is becoming normal to do. There is a reality that exists of good and evil that even most

Christians are afraid of experiencing while some Christians know that the only protection in the world of satanic powers is the Holy Spirit. If Hollywood is able to comprehend satanic powers, then it means that it is a reality already in existence to mankind.

If mankind has no knowledge of the spiritual world, then mankind does not know what is spiritually affecting him. Now unless mankind is spiritually conscious and in tune with God's righteousness, mankind would never be protective of his true reality of good and evil.

When we are talking about the spiritualism of mankind, we must always remember that mankind is limited in the physical world but more limited in the spiritual world. The only thing that does not limit mankind in the satanic world is God's divine Word; that would reconnect mankind back together with God, and that is the Holy Spirit. The Holy Spirit is mankind's eyes that gives mankind the vision into a satanic world.

Many theologians or students of the Bible might agree or disagree. All of the prophets fell short of God's will for their lives. Why do you think that Jesus was so successful with His walk with the Father? Jesus was the only one that was successful. Do you think again that it was because Jesus Christ was the Son of God, and that is what made Him successful in His walk with God our Father?

Here is what Jesus did; it is something simple and the most powerful and effective thing that Christians need to survive in their relationship with God. This thing that Jesus did is the heart and soul of the Christian faith, and it is something that mankind forgets to do most of the time. In the situations or circumstances or trials that Jesus faced,

He prayed and was consistent with His spiritual journey and walk with the Father until His death on Calvary. Jesus prayed and always made sure that He was led by the Holy Spirit before He made any move at all. Jesus interceded with the Holy Spirit.

Again, we need someone in the spiritual world to help mankind fight against the principalities and things not seen and still be able to allow mankind to stay in fellowship with God. These are the things that man cannot understand from the physical realm.

If you notice how mankind is fighting in the spiritual world but has no understanding of what is going on, it is because we do not have the Holy Spirit in our lives to fight with. We must stay consistent with the Holy Spirit and pray. That is why it is important for Christians to stay in tune with God and His Word because that is our strength and power over all of the satanic and evil powers.

The Holy Spirit understands God's purpose and reason for mankind and man's relationship with God. Why did Jesus actually die? Because He was in the physical manifestation of life, but from His death, Jesus transformed back to the physical existence of life. Everything in the physical realm exists with substance, matter, and is transformed by the authentic hands of God. That is how mankind was created in the beginning as one of God's creations.

Our physical existence is very limited. We need the spiritual essence of God because man cannot control nor have an opportunity to recognize many of the principalities and things unseen that exist. The physical world is affected by the spiritual and satanic world, but the satanic world and spiritual world are not affected by the spiritual and satanic world. What the satanic world wants is mankind's souls. Now let me say this because mankind is in the physical manifestation of life: man can only experience these things based on God and mankind's relationship with the Holy Spirit. If mankind is in consistent fellowship with God, then it is easier for mankind to have knowledge and understanding of what is good and evil.

Now when mankind is able to recognize what is going on in the satanic and spiritual world with the understanding and guidance of God's divine Word, that is when mankind is introduced to the power of discernment to recognize the principalities and things unseen of this world.

God would grant us the consciousness and courage we need to overcome our trials and temptations, even in the physical world, all because of our relationship with the Holy Spirit and the Holy Spirit's intercession with God for us.

For example, the one thing that we need to accept is Jesus's love for people. First of all, Jesus never placed Himself above others or let the people's status intimidate Him teaching and spreading of the Gospel because when you have the knowledge of God, you are not intimidated by God or any other man.

First of all, God is not a person of fear. God is a person of praise. God has the power to destroy us and the world in seconds. We fear God out of love and respect, not out of intimidation. So to fear is nothing. Man has no significant power unless God grants that power to man himself because of his commitment with God.

Jesus knows that his purpose was to save the souls of men. He knew that we had to learn humility toward each other. This alone is a virtue we must learn. It is also the spiritual essence of man's character where man and the Holy Spirit meet to become one in communion with God. This is the spiritual level that God wants us to be on with Him and the Holy Spirit.

Some people would say I have humility for my fellow brother. Now if that is the case. I would like you to look at your son or daughter and let them ask you a question: would you sacrifice your son's or daughter's life for the sins of the world or even your neighbors or even someone you might not know? God allowed His Son, Jesus Christ, to die for our sins. To let your son or daughter die for someone is one of the greatest loves of all. It is like you are giving up a precious part of yourself for that person or for people. That is what God did for us when His Son, Jesus, died for us.

Here is what I mean. Let us look at John 15:13–17, and it reads:

> Greater love has no one than this: to lay down one's life for one's friends. You are my friends if you do what I command. I no longer call you servants, because a servant does not know his master's business. Instead, I have called you friends, for everything that I learned from my Father I have made known to you. You did not choose me, but I chose you and appointed you so that you might go and bear fruit—fruit that will last—and so that whatever you ask in my name the Father will give

> you. This is my command: Love each other. (John 15:13–17)

One of the statements that stand out is when God defines our purpose in Him. We do not have to be God's servant because the servant does not know the Master's business. God wants us as we redefine our purpose. He wants to redefine who we are, based on our life commitment to him.

> For until the law sin was in the world, but sin is not imputed when there is no law. Nevertheless death reigned from Adam to Moses, even over those who had not sinned according to the likeness of the transgression of Adam, who is a type of Him who was to come. But the free gift is not like the offense. For if by the one man's offense many died, much more the grace of God and the gift by the grace of the one Man, Jesus Christ, abounded too many. And the gift is not like that which came through the one who sinned. For the judgment which came from one offense resulted in condemnation, but the free gift which came from many offenses resulted in justification. For if by the one man's offense death reigned through the one, much more those who receive abundance of grace and of the gift of righteous-

ness will reign in life through the One, Jesus Christ. (Romans 5:13–17)

One of the main things that we have to do as we try to redefine our purpose in God's consciousness is to understand the nature of sin and how important it is for Christians to understand sin.

Let us reexamine sin. We think it's wrong, but sin has shifted and repositioned the nature of our lives. Adam's sin has distorted the joy of mankind and mankind's relationship with God, but Jesus came to put it altogether again. Jesus's unselfish love gave meaning and being to our life. Let us look at the unselfish love of God that He has for mankind, especially in the book of Romans:

> You see, at just the right time, when we were still powerless, Christ died for the ungodly. Very rarely will anyone die for a righteous person, though for a good person someone might possibly dare to die. But God demonstrates his own love for us in this: While we were still sinners, Christ died for us. (Romans 5:6–8)

Before man had any consciousness of God, Jesus still died for our sin because from the beginning, God knew that the trinity would become the salvation of mankind. We came into the consciousness of God based on our direction in life, also what roads we travel and our life conditions.

Jesus died for our sins because God understood that when you recognize the authenticity of His love, the foundation has been laid because of Jesus's death which become the salvation of all men and the consciousness of their salvation.

God who is omnipotent allowed his Son to die for us. This act did not stop there. It allowed salvation to become a reality for mankind. The death of Jesus brings about deeper meaning in defining salvation. Salvation is a means to get a better understanding of God's love for mankind.

Here is what we need to understand: God who is all-powerful took his only begotten Son to die for mankind before they recognized the importance or learned about the importance of God's salvation. The problem is God is not too powerful where He does not recognize that mankind needs to be saved. Even when mankind turns their backs on God, we serve a God that does not turn His back on us. From my perspective as a human being, God has humbled many a philosopher, king, politician, and powerful leader of the world to become submissive to His Word.

God has used the uneducated men and women of the world to educate the chosen men of the world, giving the uneducated men and women the wisdom to challenge the chosen men of the world's ignorance toward God. The men in the world, after all of their sinning, hate, and blasphemy toward Him—God still has the compassion to grant them salvation.

We should appreciate God's love because even when it hurts God through our actions of sinning and unrighteousness, God still just to grants us His salvation. Always remember God does not need us. We need God. That is why I call Him an awesome God. Even through our own trials and temptations, the purpose of God's compassion has never changed. God has remained true in His Word, a blessing to a sinful world.

Many people would want to believe that they turn their backs on me. When we look at Jesus's life, we experience the intervention of God and man on a spiritual level of existence. For example, in the book of Matthew 3, the world experience is a transcending force of energy that spoke about the goodness of Jesus through the inspiration of God:

> "I baptize you with water for repentance. But after me comes one who is more powerful than I, whose sandals I am not worthy to carry. He will baptize you with the Holy Spirit and fire. His winnowing fork is in his hand, and he will clear his threshing floor, gathering his wheat into the barn and burning up the chaff with unquenchable fire."

The Baptism of Jesus

Then Jesus came from Galilee to the Jordan to be baptized by John. But John tried to deter him, saying, "I need to be baptized by you, and do you come to me?"

Jesus replied, "Let it be so now; it is proper for us to do this to fulfill all righteousness." Then John consented. As soon as Jesus was baptized, he went up out of the water. At that moment heaven was opened, and he saw the Spirit of God descending like a dove and alighting on him. And a voice from heaven said, "This is my Son, whom I love; with him I am well pleased." (Matthew 3:11–17)

When I look at John, I see the humility of God reflected upon this statement, and that is I am not worthy to carry His sandals, and He is even more powerful than one of our purposes. In life is humility in God because God can work with man better. We should not allow God to break us in order that He can get our attention. When it comes to that point God is the idea and us not allowing God to reach that point, we should listen more.

Jesus Washes His Disciples' Feet

It was just before the Passover Festival. Jesus knew that the hour had come for him to leave this world and go to the Father. Having loved his own who were in the world, he loved them to the end. The evening meal was in progress, and the devil had already prompted Judas, the son of Simon Iscariot, to betray Jesus. Jesus knew that the Father had put all things under his power, and that he had come from God and was returning to God; so he got up from the meal, took off his outer clothing, and wrapped a towel around his waist. After that, he poured water into a basin and began to wash his disciples' feet, drying them with the towel that was wrapped around him. He came to Simon Peter, who said to him, "Lord, are you going to wash my feet?" Jesus replied, "You do not realize now what I am doing, but later you will understand." "No," said Peter, "you shall never wash my feet." Jesus answered, "Unless I wash you, you have no part with me." "Then, Lord," Simon Peter replied, "not just my feet but my hands and my head as well!" Jesus answered, "Those who have had a bath need only to wash their feet; their whole body is clean. And you are clean, though not every one of you." For he knew who was going to betray him, and that was why he said not everyone was clean. When he had finished washing their feet, he put on his clothes and returned to his place. "Do you understand what I have done for you?" he asked them. "You call me 'Teacher' and 'Lord,' and rightly so, for that is what I am. Now that I, your Lord and Teacher, have washed your feet, you also should wash one another's feet. I have set you an example that you should do as I have done for you. Very truly I tell you, no servant is greater than his master, nor is a messenger greater than the one who sent him. Now that you know these things, you will be blessed if you do them. (John 13:1–17)

When I looked at this verse as a young child, I did not get this perspective from the passage. This is what I mean about the verse, but let us look at Jesus's integrity.

He knew that he was about to die and be betrayed all at the same time, but Jesus, having the spiritual integrity that He had, still washed the disciples' feet, including Judas, the son of Simon Iscariot. Although Jesus knew Judas was going to betray Him, He still humbled himself to the disciples in order to wash their feet.

Peter said, "I am not letting you wash my feet." I think Peter probably made the statement "I should be washing your feet," but Jesus said, "No, I will be washing your feet with all of the authority in the heavens who should be washing whose feet." The purpose that we have as Christians has nothing to do with power but being humble in God's grace and understanding that is why God favors our integrity and humbleness to each other and Him.

Being humble produces a certain type of faith that makes mankind submissive to whatever God's will is for him. Mankind's submissiveness to God produces enough evidence within his faith that shows him how faithful he is to God's consciousness.

Being in the state of our submissiveness shows our true divine inspiration toward God and mankind. Now the other thing about mankind's submissiveness to God is that it produces the evidence needed in mankind's faith that gives God the compassion to favor mankind.

In other words, it is because of the state of mankind's submissiveness to the Father that the Father began to provide mankind with His favor. Favor is one of God's most high and precious gifts to mankind. It comes when God is able to recognize your presence within your submissiveness to Him through your faith, and it happens because of God's grace and love toward mankind's submissiveness and God's compassion.

When a person gives up their freedom by being submissiveness to God, it brings them into fellowship with God. This comes with the faith and knowledge we have in learning God's Word as we try to define our purpose and reason in life through God's consciousness.

Now that we have become submissive to God's will in our lives, being submissive to God's will for our lives means that we are spiritual beings wrapped up in physical bodies trying to define our purpose and reason through our submissiveness toward God's consciousness. Our purpose in life has been instilled in us by God. God has instilled our purpose as Christians based on our choice. It is in our nature that God's salvation has given us a purpose to exist.

It is by our nature that we are giving the reason to choose, and it is in our choosing that our choice has a spiritual essence that God has created within us. That spiritual essence keeps us connected to God, even when we think that God never notices what we are doing or trying to achieve spiritually in our lives.

I think that man's driven purpose in God prepares him for his spiritual awareness in God salvation. Man's spiritual awareness is the direction that God has planned for mankind to walk in God's consciousness. For example, we have a tendency to ask the question, why are we here? Does God really exist? Is there life after death? Why is there so much suffering on earth? Does God really care about us?

These are questions that we ask ourselves in order to get a better understanding of who we are as we try to define what our purpose and reason is in God's grace. All of the questions I just mentioned are found in our submissiveness and consciousness in God's faith, and the answer becomes more revealing to mankind as mankind grows spiritually and matures in God's grace; the closer we become to our salvation in God.

In the book of John 17.

> My prayer is not that you take them out of the world but that you protect them from the evil one. They are not of the world, even as I am not of it. Sanctify them by the truth; your word is truth. As you sent me into the world, I have sent them into the world. For them I sanctify myself, that they too may be truly sanctified. (John 17:15–19)

We must understand that when Jesus came, He came, yes, to teach and preach the Gospel, not to change the laws of God because Jesus thinks that they might be old; but the Gospel is still relevant for these times that we are living in today, something that the churches are being faced with today's society. We are writing the Gospel to fit into society instead of allowing society to fit into the structure of the Gospel. Jesus never came to replace God's Word but to secure and enhance mankind's salvation through God's grace.

Jesus came to protect people from Satan attacking them. Jesus even challenged the tradition that man has tried to incorporate into the Gospel of God, especially when Jesus was challenging the Sadducees and Pharisees about what is traditional and what should be taught as God's wisdom and consciousness.

As Christians, how do we define our faith in God? The main thing we should recognize as Christians is we are not of this world. We cannot be conformed to the things of the world, but we can be transformed by the renewing of our consciousness in God.

Now as we define our purpose and reason through what God has willed for our lives, we get a better grasp and understanding of why we do not belong to this world but are in this world. We sometimes should have better judgment and make better choices around our life's experiences, although we wrestle with the adversities of life and try to overcome the many obstacles we have faced.

The one thing that remains constant is the power that is in God's Word. That power does not change. What that power does is bring mankind together with God. God's Word does not change. Because of God's Word and its consistency, that is where God's power lies. The strength of the Gospel lies in the consistency, meditation, and constantly studying God's divine Word. The Gospel of God is to transform the world, not let the world transform the Gospel. That is what makes the Gospel of God more imperative for man to develop his faith in God.

## THE POWER OF GOD'S CONSCIOUSNESS

One of the things that I think is challenging to the churches is people that I called runners. Runners are people who find one excuse in the church and run to the other church.

They run from church to church trying to get attention, from the members of the different congregations. They run with the attitude that they are more spiritually endowed than other people in the churches.

These are the type of people who have more excuses, than having God's divine heart in their life. These are the Christians in the churches that feed off of negative information, which stagnated their consciousness and faith in God.

Faith and they feed off of negative information in the churches. They are spiritual consciousness but not spiritually active or spiritually in tune with God's righteousness.

These are the people who have caused so much chaos in the congregations that they go to in visit these are the people that are also jealous of other believers who have been anointed by God.

These are the types of people that want to feel spiritually endowed and want the masses to worship them instead of God. They want to be the ones whom people in the churches look up to them for their own spiritual gratification instead of looking up to God for their own spiritual gratification. Nobody replaces the consciousness of God that did exist within mankind's heart, body, and soul but God our Father.

For example, many people have run from the church for whatever reason. Many of the people became runners. What is a runner? A runner is a person or people who looks for mistakes in a church or churches that they would have excuses to run from church to church. Here is what happens to them: some of them realize that after running, salvation in God has nothing to do with what church you go but how consistent your faith is and how your fellowship is with God and how in tune we are to God's Word. And again, we're also trying to use every ounce of our potential to develop and mature in the divine consciousness of God.

Many people deny the fact that God cannot define their will in life. Many people would say that they don't need God to define their purpose in life, that they can find their own purpose in life without God. Everything we do, God should always be implemented in our plans. God should always be in the center of our progress and actions.

Some people have a tendency of trying to define their life based on their career, status, and financial income. Now what we have come to experience in life is that whatever road we travel, all roads lead back to God's unchanging hands. In other words, whatever road we travel, we still at some point in our lives have to become submissive to whatever decision God has willed for us to do. We have to give of ourselves. We must always remember that we cannot serve two masters at the same time. "No man can serve two masters, for either he will hate the one and love the other; or else he will hold to the one and despise the other. Ye cannot serve God and mammon" (Matthew 6:24).

# The Spiritual Essence of Purpose and Reason

One of the interesting statements of defining our purpose has to do with how much time we put into God's Word in order for us to develop our consciousness in God's authentic Word. Our total commitment depends on our relationship with God. The more we try to improve our relationship with God, the better we become as people working our way toward God's salvation.

One of the things that I have experienced is how difficult it is for me to read my Bible. It seems that we have more obstacles distracting us than having enough obstacles to help us stay in tune with God's Word. I always wanted to improve my spiritual life as a Christian. We all want to, but finding the time and place to do it becomes a difficult task sometimes.

Sometimes it is difficult for us to set some type of structure that would make it easy for a person to structure their devotional time with God. I know sometimes when I try to do my devotions, everything gets in the way. Sometimes, in order for me to successfully complete my devotions, I have to shut the world out in order to spend my devotional time with God.

When I pray, I pray for the conditions and chaos in the world. I also pray for my friends and family. The more time I spent on devotion, the more my spiritual life became more successful in God's consciousness.

This is when the Scriptures became more enjoyable. It moved from just a duty to a history book, and from a history book to one of the most spiritual books with a transcending power of God's authentic Word, which is able to develop the consciousness of mankind to become a spiritual being.

One of the things that I have come to find out is the Bible cannot be approached like other books because the Bible is not a book of scholarly reading or atheist perspective on whether God exists or is true as the Bible says He is.

For example, a scholar reads the Bible, looking for scholarly things to report. An atheist reads the Bible, looking at the idea that God does not exist in order for them to have substantial evidence to accommodate their truth, not the atheist's truth. And the philosopher's truth, the serious truth, and a theologian truth are not God's truth; they are God's lie.

In other words, God's lie is the philosopher's truth, God's lie is the existentialist truth. God's truth brings about a spiritual consciousness that is recognized as the fear of the existentialist truth, the theologian truth, the theorist truth.

Now that is how God's truth becomes, a lie to the world. So God's truth is always a lie to the world, but the world's truth always conflict with God's truth, and this is the challenging part that mankind has to choose, and that is what is the ultimate truth that mankind has to choose in order for mankind to what is the actual truth. That is why so many libraries are filled with mankind trying to define what is the ultimate truth that exists within the universe.

That is why it's also imperative that mankind develop spiritual consciousness to the best of his or her ability in order to strengthen their faith in God. That us when we are faced with so many challenges, that exist within the world, that is why we must the Word of God dividing it in truth in love so that the truth of our reality would embrace and allow us to experience God's divine Word in our consciousness, Where we can acknowledge what is the spiritual truth in the spiritual reality of the essence and substance of God's truth.

But the atheist themselves know their truth about why God doesn't exist where he or she can satisfy their desire that God does not exist. I read God's Word to redefine my purpose and reason for my life through God's consciousness, which brings me to a better understanding of who I am in the presence of God's grace and mercy.

It's a statute. We must look at a statute from a theological perspective in order to get some clarity on God's definition and seriousness of implanting His Word. I can also look at God's Word as a statute. A statute is a formal written enactment of a legislative authority that governs a state, city, county, written to bring some type of structure to people's lives while giving them the blessings of their salvation.

Typically, statutes command or prohibit something or declare policy. The word is often used to distinguish law made by legislative bodies from case law, decided by courts and regulations issued by government agencies. Statutes are sometimes referred to as legislation or "black letter law." As a source of law, statutes are considered primary authority (as opposed to secondary authority). Ideally, all statutes must be in harmony with the fundamental law of the land (constitutional).

This word is used in contradistinction to the common law. Statutes acquire their force from the time of their passage, however, unless otherwise provided. Statutes are of several kinds, namely public or private, declaratory or remedial, temporary or perpetual.

A temporary statute is one which is limited in its duration at the time of its enactment. It continues in force until the time of its limitation has expired, unless sooner repealed. A perpetual statute is one for the continuance of which there is no limited time, although it may not be expressly declared to be so.

Before a statute becomes law in some countries, it must be agreed upon by the highest executive office of that country's government. In many countries, statutes are organized in topical arrangements (or "codified"), for example, Massachusetts General Laws 2001 or whatever it pertains to. Now the laws are publicized in things called codes, such as the United States Code.

In many nations, statutory law is distinguished from and subordinate to constitutional law. We must always recognize that everything we do in life, we must uphold God's laws. When we are able to keep God's Word in our hearts and do what is right, we are in the process of becoming a blessed people or nation in God's eye.

Even in God's statute, our purpose in life is to redefine as well as teach and shape our lives toward God's laws and consciousness. We should always allow God's Word to shape and develop our minds, bodies, and souls. Just like if we were clay being shaped by God's authentic hands, we become the potter or clay on the wheel of the potter.

We must give God the authority and power to shape us in His image, name, faith, and likeness and in His Word. The problem is that each sermon I preach, God has allowed me to live it and experience it, and now I am influenced by God to preach and teach His Word until the end of my life's journey here on earth and use our consciousness as a means to remember God's divine Word, see God's Word is stored in our consciousness, and as we stored God's Word in our consciousness. We are able to remember what God has said, and when we face a situation it is God's Word, that teaches us through our consciousness.

We must also remember what God's Word has said *to* us. We must develop a spiritual consciousness where theology, theory, and philosophy cannot penetrate. Read the book *The Theory of Theology* by James Grant.

I think the point that I'm trying to make is that if your consciousness is constantly being developed in the spiritual essence and substance of God. Then when the laws such as the Constitution, and the laws of the land, the federal laws the state law of the land through our discipline as Christians and our conscious state of mind.

We are able to obey these laws because these laws that are given to us have already been written and become a part of God's divine Word. That is why the key is discipline. Discipline is the faith in our action that produces our spiritual consciousness where we can recognize that God's Word becomes a way of life, and that way of life is a belief that creates and develops mankind's consciousness and faith in God.

And that is what gives mankind the discipline, that mankind needs to obey the laws of the land, and that is why God said surrender onto Caesar that which is Caesar and surrender onto God, that which is God, not only monetary or material possession but things. But things that are also spiritual. Those things that are also spiritual are what develop our spiritual character and integrity, which exist within our conscious state of mind that reflects God's consciousness in our life.

# Reasoning with the Scriptures

In the book of Acts 17:2–3:

> And Paul, as his manner was, went in unto them, and three Sabbath days reasoned with them out of the scriptures, Opening and alleging, that Christ must needs have suffered, and risen again from the dead; and that this Jesus, whom I preach unto you, is Christ.

There comes a time when we have to prove the existence of God's Word through our state of reasoning. For example, as faithful Christians, we have to be intelligent enough to defend God's Word against the political system of this world, which tries to rise up against God's doctorate. The political system of this world is influencing the world and some of the churches more than God's divine Word.

That is why in our society today, we have no validity not ethnicity and no unity against human beans all because we are removing God's Word from society and embracing political establishments of this world. As Christians, we are supposed to teach God's Word, to reason God's Word, to teach God's Word with power and conviction in order to let the world know that we are Christians on the battlefield for our Lord. The more we study God's divine Word the more we are prepared to be on the battlefield, for God. As long as our consciousness is transparent, it is that beacon of light for God. That is when we are confident that our consciousness is the weapon that we have to fight the spiritual warfare of mankind.

Our spiritual warfare can only make us feel spiritually equipped through the knowledge and wisdom that is in God's Word.

We must understand that we have, to have enough knowledge of God's Word to defend it and we defend, it based on the ignorance that surrounds God's Word such as the atheists, philosophers, theories, and theologians.

Using God's Word, we have to put God's Word up against every philosophical belief in the world today and still be able to prove that God does exist, and because of God's existence, He still has enough room in his heart to grant us all salvation. In the days to come, we will be persecuted for believing in God. So we will have to stand up to the world, claiming God as our personal Savior. That also means that mankind has to have a spiritual consciousness about God's divine Word.

# THE DANGERS OF OUR COMFORT ZONES

Some Christians are in a comfort zone where they believe in God, but they are not in fellowship or in tune with God. They might have faith in God, but they become so comfortable in their faith with God that it has placed them in a mental state of laziness. They have no interest on increasing their faith. They have no reason anymore to read God's Word.

Let me explain one of the most dangerous places a Christian can be in with their relationship with God and being in their own comfort zone. Some Christians have been on the same path of faith for a long time. It seems that some Christians do not have the ambition and motivation anymore to stay in constant fellowship with God. Some Christians have lost their ambition and fight for God.

So many Christians have not made any progress maturing in their Christian lives. Our number one goal in life is to perfect ourselves through God's faith. That is our number one priority.

The question that should be asked is, why do we need to mature in God's faith? First of all, we have to because it is not right to stay on one particular level of God's faith. God's faith is a process of constant growth. We are constantly growing in God's Word, and our responsibility is to change people's lives and bring them closer to God.

That is why Paul told Timothy to study to "show yourself approved of God's Word, divide God's Word, and bring God's Word into its most simple terms and meaning in life. That you, Timothy, should be able to teach the masses about God's Word, interpreting the most difficult lessons of God to the masses of people in a simple way that they can understand God's Word more clearly."

I call on the Christians that have reached a point in their faith with God where they are so comfortable that they do not want to make any progress in God's Word. How do these Christians become like that? I refer to it as the Christian's "comfort zone." Let me define it more on the next chapter.

Some Christians are in a comfort zone where they have the consciousness of God, but they are not exercising their consciousness to its fullest potential. Because over the years, they stop exercising their consciousness, and because they became comfortable in their consciousness with God, they feel comfortable where they are spiritually. They are not being challenged in their spiritual environment, so they are not growing like they should, both spiritually and physically.

Again, they might have faith in God, but they become so comfortable that it has placed them into an uncomfortable position of laziness that is able to stagnate their state of consciousness, like they are dead. Our Christian life is like a relationship we have to constantly rekindle the fire of our commitment with God. We have to do the things that would motivate us spiritually, to keep our spiritual flame burning in our hearts and minds in order that our comfort zone would not cause us to put out our spiritual flame that we once had for God. Those people who are in their comfort zone might not have an interest anymore on increasing their faith.

Sometimes it leads to those people being able to compromise God's Word to fit their comfort zones. Now just to let you know, our comfort zone is the most dangerous place to be, especially if you are a Christian. It usually happens to Christians who have been in fellowship with God for a long time and sometimes new Christians who are struggling with the idea of what to do next.

Our Christian life is just like any relationship. We become tired and slack up on our commitment in our relationships and our commitment with God as well. It seems that some Christians don't have the ambition to inspire themselves anymore for God. They have lost that burning flame that once became the light of their salvation. For some strange reason, they cannot find within their comfort zone the spark that once ignited the flame.

That spark that would once rekindle their heart and soul to burn bright enough would bring an enlightenment back into their consciousness where they can light up the world once again for God; a spark of consciousness that brings the Christian(s) that would motivate them back into perfect fellowship with God and their salvation.

So many Christians have not made any progress in their spiritual consciousness. It seems somewhere along the way, Christians are losing control over their spiritual lives. The Christian's number one goal is to create the potential to perfect themselves through God's consciousness and faith.

That faith would allow them to reach their fullest potential in God's grace that would lead them back into fellowship with God. The question that one should ask is, why do we need to mature in God's faith? First of all, we have to because it is not right to stay on one particular level of God's faith. Fellowship and worshipping with God are stages of growth and maturity.

The experience Christians have in God's faith is a process of constant growth. Christians have a responsibility to God, and that is they are supposed to constantly grow in God's consciousness while trying to change people's lives and bring them closer to God. We cannot use our comfort zone as a means to stray away from God's consciousness but as a means to rekindle our strength in God's grace.

That is why Paul told Timothy to study to "show yourself approved of God's Word, dividing God's Word and bring God's Word into its most simple terms and defining it's meaning in life to the world. That you, Timothy, should be able to teach the masses of people about God's Word, interpreting the most difficult lessons of God to the masses of people but still keep God's message in a simple way that they can understand God's Word more clearly that would allow the masses of people to embrace God's consciousness as a part of their lives."

This comes because many Christians sometimes get comfortable with their pastor's sermons and teachings. So they think and assume they do not have to study God's Word as much or just for convenient moments in their lives. Because their pastor is anointed by God, they feel they do not have to study God's Word for themselves. Now that is a dangerous place to be in with God.

Here is why: Christians must also understand that their relationship with God is personal, and no pastor can even become a substitute for Jesus Christ. The Scriptures do not allow any room for pastors to become a substitute, an imitation of Jesus Christ. Here is why your pastor is not Jesus Christ: your pastor is not your intercessor. Jesus Christ is your only intercessor and for all men and women.

Christians, we must understand and not forget that God's salvation is personal. Your salvation is not your pastor's salvation. For example, your pastor's salvation is not yours, and people (believers), because your pastor preaches well and because your pastor sings well and because your pastor's church has a large congregation, it does not make him or her a person of God. You have a lot of pastors that are very self-centered. We have to be consistent with our consciousness with God.

You have some pastors that have taken advantage of the older members in the congregation, by influencing them to give their properties to the church. You have some pastors who have used the Word of God to take advantage of other people. Some people think that being a member of a large congregation, they do not have to study God's Word.

I know that we all can agree with this, and that is the burning flame that we once had toward God. We were fired up to fight the great fight for God, and for some strange reason, our flame has burned out. Some of us have lost our courage to fight and defend our faith in God. In this case, the pastors have to be blamed because if the pastors are not growing in their knowledge and wisdom of God, then their congregation is not growing. If the pastors do not have the courage to stand up and represented God's Word, the masses of people are not going to experience or respect the power that is in the Gospel of God. That means that the church is not maturing or growing spiritually in God's grace.

The pastor's job is to continually energize and motivate his/her congregation. Remember, the pastors are the leader of their flock. They are the ones who God chooses to lead, not stagnate the congregation's growth and faith in God's consciousness.

Sometimes we think that we know enough of God's Word that we do not have to study anymore; that is where we fall into the ignorance of our own comfort zone because the other members in the church are not knowledgeable enough in God's Word to teach, quote scriptures, or preach God's Word better than the person who is in their comfort zone.

So that same person stops growing because they assume that there are not enough people in the church that are not as mature as they are or even as stimulated as they are in God's consciousness. That means that they are not growing because the pastor is teaching or the members in the church are in their own comfort zones.

The other is membership and authority in the churches. People, when they get a certain position in the church, decide that they have reached their peak, and that is when they relax and become a part of their comfort zone. Authority is a position for growth, maturing, especially when it comes to our faith in God. God has never been a God of people status. God does not choose His people based on their status or education to do His work. God chooses His people based on their commitment and faith in Him. He has always been a God of knowledge, wisdom, and faith. Our faith is our only belief and hope in God.

Christians must remember while trying to complete our faith in God, we must always try to do what is necessary for us to strengthen our faith with God. We do that through our knowledge and wisdom that we have acquired through God's consciousness.

For example, God said in the book of Mathew 17:20 that Jesus is speaking to His disciplines about their growth and maturity in God's faith. Jesus wanted the disciples to recognize their faith, that it was not where it should be for the time, that "you have been with Me and experience the many works of what I have done." Even Jesus's disciples had a problem with their spiritual maturity in God.

"You don't have enough faith," Jesus told them. "I tell you the truth, if you had faith even as small as a mustard seed, you can say to this mountain, 'Move here to there,' and it will move. Nothing will be impossible for you" (Mathew 17:20).

In this case, what Jesus is making reference to is the idea that "I am not asking for all of your time. I want you to dedicate some of your time to the Father's will for your life. Not all of your time but just a certain amount which would allow you enough faith that would allow you to grow in your consciousness which is the size of mustard seed. That you can say to this mountain 'Move,' and the mountain would move."

Just enough of your time that would allow you to develop just enough of a belief in the Father, that would generate in your hearts the confidence you need in the Father in order to increase your faith and be on the level of spiritual maturity that you should be on already. Even in our state of meditation, God is able to produce enough faith in us the size of a mustard seed that will allow us to move the mountains of the world and bring those mountains back into fellowship with God.

Man's faith in God has always been the key for man to move any mountain, not only to move this mountain that I am speaking of but any other mountains in our lives that need to be removed.

Because your faith is your power of hope; because your faith is your power of belief; because your faith is your power of strength; because your faith is power that is within us; because of your power, that power is where the source and power of Almighty God rests in the deepest chambers of our souls; we are limited in our faith and growth toward God's grace.

Most of all, our faith is where the power of God is implemented as well as teaches man about the consciousness of God. His commitment and faith toward God and the rewards of man's faith in God, such as God's salvation, grace, and mercy, this is what God has bestowed upon mankind. That is why we cannot allow anything to distract us or even stagnate our faith in God. We must always recognize that we serve an Almighty God.

We must always remember that Christ's death has paved the way for all of our salvation. Our salvation is a paid debt with Jesus's blood that He shed on Calvary. It is up to us, based on our lifestyle, to cash in on the life insurance policy of everlasting life that we have with God which leads to mankind's salvation. The only way that we can cash in on our life insurance policy of salvation is to constantly stay in God's consciousness.

This means constantly staying in God's Word. This also means staying constantly in prayer with God. This means constantly staying in meditation with God. This means constantly teaching God's Word and also means staying open and available to what God's will is for your life.

Man can never repay that debt or credit back to God. God has the means to pay God back. Mankind cannot use his influence. His power is manipulation. Mankind cannot even use his pride or his monetary gains or political gains in order to pay God back for His salvation. That can only be done by God Himself and achieved by mankind themselves. The only way man can pay that debt or credit back is to be humble to God's unchanging hands, which would allow God to embrace us in His heart.

This is what gives us a better understanding of why our relationship with God is personal. As a matter fact, we do not have the physical or spiritual strength nor do we have the physical power to pay God back for the salvation that He has bestowed upon us (man).

The majority of us has taken God's salvation for granted. Here is how we do it. We allow ourselves to reach a certain comfort zone where we become lazy and comfortable. Some Christians do not have any intention on furthering their knowledge and faith in God.

That is why many people in society view Christians as lazy. Some Christian integrity does not reflect their true faith in God. Well, what do you mean? For some strange reason, some Christians are not living the lifestyle that they proclaim they are living. Many Christians hide their sins behind the Bible and are not trying to mature in their consciousness of faith with God.

They use the Bible as a tool to manipulate the masses of people for their material gain. They make people think that their faith and life is guided toward God's direction when in actuality, they are the worst people in the world. That is what confuses the masses of people about the true existence of God. The question the masses of people have is whether or not God exists.

Some people ask that question not because they are trying to challenge God but because of how God is able to tolerate so much from the people who should be conscious of His Word and that are doing wrong. Many people in the world ask this question: does God actually exist? How come God doesn't see how these people are abusing his name and does nothing about it?

We admit that God is all-knowing, so to masses of people, if we admit that God is all-knowing and Christians are abusing his name in vain, it seems that God should have enough knowledge and wisdom to recognize the people in His faith or community that are constantly abusing His name in vain, especially those words that come out of their mouths. We must be respectful toward each other. Remember that we are brother and sisters in God's faith.

Some of them talk about other Christians, also the things that some Christians do to their family members. That is why I can tell you that some family members of people who are Christians or friends don't have an interest in church because of how Christians behave toward their friends and families.

Sometimes some Christian attitudes become more discouraging than encouraging to the masses of people they should be witnessing to.

That is why their faith has no representation of God's divine works. Many people look at Christians like those that believe in a God that does not exist, again based on how faithful our relationship is with God. People in the world do not understand the patience that comes in the process of God's forgiveness toward man. So when people experience how we as Christians disrespect God's faith, the first thing that people of the world respond to is, how could a God who is all-powerful tolerate the indecencies of how his own Christians' abuse His Word, His power, and God's name, and then take advantage of other people? How does God allow it? That is why they would say that God does not exist. God is the only one that existed before the world and mankind were created.

## THE POWER OF GOD'S CONSCIOUSNESS

If our spiritual life does not have any spiritual essence, that is a reflection of our love and divine faith in God because of how we act toward God. Then why would the masses of people want to respect God? Our behavior toward God is a reflection of our true consciousness toward how we respect the faith that we believe in. In other words, our spiritual consciousness represents the God we believe in and to the capacity of our belief in God. In other words, our lifestyle should reflect the authenticity of God's power, love, faith, and of Jesus's blood and of all of God's salvation.

Trust me, most of the time, the world is not looking for perfection in the Christian life. What they are looking for is constant stability in our lives as it pertains to our actions that reflect our faith in God's righteousness while using our lifestyles as an example of God's consciousness.

God's consciousness that we as Christians embrace, becomes a reflection of our life's condition and the foundation of God's own faith and integrity of our lives. Christians should be able to reflect all of God's attributes in their personalities. Our integrity toward God's consciousness is the reflectiveness of God's divine love for the world and those Christians who are in constant fellowship with God which comes from God's consciousness. Most Christians damage the name of God based on their integrity toward God.

Now the people in the world are not looking for Christians to be perfect but to have a sense of responsibility to the God that Christians say that they have faith in. For example, the world is looking for God's sermon through the lifestyle of Christians because it is the Christians who should have the discipline of God in their hearts. People in the world are not looking for pulpit sermons anymore.

People are using the actions of the Christians' and pastors' lifestyles as an example of showing what our faith is like toward God.

In the book of Ephesians, the Apostle Paul explains:

> Finally, Paul said, "Be strong in the Lord and his mighty power. Put on the full armor of God, so that you can take your stand against the devil's schemes. For our struggle is not against flesh and blood, but against the rulers, against the authorities, against the powers of this dark world and against the spiritual forces of evil in the heavenly realms." (Ephesians 6:10–12)

Let us look at Paul's position. What was Paul's inspired words to the Christian communities as it relates to God and mankind's faith? One of the things that is very interesting in this passage is to better understand the true meaning of God and the faith we should have in order to be granted our salvation in God.

When we as human beings fight with each other, we can better understand why. It is in the open we can see how man is able to physically hurt each other. The one thing that we need to understand is that our most serious fight is not against man. We can handle that. Our greatest fight is against the things that we cannot see and the rulers that have places in many organizations against God's divine institution of faith.

Let me reiterate the only person who is competent enough to reveal things to mankind is God through the

Holy Spirit. I think in some cases, we forget about our relationship with the Holy Spirit because it is manifested by God to keeps the presence of the Holy Spirit in its spiritual essence.

Mankind, being created in the physical existence of life, has the tendency to relate to things in their own physical manifestation of existence. This allows enough room for mankind to recognize that he is no longer fighting a physical battle but a spiritual battle of war that uses principalities and things unseen. Again, thank God for leaving us the Holy Spirit who is able to discern and intercede for man when man is fighting against principalities and things unseen.

Mankind has no knowledge of that experience. They know it exists, but mankind has no control over it, except being in constant fellowship with God.

For example, the physical battle consisted of God's Word becoming flesh. Let's put both ideas together, and that is how God's Word was able to become flesh. Does that mean that because of God's Word becoming flesh everyone who projects the image of God through God's authentic Word actually dies? Why? Because the educated man stands up against God's authentic Word, but it is the wisdom in God's authentic Word that makes mankind wise. It is the education of the world that breeds ignorance and foolishness into the hearts and souls of mankind.

Here is why God's Word makes the educated man look like they are foolish. Let me elaborate more. It seems to me that any man or woman who preaches or teaches God's Word somehow dies at the hands of the masses. Here is the reason: it seems to me that the people who walk upright in the faith of God and do not compromise their differences in God's faith in the world die. Now the question, is why? Because God's Word challenges man's education which is not the consciousness of God.

The education that man places upon society has no validity when it is challenged by God's Word. For example, in the theory of man's philosophy, in order for someone to get recognized as expected in society, we look at the status of the person. They have to have a PhD a doctorate sometimes a bachelor's degree in order to be recognized as educated.

But it is interesting that God's Word is able to bring mankind's consciousness to a level where their faith, belief, and consciousness in God places mankind, on the same level as a PhD, master's, and doctorate degrees.

What people take for granted is if mankind studies God's divine Word, the level that mankind can get from God's Word will take mankind on a level that is more educated than any doctorate or PhD.

Here is why academic institutions and degrees do not rule the world the knowledge of God is what you rule the world. That is why when someone studies the Bible and reads the Bible, it is the wisdom that is embraced in the Bible. That illuminates in us and Braden the spirit in the soul of mankind, and that is what becomes our light-bulb moment, which is able to bring mankind into enlightenment that is able to transform mankind's consciousness through God's divine Word.

And death brings you into a light-bulb moment that really enlightens mankind about their spiritual consciousness and faith in God.

It is through God's divine Word that mankind is able to elevate himself beyond the limits of societal institutions of teaching. It is God's divine Word that brings mankind into a conscious state of mind, which is able to surpass all of mankind's understanding.

It is a consciousness state that surpasses all understanding; and comprehension is the consciousness that develops mankind's spiritualism, spirituality, and discipline, through reading and studying God's divine Word. In society, we are just based on our academics; but with God, we are judged based on our spirituality and faith in God.

It has been proven over and over again that God has used the uneducated to make the educated people wise. God's wisdom uses mankind's own philosophical reasoning—such as mankind's laws, ideologies, philosophy, and theories—to actually prove the authenticity of God's Word.

# Defining Our Purpose through Jesus Christ

One of the most important things we have in this life is to experience Jesus's life and the many challenges Jesus faced as it pertains to mankind's salvation and how he sacrificed His life for mankind.

Here is why. If Jesus did not exist in the physical manifestation of life, mankind would never have the opportunity to be granted salvation.

Here is why through Jesus's life and death, we are granted salvation through God. So in order for us to have the opportunity to be granted salvation through God's divine consciousness, we have the opportunity to become like Jesus Christ and set the example that Jesus had set. If most Christians were to define their lives through the path that Jesus had walked, we would have a better relationship with God.

For example, we would be able to define our purpose in life based on what we experience through Jesus's consciousness and what Jesus has sacrificed for our lives as it relates to the salvation of God. The one thing that I want to express is that Jesus had a purpose in life, but what a painful reason and purpose Jesus had, just because of God's love for mankind.

I remember many Christians saying, "I wish I was Jesus Christ if it did not include Jesus's death." But the answer to that is that you do have the potential to be like Jesus Christ if you embrace God's consciousness and develop your faith in God.

Jesus's life was like the majority of the masses of people. He was very poor and brought up in similar surroundings like most people in the world today. It's interesting that when you show love toward people, sometimes they interpret love as an expression of weakness. People are not accustomed to genuine love like Jesus showed toward the masses that He even died for.

Love sometimes is best appreciated when we lose it and cannot get it back from the person who once gave it to us. We must remember that Jesus had no way to lay His head. So when we look at Jesus's life, we must realize that type of life that Jesus lived might not have been as exciting as we think of it being when we look at how Jesus's birth and how Jesus was born and, most of all, how He died.

Although Jesus's purpose in life was painful, Jesus had a purpose in life to do His father's will. What makes Jesus's life so fabulous is He found great joy in doing the Father's work, even knowing that he was going to be crucified:

> He left Judea and went away again into Galilee. And He had to pass through Samaria. So He came to a city of Samaria called Sychar, near the parcel of ground that Jacob gave to his son Joseph; 6 and Jacob's well was there. So Jesus, being wearied from His journey, was sitting thus by the well. It was about [a]the sixth hour.
>
> There came a woman of Samaria to draw water. Jesus said to her, "Give Me a drink." For His disciples had gone away into the city to buy food. Therefore the Samaritan woman *said to Him, "How is it that You, being a Jew, ask me for a drink since I am a Samaritan woman?" (For Jews have no dealings with Samaritans.) Jesus answered and said to her, "If you knew the gift of God, and who it is who says to you, 'Give Me a drink,' you would have asked Him, and He would have given you living water." She said to Him, "Sir, You have nothing to draw with and the well is deep; where then do You get that living water? You are not greater than our father Jacob, are You, who gave us the well, and drank of it himself and his sons and his cattle?"

> Jesus answered and said to her, "Everyone who drinks of this water will thirst again; but whoever drinks of the water that I will give him shall never thirst; but the water that I will give him will become in him a well of water springing up to eternal life."
>
> The woman said to Him, "Sir, give me this water, so I will not be thirsty nor come all the way here to draw." He said to her, "Go, call your husband and come here." The woman answered and said, "I have no husband." Jesus said to her, "You have correctly said, 'I have no husband'; for you have had five husbands, and the one whom you now have is not your husband; this you have said truly." (John 4:3–18)

Now when I look at this verse, Jesus the Son of God has walked many miles and was tired. His disciples had left him, so he decided to rest after all of that walking. He walked and left Judea and went into Galilee through Samaria. Now the interesting thing about the well is it is a well that Jacob gave to the people in the town, and he and his son, Joseph, and the cattle drink from the well. Now Jesus asked a woman for some water, and the woman told Jesus, "You are a Jew."

The reason for that statement is Jews and Samaritan don't speak or even share the Word of God. If Jews have dealings with Samaritans, they do not speak to each other. If we notice in the dialogue with the woman, Jesus is always ministering to people. The purpose Jesus uses at that particular time was the most interesting thing to the people, and that was the water. He said that the water you drink from this well will still make you thirsty.

"The water I give you will give you everlasting life," which created a curious perspective where Jesus can introduce many more questions to witness to the lady.

She asked Jesus many questions about salvation and eternal life. The woman mentioned, "You are no greater than Jacob."

Jesus never became boastful and didn't say, "I am better than because I am the Son of God." He basically tried to appeal to the woman's instinct and senses in this case, which was her getting water at the well. When we look at Jesus, we recognize that Jesus had no way to lay his head. Jesus's work took on many responsibilities in life.

For example, in the book of Luke:

> for the Son of Man did not come to destroy men's lives, but to save them."] And they went on to another village As they were going along the road, someone said to Him, "I will follow You wherever You go." And Jesus said to him, "The foxes have holes and the birds of the [a] air have nests, but the Son of Man has nowhere to lay His head." And He said to another, "Follow Me." But he said, "Lord, permit me first to go and bury my father." But He said to him, "Allow the dead to bury their own dead; but as for you, go

and proclaim everywhere the kingdom of God." Another also said, "I will follow You, Lord; but first permit me to say good-bye to those at home." But Jesus said to him, "No one, after putting his hand to the plow and looking back, is fit for the kingdom of God." (Luke 9:56–62)

How could a man serve God and not know where his next meal is coming from? The question is, did Jesus have a purpose or a meaningful life? When we look at Jesus's lifestyle, we can see how Jesus and the Father's relationship is. We can experience why the Father gave Jesus a purpose and a reason to exist. When we look at the life of Jesus and His commitment toward the Father, we realize that Jesus's purpose had to have a meaning and a purpose to exist.

From the outside looking in, the lifestyle of a Christian looks glamorous, but it has a lot of struggles and temptations that need a lot of discipline. Still, the rewards are worth the commitment with God. Jesus, even in these types of conditions, still kept preaching the Word of God, even if the truth was not being accepted. Yet, Jesus found the courage and fulfillment in preaching God's Word, even when we go into the book of Luke.

Jesus even had a strong love for the masses of people and His father in heaven. While we are in the book of John, let us look at John 14:18–31:

> I will not leave you as orphans; I will come to you. Before long, the world will not see me anymore, but you will see me. Because

I live, you also will live. On that day you will realize that I am in my Father, and you are in me, and I am in you. Whoever has my commands and keeps them is the one who loves me. The one who loves me will be loved by my Father, and I too will love them and show myself to them."

Then Judas (not Judas Iscariot) said, "But, Lord, why do you intend to show yourself to us and not to the world?" Jesus replied, "Anyone who loves me will obey my teaching. My Father will love them, and we will come to them and make our home with them. Anyone who does not love me will not obey my teaching. These words you hear are not my own; they belong to the Father who sent me. "All this I have spoken while still with you. But the Advocate, the Holy Spirit, whom the Father will send in my name, will teach you all things and will remind you of everything I have said to you. Peace I leave with you; my peace I give you. I do not give to you as the world gives. Do not let your hearts be troubled and do not be afraid. "You heard me say, 'I am going away and I am coming back to you.' If you loved me, you would be glad that I am going to the Father, for the Father is greater than I. I have told you now before it happens, so that when it does happen you will believe. I will not say much more to you, for the prince of this world is coming. He has no hold over me, but he comes so that the world may learn that I love the Father and do exactly what my Father has commanded me." Come now; let us leave. (John 14:18–31)

The love that Jesus had for the people and disciples of the day, He gave them enough confidence that He would not leave them like orphans and did tell them He would not see them nor would they see Him. Those who do not love Him will not keep His commandment. Those who love Him will keep His commandments.

Jesus, at this point, is letting people know that He was getting this inspiration from the Father. Now even in this verse, Jesus still shows His love for the Father by letting His disciples know that the Father is greater than He is. Jesus is magnifying His purpose and presence in God the Father.

But the prince of this world is coming. He has no hold over you. That is why one of our main purposes is to constantly stay in God's authentic Word daily in order to strengthen our faith in God. The more we stay in God's Word, the more mature we become. Our maturity in God's Word makes it easy for us to fight off all of our adversities and stand toe to toe with Satan's attacks, defeating everything that Satan puts before us. This is what God expects of us.

But during all this, Jesus let them know that "through the Holy Spirit, I am not leaving the people by themselves, struggling like a ship without a sail." Jesus is letting people know, "I will be there for them, even in the time of their adversities, in their sickness, even when the world turns their back on them and me because of our faith in God."

Even when your family and friends turn their back on you, Jesus says, "I will give you a rock to build and restructure your faith in God. I will give the people a comforter called the Holy Spirit who would lead them in all truth as long as we stay constantly in God's Word." This is God's consciousness.

The Holy Spirit is the advocate who the Father has sent in representation of Jesus Christ as a transcending power of energy. That same power has knowledge of man's struggles with Satan. The Holy Spirit stays in constant fellowship with God's consciousness and wisdom.

The Holy Spirit has a consciousness of man's nature. The Holy Spirit has a consciousness of man's spiritualism with God. The Holy Spirit has consciousness of man's relationship with his God.

That is why the Holy Spirit was sent to us by God. From my perspective, the Holy Spirit is Jesus with the physical manifestation of creation. The Holy Spirit carries the same connotation as Jesus Christ. As the population of mankind grew, sin itself became more propionate in the hearts of men and throughout the world.

This is when we need the physical life existence of God's Word so that God's consciousness would penetrate the heart and mind of mankind because a part of man's existence is through Jesus Christ. I think many people realized that God's Word had to become a physical manifestation of man's existence to prove that mankind cannot live his life without sin.

That man has spiritual laws that are above all of the laws that mankind established to govern society. Man even has the opportunity to be rewarded salvation through Jesus Christ's death. For example, God's Word becoming flesh also became the consciousness of mankind's salvation because of Jesus's physical existence here on earth. Let us look at John 1:14, "And the word was made flesh, and among us (and we beheld His glory, the glory as of the only begotten of the Father) full of grace and truth."

That the truth in God's Word can be lived and manifested in men lives if we use Jesus's life style is an example to modified as well as perfect in our lives after Jesus's lifestyle here on earth. This is where everything that was written down, including the Ten Commandments, had to blossom into the reality of man's physical manifestation of life. We had to experience Jesus's life style in the physical manifestation of life in order for mankind to become an example of God in the physical existence of life. Many people believe that Jesus is the human image of God's Word transforming into the human existence of life and that human existence of life is what we refer to as Jesus Christ.

For example, to prove the physical manifestation of God, we can experience that through the lifestyle of Jesus's walk here on earth with man. Jesus's life provided man with the information he needed for man to have faith in God.

We experience the truth within God's Word when He healed the sickness of men. We experience God's Word when He saves men from their sins. We experience God's Words coming to man in the sign of the burning bush. We even experience God's Son being crucified on the cross for the remission of mankind's sins. We also experience God's

Word coming alive in men hearts and souls. We even experience that if we have faith in God's Word, we can say, "Not only this mountain but any other mountains in our life be removed, and they will move."

Now the Holy Spirit is what I refer to as the unseen hand of Jesus Christ. It seems to me that the unseen hand which is the Holy Spirit has taken on the role similar to Christ without the physical manifestation of Jesus's existence. When all the time that Jesus spoke, teaching God's Word on faith and love, the Holy Spirit existed with that same faith and love we have today.

Jesus was preparing man through God's Word to develop a sense of spiritualism and understanding and consciousness toward the Holy Spirit. That sense of spiritualism was to bring man into a closer relationship and understanding with God through the Holy Spirit.

That is why I think at the point of man's existence, if anyone brings any blasphemy against the Holy Spirit, that is the one sin God would not forgive that person of because the Holy Spirit is a representation of God the Father and God the Son. It is like Jesus. It stays on earth to dwell against mankind and is in a state of energy that is consciously connected to God the Father.

Because the Holy Spirit is a representation of Christ's walk with the Father in the physical manifestation of life, if one loves the Word of Jesus Christ, then that one person or people would love their relationship with the Holy Spirit. It is very important that we develop a relationship with Holy Spirit like we did with Jesus Christ because it is the comforter that accommodates man's faith toward God. After Christ's crucifixion, the Holy Spirit became the unseen hand of God's relationship with man. For example, we only experience the Holy Spirit in the spiritual manifestation of life but not in the physical manifestation of life.

We must remember that everything that is in the physical manifestation of life, man has the potential to destroy it, even if they do not agree with who it is representing, especially when that thing has taken the responsibility to teach God's Word and become an advocate for God's salvation.

It is just like what Jesus Christ did and was crucified. So God had to position the Holy Spirit in the spiritual realm of life. That is why it is important that we stay in tune as well as develop our spiritual essence in life because it keeps us in touch with God. Most of God's revelation is revealed to man through the Holy Spirit.

Our spiritual awareness is what connects us to the Holy Spirit. During one's confession with God, that is when that person or people submits to the complete authority of God. During one's submissiveness to God is the beginning of one relationship with the Holy Spirit. The unseen hand means that the Holy Spirit is unknown to man. The Holy Spirit reveals itself to mankind through mankind's faith and consciousness in God, especially those who do not believe in God. The Holy Spirit is like a guardian angel to man. It keeps us out of trouble and reconnects us with God when we fall short of God's grace. That same unseen hand that I refer to as the Holy Spirit has reached out and hugged the hearts of men. That unseen hand has reached out and built better lives for men. That unseen hand of the Holy Spirit has reached and enhanced the spirituality of men.

That same unseen hand has wiped away the tears of many families' hearts who are suffering and bringing them into a better understanding with God. That same unseen hand has healed many people from the sickness of the world. That same unseen hand has brought us together in love and unity. That same unseen hand is a representation of the Holy Spirit that dwells in us. That same unseen hand is what Jesus meant when He said, I will leave you a comforter which is the Holy Spirit.

The Holy Spirit also supports and respects mankind's need to have a relationship with God. The Holy Spirit intercedes for man while comforting man as well. God has given mankind the privilege to communicate with the Holy Spirit, deciphering information that might be of prophecy or a message that God wants to reveal to the masses of people, especially from the spiritual world into the physical world, or even bring clarity to the spiritual essence of man's life and bring comfort to the masses of people here in the physical world.

Most Christians for some reason believe that because God grant them salvation, that is enough. They are not to do anything else; just live off of God's blessings. There is nothing to do but complain. They have no further challenges in life! Just leave everything to God, and He will take care of all of our needs.

Some Christians feel this way because of their commitment and faith in God. They should leave everything in God's hands and not worry. Always remember that in the book of James 2:14–26 (ESV), "Faith without works is dead."

Their spiritual requirements are done when, in actuality, their spiritual awareness has begun. We must remember consistently that our spiritual life needs to constantly keep improving upon God's desires for us so our faith should be proven by our works toward God.

We must recognize that in order to maintain our salvation, it is a constant battle with things in the spiritual realm and more in the physical realm as well. Satan also has a mission, and that is to get every soul that he can in order to complete his mission.

# Faith in the Midst of Our Sins

Christians must always remember that faith without works is dead. Our faith is our strength in the midst of our struggles, even sometimes when our struggles lead to our sins. Our faith is our strength that even holds us together spiritually in God's authentic hands when we are actually struggling with our own adversities.

It is through our faith in God that God is able to have compassion toward us as we wrestle and even fall short within our sins. The challenges within our sins let us know how strong we are in our faith with God and how much we have matured in God's grace and consciousness.

The things that challenge our sins lets us know how much of our free will we have given up to God and how much of our free will we are still struggling with before we surrender it all to God and how much of our human nature we have given to God. We experience this through the challenges of trials and temptations that Satan has put us through.

One of Satan's biggest strict rules toward mankind is to expose mankind's sins but not let mankind recognize Satan in the sins that he has caused mankind to do. So Satan created something called the unseen hand which is Satan's actions that he has placed to deceive mankind or try to prevent mankind from accepting God's grace and mercy.

So if Satan goes unrecognized, and mankind's sins are recognized, it seems the person who is in charge of all evil, who is Satan, has removed himself from the minds of all men who are doing evil to others. So let me summarize it all like this: the person who is in charge of all of the wrong and evilness in the world is not being recognized for the sins and chaos that he is causing or has caused.

For example, when is the last times we have heard Satan's name being called out on the pulpit? If we have been watching news and experiencing many injustices that are being done and shown on the news, the sins of people are being exposed, then the question one needs to ask is, what is going on in the world?

At one time, the churches had the answer to all of the world's problems, and now the church has a deaf ear to all of the problems and situations in the churches. At one time, the churches had the answers to the world's problems, and now the churches are functioning like they don't have the courage to fight to preserve the soul and heart of God's Word anymore.

The question is, what is wrong in the churches? The same devil that we are talking about is in the churches. Let us be honest: they assume that because they preach and teach God's Word that people do not recognize the devil that is in the churches.

The devil has moved into the organization of the churches and on the pulpit of the churches by selling the masses of people an imitation brand of the Gospel and by telling the masses of people in the church that everything they are doing is okay as long as it does not hurt nor affect others. So with that type of Gospel, as long as you don't hurt or affect others with your behavior, then your behavior is okay.

No, that is watered-down version of God's Gospel. That is not what God wants us to consciously apply to our lives, and that is not a part of God's teaching. That is the kind of teaching, preaching, and ministering that people teach to satisfy the masses of people throughout the world.

For example, we don't even hear the name of Satan being call as the devil anymore. It seems that the churches have become so afraid of the evilness in the world that they are afraid to use their faith to go face-to-face with the devil. If we have confidence in God's Word, then our consciousness should be so developed and mature in God's faith that we should have the courage to face the devil face-to-face.

What is going on with the pastors, ministers, and deacons in this world? Where is their courage to fight the evilness that they should be preaching and teaching about every Sunday from our pulpits that Jesus Christ is Lord and is the Son of God? That is why we need to have faith within our own sins.

It seems to me that our sins exist, but Satan who is causing the sins in the world does not exist because the people of God do not make Satan responsible for the evilness that he is causing in this world. Satan has always used the unseen hand to deceive, challenge, and destroy every believer's faith in God.

He is trying to destroy the lives of those people who faithfully believe in God's authentic Word. When I mention the unseen hand, I am making reference to Satan who has caused all of the sins and evilness and chaos in the world and makes it looks like he is not involved or that he even does not exist.

Here is another unseen hand approach that allows Satan to hide the unseen hand. Satan hides it when he is not being blamed for the sin and chaos in the world. The Christian Community is not making Satan responsible for his evil desires and chaos in life.

How do we make Satan responsible? We do that by calling his name and discussing Satan's actions and his state of evilness while we are giving praises to God and giving more praise to Satan. Because Satan gets afraid when the name of God is called, the pastors and ministers need to keep Satan trembling at the call of God's name. Be honest. When is the last time you've heard a pastor preach or a minister a sermon and mention the name Satan or referred to Satan as the devil?

With so much chaos going on the world, who is the cause of this mess? I can answer that question with this response, and that is no one except Satan. The name of Satan is not being mentioned. I would like to ask this question, and that is, does Satan himself still exist? Or is the evilness and chaos in the world exist without Satan or the devil's involvement? Or did Satan take a break? Or does he still exist? Or maybe sin and evilness exist by themselves?

Now could it be that some of the academic institutions are accepting the theological ideology and notions of telling their students that are majoring in divinity or religious studies that we should not mention Satan's name because it is not politically correct in the Christian Community? This could be the case that it is not theologically correct anymore to mention Satan's name in their sermons while preaching and teaching God's Word. The academic institutions, I believe, could mention to the students that it is harsh or barbaric to mention Satan or the devil's names while preaching and teaching God's Word.

People, if that is the case, we have a watered-down version, of God's Word full with a sweet water version of the Gospel. Now if that is the case, where is the power and strength of the Gospel? If that is the case, how and where do we define the strength and passion of our faith in God? I think what is happening in the churches is the churches are looking for entertainment than for God's knowledge and wisdom to be taught in the churches. It seems that the churches are competing with the world or want to be more like the world, worshipping the material possessions that God created rather than the Creator Himself. Our creator

## THE POWER OF GOD'S CONSCIOUSNESS

God has shown us love and compassion for the people in the world, just like God has done for us.

It seems to me that the churches are compromising the Gospel so much that they are destroying the soul and spirit of the churches every time the pastors, ministers, deacons try to compromise God's Word. It seems that as the churches progress in the age twenty-first century, the church is losing its flavor and favor with God. The reason why the churches are losing their flavor and favor in God's eyes is simple. The churches are not having enough control over the Gospel. The churches are saying one thing and doing another thing.

For example, the fall of the churches has nothing to do with God's doctrine or God's consciousness and His doctoring. It has nothing to do with the teaching of God's faith. It has to do with the dishonesty of the people who are supposed to be in fellowship with God. It has nothing to do with the churches not being challenged spiritually or the churches not having the answers to solve the problems that exist in the world today or with Christians not being able to satisfy people's passion in the world for God the Father. It has nothing to do with God not having love and compassion for the world.

It has to do with how Christians act like they are divine or like they are God's chosen people that they cannot recognize their own sinful thoughts. Christians are just as wrong and sometimes do worse as the people they think they are better than or the people they are supposed to bring to Jesus Christ.

We need to stop trying to hide behind the iron curtain of self-denial and admit that we are as guilty as the people in the world. It seems that Christians are persecuting the people that they should be saving. Instead, Christians are acting like the people they should be saving. Some Christians do not want to admit that to themselves this is how they are acting. The doctrine seems to be appealing to masses of people than appealing to the salvation of God.

Let me get back to my point because the pastors or ministers do not mentioned Satan or the devil's name in their sermons or Bible lessons anymore. People would assume that he doesn't exist while in reality, he does.

That is when Satan uses the unseen hand to control and manipulate the minds and emotions of the masses of people in the world and those in the Christian community. For example, to prove my point, if you're a person that watches TV and loves the so-called Gospel ministry and even in your church right now, why is it that you don't hear the name of Satan being called in the pastor's sermons?

We don't even call the name of the person who has called our own deceptions, chaos, and evilness. The person who is more deceptive than the nature of mankind, we somehow cannot find his name in the sermons of all men.

Let's us look at it from a different perspective. The church is in chaos. Some of the churches have no validity and truth in God. Here is why it seems that the people in the churches have lost their courage in God's consciousness. The people's consciousness, it seems some of them are focused more on the material possessions of this world and trying to fit Jesus Christ's message into the world.

The world is to hear God's Word so that the world can develop their own consciousness in God's grace, not to compromise God's Word to pacify the masses of the people. How would the masses of people understand and know about God's consciousness if we keep compromising God's Word?

Here is what we should be teaching and preaching: that it is through our faith in God that we are granted His grace. It is through our faith in God that we are granted salvation which comes through the blood of Jesus Christ. We should also call on Satan to prove how awesome the good of God is when compared to Satan, the devil.

You see, God's grace lets us know that when our sins get the best of us and has defeated us because of our strength in God's faith, we are forgiven based on God's grace and His mercy toward us. The faith of a person creates the discipline that a person needs to stay constantly and consciously in fellowship with God's righteousness.

When a person or people stay constantly in fellowship with God's consciousness, they are acknowledging the presence of their faith in God. Our faith in God gives us the wisdom we need to develop the courage within us that would cause us to recognize that our own will is not enough to conquer Satan's temptations, attacks, and chaos that he has bestowed upon the world. But it is through our submissiveness in God that we give up on our free will and embrace God's will for our lives.

We must understand that we have power within God's Word. That is the power that Satan knows about. Satan can never overpower those people who have faith or those people who have enough discipline in God's consciousness. The people of God should have enough discipline in God's Word where it reflects in our faith and actions toward God.

We must understand that the more the Christians work on strengthening their faith, the better they become prepared themselves not to constantly fall into sin. Now God's Word is a very serious deterrent toward sin, and it also embraces God's salvation.

Christians who only believe in the faith of God but do not work to enhance their faith or their growth and their relationship with God set a negative example for themselves and their spirituality. Those are the types of Christians that also say what should be done and do the opposite of what they should be doing. They preach a good sermon, and their actions are totally different than what they are saying.

For example, people who are not Christians would always say why go to church? Do you want me to go to church or have faith in God? To be just like you. Now that is a dangerous statement coming from someone who knows a Christian or Christians.

What makes a person who is not in the faith make such a statement is simple: the Christians or Christians are not reflecting God's integrity in their lives. The unbeliever has enough evidence from that Christian behavior to recognize the person's attitude is not of God's divine inspiration which should always be a reflection in our lives. That means that those Christians are not being in tune with God's consciousness.

They are not being Christlike to the point where someone would want to embrace the omnipotent power of God, just because of them. It means that the Christian(s) are not living the life that the unbeliever understands Christians should be living, and that is being in the image and likeness of God.

It tells me that Christians are not living up to the expectations that are required of them by God. We must always remember that our lives are a reflection of God. Now that is embarrassing to all of the Christian community when a person cannot identify with their own consciousness and faith in God.

Those types of Christians give other people in the world the impression that Christians are lazy. That Christians are unfaithful and want God to intercede for them every moment of their lives. Also, those Christians are not aggressive or progressive people in their lives at all. They are all just lazy people worshipping a God that is unseen. To them, that has no significant meaning. The atheist uses the Christians faults to justify the position of God in the world.

If you do not want to be committed to serve God, please step aside; step out of the way. Please do not give the Christian communities a bad name because of your actions not being Christlike. The world already has a negative disposition of the Christian community.

Please don't make God's faith look weak in the eyes of the world. Please stand up and represent God's salvation for your lives. Just to let you know, Christians are and should be strong people yet humble. Christians would be submissive yet aggressive for God and determined to fight and uphold the faith and salvation of God's consciousness in their lives. Christians should be a people who would die for God's Word.

As Christians, we know what we are fighting against when it comes to the flesh and blood of Jesus Christ. First, we are fighting against principalities and things unseen.

That means that Christians in the world today should know all the times that we are in spiritual war.

We should recognize that it is the Holy Spirit to intercede for us. The Holy Spirit is the protection that God has a place to protect mankind. It is the strength of mankind's faith when he is fighting in a spiritual war. We should recognize that it is the Holy Spirit that also intercedes for us, not only in our prayers but also when we ask for forgiveness.

The Holy Spirit is also our true protection that God has placed in our presence to protect mankind against the satanic world. The Holy Spirit adheres to its responsibilities in the spiritual world as it relates to the Christian community and the people of God. The Holy Spirit intercedes for mankind, especially when mankind is fighting a spiritual fight in the state of principalities and things unseen to mankind's knowledge. When I say things that are unseen or the unseen hand of God, I am referring to our state of temptations and obstacles that we are faced with.

That battle consists of things that mankind cannot see which are beyond the physical existence of mankind. Now that is a very scary thing to face. That is why we have the Holy Spirit.

When the Bible mentions about the Holy Spirit and its relationship to mankind, one of the things we must observe within the reference is how the Holy Spirit protects mankind from the principalities and things unseen.

The Holy Spirit acts as the consciousness of mankind for God. The Holy Spirit understands the nature of mankind, well enough to protect us from constantly committing the same sins against God. In order for the Holy Spirit to act as our intercessor to God, the Holy Spirit stays in tune with our consciousness to let God know where we are at spiritually and our level of maturity in the spirit. We must understand that the Holy Spirit knows what God expects from us and knows what God's will is for us, and the Holy Spirit tries through constant reinforcement to keep mankind on the righteous path with God. We must always remember that the Holy Spirit even brings us comfort, even in our state of consciousness.

When something is about to happen, it depends on the thing we are given, a warning which is the Holy Spirit. That is why it is very important that we stay in constant fellowship with the Holy Spirit.

For example, let us say that we are either on our way to work or heading out someplace important as you enter your car. It would not start. You try several times. Do you remember this example? Let me reiterate this statement. Have you ever had a problem with your car that wouldn't start? We call the car all kinds of names, lots of names—you know those names—just because the car would not start. As a person looking at this analogy, what do you think? Let me continue. Assume there is a bridge that you cross over in order to get to work. Everyone at work knows that you have to come across this bridge in order to get to work.

Remember, you are late, and you had to get someone else to ride with to work this morning. Now do you experience any form of a relationship with this situation and the Holy Spirit? Let me continue. Now you arrive at work.

Remember, you are all caught up in the moment of trying to get to work. One thing you know is that at a certain time, that bridge is crowded, so you take an alternate route. Now as soon as you get in the door at work, ten to fifteen fifteen employees approach you. Some of these people are people you see every day that you did not know really knew you on the job.

Everyone looks at you, saying, "Are you hurt?" or "Are you okay? Do you want to go back home?" or "Why didn't you go to the doctor?"

Now you become curious. Now you ask the question of the morning, "What the hell is going on?"

All of a sudden, someone tells you that the bridge you drive over every morning at the same time for work has collapsed, and many people have died.

Now it seems that the car you have called so many names has just saved your life, just because it did not start this morning. Now the major question is who told the car not to start. It was the Holy Spirit embracing the energy of the car and preventing it from starting.

The question is, why did God spare your life? Because your work was not done yet on earth. Now if God spares your life, then that means He is not done with you yet.

Always remember that faith without works is dead, and in order to get that type of favor from God, or God has recognized you within the state of favor, it means that God knows that you are consciously aware of your spiritual existence, and He has allowed the Holy Spirit to transcend His message to you because of His favor toward mankind.

We must be thankful for everything that God has given us, including yesterday and however it came to you because today, we can be removed from this earth. We must always be thankful to God for His blessings and even have the consciousness to serve Him through His grace and mercy.

For some reason, many people forget about the idea that Satan by himself is a very powerful force to contend with. The nature of mankind cannot compete with Satan's powers. Jesus knew that. That is why Jesus asked the Father to send us a comforter, and the comforter Jesus refers is the Holy Spirit.

This is why I think that God sent the Holy Spirit to intercede for mankind. The Holy Spirit is an energy that transcends into transformation of what God's will is for the Holy Spirit to do. The reason why Jesus sent the Holy Spirit is that mankind cannot grab a spirit or capture a spirit and nail that spirit on a cross or afflict bodily harm or physical harm or endanger a spirit.

I would say that the Holy Spirit has the same love and compassion that Jesus has for mankind. That is why the Holy Spirit protects us from all evilness, especially when we stay in tune with what God's will is for our lives. We must also understand that we are human beings, and the Holy Spirit is a spirit.

We must understand that the Holy Spirit knows the nature of mankind and keeps mankind's consciousness focused on God. Now the nature of the Holy Spirit is that He has a consciousness, just like mankind does, for God. The nature of the Holy Spirit is that He is a spirit that can never be touched by human hands, unless God orchestrates that to happen. The other thing is mankind cannot control the movement and emotions of the Holy Spirit enough to control His physical existence.

Here is what I am referring to. For example, mankind cannot grab or hold the Holy Spirit long enough to crucify the Holy Spirit or place the Holy Spirit on the cross.

Here is why: because the Holy Spirit exists only as a state of energy. That energy is a representation and transcending extension of God's power.

The Holy Spirit has the same character as Jesus Christ and represents the Father in the same capacity as Jesus Christ did. The Holy Spirit is a spirit that interacts with mankind by protecting mankind from Satan's attacks. The Holy Spirit has enough of a consciousness that if mankind is willing in their state of his free will to give up their free will and follow Jesus, the Holy Spirit is able and spiritually qualified to direct, lead, and guide mankind back into God's grace and righteousness.

In other words, mankind's nature does not allow mankind to control the Holy Spirit, or to elaborate further, the nature of the Holy Spirit does not allow mankind to control His nature. Here is why: when mankind was able to see Jesus Christ, touch Jesus Christ, and hug Jesus Christ and give Jesus Christ their love, that is when mankind took advantage of Jesus Christ's existence. Here is how mankind was able to take advantage of God's existence and turn it around and crucify Jesus Christ. That is when mankind was able to control Jesus's physical movement but not Jesus's consciousness and love for the Father.

This is what caused the death of Jesus Christ, so now we have the Holy Spirit who is nothing more than a conscious state of energy that is embraced into the trinity of God's consciousness. Mankind is not able to control or even touch enough of the Holy Spirit to restrain His movements. Again, just like Jesus Christ did.

That is why I have always told Christians never underestimate the power(s) of Satan, but always remember that you are more powerful than Satan because you have the Holy Spirit. Just because we might believe in a powerful God, it does not mean that we should relax and become comfortable in our faith with God. It simply means that the Holy Spirit interceded for us in order that we would control all of Satan's power of evilness and temptations that Satan tries to afflict upon us.

Satan has already perfected his craft of deception indeed. Satan had many generations of people that he had challenged in order to perfect his trickery on, and Satan is also able to work through people in order to destroy God's work and Word, especially those who actually believe and are faithful toward God. Satan knows that he cannot fight God directly and win, so he has to use human beings against human beings as a means to exercise his powers through them and in them.

We must always remember that God created Satan. So Satan does not have enough power or have as much privileges as we do with God. The only thing that we have to do to constantly maintain our power is to stay in tune with God. So God knows the nature of Satan. Mankind does not have to privilege or faith to know Satan like God does. That is why God uses the Holy Spirit to protect us from all of Satan's evil desires.

Satan had studied intensely the pride and the fall of mankind. As a matter of fact, Satan was the one who started the fall of mankind and created all the evilness needed to destroy mankind's faith and commitment with God. Satan used his evil desires to make them desirable and appealing to mankind in order that mankind would actually sin against God.

Satan has experienced studying mankind's culture from generation to generation, manipulating people through their cultures, emotions, pride, racism, and their passion for love. Even in the midst of people's history, Satan can destroy people's faith and their commitment with God. Satan disguised his approach toward mankind in many social settings that are unrecognizable to mankind, but it is very easy to manipulate the mind of mankind.

We are living in time where signs, symbols with many secret social institutes that are determined to run and rule the world, and the messages that Satan uses would be deceptive to mankind and their faith in God. Satan's first approach is to make God's faith an illusion of nothingness and to make people assume that God does not exist or God does not exist the way the Christian people say He does.

To be honest with you, this is what is happening in the world today with the churches right now. And the churches will be his major illusion of deception and nothingness. Our senses, it seems, are focusing on what sounds good and appealing instead of focusing on whose sermon is truthful and is concrete enough in their teachings about God's consciousness and what God's will is for us to do.

Satan's deceptions are hidden in our social structure, religious structure, and most of all, our economic structure and sometimes in codes and symbolism that we overlook every day. Those people who are deceived by Satan are highly rewarded for their membership with Satan as it pertains to deceiving and manipulating mankind through signs and symbolism.

It seems that God's doctrine became a watered-down version by the same people who have been worshipping

God for years. Some of them, in the spirit of God's faith, are still drinking milk when they should be eating solid meat. People who actually are affiliated with Satan would be manipulating the media where they would be saying in the media, "I cannot believe my parents believe this stupid doctrine about God."

It would be flashing all over the media. The idea is to get in the minds of people that religion is not important. Religion starts to lose its foundational structure and its content because many of the social institutions already have implemented their structure in God's doctrine. How was that done? That was done based on Satan's actions and what Satan used, the tool to manipulate the masses of people which would cause them to deviate from God's divine doctrine. Satan has a tendency to appeal to the materialistic, pride, and selfishness of mankind's ego, and that is what disturbed and manipulated the consciousness of mankind so much that mankind became stagnated in their faith toward God while God's grace appeals to mankind's salvation in God.

# The Definition of Consciousness

When we talk about consciousness, what are we referring to? We are referring to information that brings mankind into a state of awareness, and understanding about life and God.

That state of awareness and understanding is the information that we learn or acknowledge from a particular subject or thing. Now that that particular subject or thing is what brings mankind into a state of consciousness and awareness with God.

Now that awareness brings about an understanding, now that is the knowledge, and information, which mankind has developed from a particular, subject or thing. Now the information that mankind has studied, researched, and understood becomes mankind's subject.

Mankind's subjects or subject has to do with what mankind has been studying in order to enlighten or bring mankind's awareness to mankind either in the spiritual realm or through the physical existence of mankind.

The subject or subjects is what mankind wants to study in order for mankind to become knowledgeable or enlightened about the particular subject or subjects, which mankind is studying, is what I would like for you to do while reading this book or making progress in reading this book.

In this case in the book, mankind's subject is nothing more than God's divine Word. In other words, the subject of this book is acknowledging God's awareness through the consciousness of mankind and using God's divine Word as the subject, which can transcend and transform mankind from physical reality into spiritual enlightenment of God's consciousness.

That is what, I am referring to as the subject, which mankind has to understand, is nothing more than the scriptures, which is God's divine Word. Now for mankind to develop their consciousness, about the subject or thing that they are studying, or were studying, or trying to enlighten themselves about. In this case, let me repeat this: I am referring to God's divine Word, which I sometimes refer to as the scriptures.

As mankind develops in their conscious state of mind. Now what mankind is developing, is what mankind can retain, in their conscious state of mind. Now, this type, of information is what, mankind can gain, knowledge, understanding, and comprehending as God's divine Word.

As mankind tries to embrace the information that is in God's Word. The information that mankind is trying to embrace and analyze, is embraced and kept in mankind's mind.

The mind of mankind is the storage house that retains all of mankind's information, good and bad, that is what makes mankind's mind become the storehouse, of all of mankind's information, even the good and the bad experiences that mankind has acquired in this life becomes a part of mankind's consciousness.

Now mankind's consciousness is the awareness, which acknowledges all of mankind's good and bad experiences and information.

Now mankind's consciousness is the awareness that brings mankind into the enlightenment of mankind's spiritual consciousness is the knowledge that develops mankind's consciousness is the information, which comes from God's divine Word.

Mankind's consciousness is the awareness that guides mankind into all of God's spiritual qualities, those qualities of God are what start to develop mankind's spirituality and righteousness. Along with Mankind's integrity, and character, which develops the actions of mankind's faith.

It is mankind's consciousness that brings mankind into all of their own spiritual experiences, which develops and enhances mankind's consciousness through God's divine Word.

Now mankind's enlightenment is the awareness that brings mankind into their own spiritual experience, which can develop mankind's spiritual consciousness. Mankind's spiritual consciousness and enlightenment come from mankind studying the scriptures and praying to be in constant fellowship with God.

Now mankind's consciousness is what formulates into forming and creating a belief about how mankind perceives information or how mankind disagrees or agrees about a certain opinion or about how mankind can perceive or discuss a particular subject or topic in life or anything.

Now in this book, the awareness, belief, or opinion that I am talking about is how God's Word can bring mankind into an awareness, which can transform mankind into becoming a spiritual being.

When mankind is given or receiving information, that information mankind brings mankind into their enlightenment or awareness is nothing more than mankind's consciousness coming into its spirituality.

Now that enlightenment or awareness that mankind receives from God's divine Word is what brings mankind's character and integrity, into a faithful relationship with God. In other words, when mankind embraces God's authentic Word as a way of life, from studying or reading God's authentic Word, this is nothing more than the exaltation and manifestation of mankind's belief in God. That belief is what shapes mankind's faith and confidence in God. All of this is done through mankind's consciousness of God.

Please stay with me, and let me make this point about our spiritual consciousness. We must acknowledge that how mankind behaves or acts is nothing, more than an expression of mankind's faith in God.

Mankind's faith in God is inspired by mankind's consciousness. Mankind's spiritual consciousness is nothing is no then more than mankind's awareness. Now mankind's awareness is nothing more than mankind's consciousness.

Now let us look at the human body. The human body houses and stores all of our information in it, even information, which is intellectually discussed such as in academic settings, college and university, and also those sociable conversations that we would have with each other and whatever we understand, or comprehend, from what we experience in life or, let me reiterate, the information that we gathered from our experiences.

I mean the information where we try to define the true reality and spirituality of our life. It is all a state of mankind's consciousness. Now the mind is the storage house, which stores all of the information, that comes into the human body.

Now when mankind collects the information, that comes into the human body, the human body is enlightened mankind's awareness about God, and bring mankind into a spiritual consciousness with God.

At this point in our life when we beg to rationalize the information, interpret, comprehend, understand, all of that is done in mankind's state of consciousness. Now this is done especially when mankind begins to read and study the Word of God.

Now the mind storage the information, but all of the rationalization, interpretation, experiences, comprehension, understanding, and analytical perspectives are the processing of information, which is done in mankind's state of consciousness, and to me, this is where mankind's spiritual consciousness takes roots. This where

This is also where mankind can rationalize, interpret, experience, comprehend, understand, and use their analytical perspectives to reexamine the information that is in God's authentic Word. All of this is done through mankind's state of consciousness.

Now as mankind can rationalize, interpret, experience, comprehend, understand, and use their analytical perspectives to embrace God's consciousness through reading, studying, rationalizing, interpreting, experiences, comprehending, understanding, and using their analytical perspectives to get a better understanding of God's Word.

Now that is when mankind embraces God's Word and while mankind is wrestling with God's Word trying to make a decision on whether to apply God's Word as a part of mankind's way of life.

Now that is when mankind's consciousness starts the beginning of the spark that starts to ignite mankind's consciousness to keep burning in the hearts and minds of mankind's spiritual essence and substance, which begins to take root in God's divine Word.

It is at this point and time that God's Word encourages mankind's spiritual consciousness is being developed and inspired by mankind to become spiritually conscious and faithful in the Word of God.

The concept of what we need to do is express more of our faith. We must remember that our faith does not take the place of our consciousness.

Mankind's consciousness introduces mankind to God's faithfulness. Here is how God's faith is introduced to mankind: through mankind studying God's divine Word and the information that mankind receives from God's Word, creating and producing the information needed to create, develop, and mature mankind's faith in God.

Our faith is the actions of what mankind believes in. That belief that mankind has believed in is nothing more than God's faithfulness. God's faith is the belief that expresses mankind's actions and behavior.

Now someone might ask the question. It seems that when I discuss consciousness, it seems like you are talking more of mankind's mind. Mankind's mind is the storage house that can retain and keep the information needed to develop mankind's confidence in God's consciousness.

Now the information that mankind has retained and kept in their minds and hearts is information that we use when we are in a position to teach and to preach. That same information that mankind teaches to the masses of people, is the same information that mankind teaches and preaches from is the same information that develops and matures mankind's consciousness and experience in God's divine Word.

Now that we might need to overcome our temptations, even when we are challenged by adversity in life, that is nothing more than a spiritual war where our only weapon and protection is our spiritual consciousness that receives one again from God's divine Word.

When we are in a spiritual war, all of the information that the mind has retained or stored in our minds acknowledges to us what information we need for us to defend our trials and adversities in life.

In other words, our consciousness brings us into the reality of the type of information we need to protect ourselves from our spiritual warfare, that we are faced with and is in constant battle fighting, and that is how mankind's consciousness works to me as it pertains to God's divine Word and mankind's spirituality and enlightenment of God's divine Word.

All of the information that mankind has gathered brings mankind into a conscious state of mind, which is mankind's awareness. Now mankind's awareness is what develops mankind's spiritualism.

Now our awareness that comes from our conscious state of mind brings us into an enlightenment state of knowledge, and that knowledge is displayed through our conscious state of mind. Now our consciousness state of mind is the awareness of the knowledge, and wisdom we gather from God's Word. Now mankind's awareness is having the confidence, knowledge, wisdom of God's authentic Word.

Now as our consciousness increase in God's wisdom and knowledge. God's wisdom and knowledge bring mankind into their spiritual consciousness, and mankind's spiritual consciousness is acted out through, mankind's awareness, of how mankind interprets, acknowledges and comprehends, that mankind has learned through God's authentic Word.

Our consciousness is what we used to understand comprehend and acknowledge, the true reality and existence of both the physical world and the spiritual world. It is in our minds where that information is stored, until it is needed by our actions, to challenge, or defend the principalities, and the things that are unseen to the human experience but still exist in the physical realm of mankind's existence and reality.

For mankind to better understand their spiritual consciousness, mankind must first be challenged, first by their adversities, and trials in life. Our adversities and trials in life are what challenge our choices and make us decide what roads we should travel in life. Our adversities and adversaries, that we faced in life, also help us define our true purpose and reason for living.

That is why we must study God's Word because it is through God's Word that helps us even when we are going through our adversities and adversaries, which we are faced with.

Now if our faith and consciousness state mine is grounded in God. Then whatever adversities or whatever adversary that we stand up and face, we will always make the right decision, even in the state and time of our adversities and our adversaries. We will always overcome them.

As long as we stay consciously in the spiritual realm, of God's divine Word, and ask God to protect us and deliver us through our adversities and adversaries, we will always deliver us even if the outcome of whatever we are praying, for is not what we expected, or want God will always answer our prayers.

That is what strengthens, and directs our consciousness state of mind, to have enough confidence in God's Word, which would be able to faithfully and spiritually deliver us from situations or circumstances we face.

Our choices that we make amid our adversities give us the experience we need to make better decisions, which affect us and let us know, how well we can face, our trials and adversities, and it is the state which mankind uses to decide their spiritual growth and maturity, all of this is done through mankind's consciousness.

Every decision we make in this life must be determined by mankind's consciousness and mankind's interpretation of God's divine Word. We also understand and interpret. That is what develops our inner peace of mankind's spirituality and submissiveness toward God. Is the confidence of knowing that whatever situation we are faced with God is always willing and able to deliver us from any harm that we are facing.

When we talk about spiritual consciousness, we are referring to the idea of how that person or people have embraced the power of God's Word and how that person or people uses the Word of God to develop their own spiritual life and consciousness in God.

I remember someone asked me, a question about consciousness, and that is if a person is conscious, can that person be a failure in life? Yes, as a matter of fact, our failures in life help us develop our spiritual consciousness, in our life. It seems that people seek God in the most difficult times of their life and adversities and when they think they are being destroyed by their trials and adversities.

Here is what I mean: Our consciousness is developed through our failures. Our failures are our strength and foundation that help us develop our spiritual consciousness. There is nothing wrong with failure. Failure is nothing more than improving on what has caused, you to fail in the first place, or what is challenging you or stopping you from becoming successful in life especially in the things that you want to achieve success in.

We must understand that our failures in life, can only be defeated based on our spiritual consciousness. Our spiritual consciousness is our true awareness, that strengthens our faith in God. Everything that we have done, physically, consciously, and spiritually, is the experience, that teaches, us the importance, and significance of our faith in God.

We must also remember that every adversity or adversaries we face in life in the midst of us struggling with our adversities and adversaries, we are developing the knowledge and wisdom of our true spiritual reality, of what this life, means to us.

Although our true reality can destroy us, it is through the spiritual and physical battles that we find strength and confidence in the power of God's consciousness. That power that is in God's consciousness is the power that develops our faith in God. And as our faith grows, our confidence grows, and that is what develops our spiritual consciousness in God.

It is the experience that we wrestled with, that teaches us through God's divine Word, how we should respond and overcome our adversities and adversaries. That is what gives us power. Through our faith in God, to grow and

## THE POWER OF GOD'S CONSCIOUSNESS

mature faithfully and spiritually in our faith, and in our consciousness with God.

What is consciousness? I know you referred to consciousness as an awareness. Now, Mr. James Grant, can you use another perspective in which you can define consciousness?

Yes, consciousness is the power and knowledge we need to overcome any adversities or adversaries that we are faced with, especially those adversities and adversaries that accrue in our physical and spiritual life.

Our consciousness is the energy and power that develops, educates, acknowledges. God's consciousness comes through God's divine Word. It is through our knowledge that we have comprehended, and understood, through God's wisdom, that gives us the power, that exists in every human being's inner self.

The inner self of every human being's life is the experience and knowledge, where, every human being has houses and stores all of the information, that they have gathered from God's divine Word.

That knowledge and wisdom, that we gather from God's divine Word. It is retained and stored in the inner chambers of mankind's soul and spirit. This is where the power of our faith and consciousness, in God, lies just in mankind's spirit and soul until he or she, is ready to do battle against their adversities, and their adversaries, and the principalities and things that are unseen to mankind in this life. The power that comes

The good and bad experiences still enhance our power and strength in God. Here is what I mean, how because as we study God's Word gives us the power and wisdom to even challenge and overcome our adversities through our conscious state of mind.

The power that mankind uses to develop, their consciousness, and strength in God, comes from God's Word. It is the wisdom, and spirituality, which manifests themselves, in the wisdom, and power that comes from God's divine Word, is that gives mankind the strength, that mankind needs. For mankind to have enough confidence, in their faith with. All of this is done through mankind's spiritual consciousness and faith in God.

It is that power and strength, that keeps mankind in constant fellowship with God. Here is what I mean: Our knowledge brings into fellowship and worship with God. It is the knowledge, which brings about our understanding, and fellowship with God.

That is also what gives us, the power that we need to overcome any trial or obstacle that we have faced in our lives. It is mankind's consciousness and faith that becomes mankind's weapon of destruction toward the evil desires of this world, as well as the principalities, of this world.

I remember someone asking this question: Can someone who has failed in life, become successful in life? First of all, for anyone to become successful, it starts with the person's consciousness. Our consciousness has to do with mankind's awareness of life and mankind being able to develop the discipline needed for mankind to become successful.

Failure comes when someone is trying to destroy another person's motivation and drive. This happens because someone or people might know your potential, and because they know your potential, they might want you to be in that position. This is what I call jealousy is an emotion, that is very deceptive.

Here is why jealousy is deceptive: it is because of how it is polished up in other people's personalities.

Here is what I mean: Jealousy never notices. Jealousy is never noticed by a person's personality.

We all can recognize our enemies right away and from far away but we can never recognize those who are jealous of us until their actions display how much hate is in the jealousy for us.

People will exercise jealousy at the wrong times, inappropriate places your enemies you know will destroy you at the split of a second show you're always building your guard up people who are jealous of you has a personality where they don't act out they jealousy until they are ready to strike like the snake that they are.

Now that is why it's imperative that we stay spiritually in tune and conscious, because whatever size, or whatever the cause is, our spiritual consciousness, gives us the insight to recognize, the jealousy, and hate that people feel and have toward you.

When you embrace God's Word into your heart and mind. That is when God to you start to develop your spiritual consciousness in God. When a person develops their consciousness in God. That person or people are developing the discipline need to recognize that failure is nothing, more than a chance to try and recuperate, pray and use your consciousness to get up and do better.

The word failure should be substituted for, trying to find a different way to approach the roads to your success, because you have come across so many detours in life.

Even writing this book I have come across so many detours in my life, that I have come to accept them. I even struggle with them through pray and constant fellowship with God. I have learned to accept failure. Failure is one of those things or circumstances, which I use a lot to pray and develop my spiritual consciousness in God, in most cases through the failure I have experienced more pain and suffering, that comes with my failure.

Once again, through my failure, I have experienced so much pain and suffering, but the pain and suffering that I have experienced from my failures have allowed me to develop a deeper consciousness, which I refer to as my spiritual consciousness.

This developed within, my character and integrity, enough confidence, and courage to face my fears, and fight my fears, and that is what causes me to become victorious and overcome, all of my failures, which cause me so much pain and suffering, in life.

But through the courage and strength that I have developed, to fight my failures, in life, is the consciousness, that God has placed in me through His divine Word, which develops enough faith in me to overcome all of the failures.

The one thing with failure is that the people you know might not want you to succeed spiritually, economically, socially, politically. Here is why sometimes people feel more comfortable seeing and experiencing you in the same position that you are trying to grow from or move on with your life and mature to do better things in life.

People hold you back because you might inspire them to become responsible and exercise the discipline needed, for the reason why they are not growing spiritually. You might recognize the jealousy of others, all because they are cough in their hate and jealousy toward you that you might recognize it because you are trying to grow spiritually.

Failure is when you stop trying when a person stops feeding their potential to become successful spiritually. When you stop doing everything in your power not to become successful.

Obstacles, trials, tribulations, adversities, and adversaries are the things that make it very difficult for people to become successful spiritually. These are the things that dominate and control our emotions.

Let me also look at it from this perspective for me to define my purpose and reason why I have to be able to define my purpose and reason in life everything we do or what we to achieve we have to have a purpose and reason. I must say that all human beings do exist in this life.

It takes more courage to challenge to know where one is trying to define a spiritual consciousness and spirituality challenge the face of the obstacles I will consciousness is what gives us spirituality belief to define who we are as individuals in this life.

Grow up the spiritual conversation to challenge so that we can still define who we are

She read my social experience ourselves growing this gives us the spiritual consciousness that we need to achieve the things that are needed to improve who we are spiritually and for God.

We must also see ourselves maturing as we progress in the consciousness of God the experience of maturity and the development of a spiritual consciousness helps develop or in the self or inner self is the strength of where we grow and nurture our growth in God.

And as we go back into the world we realize that we become a different being through, the essence and substance of our faith, and that is where people experience their spiritual growth and spiritual potential. All this is done through our state of consciousness, which is the awareness and the development of how we progressed spiritually and consciously in God's faith, grace, mercy, and salvation.

# Developing Confidence in Our Spiritual Consciousness

Have you ever experienced so many people talking about what they could be, what they want to do, what career they want to achieve in life, and most of all how much money they want to make? People want to know or think about what career they want to become successful in. All of these things are controlled by mankind's consciousness and mankind's faith in God.

People sometimes are more concerned about who loves them and appreciates them. For example, like our families and friends. Some people are trying to look for gratification and approval in the wrong places in life.

The only place we can find gratification, through God's Word, and our faith in God. God's divine Word and mankind's faith are what develop and transform mankind's consciousness from the physical reality of life into the spiritual manifestation of life.

The only person that can give you that gratification and approval, that you need is God Himself, in order to become successful in this life is God. Your success might not be what God wants you to have. That is why people waste so much time in life, trying to do what God has not called them to do.

We experienced this in the universities, colleges where people have their own minds and hearts made up to major in a particular major, and after a while, they realize it was not for them. It is because God was not calling upon you to major in those things. What God calls you to do makes you feel more comfortable and spiritually encouraging.

God has a different anointing for you which is different than what you think, you should do what God has called you to do. If you stay in tune and in fellowship with God He will anoint you and let you acknowledge spiritually and consciously, what your true calling is in life.

When we look into the world we experienced a world where people are in a state of confusion, chaos, politically, economically, spiritually, socially, religiously, academically, but the world arrogance and pride, would not admit that their own stupidity and chaos, is slowly leading the world into its own state of destruction. Very slowly, where the world thinks, that they are mankind progress, but the world is causing its own chaos and destruction to themselves.

Satan is doing it slowly, where people get so comfortable, where they cannot experience or recognize the destruction of the world's own chaos. We need to let God's consciousness be in every four corners of the universe and world.

Here is why we need to bring God back into our homes, schools, and also back into our churches without walls and with walls. These places, because some people's consciousness is not spiritually driven anymore, we need to develop more of our consciousness in order for us to find our way back home to God spiritually and consciously.

The decisions that people are making in our society, that does not relate to God's divine Word. Because God's people are standing strong, and courageous it seems that God's people are losing their, faith and spiritual consciousness in God.

It seems that the people in the world are having more of an influence on the masses of people, than those people who actually believe in God's divine Word. Especially, once again those people who don't believe or have faith in God's Word, are the people who are actually influencing and giving their perspective on how life should be in the world than the people who actually believe in God.

The world is teaching us that, as Christians

It seems that most Christians are embracing the world views, and perspective on life, instead of God's perspectives on life. It seems that God's Word and consciousness are restricted. Why is the voice of God's Word not being heard? I have the opportunity to live long enough to recognize that if we implement God's Word in our lives, we would have better choices and a better way of life.

Here is why because the people who study God's Word are not influencing the masses of people. It is because the people in the churches and those who believe and have faith in God are becoming very fearful of standing up for God, and those same people are not living up to the discipline that God expects of us. One of the main priorities of God's Word is the discipline that is implemented in God's Word for mankind to obey.

In other words, those people who believe in God, have a difficult time, believing and living up to God's expectations, of what God wants of them, or what God expects them to do. It seems that even God's people are living up to the world's expectations than God's. Some of them preferred to fake the faith in God, instead of living by the faith and consciousness of God.

Those people who disagree with God's divine Word, those people's thoughts seem to be destroying and failing the minds, and hearts of mankind. Yet mankind prefers to be entertained by every ounce of the negative information that is coming from the world than the positive information that is coming from God's divine Word.

I think mankind needs to develop its spiritual consciousness more. With our fear and timberline, because in God's divine Word, He does not teach us about fear. Our faith and consciousness are enough for mankind not to have fear in their hearts if they are believers in God's consciousness. Especially those men and women who are representing God.

## THE POWER OF GOD'S CONSCIOUSNESS

We are in frivolous times, it seems mankind are not having any serious purpose or value in their life. It seems like mankind is just existing, without a purpose and reason to live and enjoy life. It seems that mankind is in a serious state of being carefree, and not serious about anything in life. Mankind is not respecting each other. We have too much hate and less love for each other.

The question someone might ask is why is the world in this type of state? And it is simple, mankind is drifting away from God's divine Word, and as mankind are slowly drifting, away from God's divine Word. The world itself is beginning to lose its reason and purpose, for why the world itself is existing, in this life. That is why we are faced with so much hate, pain, suffering, and the distraction that is coming from the world.

I think the world needs a spiritual cleansing of God's authentic Word. In order that God's consciousness, which comes from God's Word, would be embedded and implemented in the masses of people's consciousness. Where they would be willing to revitalize, and give the world a refreshing, and replenishing, new birth, where mankind rich or poor can enjoy and love each other like God loves us.

Now that would bring a new meaning to the world's standards of living where our lifestyle can actually manifest the transparency of God in our own state of consciousness and love.

This will allow mankind to develop, their own spiritual consciousness. I mean a spiritual consciousness, that will destroy the evilness, and sinful nature of mankind's imperfection, and the distraction, that causes sin and fall short of God's love, grace, and mercy.

That mankind has caused themselves and other people in this world. Once again the reason we have all of this chaos in the world. It is simple, It is all because mankind deviates from God's divine Word, and discipline. Now in this time, now the consciousness of mankind's thoughts is still in a state of chaos. Just because we adapted to the culture and materialism of this world.

We need to allow God's anointing people, to rise up and speak out for God, and not become fearful or intimidating, but be able to stand strong, and firm for God. I hope those people are spiritually consciousness, of God's authentic Word. We need those people to start to implement God's divine Word, back into the world, in order to develop mankind's consciousness, in God.

Our spiritual consciousness needs to be guiding us, instead of the world's perspective guiding us about what our life should, or is about. God's, word should be leading mankind from the cradle to, the grave, back to heaven. Our life as Christians should be the example, that is leading the masses of people back to God, and the voice that is leading the masses of people is nothing more than God.

Once again, I think the reason and meaning are that we are afraid to stand up, as Christians, and stand firm as Christians for God's consciousness and His compassion, love, and salvation for God.

We must remember that the Christian life is not a life of convenience, it is a life of hard work, discipline, and dedication to God. The Christian life is a life of hard work and dedication. Now that dedication and hard work, is what develops the integrity, love, and character of God's people.

Even in the midst of our adversities and adversities of this world. God is constantly challenging our state of consciousness through the obstacles and circumstances that we are faced with and what we are being faced with in our future life.

What we need to know is that God's Word is the only thing that can define mankind's purpose and reason for living. Mankind's life can only be defined through God's Word. It is through God's Word that mankind is able to develop their own consciousness, and it is the state of our consciousness which we are able to define as our true purpose and reason for living.

We must understand that the Word of God, is the key which, opens the door to mankind's spiritual consciousness, especially when it comes to mankind trying to define their true purpose and reason for living. Now the simplicity of mankind's purpose and reason for living is best to express and experience through God's authentic Word.

That is where the truth comes from that develops *The Power of God's Consciousness*. *The Power of God's Consciousness* is a book written to transform lives through awareness which brings about the true consciousness that is in God's divine Word.

The first process of mankind knowing what their true purpose and reason, is in life. First by trying to get to know the person, who created you, and me, by bringing us forth out of our mother's womb. That is the physical reality and substance and essence of mankind's nature in trying to develop their own consciousness in God.

Now the more you become submissive to God, and read and study God's Word, the easier it is for mankind to define their true purpose and reason for living.

The more we submit to God, the easier it is for us, to define our reason and purpose for living. Our submissiveness to God is the state in which mankind's purpose and reason in life are revealed to them through their consciousness state of mind.

God can always work and develop a submissive heart, and a caring heart, that is able to give mankind a better reason and purpose to live a better life.

It is at this point in our submissiveness state of consciousness that mankind is able to develop and experience what God's consciousness means to them and what mankind's true purpose and reason are for them to do in this thing we call life.

As mankind tries to define their reason and purpose in life. That is when mankind's faith also becomes the test that is able to define mankind's purpose and reason in life, through mankind's spiritual consciousness and enlightenment.

The best way to define what mankind's purpose and reason are in life is through mankind's trials, adversities, and temptations in life. It is at this point that determines mankind's purpose and reason for living, and it is all done through mankind's faith in God our Father.

# THE SCULPTOR'S CONSCIOUSNESS OF MEANING AND BEING

There was a tree that I was told was around Boston College School of Theology since the the 1800s. I was also told that the tree died of tree cancer. Now that reminds me of my life being dead to sin, and now the only time, that my life has meaning and being is through God's divine Word.

It is through God's divine Word, that gives mankind enough knowledge and wisdom, and it is through, that same Word, which gives my life its true meaning and being in life.

It is through God's wisdom and knowledge, which is constantly redefining, and redirecting my life, which through God's anointing for my life, and that is what, also bring me into The Power of God's Consciousness, and it through God's consciousness, which gives mankind's life, its true meaning and being in life.

I want to acknowledge as well as bring to your attention, which I am one of the Greenline operators for the MBTA System. The tree that was dead, had no meaning and being to exist because it was dead. The meaning and being of the tree came to life. The sculpture with his chisel and hammer created an image that brought the dead tree to life.

That image was Mary, Joseph, and Jesus Christ. Every day I drive that tree it reminds me of my faith in Jesus Christ. The meaning also reminds me of my salvation in Jesus Christ.

But the sculptor gave the dead tree meaning and being to exist. One of the things that I want to bring to the attention of people is when we think that our lives have no significance or importance to the life that we live.

Especially when we feel that we are broken and dead, and we have nothing to contribute to life, and all of the efforts that we put into life cause so much pain and suffering. Until we feel dead to the reality of our own existence.

Somehow I feel like that dead tree, being dead to the reality and existence of its own life, and then one day God's authentic Word, touch the inner core of mankind's consciousness and giving mankind a thought. It is that thought which transcends like a spark that ignites the souls of mankind like a light.

Now that spiritual light burns like a flaming fire which burns in the heart, soul, and mind of mankind's consciousness, and the spiritual enlightenment of mankind's consciousness, is what develop mankind's faith, and that is what brings mankind into fellowship and intonement with God our Father, and that is what gives mankind their true meaning and being in life, but mankind's meaning and being can only happen through God's authentic Word.

Anytime mankind wants to give their life a new meaning, or even try to redefine their life, by giving their life a new direction. Mankind can only experience that direction through their meaning and being in life. Now that can happen when mankind embraces the Word of God.

When mankind embraces the Word of God, mankind is embracing the knowledge and wisdom of everything that exists in the heavens and the earth that only God has for those who study His Word in faith, in truth, and in discipline.

The only thing that is able to transform mankind from a mere physical being into becoming a spiritual being is God's wisdom and knowledge. This is written in God's authentic Word. God's authentic Word is able to change and transform mankind's ways of life and bring mankind into a spiritual being with love and harmony for their own God.

That spiritual being that mankind wants to transform themselves as is transforming themselves into becoming can only be achieved by studying and being able to exercise the discipline, which exists in God's Word, every day and night.

When mankind studies God's Word, it is God's Word that speaks to the hearts and minds of mankind. God's Word is speaking to the heart and mind of mankind. It is God's Word that is shaping and carving, mankind's heart and mind, into a transforming state, where mankind is able to develop their consciousness, through God's divine Word.

When God's divine Word changes mankind from a sinful nature and imperfections and then brings mankind, into becoming a spiritual human being. That is where the power of God's Word begins to develop and take root in mankind's consciousness for God. It is at this point, which mankind begins to experience, shape, and develop their true spiritual consciousness and enlightenment through God's Word.

I look at the tree every day I realize that the tree was not significant or ahead of me all because it's standstill and it never moves yes it was dying but isn't it amazing that even in our lives as we become dead to sin as we study God's Word revitalize is defined as and give us a Meaning and a Being to exist

Instead mind the consciousness of the sculptor just like God did when the universe had no form, or significance meaning, or being. Instead, God through His consciousness ends up giving nothing from the universe meaning and being in life. Mankind is a part of that meaning and being, which the universe was one a part of that nothingness. God even gave mankind meaning and being to even exist with the stars, and the constellation of the universe.

I see that same perspective and experience of some things, which have no significant meaning at all, can still exist from the state of nothingness, in order to become something with, such profound spiritual enlightenment, significance, where God is able to give that thing, or all things that exist from nothingness, to become that spiritual consciousness that thing or things into existence, where God is able to give that thing a meaning and being in life.

If you don't believe me ask yourself the same question you were once in a state of nothingness; and you now become transformed from substance, matter, and form. God has taken and given you nature, and that nature that God's hands have authentically given to you, all of us meaning and being to exist. Now that meaning and being out of God's consciousness.

The problems that we face sometimes become like a big tree. The rock is the problem of the world that occurs in our lives. It seems that some of the boulders, we cannot move, even sometimes when we have faith in God.

Our experience in life is not giving us enough insight. Where we can actually use our consciousness, as a means to develop, and justify the power of our faith, that we need in order to overcome the obstacles. This is the big rock in our lives, which represents our trials, tribulations, adversities, and adversaries in this life.

We realized, that in order to be able to remove this burden and try to figure out the reason and a purpose why this burden is accruing in our lives once again the burden that is in our lives is the representation of the rock.

The rock, in this case, is our trials and tribulations which continuously stand still in our life by constantly distracting and challenging our spiritual consciousness and way of life. Our faith in God once again is the action that we used in order to chisel, away each day that we are facing our adversities in life.

It is God's Word that shapes and carve, our lives just like a sculptor are able to transform a rock or wood by shaping and transforming that rock and wood into shapes that we can recognize their shapes, the shapes of rock and wood is what gives it purpose and meaning life.

That is how God gives our life its true meaning and being, through our consciousness in God. That is how God's Word shapes mankind's consciousness, and that is when mankind is able to find its true meaning and being in life.

Our lives are in our state of consciousness, just like a sculptor is able to transform, our lives. and as the chisel shape and color of the stone, it is teaching us how to define our true purpose, and reason to exist in our life.

The Word of God is an example of how the sculptor chisels away at the rock to create an image, that people can recognize, what the image is. When people can recognize the image, of the sculpture work. That image defines the nature, purpose, and reason of what the image represents.

Now the chiseling of sculpture is like, what God's divine Word is to us. Here is an example: as we study God's Word and receive the knowledge from God's Word, the knowledge that we receive from God's Word becomes the chiseling work of the sculpture.

That hard work that the sculpture has done to bring that image of the wood or stone to life. The hard work of the sculptor is like us reading and studying the Word of God, and as we read and study God's Word, the message in God's Word and the knowledge and wisdom we embrace from God's Word. The messages that we embrace from God's Word by studying are what also define who we are as a person or people who believe in God.

The message that we receive from God's divine Word, is what develops our spiritual consciousness in God. As we study God's Word, we must recognize that studying God's Word every day, and praying every day, and trying to walk and live a righteous way of life. Is the same example of how the sculptor has to work so hard, to bring something from nothing, into becoming a true way of life.

Here is what I mean: as the Word of God chips away at us, the chipping away is representative of how God's Word. God's Word is shaping us, something similar to when the sculptor is shaping and craving the image in life.

Now the knowledge we need from God's divine Word. The teaching, and preaching of God's divine Word, is what is shaping us to become better human beings, spiritually with a consciousness to serve and worship God.

The studying, the discipline, and the faith, we have to go through to implement, intense studying is what brings our consciousness, in alignment, with God's fellowship, mercy, and grace. Now in order for us to develop our consciousness in God's divine Word. We study and work in the shape and image that the sculptor does in order for us to truly develop our integrity and consciousness in God.

That is what develops our true purpose and reason for living. We must always remember to do what is needed of us. In order for us to develop our consciousness, in God, in order for us to be able to know what our purpose and reason are in life.

Now the shape of the image of the rock, or wood that the sculptor is trying to bring into existence, is the awareness, of having the knowledge to predict and predestine, what the image is that the sculptor is trying to bring to life, in order to give the image a reason and purpose to exist.

Our consciousness is what is give us the knowledge, to bring our trials and tribulations in our lives to a point where we can use our trials and tribulations, spiritually to shape and structure the image of this rock and bring it into a more realistic perspective of life.

This means this rock is the trial that causes us so much pain and suffering in our lives. And God's Word is the antidote that builds up our resistance and strength through our consciousness and faith, in order for God to let other people recognize our potential within ourselves spiritually and consciously.

Now in order for us to overcome our trials in this life. We have to become spiritually consciousness, of our minds and our actions, which strengthen our faith in God. Here is what I mean: Faith is the action that exercises our belief in God. Now that belief, which we have been rewarded through God's consciousness, gives us the power we need to transform our lives through God's divine Word.

Now let us look at a rock, that becomes one of the biggest boulders in our life. Now that rock is like a mountain. But that mountain is symbolic of the adversities and adversities, that we face in our lives. Now we must look at the rock, as an example of our trials, our and our tribulations, and our adversities, and our adversaries in life.

Now as we embrace God's divine Word, we must become the sculpture, of our life. This means that the rock is our adversities, that exist in our lives every day. Now we need a chisel, that chiseled represents the Word of God. It is through that chisel or chiseling that we begin to direct or redirect our lives through our spiritual consciousness in God.

When we are faced with our problems, and adversities in life I am referring to those trials and adversities that would almost destroy, annihilate, or even ruin, our consciousness and faith in God. I am referring to hard trials in life that would destroy our faith in God.

Now the chiseling or chisel is the word, it helps now as the Word of develops and shapes our consciousness, that is the same way that the chiseling and chisel shape our consciousness of who God's Word shapes, now at this point in our trials and adversities we can experience the light at the end of the tunnel.

Our consciousness is beginning to shape, our lives, and that is what brings our obstacles and adversities into a state where we can experience, through our consciousness and faith, how God's Word has protected and worked through in the midst of our trials and adversities.

Just like the rock does not move it is the same way with our trials and adversities in life. They will come in different ways, even the death of close friends and family. They don't move unless we are consciously and faithfully willing to use God's divine Word. God's as we study God's Word is what shapes and defines our purpose and reason for living.

God's Word is the chisel, that we used, in order for us to chisel our away at the rock, which is causing us so many adversities, and adversaries in life. Now our adversities, and adversaries, Which are the adversities, and problems, that we face in life.

The image or the shape that the sculpture is chiseling away at, we must keep in mind, that every stroke of the chisel is defining our meaning and being in our lives. Especially in the midst of our trials, and adversities.

When we can identify the problems, which becomes our own trials and adversities in life. That is when we can define the image of the sculpture. That image of the sculpture, at every stroke, is nothing, more than identifying the meaning and being of our own trials and adversities in life.

Once again every stroke, which comes from the chiseled, of the sculpture is defining the meaning and being, of the image, which the sculpture is trying to create, for the masses of people, hoping that the masses of people can recognize, identify, and know. What the image is that the sculpture is creating, or can the image that the sculpture is trying to create, can the masses of people identify the image, which the sculpture has created?

For example, here is what I mean, our life can only have meaning if we can first identify the problems in our lives. Especially, those trials and adversities that are causing us, not to succeed spiritually and consciously. When the sculptor, chisel the rock, hit the rock or wood and beat the rock or wood in order that the sculptor, would bring to life the image, and character, of the thing, which the sculptor is trying to create.

We must also remember that each stroke, each hit, each chip that falls on the ground from the sculptor's hard work and determination is nothing other than mankind's trying to give their life reason and purpose to exist.

The rock or the wood. That sculptor's stork that sculptor chisel thought while trying to create and develop an image that can give the image a Meaning and a Being. Represents, God's Word. Each verse we read, every time we study, every time we pray, every time we sing a hymn, teach, or even preach, We are identifying as well as acknowledging God's consciousness, and presence, in our lives.

When we are able to acknowledge and identify God's consciousness, in our life, that is when we are able to manifest, through mankind's integrity, and way of life God's compassion, and God's consciousness in our life. Those attributes from God's divine Word that mankind acquired from God's divine Word are what build mankind's attributes, integrity, and examples of who God is in their life.

For example, the sculpture does the same thing that God does when we study, preach, teach, God's Word. As the sculptor, chisels away at the rock or wood in order to identify to the masses of people, his or her creation of the image of the wood or rock.

The sculptor is also trying to give a purpose and reason for why he or she created the image. The reason why the sculptor is creating the image is to bring that image meaning and being in life. So that mankind can identify the image. The image defines what our meaning and being are in life.

We must also understand that whatever image that we are created to be by God or sculptor. Our image, also defines what our true nature is. That the sculptor is trying to give to the image a purpose and reason, which is to bring life to the creation that the sculptor and God have created.

Whatever God, and sculptor created in their consciousness, it gives that creation and image nature to exist. That image that has been spiritually by its creator defines the nature of the creation, that God and the sculptor have created.

That is the same example of how God, has become the sculptor, and creator of all men and women in the world. Through the nothingness, which once existed in the universe. That nothingness is what God has created mankind from, and that is what God caused the nothingness of this world, to become, manifested as the something of this world, in my own true state of reality, which we all are now, existing, and experiencing, as life.

That is why once again everything that God, the sculptor created has a reason and a purpose to exist including you and me. That meaning and reason can only be defined through carving out and chiseling, out based on our adversities, and trials. In other words, every time we face the adversities and trials that we faced in life.

We starting to begin, to understand the circumstances and situations that are causing so many of our trials and adversities in life. That is when we begin as men and women of God to completely understand and comprehend why we are being faced with so many adversities and trials in life.

Now when we are able to comprehend and understand our adversities and trials in our life. The understanding and comprehension create an image that brings the meaning and being of trials and adversities. Which we are facing, through our own adversities and trials in life.

The being is nothing more than acknowledging the meaning, that is causing our problems and circumstances in life. I mean especially those circumstances, and trials that are already here to impact our life.

The reason that our existing, within our trials, is to help us get a better understanding, of the circumstances that are causing our trials to impact the reality and spirituality of our lives.

Now the impact of our trials is to help us get a better understanding of our reality and spirituality, and strength of our faith, and consciousness in God our Father.

The meaning of our trials and storms in our life is to, is to protect us from the situations, and circumstances, that if we were not protected, the situations or situations would have destroyed, or killed our relationship with God.

That is why every trial we face or go through there's a reason and a purpose for the way that we go through our trials. Now that purpose and reason are given to us during the time that we are experiencing our trial and at the end of our trial. Our life and creation are defined through our consciousness and faith in God.

Life itself along with oxygen and water is the substance and matter which creates and forms mankind's life's true existence. It is the tissue of life, and form, which is the body.

Those are all physical creations that exist in our physical life, but because we exist physically, it does not mean that we cannot exist spiritually and become one with God our Father.

We are able to do that through constantly being in tune with God and developing, and maturing in a spiritual state of consciousness. Our spiritual existence comes when we study and teach God's Word. The power of mankind's spiritual consciousness is in the studying, interpretation, and living the lifestyle of God's divine Word, out both physically and spiritually in our lives each and every day.

The courage, of mankind, is when mankind, is able not to have fear, but to have the courage and the power to develop the strength of mankind, and not being able to compromise the Word of God, for the convenience of the masses, but always speak the truth of God, even if you are hated by the masses of people. The masses of people cannot grantees your and my salvation. So it's better to be hated by the masses of people but the love and blessed by God.

When we learn about God's divine Word, we are learning how to comprehend, interpret, and understand, the information from God's Word. Now that information that is in God's authentic Word is created to transform and transcend, ourselves to become spiritual human beings. With a divine consciousness and enlightenment. In order for me to teach and preach God's Word to the masses of people.

This means that God has created everything from nothing and gives nothing a reason and purpose to exist. That is why we must recognize that we serve a powerful God. Because we serve a God that has power as we transition and transform ourselves in God's divine Word. The power of God is what strengthens us in our consciousness and faith in God. It also means for us to have the same power of God.

That power that God still has is what develops our state of consciousness. It is through our state of consciousness, that the actions of our faith, introduce us to the power of God, and it is in the state of mankind's consciousness that mankind stores and keeps. The experiences, which mankind has learned, and understand through God's divine Word.

Now that information that mankind has gathered, and embraced from God's Word is what creates, God's knowledge and God's wisdom, transcending, in the consciousness of mankind's mind. When God's Word, transcends in the consciousness of mankind, it creates an awareness, which becomes, the creation, and actions of mankind's faith, and that is also what develops.

The power that is in mankind's consciousness, which comes with the discipline of mankind's faith. That discipline of mankind's faith is what gives mankind's the power that comes from, the words of God, but is transcended, and transformed, into mankind's Consciousness. We must also remember that those are the same words, that God used to speak everything that was nothing into existence, including the world and every human being.

We must also remember that when we become submissive to God, we are placing ourselves, to become in the image and likeness of God. That image and likeness of God are what develops our consciousness of God, and it is at that point that mankind develops their own spiritual consciousness in God, and that is what gives us the power we need to overcome any obstacles and adversities in our life.

We must understand that from nothingness came something. That nothingness becomes something that exists within our own reality of consciousness. We can only understand and comprehend what actually exists within the reality of our own consciousness. The reality of mankind's consciousness is what mankind can comprehend, understand, create, which is our spiritual consciousness.

Now can mankind and God be on the same level of creation? Of course not. God is the creator, which is called *Bara* from the Hebrew word. This means that there is only one creator, which is God. No one or nothing has that power, to create out of nothingness comes something into existence. Not even mankind. The definition means out of *Bara*, and it also means to create out of nothingness, come something that only God Himself can do, create, or bring into existence.

Bara is the original Hebrew word, that is only given to God, and no one else. No one else has the consciousness, to create or bring anything into life from nothingness, as God did.

Everything that mankind invented, or think they created, comes from, or is used from the raw materials, materials, substance, matter, and form from everything that God has already created, for the convenience of mankind, and it is through God's creation.

Mankind is able to invent many things like the cell phone, TV, building of wood and brick all because God has given during our creation the consciousness to develop in our mind, anything that would make mankind, progress, and develop their future, in a way that is convenient, for themselves and others.

Now when I use the word fearless or God's fearless power. What I am referring to is the God that we serve has so much that is powerful enough to destroy the enter world in the twinkling of an eye, and still, He has enough compassion to forgive mankind of all their sins and not kill mankind because they let God down.

## THE POWER OF GOD'S CONSCIOUSNESS

Yet God is more forgiving than mankind, who is never as powerful as God. Yet God is always willing and able to forgive mankind while mankind is always willing to hurt, kill, and destroy each other. Here is why God is able to forgive mankind and destroy or kill off the human race: it is because of something called compassion, grace, mercy, and love.

Mankind has the consciousness to develop the same attributes, to forgive, mankind has the grace, mankind has the same mercy, and mankind also have the ability through their consciousness to develop the same love like God, which can only be achieved through mankind's consciousness that mankind learns and comprehend from God's authentic Word.

The Asah is very important to defining *Bara*. *Asah* means "out of something." Mankind is able to create something. Now God on the other hand is out of nothingness. God is able to create, something. Now that something was the world and mankind themselves. The Asah mean inventors, once again the inventors bring things into creation already using all of God's creation.

We must never forget that the meaning and being of our life is what developed our spiritual consciousness. Our spiritual consciousness is to seek and try to develop our lives, in order for us to identify our true meaning and being in this life.

The other reason is to love and appreciate each other and try to develop our consciousness, to become spiritually enlightening, and in fellowship with God.

The way that God has loved us, and appreciate us, even in the state of peoples' imperfections, and sinful nature. We have to develop, our own consciousness, through whatever we do to become like God. We have the potential to learn and develop, the same consciousness that God has, only through God's divine Word.

It is through God's Word that mankind is able to develop its own Godlike spiritual consciousness, which we gathered from God's divine Word. That is where mankind is able to love each other, unconditionally, and understand each other, beyond what mankind is able to understand and comprehend, as his or her nature and existence.

Mankind's spiritual consciousness is what teaches mankind to love each other, through mankind's own imperfections, and through mankind's sinful nature. Now this is the key, which gives us the light-bulb moment, is when we embrace God's Word. Now as we embrace God's Word, we are becoming a new creature, that new creature means that we are moving, from the mere physical existence of life, into the spiritual realm, of life with God.

This can only be achieved through mankind's spiritual consciousness with God. When mankind is able to embrace, and comprehend God's Word Spiritually. It places mankind in a spiritual state of consciousness. When mankind is able to embrace the spirituality that is in God's Word.

That is when mankind becomes a new creature. Mankind becomes a new creature because God's Word is spiritually motivated. That spiritual consciousness and essence are what gives mankind their spiritual essence and substance, to look at life in a more spiritual perspective than in the physical reality that we exist in.

What this simply means is that mankind, are all physical human beings, which have the potential to become spiritual beings. How does mankind, makes the transition to becoming a spiritual human being.

It happens when mankind is able to develop, their own consciousness, in order for us to come into our own state of awareness where we can continuously develop and embrace who we are spiritually by redefining ourselves through God's wisdom and knowledge.

# GOD BEING THE SCULPTURE OF MANKIND

We must remember that our trials, tribulations, and temptation challenge our faith in God. It is God's Word that is the rock that helps mankind to stand, firm in our state of spiritual consciousness.

Now we must remember that we are trying to define our purpose and reason for living. The only way that our life has a meaning, and being, can only be achieved, through mankind being submissive to God's will.

I am employed with the MBTA. I am one of the operators, who are employed by the Green Line. One I saw a big tree, old in age. I was told by one of the passengers, that the tree existed since the 1800s. I was told by the same passes that the tree has tree cancer.

Because of its health conditions, I was told the tree had tree cancer. I kept looking at the tree, every time I ride by the sick tree. Just like some of us are killing ourselves to sin, and we are dying, our life like that tree has no meaning to itself and life.

Just like some people who are addicted to drugs, alcohol, marijuana, cocaine, and other substance that might cause their death. The majority of times people who are on drugs seem just like the tree their lives have no meaning or being.

We might even think that they should be dead when in reality we as Christians, men, and women of God should never judge a person, people, or family based on their living conditions.

I want to make this point we are the children and men and women of God. God who has created us has accepted us and loves us even based on our own life conditions and through studying God's divine Word. We should have developed enough of our spiritual consciousness, to know that we have to love everyone and everything, just like God has loved us.

When God created us from nothing our life had no meaning or being some of us became like the tree. We were once alive but we used drugs to destroy God's creation, and the meaning and being of what God has created us to be.

As we start studying God's Word and developing our consciousness in God's Word. It was God's divine Word, which became the sculptor that gave our sinful nature and imperfection of our life that we were living, like a drug addict, and as the drugs continuously destroyed our life, we were dying a physical death.

Just like the tree did. The tree was once dead; but the sculptor, who was just like God, gave the tree a new meaning and being life. We at one point and time were dead, but it was through our sinful nature and imperfections, that God's Word gave our life meaning and being in life, by developing our consciousness.

Once again, when we talk about the meaning and being, of or our life, having a purpose or reason for us to exist. The meaning and being in mankind's life can only be defined through God's divine Word. We must remember that God is the sculptor of our lives, and it is truly God's Word that gives our life its meaning and being to exist.

Now let us assume that we have a big rock that is preventing us from reaching our spiritual potential, or is preventing us from developing our spiritual consciousness. The reason why this rock is preventing us from reaching our spiritual potential, and our spiritual consciousness, is because we are experiencing so much, adversities, trials, and temptations in life.

Now we must remember that our trials, temptations, and adversities represent the rock in our life that causes us so much pain and suffering. And if we look at sculptor, before he or she completes, the job it looks, like he or she is destroying the wood or the brick.

That is why God places trials and temptations in our lives because the trials and temptations seem like God is using our trials and temptations as the sculptor uses his or her chisel in order to chip away at wood, or the stone.

The sculptor chips away at the tree, or the brick, in order to bring that image of the tree and rock to life. When the sculptor uses the chisel, every blow, from the chisel, and every chip that falls on the ground, from the tree or the rock.

It looks like the sculptor is causing more pain and suffering to the tree and rock than trying to develop an image that has a meaning and being. Every chip and blow from the sculptor's hands, of the axe or the chisel the tree or rock. Sometimes it looks like the sculptor is destroying the tree, or rock than trying to create an image with meaning and being in life.

I know we feel that way sometimes when we go through our trials and temptations. It seems like God does not have any compassion and love for mankind, or God actually forgot about me, struggling with some difficult trials and temptations. I mean the ones that actually hurt and caused pain and suffering.

For example, the rock is the trials and tribulations that we face every day. As we face our trials and tribulations in life. We must also understand that each trial or temptation we face defines, our reason and purpose in life.

Let us look at it from this perspective, and that is our faith, which is the work that we need to do in order to shape our integrity and personality. Now our consciousness makes us aware of the image, that we trying to create, in order to give that image meaning and being. Assume that there is a big rock as big as a mountain and that rock is the representation of the trials tribulations and temptations that we face in life.

The tools that we use to give the rock a reason and purpose for mankind to enjoy the purpose and reason which gives the rock a purpose and reason, to exist, is based only on its image and shape. The image and the shape are the reality of our nature. That rock becomes an example of how God is able to take us and define our purpose and reason for living.

Especially, when it comes to our trials and tribulations in life why trials and tribulations in life are the representation of the rock. Now our faith is the work, that we do in order to shape and redefine. The image in which we are creating the rock gives the rock a reason and purpose to be what it is to exist to be.

Now who we are is defined, through our trials, tribulations, and temptations. Our trials, temptations, and adversities in life are nothing more, than what we experienced, or similar to the huge tree or rock, that the sculptor, trying to shape or make an example of.

I will make another example: Trials and tribulations and temptations and adversities are the big rocks that stand in the way of mankind developing their consciousness and faith in God. The wood and the rock are what challenges our faith in God.

Now God's Word and mankind's actions are the faith that directs mankind to bring that rock into an image, that mankind is able to define by looking at the rocks. The image of the rock is what tries to define the true character and purpose, of why that image is being carved into life, or why that image of the rock is being carved into an image that mankind understands and recognizes as a part of his or her existence in life.

As the sculptor scalps and curves the image into the rock or tree, that is what gives the image of the tree or rock a reason and a purpose to exist. Now that reason and purpose exist are what we understand the shape of the rock to become.

Our purpose and reason in this life can only be defined if we allow God to be our sculptor. If God is the sculptor, His Word is the chisel and a hammer that the sculptor, who is God, has to use His Word, which is the chisel and hammer that gives our life a new meaning and being in life, especially when we try to comprehend and acknowledge God's divine Word in our hearts and minds.

The key is to always remember Is our trials, tribulations, and adversities are always redefined, through every test, and trial that we encounter and go through in life, and that is what strengthens and matures us in God's righteousness.

We face in life but the tools that we use to physically scalped the rock, and constantly edging and edging. The edging and edging are what start to define the image of the wood or rock. In order for the rock to take on the shape of the image of the rock, it has to be developed by the consciousness of the artist or sculptor.

Now the shape that the sculptor created to form the image of the rock, it is that shape that the sculptor invented or created is what actually defines the meaning and being of the things. The image that the sculptor has carved out is what basically defines the meaning and being of the tree's and rock's true purpose and reason for living.

The tree and rock are the trials and tribulations that we face every day. The chisel is like the Word of God. When I say that, the chisel that the sculptor uses should remind us of God's Word. It is because of God's Word. As we study God's Word, we are being created and transformed in the likeness and image of God. As human being transformed in the image and likeness of God.

It is God's Word, which chisels away at our heart developing our consciousness, and faith in God. Every time that we read and study God's Word and we embrace God's Word in our consciousness, hearts, and mind. Here is how our life gets its mean and being from mankind. First of all, every time that God's Word, is able to correct, the wrongs that we are doing.

We must always remember that God's Word is the chisel that the sculptor uses in order to give his or her wood and brick. It's the true meaning and being in this life. We must remember that God's Word is like the chisel or the tools that the sculptor uses to bring life and meaning to his or her creation.

Every time we become submissive to God's Word, we become closer to God; every time we do wrong, God's Word puts us back on track spiritually. It is God's Word that brings us back into fellowship and harmony with God, and it is through mankind's consciousness. It is through mankind's consciousness which brings mankind's sinful nature and imperfections, which causes us to sin.

We must also understand that our sins do stop at our sinful nature and imperfections, our sins are forgiven through God's grace and mercy. It is through God's authentic love, and forgiveness that God is constantly, able to forgive mankind and still allow mankind's life to still have a meaning and being in life.

Every time that mankind sins, and allow his, or her imperfection, and sinful nature to take over their hearts and mind, and causes mankind them to sin. It is through God's consciousness, which allows God, through His grace and mercy, to be the Person, who has potential, power, and authority to forgive mankind, of their sins.

When we embrace God's message and knowledge, which come through His Word, which transcends into our conscious state of mind. We must recognize that our consciousness gives us the potential and the opportunity to give our life its meaning and being in this life.

Now through God's forgiveness, and salvation, even when we are faced with our adversities, and our imperfections, and our sinful nature. God is still, able to forgive, us of our life, and still be able to our life, its true meaning and being to exist.

Now the chiseling that the sculptor is doing to the tree or rock is the same thing God is doing to us.

For example, every stroke of the sculptor chiseling away and hammering away, at the tree and the rock is redefining the tree and the rock and bringing, the tree and the rock into their own image. That image is what gives the tree or rock its meaning and being in life.

It is the same with mankind's creation. It is like God's Word is the chisel and the hummer the tree and the rock is like the adversities and adversaries that we face in our life. We must also remember that every adversity, and adversary we face is like the chisel and hummer that is constantly challenging and beating us, to use our consciousness, to redefine our meaning and being in life.

The only way that we can define our meaning and being in life is through constantly maturing and developing in our own state of consciousness. We have to become the sculptures of our lives through God's Word.

We must let God's Word become the chisel that constantly shapes, carves, twists, bends, twists, and turns the tree and rock in order for that rock or tree to take shape as that rock and tree take on its own shape.

Each trial, and tribulation that we face and become successful over, is developing our own state of spiritual consciousness. I was spiritual consciousness gives us the strength and courage to overcome the adversities, and adversaries, that we are facing in this life.

Our consciousness acknowledges to us that we are winning the spiritual battle over Satan's evil desires. Every time that we are able to stay in tune, and in constant harmony and fellowship with God through His Word. We will always win the fight and battle over Satan.

God's Word is the two-edged sword, which cut and destroy Satan's evil desires, for mankind. If mankind picks up God's divine Word in order for mankind to stay in tune and in fellowship with God.

As long as mankind is able to stay in tune, and in fellowship with God. That is when mankind is able to win the battle that exists between mankind and Satan.

Mankind can defeat Satan, all the time, as long as mankind stays strong, firm, and transparent constantly in God's consciousness. We will always find the courage, and power to overcome Satan and to overthrow Satan's evil desires.

The best way to phrase this is to say that mankind is able to find a reason and purpose in life through their adversities. It is through mankind's faith in God that mankind's faith is what starts to define mankind's reason and purpose in life, especially when mankind's heart and mind are fixed on God's authentic Word.

## About the Author

### *Work*

My name is James Grant. I am originally from Barbados, West Indies. I worked over twenty years in law enforcement. I was recruited by the state police and worked for the Department of Correction. I received a certification to teach middle school and high school at Boston public schools system. I became an assistant principal of John D. O'Bryant at Madison Park High School summer program. I also became a supervisor of the security department of Division of Transitional Assistance (DTA). In Roxbury,

Massachusetts, I also worked with the Massachusetts Bay Transit Authority (MBTA).

## *Education profile*

I attended St. Patrick's Grammar School, Julia Ward Howe School, and Sara Jay Bakker Middle School in Roxbury, Massachusetts. I also attended English High School, Roxbury Community College, Northeastern University, Roxbury Community College, and University of Massachusetts in Boston.

I am also a member of Twelve Baptist Historic Church in Roxbury Massachusetts. I presently serve as a deacon.

I am also a published author of the book titled, *Women Are God*. Also *the Power of God's Consciousness* would be in publication and should be available on June 2022. *The Theory of Theology* should also be available around June 2024.

I worked many of the campaigns; these are some of the people I support even as a child growing up in Boston, trying to give my community a positive social and economic life. Senator Bill Owens Campaign, Shirley Owen Hicks, Campaign Royal Bolling, Campaign, Bruce Bolling, Campaign, Bruce, Mark Bolling, Michael Flaherty Campaign, Deval Patrick Campaign, Elizabeth Warren's Campaign, Joe Kennedy's Campaign, Charlotte Golar Richies' Campaign, Michael Capouano's Campaign, Michelle's Wu's Campaign, Ed Markey, Tito Jackson's Campaign, Rachel Rollins' Campaign Annissa Essaibi George's Campaign. Member of Twelve Baptist Historic

Church Deacon, The Caribbean American Political Action Committee. Greater Boston Legal Services.

I was also interviewed by Governor Deval Patrick Cabinet, for the sheriff's position that Steve Tompkins is presently the sheriff of.

When Deval Patrick was running for his second term as governor, I headed up the security team, which facilitated the CIA and FBI and the city and state police departments. This was when President Barack Obama came to speak at the Hines Auditorium to support Deval Patrick's second term running as the governor of Massachusetts. Member of the Caribbean American Political Action Committee.

I also did the community walks with the Boston Police Department, State Police Department, Massachusetts Transit Police Department, the pastors and ministers of the community, and the political candidates, all of the political candidates and campaign staff of these candidates I walk with during our walk and pray in the communities of Boston.

I also did the 7:00 a.m. prayers in the communities of Boston, where these events took place for the COVID-19 patients, families, friends, medical staff, and the first responders. Also the gang shootings, which accrued, crimes in the communities, this was done on Sundays mornings before the churches were opened for their morning service.

I also design a T-shirt for the Million Man March, Million Woman March, the Million Youth Marche. The Million Woman March inspired me to write a book called *Women Are Gods*.

I also won the golden key award for photography, which competed throughout America professional photographers. I was a student at English High School. I won the Golden Key Award for photography. I won this when I was student at English High School.

Mental health, education, elderly people, the veterans of America, Foreclosure Statutory Redemption Law, Prison Reform, MBTA, Massachusetts Bay Transit Authority, and any organization to make the transporting system become green with buses, trains, and trolleys. I think it is very imperative that we look into the MBTA becoming green.

## *Political status*

Love is the emotion, which fuels the spark of mankind's compassion. Now the spark, which fuels mankind's love, develops and creates compassion in our hearts.

Compassion is the desire that we have to want to make a change to help others who cannot help themselves.

Compassion means that somehow God has placed me in authority and gives me the power to bring about a change for others. Let me reiterate that. Compassion is the emotion, which God has placed in us and gives us the authority and power to bring about a change or changes for others.

Compassion is an emotional state, which is nurtured by God and given to mankind to develop their own consciousness, to help others to develop and enhance their own life condition, to become better, and to love each other.

In other words, compassion is the spark, which creates the fire that burns in the soul of men and women, especially when they are motivated, determined, and persistent to bring about a positive change in the lives of others even to change the negative and bad conditions, which impact the life conditions of other people's lives.

Compassion is an emotional state, which is nurtured and preserved. Now nurturing and preserving is like God. It is like God preparing you for a time of season, which means a time of now.

Compassion is the emotion, which fuels our love, confidence, and courage that we need to make the necessary changes, which would impact others' life condition in a positive way.

We must also understand in order for us to bring about a change in the world, neighborhoods, communities, which would impact people's lives and schools.

It is that love, compassion, and change become the spark that burns like a flaming fire, which burns deep within the spirit, mind, body, and soul of every human being to make the sacrifices needed, to create a positive change which would bring love, compassion, and change in order to create peace among the people in our communities.

Love, compassion, and change bring peace and joy or place more joy in the hearts of people in order to exercise enough strength and power to bring people into a state of love, compassion, and change.

I would help the city, state, federal, electoral candidates, or any organizations to create a positive change in the Boston neighborhoods and communities.

I would work also with those organizations that might disagree with my decisions so that I can learn why they have disagreed; I can also learn and understand their perspective as long as they have the interest of Boston's communities and neighborhoods.

Whether they agree or disagree, the key is to get the information that is transparent enough to create the changes that are necessary for us to have a better community and neighborhoods for Boston's residents, families, friends, visitors.

The men and women in the military have fought many wars to protect and serve our country's freedom.

When the war is ending for American citizens, that is when the men and women are fighting a silent war that is the experience, drama, and repercussion, of the men and women military experience, which is contributed to the pain and suffering that they have experienced, being afflicted on them or military colleagues during wartime.

Love is a powerful emotion, and if it's handled right, it can change all the evilness in this world, all the hate and racial tension.

Here's what I mean: love is an emotion that sparks one curiosity that creates the desire of compassion. Compassion is that spark that burns as a small fire, a true love that sparks and becomes a blazing fire that is able to burn in the hearts and souls of men and women to create a positive change.

Within the communities and neighborhoods of Boston, in order for anyone to make a change, one must learn not to accept the position that they're in but try to strive for the better and, while striving for the better, contribute back to your community and neighborhood's compassion and know that we have the authority and the power to create a positive change for our families and communities in our neighborhoods.

That's smart because the blazing fire is the consciousness of mankind; acknowledging that through his or her compassion, we can make that change that is necessary to bring about a better community. It is the spark that settles in our subconscious mind and house in our soul, challenging us through our love compassion and changing us to do what we can do that is necessary to bring happiness to our communities and joy to our communities and families.

Another thing that we must look at is that when you vote for me, the work that I will do will give you enough confidence to know that you have given me the power and authority; it makes changes for this community, that power that you have voted, that your single vote has given me the opportunity to exercise my love, my compassion and to create the changes that are necessary for us to build a bigger and better society in America today. We can just sit back and figure out what it was like, but now we know what it is like to enjoy a peaceful, striving community of love, compassion, and change.

Those changes are the political, economic, and social conditions that our society faces at this particular moment, and we should know the sacrifices that we have to make in order to make a positive change for our community and that is why I think that I would be a better candidate for senator where we can pass laws to ease the burden and cut down on the cry to basically pay attention to mental health and try to develop and pass bills that will facilitate our elderly and let us not take out a backup lash or a bad look or ignore all political candidates especially the militaries who have fought blood, sweat, and tears to keep the American democracy alive in our hearts, minds, and souls and to enjoy the freedom that comes with our democracy.

You must also look at the statutory redemption to make sure that people can stay in the house longer because of the emergency situation and especially because of Covid; we have many jobs that were cut back, and many people could not afford a mortgage but lower them a year and a half to let them get back on their feet.

We also have to look at the minimum wage to increase it as well; that way, people can afford a housing in Boston.

## My perspective and reflections

*Education.* We need to engage our children in more activities to keep their minds focused on athletics, job programs, trades school, home economics, work on hands with many professional careers and get paid for working in these professional feels they should be a grant given to these children that is working to gain an experience in the career field day; this should be a part of all children's curriculum—professional field program.

We also need to develop more programs such as vocational programs, and it should be a collaboration of city and state coming together to finance these programs. The focus of these programs are consistency, discipline, and patience. With the knowledge implementing in these programs for children in these programs, to start their own business.

*Mental health.* To develop laws which would protect those people with mental health conditions, we have to stop the abuse of the mental health patience.

We should also make sure that families are compensated for the medication and living expenses and family members who take full custody of their own family members with mental health issues. This should never be a privileged package; it should be given to all families.

We should not make it difficult for those families to be compensated financially and also make sure that the medication is being distributed to the mental health patients without any financial hardship.

*Education.* We need to develop programs that would help prepare a better environment for our children's learning. We also need more schools to develop programs for students that have an IEP. Have a son that has been on the IEP so that these children don't feel complacent or are being taken advantage or misunderstood in the schools that they attend.

*Veterans programs.* I don't think that we give enough support and attention to the men and women who fought the wars and who protect and uphold our democracy, the constitution of the United States of America. When the wars of America are over, the men and women in America are still fighting a psychological war of silence.

Families and friends have come to experience. That silent war is also a war where veterans feel neglected in America—the same country they fought to protect American's democracy constitution and Bill of Rights.

*Boston public school teachers.* When I was teaching in the Boston public school system, I had to use my own salary in order to purchase learning materials for my classroom.

Many teachers bought their own supplies. The money that they use is not tax deductible or do they get compensation back for the materials that they have purchased for the students.

I know that Boston public school teachers need a salary increase to compensate for the financial loss of supporting the students in their classrooms.

Teachers also need more protection and security in the classrooms. Many teachers are assaulted by students. Some teachers are afraid of teaching in their own classroom. We need to create a more comfortable environment for the teachers and protect them from the students.

I would work with anyone who is willing to develop more trade schools and vocational schools; not all children have the academic ability to survive successfully in college or university environment.

*Universities and colleges.* I am against children and families paying for higher education. I believe on a college or university academic level of education, no child, who attends college or universities, should have to pay for an education; all students should be tuition free. I am a living example of that experience.

Knowing that the student's family already pays both federal and state taxes to the government, it feels like we are paying twice for the same product. We need more vocational schools.

*Statutory redemption laws.* To allow people to stay in their homes longer than is expected by other financial institutions, even during the foreclosure processors.

*The elderly people.* Allowing them to be able to pay for the medication because they either are retired or on social security income is not enough for the elderly. So they shouldn't be paying those tremendous amount of money for medication.

*Union representation.* We need to strengthen the unions and allow people to keep their jobs and increase their salaries. We need to fight hard for unions representation in the work places.

We also need to increase the minimum wage.

*Crime prevention in our communities and neighborhoods.* Coming up with different types of programs from the state and city collaborating together to bring about a change in crime prevention.

We need to facilitate programs that would be able to cut down on crime in our community. We also need to increase the activities in the YMCA, the Boys and Girls Club of America.

The programs should be supported by parents and communities in order for these programs to become successful in our communities and neighborhood.

We should support our youth athletic programs just like any professional sports, like the pro games: basketball, football, soccer, cricket, boxing. If the children in this case see that we are supporting them, it might be the beginning of cutting down on a lot of crime rates in the community. I think the first priority should be your future instead of professional sports.

*Police crime prevention activity.* I think all schools from kindergarten, middle school, and high school should develop a curriculum where the police department should collaborate with the school a couple of days a week to talk about their experiences as a police officer.

It would develop better relationships between the police children and also communities. It can also be done with other careers. EMS, lawyers, doctors, carpentry, the companies that participate in this program should also have a tax break.

*MBTA (Massachusetts Bay Transportation Authority).* I would support any program with MBTA that has to do with keeping the emissions of the MBTA green.

*The department of corrections.* We need more classes on crime prevention and how to prevent the escalation of inmates and officer relationships in the prison system.